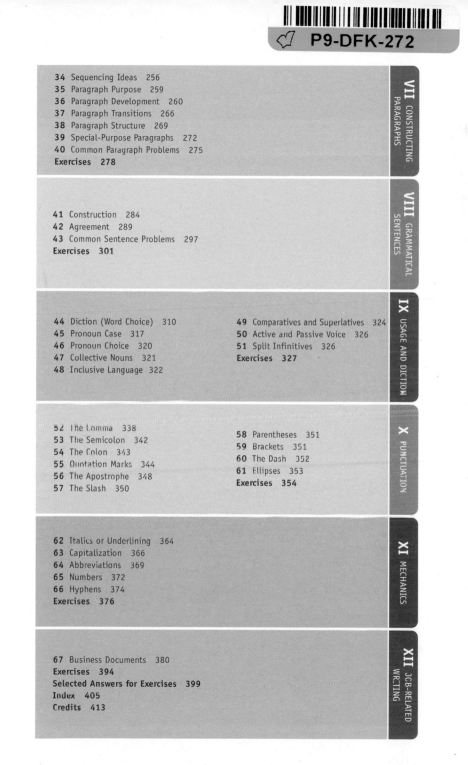

A Canadian Writer's Guide

Fourth Edition

Jack Finnbogason
Kwantlen Polytechnic University

Al Valleau
Kwantlen Polytechnic University

NELSON / EDUCATION

NELSON / EDUCATION

A Canadian Writer's Guide, Fourth Edition

by Jack Finnbogason and Al Valleau

**Vice-President and
Editorial Director:**
Evelyn Veitch

Editor-in-Chief:
Anne Williams

Executive Editor:
Laura Macleod

Marketing Manager:
Amanda Henry

Developmental Editor:
Theresa Fitzgerald

Permissions Coordinator:
Jessie Coffey

**Senior Content Production
Manager:**
Natalia Denesiuk Harris

Copy Editor:
Margaret Crammond

Proofreader:
Lisa Berland

Indexer:
Edwin Durbin

Production Coordinator:
Ferial Suleman

Design Director:
Ken Phipps

Managing Designer:
Franca Amore

Interior Design:
Peter Papayanakis

Cover Design and Image:
Glenn Toddun

Compositor:
Carol Magee

Printer:
Transcontinental

**Library and Archives Canada
Cataloguing in Publication Data**

Finnbogason, Jack, 1942–

    A Canadian writer's guide /
Jack Finnbogason, Al Valleau. —
4th ed.

Includes index.
ISBN 978-0-17-650032-0

1. English language—Rhetoric.
2. English language—Grammar.

I. Valleau, Al, 1946– II. Title.

PE1408.F45 2009   808'.042
C2008-907772-5

ISBN-13: 978-0-17-650032-0
ISBN-10: 0-17-650032-4

TABLE OF CONTENTS

III   RESEARCH ESSAYS

IV   DOCUMENTATION

V   BASIC GRAMMAR

VI   SENTENCE ELEMENTS

VII   CONSTRUCTING PARAGRAPHS

XII JOB-RELATED WRITING

PREFACE TO FOURTH EDITION

We find it interesting that, with this fourth edition, we are into this text's second decade yet still need to begin with the statement "This is a Canadian text." In 1997, when this guide first appeared, it was virtually the only fully Canadian text of its kind that was coil-bound and tabbed. There were many "Canadianized" texts then available for instructors and students but few that had been conceived and written entirely by Canadians. That situation has now changed considerably.

We have, again, with revisions and the addition of new material, attempted to make our material current, relevant, and accessible. Nelson has added colours, so the text will now be multi-coloured to enhance the presentation. In addition, a simpler chapter numbering system has replaced the third edition's number/letter scheme, and a new tab system has been introduced.

LAYOUT AND CONTENT

We have kept the basic twelve units of the book, but we have reorganized those units. The book now begins with units on the writing process, academic writing, research, and documentation. The second segment of our text addresses basic grammar, sentences, and paragraphs. The third segment covers grammatical sentences, diction, punctuation, and mechanics. The text ends with a chapter on transactional writing. We have made this organizational change to separate the material on grammar and usage from the units on academic and transactional writing.

In preparing this edition, we also focused on changes suggested by our reviewers, on updating, and on new elements. Our revisions include the following:

- a new unit on academic argument
- the incorporation of the changes in MLA style that were part of the publication of the seventh edition of the *MLA Handbook* in spring 2009; in fact, Nelson held up publication of this fourth edition to ensure that these changes could be included
- the addition of Columbia Online style to our documentation chapter, making our book the only midsize text that includes a full treatment of all five documentation styles
- a reorganized discussion of plagiarism and how to avoid it
- a new section designed to assist students in evaluating online resources
- restructured, updated, and new exercises to accompany the chapters
- a new, colourful interior design to add life and contrast to the text
- a new and expanded workbook available from Nelson to allow students to work on both grammar and content

We attempted to keep the guide the same length because we think students see this size as friendlier and easier to transport. However, the addition of two large units (on academic argument and on Columbia Online style) means the fourth edition will be approximately 10 pages longer than the third. We have attempted to preserve all the strong features of previous editions—the emphasis on writing as a process, the presentation of grammatical matters in accessible language and format, the inclusion of exercises within chapters, the ESL tips, and coverage of current practices and conventions in academic writing.

We would like to draw your attention to three elements in this edition:

1. A special website designed to extend the text with interactive exercises and additional materials. Materials previously located inside the text have been moved to the website. You will find coverage there of dictionary use and spelling as well as a special unit on the job search, including how to design and craft a cover letter, prepare a résumé, and handle an interview.

2. Greater attention to the influence of the computer on research and writing practices.

3. Completely new segments on Columbia Online style and academic argument.

RESEARCH AND STYLE

The fourth edition retains the units on MLA, APA, Chicago, and CSE (formerly CBE) styles and adds a new unit on Columbia Online style. The chapter on documentation now occupies over twenty percent of the text, in large part because of our insistence on furnishing many examples of how different texts should be cited within the five possible styles.

We have maintained currency by using the most current guides as references and by referring to online sources so students can check for themselves what current practice is in their discipline. This is particularly important for APA, where formats for citing online references are still stabilizing. We include any changes coming from the issuing of a new edition by CSE for the sciences, a new unit on online style from *The Chicago Manual of Style*, and the increasing acceptance of *The Columbia Guide to Online Style*. Most importantly, we held up publication of the fourth edition to be certain we would include changes in practice arising from the publication of the seventh edition of the *MLA Handbook*.

THE EXERCISES

The primary change in this area has been to update certain exercises, revise others, and create new ones where necessary. We have retained the practice of placing the exercises at the end of chapters and including selected answers to those exercises at the end of the text. Instructors may obtain the complete answer key from Nelson when they order class sets of the guide.

ESL CONCERNS

We have retained the use of icons to guide ESL students to detailed discussions of special grammatical issues.

YOUR FEEDBACK

In creating this new edition, we concentrated on responding to what our reviewers told us and what we believed students would find illuminating and useful. We hope this edition assists you in one of the most challenging tasks in postsecondary education, that of helping students to write with clarity, confidence, and passion. We also hope to hear from you about areas that still need improving, about any errors that you may discover, even about elements that you think work well. Please contact us either through the website or through Nelson.

ACKNOWLEDGMENTS

We must begin by acknowledging the many colleagues and the fourteen thousand students in Quebec, Ontario, Manitoba, Alberta, and British Columbia who taught us much of what we know about writing and writing instruction.

Secondly, the Nelson team has been an essential part of developing the book. We particularly want to acknowledge Anne Williams, Laura Macleod, Roberta Spinosa-Millman, Theresa Fitzgerald, Natalia Denesiuk Harris, Kristiina Bowering, Ferial Suleman, and Peter Papayanakis, all of whom played important roles in this project.

Our thanks also go to three of our librarians at Kwantlen, Jan Penhorwood, Jean McKendry, and Chris Burns, who were very helpful in guiding us through the changes that have occurred with search and meta-search engines, and with data bases and service providers. More and more, libraries are relying on online access to journals, and we quickly realized that our librarians had a stronger grasp of the changes in these areas than we had. As well, our thanks to those instructors who took time to review the manuscript during its development: Dale Bradley and Caroline Whitfield, both of Brock University.

This edition has a unique quality in that the two of us were aided by the insights of our daughters, Geneviève and Signe, who reviewed the text to make sure it reflected current student research and essay-writing practices. Both of them are enrolled in graduate studies programs, and we have learned from them new ways in which the computer is becoming an integral tool in researching, drafting, and writing. It is a pleasure to say that this text truly is the product of two generations of Finnbogason/Valleau thought.

Finally, to our wives, Marsha and Yit Shang, thank you for tolerating us when the book occupied too much time and space. Without your tolerance and understanding, we would never have been able to complete the project or relegate those endless piles of paper to their rightful place.

The Writing Process

Over three thousand years ago, Greek thinkers believed that the process of composing (whether in written or spoken form) could best be studied by breaking it down into three stages: invention, disposition (organizing and writing), and style (manner, tone, voice, level of diction, and rhetorical strategies). The comparable stages today are *prewriting, drafting, and revising,* and every writer faces the challenge of successfully managing each element in composing an effective paper. We also know now that these activities are actually recursive in that writers perform them simultaneously and repetitively. As a writer, you need to develop and refine the skills and abilities associated with each of these activities to improve your range, competence, and clarity.

1 PREWRITING I: THE BASICS

Typically, when you first sit down to write, it is in response to an assignment, whether it be a report, a review, a summary, or an essay. The basic questions that confront you at the beginning of a writing project are related to five main elements: *purpose, audience, stance, research*, and *outline.*

1-a Purpose

To write well, you have to understand your aim or intention. You need to know if you are writing to inform, persuade, describe, narrate, summarize, define, explain, recommend, or compare. The following guidelines will help you to articulate the purpose of your assignment.

- Read the instructions in the assignment carefully.
- Underline the key verbs in the assignment. (See Chapter 13 for information about verbs you are likely to encounter in assignment instructions.)
- Ask a classmate what he or she thinks the purpose of the assignment is.
- Learn to distinguish the demands of different types of writing. For example, a *report* asks you to identify a problem and make recommendations for solving it (see Chapter 67); a *comparison* asks you to examine two or more topics to find similarities and differences; an *analysis* asks you to examine the elements or parts of a topic and study their relationships.
- Make a rough outline of your intended response to the assignment and ask your instructor for feedback.

1-b Audience

It is important for you to know your audience and how that audience might influence your approach. If you are writing an assignment for a class, your audience will most likely be your instructor. If you are asked to write a report that will be read by a wider audience, you need to ask yourself questions about its members. Will they be informed or unaware? hostile or sympathetic? attentive or easily distracted? A clear understanding of your audience will smooth your progress through the subsequent stages of the writing process and help to ensure that the prose you produce is neither lifeless nor inappropriate in diction and voice.

1-c Stance

Stance is a complex but important part of writing. To understand it fully, you first have to know that your relationship to your audience creates your *voice*, and your relationship to your topic creates your *tone*. Figure 1-1 illustrates the relationship between topic and tone, and audience and voice. How you feel about your topic supplies your tone, while how you see your audience—and, more particularly, how you want that audience to see you—creates your voice. A writer's stance, then, is the combined effect of voice and tone. If you are certain of what your voice and tone should be, you will not have problems with stance.

Figure 1-1 Writer's Stance

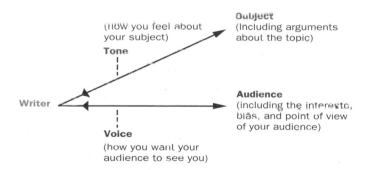

Subject
(Including arguments about the topic)

(how you feel about your subject)
Tone

Writer

Audience
(including the interests, bias, and point of view of your audience)

Voice
(how you want your audience to see you)

You will find that it is hard to write an essay response on a topic until you have decided on your stance. Your tone begins with your first sentences; your voice is a product of your first paragraphs. Therefore, it is important to decide your stance before drafting your essay.

1-d Research

One of the first questions you must answer in the prewriting stage is whether you need to conduct formal research or whether the information you already possess is adequate. There are a number of prewriting techniques that will help you discover what you already know and feel about your topic. Any research that needs to be done should be well under way before you begin work on the outline of your essay and start a first draft. For information about the research process, see Chapter 15.

1-e Outline

One of the first prewriting techniques most writers learn is outlining, the means by which a writer first defines concretely the theme, parts, and sequence of his or her paper. An outline is a sequenced description, using words, phrases, or sentences, of the paper's thesis and support. An outline is the best way for a writer to capture an initial sense of what the paper will do and how it will do it.

The best time to write an outline is after you have gained at least a preliminary sense of the facts and issues that form the basic material of your essay. If you attempt to outline before you have done any preliminary study of the topic area, your outline will probably be too general. You are also more capable of sketching a useful outline once you have formed at least a preliminary position on your subject. Generally, the less that the subject has crystallized in your head, the less formal your outline should be.

You may wish to begin with a **scratch outline**, one chiefly built on single words or, at most, short phrases. This kind of outline is exploratory, in the same way that mind-mapping (p. 7) and branching (p. 8) are. You are really attempting to reduce the information you have accumulated from your initial reading to some kind of purposeful form.

Assume, for instance, that you have become interested in the 2007 news story concerning the shipment of tainted pet food to North America from China. You were shocked that a major North American pet food supplier, Menu Foods of Toronto, had distributed pet food that poisoned the pets that ate it; the toxicity was caused by melamine, added to the food by Menu's Chinese supplier. You read more about the matter in magazines and other media. You now have a grasp of the what, the when, the where, and the who. But it is the why that interests you more. This is an appropriate moment to organize the content and perspectives you have acquired into a more purposeful form. You are ready for a scratch outline. The following is a possible result:

- pet food from Chinese suppliers to North American sellers
- pets sicken, and some die
- issues?
- source of poisoning
- the blame game
- simple blame vs. complex blame
- background first
    - massive recall (60 million cans/pouches)
    - the culprit: wheat gluten tainted with melamine
    - a key company, Menu Foods
- do causal analysis

The main thing you have accomplished with the scratch outline is the isolation of your purpose. You are not interested in simply following the early newspaper accounts that turn the Chinese suppliers into the source of the sickening and dying of North American pets. You also want to check on the accountability of the companies in North America that both ordered and sold the pet food and then issued the recalls. You wonder too if the pet owner's wish for bargain prices has an influence on the choice of questionable producers.

Although the scratch outline is an informal outlining method, you can also use the **formal outline** method. A formal outline will be useful to you if you are writing a lengthy paper or if you want a clear plan before you move from an early draft to a finished draft.

Formal outlines can use words, phrases, or sentences. They do, however, adhere to an established format. Formal outlines use the following structure:

- thesis statement: introduction and backgrounding of main claim
- body of essay
- final position: restatement of thesis as presented and shaped by body of essay

Applying this model to the subject you want to write about might yield a finished outline like the following:

Thesis: Although the preliminary tendency was to blame the Chinese supplier for the tainted pet food that killed a number of North American pets, we must agree that Canadian wholesalers and North American consumers should share that blame.

I. Background of the pet food crisis of spring 2007
   A. Use of Chinese suppliers
      1. Size of North American pet food business
      2. Concentration of North American pet food business
         a. Menu Foods of Toronto as an important example
   B. The progression of the pet food crisis
      1. Reports of poisoning
      2. Recall of tainted pet food
      3. The blame game
         a. Chinese suppliers to blame
         b. Slowness of North American companies to respond
         c. Differential response of pet food stores

II. Roles and responsibilities of pet food retail companies
   A. Menu Foods: a North American example
   B. Procter and Gamble: a North American example

III. An analogy: lead paint and Christmas toys
   A. Chinese share of North American toy industry

      1. How the 92% happened
      2. The contractual relationship of Chinese toy maker and North American seller
      3. Mattel toy recall
    B. Recall
      1. Recall issued
      2. Media response
      3. Film at 9: Chinese factory conditions and practices
      4. Who's checking: a look at the relationship between maker and seller
  IV. Where should the blame be assigned?
    A. A case against the Chinese supplier
    B. A case against the North American seller
    C. A case against the North American consumer

Final position: When we investigate the tainted pet food scandal and then widen our focus to include another instance of Chinese producers shipping dangerous toys to North America, we find that there is no single villain here. It is easy to blame the Chinese producer, but why was this activity assigned to Chinese producers by North American companies? And if the sole reason was to save money, why didn't the North American company take sufficient pains to ensure the cheaper product was safe? It appears there is quite enough blame here to go around.

This sample is written in phrases. At their most formal, outlines are written entirely in sentences. The discipline this introduces, the need to name an agent and an action in each part of the outline, will give you the fullest possible overview of your analysis or inquiry. A brief look at the model presented above will show you how easily it can be converted into the most formal of outlines, the sentence outline.

Generally, remember that the outline is a formal prewriting activity and most suited to larger assignments. If the essay you are writing is only going to be three or four pages, outlining is probably not a useful aid. If you are engaged in a research essay or an extended semester paper, outlining can be a genuine help. You still need to allow for the fact that, once you start drafting your paper, you may still reorder your topics and paragraphs. For more on outlining, see 18-a on page 86.

2   PREWRITING II: TECHNIQUES

During the prewriting stage, you can explore the topic you wish to write about by using one or more of the following techniques: *brainstorming, mind-mapping, freewriting and looping, branching, the pentad,* or *topic analysis.* While some of these techniques focus exclusively on helping you to generate information about your topic, others go beyond that purpose by initiating the sorting process through which you will later organize that generated information.

2-a Brainstorming

Brainstorming is an exercise in free association that involves listing your responses to a topic. As you perform this activity, do not pause to reflect on organizational considerations such as the order of the ideas and the relationships between the ideas. Simply list as quickly as possible all the ideas and associations that come to you. If you were asked to write a short report on the problems that part-time work creates for students, you might produce a list such as the following:

- the company each person works for
- types of jobs people work at
- how each person feels about his or her job
- whether the job is related to each student's field of study
- number of hours each person works per week
- number of courses each person is taking while working
- number of hours each person puts into course work per week
- reasons why each person finds it necessary to work
- amount of money generated by part-time work
- cost of a college education
- grade point average of each student before and after acquiring a part-time job

2-b Mind-Mapping

Mind-mapping involves creating a *visual representation* of the relationships among ideas. To create a mind-map, take a blank sheet of paper and write your topic in the centre of the page. Draw a circle around the topic. Then write down the major ideas associated with the topic, circle each idea, and draw lines connecting the ideas to the topic in the centre. Next, write down minor ideas that relate to the major ideas, circle the minor ideas, and connect them to the main ideas. If even more specific ideas occur to you, record those ideas and connect them to the minor ideas. Continue this process until you run out of ideas. A mind-map of the problems that part-time work creates for students might look like the one shown in Figure 2-1.

Brainstorming and mind-mapping both operate on the principle of association, with one idea triggering another. However, mind-mapping goes a step further by requiring you to exhaust each associative cluster before you move to a new cluster. In this way, you simultaneously discover and organize.

2-c Freewriting and Looping

Freewriting and looping are prewriting exercises that help you to define your stance; they also generate a surprising amount of detail that may prove useful at a later stage in the writing process.

Figure 2-1 Mind-Map

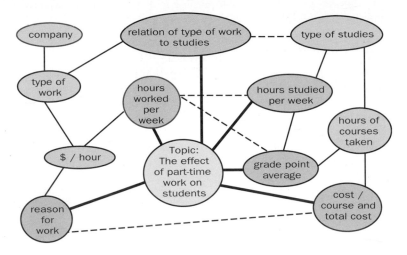

Freewriting silences the internal critic that hovers over all your writing efforts, allowing your true feelings and natural voice to emerge. The process is simple. Set a time limit of five minutes or so and write continuously about the topic, never letting your pen stop. If you cannot think of any ideas, keep writing *thinking* or *can't write* until something does come to mind.

Looping is a more directed form of freewriting. Imagine that you are writing an essay on Louis Riel. You may not know what position you want to take even though you have done some preliminary reading. Looping is an ideal method for exploring how you feel about a topic. First, produce a statement (e.g., "When I think about Louis Riel, I think …") and spend five minutes freewriting about that statement. Next, read what you have written and isolate one sentence, image, or phrase that surprises you the most. Use this unexpected element as your starting point for another five minutes of freewriting. Continue this process until you reach a point of diminishing returns. Do not overdo this exercise; it is effective only when you are fresh.

2-d Branching

Branching is a variation on mind-mapping. The chief difference is that branching proceeds in a much more linear way. The first step in branching is to break your topic down into as many parts as suggest themselves to you. If your analysis were to produce five topic parts, you would be left with five branches to explore. To the right of each branch, you would add new branches consisting of supporting ideas. A branching exercise based on the example topic of Canadian multiculturalism is shown in Figure 2-2.

Branching gives you a better understanding of how the constituent parts of your topic relate to one another. It also gives you a clearer sense of any gaps in

Figure 2-2 Branching Diagram

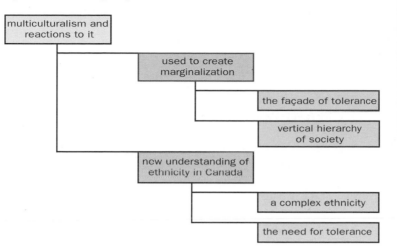

your knowledge of the topic, thereby allowing you to identify areas in which you need to do more research.

2-e The Pentad[1]

The pentad is a set of five headings that helps you to discover, classify, and organize the relationships among the main parts of your topic. This prewriting technique emerged in part from the work of the American literary critic Kenneth Burke and in part from the traditional questions of journalism—*who, what, when, where, how,* and *why.* The pentad, which is based on Burke's five terms (listed below), is a useful mechanism for generating additional details when you are writing an essay about people and/or events.

TERM	DEFINITION	ACTION
ACT	the "what" of an event	the central act, what happened
SCENE	the "when" and "where"	the background of an event, including the physical space and the time in which the act occurred; includes the culture of a place and time
AGENT	the "who"	the person or persons or key force involved in the central event
AGENCY	the "how"	the means by which the act or event was accomplished
PURPOSE	the "why"	the intended objective or end; the reason the act was committed or the event occurred; the purported aim of the action

[1] Adapted from W. Ross Winterowd, ed., *Contemporary Rhetoric: A Conceptual Background with Readings* (New York: Harcourt Brace Jovanovich, 1975), 155–62.

To do a pentad analysis, simply write down each of the five terms as a header and then list under each term the details that come to your mind. If you were working on a topic concerning the banning of toys produced in China, your Pentad analysis might look like this:

- Act (the what)
  - the recall by Mattel of toys made in China because of their high lead content
- Scene (the where, the when)
  - the United States and Canada, 2007
- Agent (the who)
  - Mattel, followed by the U.S. Consumer Product Safety Commission
- Agency (the how)
  - Mattel's creation of the specifications for its order of dolls, toy soldiers, etc.
  - the issuing of recalls first by the toy maker Mattel and subsequently by the U.S. Consumer Product Safety Commission
- Purpose (the why)
  - to guarantee the safety of children; the chief target of the recalls were toys aimed at young children who might put them in their mouths; the source of the lead content was paint

Listed below are the ten possible pairings (or *ratios*, as Burke calls them) you can use to explore a topic that involves actions or people.

Act–Scene	Scene–Agent	Agent–Agency	Agency–Purpose
Act–Agent	Scene–Agency	Agent–Purpose	
Act–Agency	Scene–Purpose		
Act–Purpose			

Burke's ratios allow you to examine in a systematic fashion the relationships among the main parts of your topic. For example, *Act–Purpose* forces you to answer central questions about the event and its intent, while *Act–Agent* yields useful connections between the event and the person or force that caused the event. By analyzing these and other ratios, you may generate additional details as well. An analysis of *Agent–Purpose* and *Agent–Agency* with respect to our banning of toys example might yield a list similar to the one shown in Table 2-1.

TABLE 2-1 Pentad Analysis

ACT	PURPOSE
Mattel's recall	• to protect its reputation in the toy market • to project the entire blame on the Chinese manufacturers • to protect children from harm

AGENT	AGENCY
Mattel	• sign contract with Chinese producers • control costs of product with contract • specify delivery timetable, etc.
Chinese producers	• specify payment amounts and schedules • cover any quality assurances • include all specifications on product

2-f Topic Analysis

Called *topoi* (topics) by the Greeks, topic analysis is a prewriting technique that involves using a set list of questions to generate details about your topic. The activities associated with topic analysis (comparing, contrasting, defining, classifying, and so forth) require you to examine your topic carefully. The sample topic analysis questions that follow are adapted from a list prepared by the American rhetorician Richard Larson.[2]

Exploring a single item

- What are its physical characteristics?
- From what perspectives can it be examined?
- What is its structure?
- How are its parts put together?
- To what class does it belong?
- What uses does it have?
- Who uses it?
- Who or what produced it?

Exploring an event or process

- What happened? (Be precise.)
- What circumstances surrounded this event or process?

---

[2] Adapted from W. Ross Winterowd, ed., *Contemporary Rhetoric: A Conceptual Background with Readings* (New York: Harcourt Brace Jovanovich, 1975), 144–54.

- What were its causes?
- What were its consequences?
- Who or what was affected by it?
- What class of events or processes does it belong to?
- Is it good or bad, desirable or undesirable? By whose standards?
- How do you know about it? How reliable is your information?
- To what other events is it connected?

Writing about abstract concepts (such as socialism or capitalism)

- To what items, group of items, events, or group of events does the word connect?
- What characteristics must an item or event have before this name can be applied to it?
- How do the characteristics of this item or event differ from those of other items or events included in the same class?
- How has the term been used by writers you have read? How have they defined it?
- Do you feel positive toward the item or event named by this term? Negative? What standard inclines you to feel this way?

3 PREWRITING III: SKILL DEVELOPMENT

3-a Reading Skills

Reading is an integral part of the research process and, by extension, prewriting. To be an effective reader, you must first understand *why* you are reading. Your purpose may be as simple as familiarizing yourself with a text or as complex as gaining different perspectives on a topic.

The further you get in your education, the more you shift from reading for information and understanding to reading critically. The latter is more demanding, for it assumes you come to the text with an understanding of the topic. Whether the subject area is English, sociology, business, technology, or applied science, you are asked to use the knowledge you have and apply it to the text. You have to be wary, though, for the text you read may be flawed, or it may present an argument that you do not accept. This is where critical thinking comes into play. Do not accept what others have written without being critical. All writers are subject to bias and faulty logic. Use the following questions to help you become a critical reader.

- What is the writer's purpose?
- Does the writer have a concealed purpose or unannounced bias?
- What do you think the writer's key assumptions are?
- Is any pertinent information ignored?
- Does the point of view distort the material?
- Is the material current?
- Has the writer acknowledged any opposing views and dealt with them?
- Are there any logical problems with the material?
    - Are there close relationships between the points?
    - Is the treatment of the material comprehensive?
    - Are cause-and-effect relationships logical?
    - Does the material include any fallacies or unsupported generalizations?
- Does the author expect you to know anything about his or her topic? Do you?
- How does what you know about the topic differ from the information the author presents?
- Does the author support his or her opinions with evidence? Is the evidence convincing? Is it current?
- Is the author an expert in the field? If not, what does he or she know about the field?
- Is the material based on *primary evidence* (the evidence of the author) or on *secondary evidence* (the evidence of others)? If the latter, are the "others" experts in the field?

Techniques such as *previewing, skimming and scanning, highlighting,* and *note-taking* provide concrete assistance as you engage in the reading process.

PREVIEWING

Before you read a book or an article, you should preview it. Previewing ranges from looking through the table of contents or index of a book to scanning the headings and illustrations of an article. Previewing is an invaluable research tool, for it makes it easier to gauge whether the material you are considering is closely linked to your topic. In this way, previewing helps you separate essential information from nonessential information.

SKIMMING AND SCANNING

Skimming and scanning a text go hand in hand with previewing. Whereas previewing a text focuses on particular items, such as a book's index, table of contents, and headings, *skimming* lets you move through the text by reading the first sentence of a passage and quickly assessing the passage's content. You do not read every sentence when you skim a passage; you simply focus on phrases and important terms to arrive at a quick picture of what is in the passage. If you think the passage is of value, you eventually go back and read it carefully. *Scanning* a passage has the same effect. In scanning, you use your finger, a ruler, or a mouse cursor to guide your eyes down the centre of the page. When you do this, you are not reading individual words; rather, you are gaining a quick impression of the content of each line of print.

When you are doing research, you do not have time to read everything fully. It is more sensible to get an overview of your resources so that you can choose the material you think is most appropriate for your purposes. By skimming and scanning material, as well as looking at the table of contents, index, and topic headings, you can make a quick judgment about the material's usefulness.

HIGHLIGHTING

Highlighting or underlining by means of a highlighter or a pen is an effective way to show the important points in a passage. However, it is recommended only if the material in question is your own property; if you are using a library book or periodical, you should photocopy the material before marking it up.

What you highlight will depend on your purpose. If you read a passage with a specific purpose in mind, that purpose will lead you to different information than might have attracted you had you been doing a general reading. Understanding paragraph structure can also help you decide what to highlight. A paragraph's main idea usually appears in the first or last sentence of the paragraph. (For a discussion of paragraph structure, see Chapters 34 and 38.)

Another form of highlighting is the marginal note. The following passage,[3] which comments on the theme of nationalism in Guy Vanderhaeghe's *The Englishman's Boy*, illustrates how to highlight a text using marginal notes. The marginal notes identify the main idea of each paragraph in the passage. Appended to some of the marginal notes are asterisks, which indicate the relative importance of the paragraph; the greater the number of asterisks, the greater the paragraph's importance. Additionally, some of the notes have questions attached to them that reflect a critical response to the paragraph's claim. Marginal notes therefore allow you to track the writer's analysis and respond critically to elements in that analysis.

---

[3] Reinhold Kramer, "Nationalism, the West and *The Englishman's Boy*," *Essays on Canadian Writing*, Spring 1999, 5–6.

**
Nationalism's
contradictory
positions and
relation to the
novel

First, nationalism
must be evil.

Are such moral
categories useful
in examining the
novel?

Second moral
category:
nationalism is good.

Example: Canadian
nationalism in
regard to US
nationalism

Example: Harry's
rejection of the
American market
****

The effect of
America on
Canada

Is this true in
Vanderhaeghe's
novel?

Nationalism leads . . . to two contradictory positions. First, nationalism must be evil; its military, economic, and cultural forces, signified by Hardwick and Chance, raid across borders. The Western in particular must be evil because it justifies imperial violence by tying it to a nationalist myth of the frontier, and because, in the words of David Lavender, "the leaning gallows, the whistle of wind through the lonesome places, the grim march of the defenders to the place of retribution—the costuming always wins" (153) against Bills of Rights and against (Canadianists might add) national sovereignties.

Second, . . . nationalism must be good; it speaks the counterword to America when E. D. Blodgett, for example, claims that Canada is antifoundational, having no precise moment of birth (147–48). Canadian nationalism is the counterattack against cross-border resource shopping trips: "I am the space you desecrate / as you pass through" says Atwood's backdrop to the cowboy (57). . . . At the end of *The Englishman's Boy,* Harry is ineffectual but morally superior; he has rejected the American market and has done what Claude Jarman Jr. should have done: gone home with mom. And it's hard for Canadianists to quarrel too loudly with either those who disparage nationalism or those who praise it, since the "knavish tricks" from the south more than anything have given life to Canadian nationalism, and we owe our jobs to that nationalism. It is true that there are those, Blodgett usefully reminds us, "who do not readily accept either nationalist or federalist models" (157). Still, no Massey Commission, no Canada Council, no New Canadian Library: no us.

*****
Cosmopolitanism and postcolonialism, two critical theories and their relation to nationalism

Is nationalism, as Hobsbawm suggests, no longer a force? If so, is Vanderhaeghe's novel utilizing a perspective that is no longer relevant to most Canadians?

Wishing somehow to reconcile the contradictory positions (that are of course not unique to North America), cultural theorists generally arrive at either "cosmopolitanism" or "postcolonialism." Cosmopolitans tend to dismiss nationalism as an archaic and quasi-religious stage through which we must pass as quickly as possible in order to arrive at a benign world culture. Cosmopolitans reconcile the two positions by making all nationalisms, theirs and ours, evil. Theirs is evil, as we all know; but ours is evil too—we just haven't recognized this yet. Political scientist E. J. Hobsbawm argues that nationalism is artificial and inauthentic, no longer the historical force it was between 1789 and the 1960s. His first and most convincing argument is empirically based. Most independence movements after World War II were cross-tribal and therefore effectively internationalist; only about 12 of 180 nations are based upon a single ethnic or linguistic group; more and more small states are dropping nationalist goals by aligning themselves with groups such as the EC; the use of lingua francas is on the increase; multinational capital is forging a global economy over which even powerful nations have little control. At the same time, he admits that nationalism is "inescapable," that it is a way of asserting one's precedence in an era of meager resources, that there is now just as much nationalism as there once was, and that it is still prominent in world politics (169, 174, 190–91). . . .

NOTE-TAKING

Although most students have learned to take notes from a classroom overhead, a blackboard or greenboard, or a slide presentation, fewer have mastered efficient note-taking from a speaker, an oral presentation, or a discussion. The same challenge occurs when students are taking notes on highlighted material, trying to make notes that are both brief and sufficient. Additionally, you need to consider how you will preserve the notes. The dominant choice now is storage in a file in your computer; this choice means you have to make an initial decision about what you will name the folder where the file will be kept before you start your initial note-taking. When actually taking your notes, consider the following factors:

1. *Are the notes connected to a text?* If so, be sure to make a record of the author, the book/article/essay title, the library information or URL, and the page or paragraph number of the text. You should record whatever information will be necessary to write a bibliographic reference if you use the material in an essay. For more information about the mechanics of and options for note-taking, see Chapter 17. In addition, ask yourself the following questions:

   • Are there any definitions or facts I should record?

   • Does the material cover what I thought it would, or does it cover ground I was not expecting to cover?

   • Is there anything in the material I do not understand?

   • Do my notes cover the material? Can I cover it in a different way?

2. *Are the notes connected to group discussions or lectures?* If so, ask yourself the following questions:

   • What is the topic of the discussion?

   • Am I responding to a set of discussion questions?

   • What have I highlighted as the main ideas?

   • Are there any cross-references to a text from the discussion or lecture? (If there are, note the page references and highlight the passages the discussion focused on.)

3. *Are the notes intended as primary work for an assignment?* If so, and if that assignment is an essay longer than four pages, you should set up a separate folder for that assignment. Then each set of notes you take on your resource reading can be stored in separate files in that folder. For more information about the note-taking process, see 16-b.

OTHER CONSIDERATIONS

When you are reading, you should also take into account the following considerations:

1. *Personal experiences.* Do you have any experiences that illustrate or describe something about the topic? Your personal experiences may have as much validity as those of the people you read.

2. *Emotional response.* What are your feelings about the topic? It is important to remember that your response to a topic is emotional as well as intellectual. Knowing how you feel about a topic often helps you overcome your

biases, just as knowing what an author feels about a topic helps you respond to his or her comments.

3. *Fact and opinion.* Remember that writing is a combination of fact and opinion. *Facts* deal with people, places, objects, occurrences, and processes that exist or did exist. Although it is possible to have an inaccurate statement that purports to be a fact, a fact's truth or falsity can be proved by objective means.

   Opinions, on the other hand, may be based on facts, an evaluation, an attitude, a probability, or even a belief. However, a statement that is based on attitudes or evaluations of facts is an opinion even when it is generally accepted. Similarly, statements concerning the future are statements of opinion even when they are probably accurate. For instance, a prediction about a plane's departure time is an opinion; once the plane has taken off at a given time, you are dealing with a verifiable fact.

   Be critical of others' opinions. You may find it necessary in your notes to include a judgment on the quality or validity of the opinion you summarize. The fact that an individual is an expert in one field does not necessarily make his or her opinion valid in another field. Ensure that all opinions are substantiated by supporting details and a sound argument.

4. *Organization.* In order to make both summarizing and critical notes on the same page, divide your page in half and place the summary notes on the left side, the critique of those notes on the right. If your notes are electronic, use the table function of your computer to create a table with two columns and as many rows as you need. This simple manoeuvre allows you to concentrate only on summarizing initially and leave your critique for a later time.

3-b Listening Skills

Listening skills are as important as reading skills. You need those skills in order to gather information in various situations. Besides classroom situations, where you listen to a person give a lecture, you may be faced with a discussion, an interview, information on an audio, or videotape, or even information on a live radio or television broadcast. You have to be adept at using your listening skills. Here are a few questions you can ask yourself to judge whether you are a good listener, an active listener, a critical listener:

- What is the main idea the speaker is presenting?
- Are there any supporting facts I should be taking note of?
- Can I predict what the speaker is going to say next or how he or she is going to conclude?
- Do I have any questions about the material? If so, what are they?

- Can I apply the material the speaker is presenting to other material I know?
- Is there any material I disagree with? Why do I disagree with it?

A good listener has to learn not to be distracted by the delivery of the material. It is too easy to be won over by a dynamic presentation of mediocre material and alienated by a drab presentation of first-rate material. Resist the temptation by remembering that your primary concern is content, not delivery.

3-c Critical Thinking Skills

Critical thinking refers to a set of reasoning skills that help you analyze any topic. These skills are important for success at college or university; they provide an essential aid to generating the information and perspectives necessary to a persuasive essay. Critical thinking skills include *inference, causal analysis, summary, analysis, evaluation, synthesis,* and *the Toulmin model.*

INFERENCE

An inference is the reasoned product of two or more facts. It is one of the most basic mental operations you perform in moving from fact to premise, and it is the core of what you do when you use the Toulmin model. If you know factually that the average attendance at hockey games improved following the 2004–2005 lockout and the owners' profits increased, what inference might you draw? If you know that the American emphasis on biofuels advanced significantly in the past twenty months and that the price of corn increased in the past eight months, what inference might you draw? You also need to check whether the logic that allows you to make an inference is self-evident or whether you need to explain it in some detail. Increasing your skill in drawing inferences will increase the persuasive force of your writing.

CAUSAL ANALYSIS

From an early age, you attempt to identify causes and predict effects, two related mental operations. You engage in this particular mental operation frequently enough to call it a basic critical thinking tool. The problem, of course, is that the mere connection of two events in time is not enough to merit calling one the cause of another. There are two key elements you need to learn. The first is the ability to discriminate among contributory, necessary, and sufficient causes. A *contributory cause*, as its name implies, is one that assists in the creation of an effect but is not sufficient by itself to produce that effect. A *necessary cause* is one that must be present if an effect is to result but is not by itself sufficient to produce that effect. A *sufficient cause* is the cause or causes that, alone or working together, will ensure that a certain effect is the result. A primary objective of causal analysis is to identify sufficient cause.

To return to the biofuels example, you might identify the American government's emphasis on these fuels as an alternative to oil as a *contributory* cause for the rise in corn prices. That emphasis, of course, issued from the simple fact that America relies on outside sources for most of its oil. The direct conversion of American corn production from principally a food product for cattle and humans to a key component in ethanol would qualify as a *necessary* cause, as it ensures that the area devoted to producing corn for food will shrink and that shrinkage will increase its price. To establish *sufficient* cause, you would want to include the influence of government financial inducements to increase ethanol production, the current popularity of alternative fuel sources in North American thinking, and the pressure on automakers to be seen as socially responsible while still selling vehicles with high horsepower.

The second key element is to learn to distinguish among *immediate* causes, *intermediate* causes, and *remote* causes. These three terms refer to how close in time a cause is to an effect. You need to discipline yourself to list all the causes you can think of with these three headings as your organizing tool. You will be surprised how often a remote cause turns out to be more important than an immediate cause. The earth tremors that are part of an earthquake, for instance, are not as important to that effect as are shifting plates, a decidedly remoter cause.

Challenge yourself to work with the basic tools of causal analysis until you are skilled at them.

TIP

Use the immediate/intermediate/remote categories to list all the causes you can think of. Then apply the contributory/necessary/sufficient categories to select and develop the causes you want to include in your overall analysis.

SUMMARY

Summarizing is an essential skill for first- and second-year students. Its first purpose is to test your critical reading skills, because it requires you to present the essential matter from a text in your own words in a quarter to a third of the space occupied by that original text. A successful summary therefore retains all the essential matter from a text and filters it through your own language. This filtering action clearly displays the exactness of your understanding of the text being summarized, and this overall process allows you to absorb, reflect on, and present the core meaning of that text. Any longer essay assignment you receive will require you to use your summarizing skills with economy and speed. For that reason, you need to refine and improve those skills.

For a more detailed account of the elements involved in writing a summary, see Chapter 9.

ANALYSIS

Analyzing means "taking apart." Whether you are analyzing a poem, a political campaign, a historic event, or a natural process, you must take the topic apart and study those parts before putting them back together again. This process involves a three-step approach.

1. Divide the topic you are analyzing into its constituent parts.

2. Study the individual parts to see what each contributes to the whole.

3. Reassemble the parts into the whole, commenting on the connections between the parts and the whole.

EVALUATION

An evaluation states why something has, or does not have, value. It is not enough to assert that a particular movie, television program, or fast-food chain is "good" or "bad." You have to demonstrate, as concretely as possible, some grounds that support your claim or thesis. Here are four basic steps you should follow in writing an evaluation:

1. State your claim.

2. Present criteria to provide an objective test of your claim.

3. Apply the criteria carefully and thoroughly

4. Restate your claim, but now as a proven rather than merely asserted claim.

SYNTHESIS

Synthesis is the reverse of analysis. To synthesize, you must put things together rather than take them apart. A typical synthesis involves assembling and presenting the views of three or more informed people on a particular topic. A critical synthesis requires you to do more than point out areas of agreement and disagreement among your sources; you must also indicate which view(s) you support and why. A synthesis tests your ability to summarize views briefly and successfully and to keep many positions clear for your reader while also advancing a single dominant perspective.

THE TOULMIN MODEL

As a postsecondary student, you will be asked to write many forms of argument, from literary analysis through history papers arguing a particular interpretation of events to social sciences papers changing data into premises or positions. In *The Uses of Argument*, Stephen Toulmin proposed a break with the classical model of deductive reasoning and suggested a simpler model for proving or disproving a proposition. His model has six key terms and revolves around two core terms, *data* and *claim*. For a full explanation of this model, see 8-b. Below you will find a sample outline of a Toulmin argument.[4]

Data ———————————————— **Qualifier**
(Between 1976 and 2004, the after-tax income of Canada's rich increased from being 8.1 times greater that that of Canada's poor to being 9.9 times greater)

(It is probably fair to say)

So **Claim**
(The actual disparity in wealth in Canada is overstated)

Since **Warrant** ———————————————— *Unless* **Rebuttal**
(The after-tax statement of income is a more reliable measure than the pre-tax statement)

(The amounts involved in the incomes of the rich are so large as to make this form of measurement questionable)

Because **Backing**
(Our progressive tax structure takes more taxes as the income being taxed grows larger)

---

[4] Adapted from Stephen Edelston Toulmin, *The Uses of Argument* (Cambridge, UK: Cambridge University Press, 1958), 105.

Once you have completed your prewriting activities, you are ready to write your first draft. Do not aim for perfection at this stage. Experienced writers know that trying to create a finished essay in the first draft can stifle a writer's natural voice and impede the flow of writing. A clear understanding of the conditions in which you write will help to smooth your progress through this challenging stage of the writing process.

4-a Writing Preferences

Some writers are happiest writing quickly. Others tend to be more reflective and build their work slowly. It is important to understand and work according to your own idiosyncrasies and preferences as a writer. If you are most comfortable writing one part of your draft at a time, then do so. If you prefer to complete your first draft at a single sitting, then feel free to use that strategy. On the other hand, be wary of counterproductive habits. If you rush through your first draft too quickly, you run the risk of leaving out important elements of your argument or failing to develop your points fully. Conversely, if you proceed too slowly and are preoccupied with such details as spelling and mechanics, you may end up with prose that is choppy and lifeless.

4-b The Importance of Routine

You should establish a routine for drafting. Routine includes the order in which you do tasks. Whereas some writers like to begin with an easy task and thereby build confidence, others prefer to dispense with the most challenging tasks first. Ritual also has to do with where you work, when you work, and what kind of atmosphere you work in. Some writers work best if music is playing in the background; others require silence. Some writers like to have their reference materials spread out on their desks, while others abhor clutter. There is no right way or wrong way to write, but consistency is important. Establish a routine that suits you, and stick to it.

If you have trouble starting, you might try one or more of the following strategies:

- Review the work you did in the prewriting stage.
- If you are feeling overwhelmed, focus on one aspect of the task rather than the task as a whole.
- Reflect on the goal of your task if your inability to start has to do with the fact that you have lost your sense of direction.

Once you have completed your first draft, set it aside for a few days. When you revisit your draft, you should do so with a more critical eye. Your editing will be more effective if you focus on one facet of your draft at a time. Four editing activities that will help you do this are the *structure sweep, the development sweep, the special-paragraphs sweep*, and the *proofreading sweep*. (For further information about these editing tasks, see Chapter 19.)

5-a Structure Sweep

The most efficient way to start revising your first draft is to do a structure sweep. When conducting this kind of editing sweep, ask yourself the following questions about the draft:

- Does each paragraph relate clearly to the preceding paragraph and to the following paragraph?
- Does each paragraph have a focus and a purpose?
- Does each paragraph connect to and advance my thesis?
- Is my argument balanced? Are all of its parts equally developed?

An easy way to check your answer to these questions is to use different-coloured markers or your computer's highlighting feature to identify the main claim in each paragraph and the transitions between paragraphs.

5-b Development Sweep

The goal of a development sweep is to verify that the ideas in your draft are supported sufficiently. Using a pen, a highlighter, or your computer's highlighting feature, identify the sentences that define, illustrate, or otherwise support the main ideas you selected during the structure sweep. If your underlining or highlighting in a particular paragraph yields only one or two supporting sentences, that paragraph's main idea is probably not adequately supported.

5-c Special-Paragraphs Sweep

The focus of a special-paragraphs sweep is the introduction, the conclusion, and any other special paragraphs you have written. To begin your special-paragraphs sweep, ask yourself the following questions about the introduction:

- Does it capture the reader's attention?
- Does it clearly establish my claim (thesis)?
- Does it define difficult or challenging terms?
- Does it provide the background necessary to a successful argument?

Next, respond to the following questions about the conclusion:

- Does it restate my claim?
- Does it summarize the main points supporting my argument?

- Does it reiterate the general significance of my topic?
- Does the last sentence express an appropriate note of finality?

In a short essay, a summary in the conclusion may not be necessary; in a longer essay, however, such a summary is a standard element.

5-d Proofreading Sweep

The purpose of a proofreading sweep is to eliminate errors in usage, spelling, and punctuation. (For information about checking for formatting errors, see 19-d.) Here are some guidelines to assist you with the process:

- Read your essay aloud. Some errors or omissions become more obvious when you hear them.
- After obtaining your instructor's approval, have a fellow student proof-read your essay.
- Set your draft aside for a few days and then return to it. Gaining distance from your essay generally leaves you in a better position to spot errors.
- Use past graded assignments and the errors chart (see Chapter 12) to determine what your most common errors are. Use your awareness of these errors to make your proofreading sweep more efficient.

THE WRITING PROCESS: HIGHLIGHTS 6

Writing an essay can be an overwhelming task unless you use a system. Breaking the writing process down into its three basic stages—prewriting, drafting, and revising—and developing the skills and techniques associated with each activity will help you to move through the process methodically. Below are some fundamental questions you need to ask yourself about each stage of the writing process.

PREWRITING

- Have I considered all possible sources for material?
- Have I gathered all the material I need for this project?
- Have I organized the material I gathered?
- Have I decided which material is essential and which material is unnecessary?
- Have I taken a position on my topic?
- Have I narrowed the focus of my topic?
- Do I have a claim (or thesis) that I wish to make?

DRAFTING

- Am I using the organizational structure I developed for my topic?
- Am I developing each of the points in my analysis?
- Am I using illustrations and data to support my claim?
- Am I keeping paragraph and topic unity in mind as I write? (For a definition of paragraph unity, see page 256.)
- Am I keeping in mind the purpose of each paragraph?
- Am I connecting each paragraph to my claim?
- Am I using quotations where needed?

REVISING

- Am I using all four editing sweeps to check my work?
- Am I looking for errors I commonly make?
- Am I examining the work to see if it has unity and coherence? (For a definition of paragraph coherence, see page 256.)
- Have I developed each part of my analysis?
- Are the parts of my analysis balanced with one another?
- Are my claim and conclusion appropriate for my analysis?

EXERCISES

EXERCISE I-1 PREWRITING ACTIVITIES

Assume that you are in the first stage of the writing process. Read the list of topics below and choose the one that most interests you.

> Dreams: The Psychological View of Their Significance
> Transition Time in Television: The Rise of Televised Poker
> Private and Public Health Care: A Position
> Student Debt: The Impact of Increases in Tuition and Living Costs

To discover what you know about your chosen topic and what your position on it might be, work through as many of the following activities as you can. Remember that the key to effective prewriting is to identify your audience and your purpose, to discover your position on your topic, and to begin generating the information you need for a successful essay.

1. Define your purpose, audience, and stance.

2. Brainstorm your topic. Remember that your objective in brainstorming is to generate ideas, not to organize them.

3. Create a mind-map of your topic.

4. Engage in either freewriting or looping. Use the results to fine-tune your definition of your stance.

5. Apply the pentad to your topic. First, create a list based on the pentad's five terms or headings. Next, create a list based on Burke's ten ratios.

6. Using the information you have gathered through the mind-mapping, freewriting or looping, and pentad activities, apply the branching technique to your topic.

7. If you are not satisfied that you have discovered all you know about your topic, answer the relevant topic analysis questions listed in 2-f.

EXERCISE I-2   CRITICAL THINKING

Critical reading and thinking are essential skills in your approach to writing essays. You use these skills to create content, to read your resources critically, to construct claims that form the core of your paragraphs, and to assist your editing. Another key skill is pattern recognition connected to analysis. In short, we see the pattern and then we analyze what it tells us. In the following exercises, you will need to practise your pattern recognition skills. Some of the exercises are based on the sets of facts that follow.

THE FACTS

The data in the sets of facts below are drawn from newspaper reports, Statistics Canada publications, a book, a magazine, and other sources. Examine these sets of facts closely. Try to discover any patterns that announce themselves. Every time you find one, write it down and check to see if it is really there. Some but not all of these patterns are stated in the presentation of the facts.

(1) Distribution of Personal Wealth* among Families in B.C., 1999

	TOTAL WEALTH OF GROUP	AVERAGE WEALTH OF FAMILY UNIT	DISTRIBUTION OF WEALTH
All family units	$423,494,000,000	$251,235	100%
Poorest 10%	($1,371,000,000)	($8,126)	(−0.3%)
Second	$445,000,000	$2,633	0.1%
Third	$2,016,000,000	$11,998	0.5%
Fourth	$5,503,000,000	$32,496	1.3%
Fifth	$11,553,000,000	$68,843	2.7%
Sixth	$20,715,000,000	$122,747	4.9%
Seventh	$31,569,000,000	$187,168	7.5%
Eighth	$47,752,000,000	$282,069	11.3%
Ninth	$73,946,000,000	$439,594	17.5%
Richest 10%	$231,367,000,000	$1,378,534	54.6%
Poorest 5 Groups	$18,146,000,000		4.3%
Richest 5 Groups	$405,349,000,000		95.7%

* Note: In Table 1 and Table 2, "Personal Wealth" means the total wealth of a family unit, including salaries, house, cars, and any other wealth.

(2) Regional Differences in Personal Wealth, 1999

	AVERAGE WEALTH	AVERAGE % OF NATIONAL AVERAGE	GAP AVERAGE FOR RICHEST 10%	FOR POOREST 10%	BETWEEN RICHEST AND POOREST
British Columbia	$251,235	126%	$1,378,534	($8,126)	$1,386,660
Prairies	$221,110	111%	$1,088,364	($7,096)	$1,095,460
Ontario	$213,114	107%	$1,135,499	($5,655)	$1,141,154
Quebec	$155,189	78%	$868,517	($7,067)	$875,584
Atlantic	$122,798	62%	$604,669	($8,227)	$612,896
CANADA	$199,664		$1,059,423	($7,110)	$1,066,533

(3) Income Shifts, 1989 to 1998

In the decade from 1989 to 1998, there was a dramatic shift in how much income families brought home in earnings—including salaries, investments and private pensions, but excluding welfare, Canada Pension and other government payments. Families with two or more persons are broken into five equal segments, each representing 20 percent of the total number of families. Average pretax incomes, in constant 1998 dollars:

SEGMENT	1989	1998	% CHANGE
Poorest	$10,388	$8,627	−17%
Lower-Middle	$31,427	$27,486	−13
Middle	$48,776	$46,835	−4
Upper-Middle	$67,790	$68,505	+1
Richest	$114,178	$124,681	+9

(4) Income and Taxation Gaps, Canada and the USA

- From 1999 to 2002, the richest 10 percent of Canadians increased their share of the nation's total income from 31.7 percent to 35.7 percent.
- In 1976, the wealthiest families grossed 31.2 times the income of the poorest families; in 2004, they grossed 81.7 times the poorest incomes.

- When the comparison shifts to after-tax income as opposed to pre-tax income, the ratios change. Between 1976 and 2004, the gap between the richest and poorest saw the top earners move from 8.1 times the incomes of the poorest to 9.9 times the incomes of the poorest.

- Between 1996 and 2005, the percentage of Canadians living below the poverty line moved from 15.8 percent to 10.8 percent.

- In 2002, 52.6 percent of all federal taxes were paid by the top 10 percent of income earners; in 1990, that group paid 46 percent.

- Between 2002 and 2005, the income of the top 1 percent of earners in the United States increased by an amount larger than the *entire* income of the bottom 20 percent of earners.

Source: *Maclean's,* 18 June 2007

EXERCISE I-3   ANALYSIS

Choose two of the following questions and write a response of two to four paragraphs on each.

1. Explain why the minority of taxpayers in Canada pays more taxes than the majority.

2. Using the data available to you, what do you believe are the principal reasons for the income disparities revealed by the data offered here. Include in your response your view of whether the data is skewed or not.

3. Given the data here on income distribution, what would you expect its influence to be on attendance at institutes? colleges? universities? private training schools?

4. Explain whether the differing valuations of the Canadian dollar during the period referenced would have an effect on income distribution.

5. Pay particular attention to the data in Table (1); choose two patterns that you discover in that table and comment on each in a single paragraph.

EXERCISE I-4   INFERENCE

In this exercise, you will use your skills in creating inferences. Remember that an inference is a general conclusion based on two separate facts. The facts are given to you here in the sets of data. Write two paragraphs based on the data supplied.

(a) In the first paragraph, choose two facts from the data and use them to support your inference. State the facts first, followed by the inference. If you feel it is necessary, explain how the facts support your inference.

(b) In the second paragraph, state your inference first and follow that with the presentation of the two supporting facts. Again, if necessary, supply the reasoning that links the facts to the inference.

EXERCISE I-5   SUMMARY

The activities in this exercise require you to use your summarizing skills. For more on summarizing, refer to pages 54–55 in Chapter 9.

1.   Write a summary of the Reinhold Kramer excerpt on pages 15 and 16.

2.   Write a summary of a two-page excerpt from a text you use in one of your other courses. If you submit this exercise to your instructor, include a copy of the excerpted pages.

EXERCISE I-6   SYNTHESIS

Write a brief synthesis. In it, attempt to amalgamate the income data supplied above. See if you can reconcile income distribution disparities with social health.

EXERCISE I-7   CAUSAL ANALYSIS

Use the facts below to write a brief causal analysis of the 2007 die-off of bees in the United States and the subsequent decline in agricultural output. In your analysis, suggest why the first causes identified were so wrong.

In the September 7, 2007, issue of *The Globe and Mail*, an article was included in the Agriculture section (A3) that summarized the current understanding of the lead cause behind a significant die-off of honeybees in the United States. During the first period of recognizing the threat, it was assumed that the colony collapse disorder was affecting both American and Canadian bee colonies. By the time this article appeared, Canadian authorities had made it clear that bees in Canada were not affected. The following are selected facts from that article.

- The first causes suggested for the die-off, once its extent was known, were
  – the presence of radiation from proliferating cellular phone towers dis-oriented the honeybees and caused them to die while foraging for nectar, and
  – genetically modified crops were poisoning the bees.
- The widespread alarm in the bee industry was based on the fact that bees are essential for propagating many crops. The absence of bees for propagation threatened agricultural produce worth $15 billion.
- A team of scientists established that the cause of the colony collapses was Israeli acute paralysis virus.
- The scientists speculated that the virus arrived in the United States in 2004 with Australian bees imported by American beekeepers wanting to expand their hives. The American agriculture industry had lobbied for this importation as a way of increasing the bee colonies' capacity for pol-lination, and, in particular, for increasing the production of almonds.
- Canada does not allow the importation of whole colonies, only of queen bees, and Canada has been free from the colony collapses troubling American beekeepers.

- Australian bees are not affected by the Israeli virus; scientists speculate that this is because the bees do not have varroa mites, which are found on North American bees and which suppress the immune system of bees.

EXERCISE I-8   SYNTHESIS

Examine the tables and data and assess what has happened over time to the distribution of income in B.C. and Canada.

Write a short essay supporting either

1. the claim that the inequality of wealth distribution is a harmful social fact, OR

2. the claim that unequal distribution of wealth in Canada is a necessary and socially productive fact.

Academic Writing

Plagiarism is a problem directly associated with academic writing. If you are writing an essay on a general subject, you are far less likely to feel the need to locate and use formal secondary sources. Most academic papers, however, begin with the assumption that you will supplement your own knowledge of the assigned subject through research. It is this expectation that leads to plagiarism.

7-a Definition

According to the *MLA Handbook for Writers of Research Papers,* Seventh Edition, the term *plagiarism* derives from a Latin word that means "a kidnapper." It is the writer's kidnapping of someone else's work and the offering of that work as his or her own that is the fundamental element in all cases of plagiarism. This kidnapping is both a theft of another person's work and an intended deception of the paper's audience into believing the work is the writer's. This double act, therefore, explains why the academic community takes cases of plagiarism so seriously.

The public profile of plagiarism has risen sharply in recent years. We now witness several high-profile Canadian postsecondary institutions requiring student writers to furnish proof that their submitted papers contain original work with all borrowings properly attributed. Previously, the onus rested with the faculty member to establish, objectively, that plagiarism had occurred in the writing of the paper. At one institution, students have to submit verification that submitted papers have been scrutinized by Turnitin, one of the software packages designed to check for elements of plagiarism in a paper.

7-b Context

If the incidence of plagiarism in the postsecondary system is, in fact, increasing, and we are not simply experiencing an increase in our awareness of the phenomenon, it's fair to ask why. Among the leading reasons would be

1. *The influence of electronic resources.* The Internet has changed the student's life. Twenty-five years ago, the resources students used to write postsecondary papers could all be found in the library. Students became familiar with the Library of Congress organizing system libraries used and knew the areas of their chosen disciplines. They relied on handwritten notes and research done in books and journals. The computer changed all that. Now students can search for resources in the comfort of their homes and keep all their notes and drafts in electronic folders and files. This also means students are frequently going to rely on electronic source material, as they have often been urged to do. If their notetaking is careless, they might offer the wording of the source as their own. They may even believe that the electronic resource is public property and therefore not in need of citation. Ironically, the same electronic network makes it far easier for instructors to check a student's paper if they feel plagiarism has occurred. All they have to do is enter suspicious strings of words, and the electronic sleuth, whether Eve2 or some other

scanning program, will instantly identify the source the student has used if that wording is identical or strongly similar. The computer can hold thousands of sources in its files and use its scanning and pattern recognition capacities to identify plagiarism in seconds.

2. *Increased costs of postsecondary education.* Anyone who reads the daily paper knows that the cost of tuition at Canada's postsecondary institutions is outstripping both inflation and most previous periods of inflation in tuition costs. Much of this is the result of the downloading of costs from provincial governments to institutions, but that doesn't change the facts of the increased cost and the pressure it places on students not to fail and waste the money they spent to attend a postsecondary institution.

3. *Increased enrollments in postsecondary institutions.* Even though we are now undergoing a period of adjustment, with declining K–12 cohorts of students in most provinces, the overall rise in postsecondary enrollments has been considerable in the last twenty years. This places pressure on students to get better marks to ensure their place in the program they want to enter.

4. *Increased competition for grades.* The fact that more students have been trying to get in to postsecondary institutions increases the use of grades as entrance filters. Even with that pressure easing at present, students still believe they need to maximize their chance of entering the program they want through better grades. One possible product of these pressures is plagiarism. And, if it is not discovered immediately, a student can believe it's a reliable option.

5. *Levels of student ability.* With almost half the university-level population now attending a postsecondary program, it is probable that the overall skill level of the entering undergraduate population is lower. That decline would show up in the level of reading, writing, and analytic skills possessed by students when they enter. After they begin postsecondary education, they also discover that the pace of their education has quickened and the level of assistance available to them has probably declined. This reality has led to many institutions adjusting their entrance requirements, expanding their services for learners, tightening prerequisites for entrance to certain courses, and other responses. It is possible that more students are trying to write sophisticated papers without all of the skills such papers demand, and that fact can also lead to plagiarism. Postsecondary instructors know that plagiarism is often an act of desperation.

6. *Time-management problems.* If it is true that more acts of plagiarism are acts of desperation than conscious attempts to deceive, then it is not surprising that students who feel their talents are more modest than what is demanded by an academic paper will be tempted to submit the work of others to buttress their own. If the student is working fifteen to

twenty-four hours a week part-time, as many students do, the pressure increases. Adding a time bind to anxiety about ability can lead to plagiarism as a response.

7. *Cultural differences.* The student may come from a context in which it is both appropriate and proper to repeat the words of an expert or learned person as a sign of respect. It is relatively easy to move from this experience to an act of plagiarism and for the student to be residually puzzled by the depth of the response to that plagiarism.

8. *Increased formal attention to plagiarism.* Most postsecondary institutions have identified plagiarism as a serious problem. There have been highly profiled cases reported in newspapers and nightly news reports. In response to that, institutions create policies and purchase the software necessary to discover any plagiarism occurring in papers and assignments. This increased attention means more acts of plagiarism are detected, and the public continues to see it as a significant problem.

Given that the context in which plagiarism occurs is a complex one, it is often not sufficient simply to tell students not to plagiarize. Most institutions also give entering students a copy of their policy on plagiarism. It is common for that policy to include the penalty of a grade of zero on the paper for a first offence, zero in the course for a second offence, and possible expulsion for a third offence. Given these multiple warnings, it remains startling that such a large number of students annually commit plagiarism.

7-c Practical Examples of Plagiarism

The following represent examples of plagiarism. Each of these examples has actually occurred and represents one form of confusion about what constitutes plagiarism.

a) *But I didn't plagiarize; I just gave my paper to my study partner.*

It does constitute plagiarism in most institutions if an instructor discovers a paper essentially copied, in whole or in part, from another submitted paper. The circumstance is analogous to a student in an exam cheating by looking at another student's exam with that student's compliance. You should know that the penalty for plagiarism in this case is applied to both students and not just to the student who actually copied the paper.

b) *I was just using notes I had borrowed; how was I to know the notes weren't the original work of the student who lent them to me?*

Again, this is an act of plagiarism whether you knew the notes were paraphrases of someone else's work or not. In this case, however, the student who lent the notes is not guilty of plagiarism.

c) *This data was on the Web; as such, it was in the public domain or common knowledge. So my use of it can't be plagiarism.*

Wrong. Specific data is rarely common knowledge. You would have to show multiple instances of the data being published in accessible sources, such as newspapers or mass circulation magazines, for your defence to be acceptable. Whenever you use specific data from a source in a paper, cite that source.

d) *I have had help from tutors before, including fixing up my sentences and suggesting better wording.*

This still constitutes plagiarism, from the root definition of "using someone else's work without acknowledging your source." A tutor should know better than to do your writing for you, but, if this does occur, you need to acknowledge the assistance. Better still, to avoid unpleasant repercussions, you should ask your instructor what editing help, if any, a tutor can give you. Some institutions forbid such help.

e) *Come on; I only used a couple of phrases on my second page and a sentence or two later. The rest is all my work. So it's ridiculous to call this a plagiarized paper.*

It doesn't matter how much plagiarism occurs. It only matters that you have plagiarized. There is no ascending scale of penalties, with higher deductions as the proportion of plagiarism increases. One sentence, or even just a phrase, is enough to earn the penalty. Cite the source and avoid that penalty.

f) *But I never used the original wording; I was just copying from my notes, and you can see that I used my own wording when making those notes.*

Again, that doesn't matter. The act of plagiarizing is the act of offering someone else's work as your own. If you use the structure of the person's analysis or the same examples in the argument or the same sequence of points, it doesn't matter that you substituted your own words. The same principle applies when you borrow someone else's statistics or data.

g) *I am not guilty of plagiarism. Look in my bibliography; I included the titles of the two works that I used as resources in the actual writing of my paper. So I have attributed my sources; I just did it a little differently than the way you are talking about.*

It's still plagiarism, despite what former Alberta Premier Ralph Klein might think. His was a highly publicized case in which he copied material word for word from a website and assumed a general bibliographic reference would take care of everything. The fact is that you have to cite each borrowing, whether a direct quotation or a summary or a paraphrase. It may even be only borrowed data that you are acknowledging a source for. If there's no citation of the borrowing at the point it occurs, you are committing plagiarism and are relying on your instructor either not to notice what you have done or to allow you a chance to re-submit the paper with appropriate citations. In most cases, that will not happen.

The rules are fairly simple when it comes to plagiarism. No argument after the fact is going to change the reality that you used someone else's work and did not acknowledge the borrowing. At best, the writer who attempts to offer another's work as his or her own is gambling on the inattention of the instructor. Review and master the basic guidelines below governing the appropriate uses of borrowed materials.

What does not need to be cited as borrowed material?

1. Obviously, the first answer is your own insights and understanding, expressed in your own words. Even before you commenced your research, you will have had your own thoughts and assumptions concerning that subject. They do not have to be cited. Even following your research, you will continue to have certain perceptions that are your own. The only difficulty arises when you think an original position you held has been significantly modified by your reading; at that point, you may have to include a general acknowledgment of your principal influence or influences.

2. You also do not need to include a citation for anything that can legitimately be described as common knowledge or information within the public domain. What you do have to understand is what qualifies as common knowledge. If something has appeared in multiple public sources, such as newspapers and magazines, then it is common knowledge. Some authorities suggest a minimum of three publicly accessible sources, but your common sense will assist you on this issue. It is common knowledge that before the NHL owners started the 2004–2005 season, there were threats of an extended lockout because those owners wanted to gain a salary cap similar to the one that prevails in the National Basketball Association. But it is not common knowledge that a certain team lost a certain amount last year or that only six teams formally announced a financial surplus at fiscal year-end. Equally, it is common knowledge that many scientists believe global warming is occurring and that the principal cause is pollution arising from human activity. It is not common knowledge, however, that the cost of implementing the Kyoto Accord is greater than any measurable returns for the next one hundred years. When it comes to specific information such as this, your common sense tells you that it is not likely to be common knowledge. As such, its source needs to be formally referenced.

What do I have to cite in a note or a parenthetic reference?

1. Ideally, you have maintained your notes for your essay in such a manner that you can quickly distinguish a quotation from another form of note.

You should, in your notes, use quotation marks and a distinct colour of highlighter to denote direct borrowings from your readings. Remember, each quotation has to be formally acknowledged by quotation marks or segregation from your text by indenting, and a note or parenthetic reference.

2. You must also acknowledge, in citations, all paraphrases and summaries you have included in your paper.

3. Include any note you obtained from a fellow student, a tutor at a learning centre, or any other information that you cannot fairly describe as part of your common knowledge. Write your citation in such a way as to reflect fairly the source of your borrowing.

4. Provide a citation for materials gathered from factual sources, encyclopedias, and specialized dictionaries, whether in paper or electronic formats.

5. Formally acknowledge all materials you used from your online sources. Before deciding on what your online sources will be, review the advice about assessing online sources in 15-d.

WRITING THE ACADEMIC ESSAY

8

The experience you gained in high school with papers is useful for the research protocols, planning skills, and organizational experience you gained in dealing with more extended essays. Sometimes, however, students get the sense that a research assignment is an "encyclopedia essay," where the task is chiefly to take information from one place and transfer it, slightly modified, to another. Academic essays, however, expect you to use your research to supplement the knowledge you already have and to support your own perspective.

Writing an academic essay normally requires you to demonstrate some mastery of the perspective, analytic skills, and method intrinsic to the discipline that assigns you the paper. Your instructor will grade your essay on more than your personal knowledge, passion for the subject, and general writing skills, even though those talents will assist you. You will be expected to demonstrate that you understand how to write, reason, and prove your claims in a way that is consistent with the practices of the discipline.

8-a An Overview

A good place to start in understanding the expectations of academic essay assignments is the purpose of the essay. Generally, you will find three leading purposes.

INFORMATION ESSAY

The first, and possibly the simplest, purpose you will encounter is the "information" essay. It may be a review of the literature in a specific area. That kind of assignment asks you to give a brief summary of the literature on a particular subject. You will normally be given more restrictions than simply to "review and summarize the literature on dreams in the past five years." You might be asked in a labour relations segment in a business class to summarize the gains made by General Motors and other American car builders in the negotiations conducted with labour unions between 2005 and 2008. Or your political science instructor might ask you to explain the changes made by the federal Conservatives in the past four years to payments made to the provinces. A history instructor might require you to write a comparison of the foreign policy of Bill Clinton and that of George Bush. The "information" essay has the common purpose of asking you to research a focused subject and summarize what you learned. When you are writing it, however, you need to remain aware of the expectations of the discipline that assigned it and the critical perspectives appropriate to that discipline.

ANALYTICAL ESSAY

A second kind of purpose for a postsecondary assignment might best be described as analytical. This assignment requires you to invent your own analytical framework and methods, and that is one of its most challenging features. Analysis is the art of deconstructing a subject, understanding the parts of that subject, and understanding how those parts interact. An English instructor may ask you to analyze two of Keats's odes, stressing their common features and themes. A psychology class may require an analysis of the Stanford prison experiment and what it tells us about how we depersonalize a human subject. If your marketing professor asks you to analyze the marketing strategies of Subway and McDonald's, you need to take apart the strategies of each company and relate those strategies to their intended audiences. You might even go further and discuss the utility of those strategies. On the surface, an analytic essay asks you to separate a subject into its constituents and say something about how those constituents interact, but the purpose is generally not limited to the "taking apart" phase. You will often find that the subject you are given is asking for more than simple analysis. The psychology example above shows that. Nevertheless, many of the essay choices you will encounter have an analytic purpose.

ARGUMENT ESSAY

A third kind of academic essay assignment is "argument." Sometimes this purpose is signalled directly with words such as "agree or disagree and discuss." However, even an assignment in an American history course asking you to discuss whether the Civil War originated chiefly from social, economic, or political causes is essentially an argument. You may even discover that an essay assignment that appears to be an analytical assignment can be converted into an argument. Many writers find it easier to write from an argumentative edge; you should, of course, get your instructor's agreement for such a shift. The next unit will have more to say about arguments and how to write them.

Breaking all your assignments into three purposes involves some simplification. A business class may assign you a statistical topic, but even that will involve some analysis. It is always helpful to make sure you understand the purpose of a writing assignment and what is involved in fulfilling that purpose.

8-b Academic Argument

In postsecondary institutions, essays are a standard means of evaluating students in the humanities and social sciences. The three most common kinds of assigned topics for essays are **information**, **analysis/inquiry**, and **argument** topics.

Perhaps the most frequent demand you will face is to research a subject and take a **position** on an issue or issues within it. Argument essays can range from a causal analysis in history to a critique of a major theme in a literary work. In the social sciences, essays in psychology and sociology frequently ask you to evaluate the principal features of a subject and choose a position regarding one of those features. Social sciences essays also ask you to support a reading of data compiled from a survey or questionnaire.

KINDS OF ARGUMENT

There are three kinds of arguments we can construct: arguments of **fact**, **value**, and **policy**. The argument of **fact** addresses questions of how something happened, what causes precipitated an event, how a subject is constituted, what the subject relates to or influences, and so on. When you are stating the major causes of the 2008 recession in the United States or the reasons why the Canadian government could have foreseen the problems that would arise from the engagement in Afghanistan, you are writing an argument about **fact**. This is also true if you are writing an assessment of human dreaming or of the excesses caused by our multicultural policies.

The argument of **value** specifically addresses the value of your subject, its worth according to the criteria you adopt and apply. The key to a successful argument here is to create sufficient **criteria** and apply them rigorously to make your position persuasive. If you wished to argue that *No Country for Old Men* deserved the Academy Award for best film of 2007, you would need to include more criteria than simply its handling of violence and its insistence on a particular moral position. Your criteria have to include the elements you believe made the film worthy of the award, including cinematic and thematic values.

The argument of **policy** directly addresses the question of what we should do in response to a problem or issue (the subject). As you know, elections are, in part, arguments of policy, especially when it comes to matters of finance, environmental decline, health delivery, and foreign policy. In building a policy argument, you have to clarify why some choices are wrong and others are right. You must also offer reasoned, fact-based arguments for your position in favour of a specific choice of action.

Take, as a single example of how these different forms of argument apply, the health arrangements wherever a provincial government is moving from a local to a more general model of health care delivery.

- An argument of **fact** might ask where a regional model of health delivery came from and how its delivery model differs from the previous arrangement of hospitals having individual budgets assigned by a provincial authority.

- An argument of **value** might examine the positions Canadians hold about the best way of guaranteeing universal public access to health care and argue for one of those positions as having the highest worth. This could, in turn, be applied to the different delivery models.

- A **policy** argument might argue for infusing some degree of private health care into the public model as a means of controlling costs. This argument would necessarily involve you in the debate about universal public health care and how it should be managed.

THE CLASSICAL MODEL OF ARGUMENT

One of the first models of argument that we can learn from is the **classical** or **ancient** model, seen as having either a five-part or a seven-part structure. What we should primarily learn from this model is the importance of establishing the **background** and context of an argument first before entering the **body** or content part.

The Greeks believed that the argument's beginning had three necessary parts, with the first being the **background** to or **context** of the argument.

- In presenting the context, you accomplish the necessary task of **clarifying** for your reader the events or circumstances behind the debate. If we return to our earlier example of the argument in Canada over the delivery of health care, we would therefore begin by sketching how we moved in the 1940s and 1950s from a user-pay model to an insurance-driven model predicated on the belief that all citizens, no matter their age or financial condition, have an equal right to care. We might have to go right back to the first Saskatchewan form of this model in describing the background of the traditional delivery model. We would also need to describe how there began to be trouble funding that model successfully in the last quarter of the twentieth century and why debates arose over alternative delivery models.

- We would next sketch the major **positions** taken on the issues of adequate funding and successful delivery of health care in the past decade. The ancients would insist on this background as an essential prelude to the writer's announcing a particular position.

- Finally, with background established and major positions identified, the reader would be ready for the position you will be supporting. The **major claim** and a **preview** of the argument would be the third element in a classical argument.

The opening of an argument in the classical style would therefore have three distinct parts, answering three distinct questions:

1. What are the **background details** or context of this argument?

2. What **positions** have arisen with respect to the issue/argument?

3. What **thesis** are we going to take and how do we intend to support that thesis?

These opening parts would be followed by the **body** of our argument, which would require your mounting both a "**confirmation**," or "argument for," and a "**refutation**" or "argument against." The arguments for the central claim or thesis always dominate; they are, in turn, built upon individual claims that logically support the main position.

The Greek and Roman orators and writers knew that a complete argument had to directly address the **position of the opposing side** also. In fact, what they called the appeal to ethos (the integrity of the writer) demanded a fair recitation of the opposing position. The successful argument might even make concessions to the counterargument, since it is rare that a position has no merit. Generally, in writing (or speaking) a refutation, the ancients would first state objectively the opposing position and then suggest reasons why there were problems in maintaining such a position.

It is common for writers to neglect the importance of **refutations**. However, an argument is incomplete without paying attention to the other side. It is simply good practice to do so, but it must be managed in a way that does not give too much prominence to the counterargument. Frequently, that can be accomplished by dealing with it first in the body of the argument and then moving directly into paragraphs of **confirmation**.

In the classical model, the argument's conclusion has two central tasks, to **summarize** and to **restate**. Simply repeating what you have already said in multiple paragraphs will not hold your reader's attention. You need to select the key claims upon which your position rests and find new language to repeat them. In concluding, you also need to focus on your **central claim;** unless you have a **policy** or **action** to recommend, your thesis is normally your last sentence. Some writers like to end by suggesting the general **importance** of the issue being addressed.

We are unlikely to follow the classical model of argument exactly in our academic arguments. However, this model reminds us, with its seven (or five) parts, what the tasks of a successful argument are:

1. Do not normally plunge into the **central claim** of the argument; instead, first establish the **context** of the argument, the domain in which it exists.

II
ACADEMIC WRITING

2. Include a **narration of the facts**, a full backgrounding of the issue that you are about to take a position on. This both establishes context and gives you a chance to select what you believe the most important facts are. A narration of the facts also allows you to begin in a relatively **neutral** domain.

3. Once the context and background are established, give a full statement of the thesis, the **central claim**, which is the natural bridge into the body of the argument. If the argument is a longer one, you may also wish to follow with a **preview** of the argument's claims as part of the thesis paragraph.

4. Include **counterarguments** as well as **positive arguments** in the body of the essay. As such, there are at least two parts to the body, the essay's longest unit. Remember that the counterargument should never obscure or receive emphasis equal to the emphasis on the positive argument.

5. Focus the ending on the argument's position. **Summary** naturally precedes the repetition of the **central claim**, but it is the claim that should receive the principal emphasis. Finally, you may also want to suggest an **action or actions** that may be taken if your argument is an argument of **policy**.

ARGUMENT AND ITS APPEALS

An argument has a beginning, a middle, and an end, as we can see when we examine the classical model of argument. Arguments also employ different kinds of appeals. We should remember that the root meaning inherent in the word *argument* is "to move the audience from one position towards another."

The ancient terms for the basic appeals the writer can make are *pathos, logos,* and *ethos*—the appeal to **emotion**, the appeal to **logic**, and the appeal to **integrity**.

- We expect the appeal to *logos*, or **reason/logic**, to dominate our arguments in an academic environment. As such, we build our paragraphs around claims, data, and warrant (using the Toulmin model), or claims based on inductive or deductive logic (using the more traditional terms). We also use expert witnesses, sampling, survey, and other reason-based means to support the claims underpinning our position.

- We should know, however, that argument often includes **appeals to our feelings** and to our **trust in the speaker/writer**. Political campaigns or magazine ads are excellent venues for the appeal to *pathos*, since both political parties and advertisers know that it is easier to motivate us through our emotions than through our mind. A quick survey of ads for cars or clothes or cameras will remind us that sellers want to get to our desires, not to our mental capacities. You may wish to include an appeal to emotion; however, academic argument values claims supported by facts, data, and reasoning, so that appeal must be dominant.

- The appeal to *ethos*, or the "good person" argument, is subtler, but it essentially involves speakers/writers asking us to believe them because they are honest and have our best interest at heart. In an argument, when we concede a good point to the other side of the issue, we may also be appealing to ethos because such a concession reinforces in the reader a sense of our **fair-mindedness**. Equally, when we take the time to provide a full background for the issue we are examining before we state our position, we leave an impression of impartiality. Generally, writing that relies on reasoned positions rather than slanting or absolute statements is more likely to create an appeal to ethos and give the general sense of a fair-minded writer/speaker who can be trusted.

INDUCTIVE AND DEDUCTIVE REASONING

The earliest means of appealing to logos was through what came to be called **inductive** and **deductive** reasoning. **Inductive reasoning** began with particular examples and attempted to use them to support a generalization. Individual examples were analyzed to discover a pattern, and the pattern, once discovered and supported, provided a basis for the generalization.

In the current argument for global warming, for instance, scientists compare the average warming effect of the past two or three decades with the fluctuation of temperatures over a similar period earlier in the twentieth century. The difference between these two periods is then used to support the generalization that the Earth is getting warmer. Even the more limited use of data based on the annual shrinkage of glaciers in the extreme north or south is an instance of inductive reasoning: one would examine the particular instances, discover the pattern in these particulars, and articulate the general claim that the particulars support. Even the movement of polar bears away from a traditional habitat can become a meaningful particular supporting the global warming generalization.

The strength of an inductive argument lies in the **comprehensiveness** and **representative** nature of the examples it employs to support its claim or claims. The tests you need to apply to your examples include the following questions:

1. Are my examples representative rather than specialized?
2. Are my examples sufficient to support my claim?
3. Are my examples random ones rather than specially selected ones?
4. Are my examples typical and various? (Ideally, your examples should show some variety.)
5. Does my claim go beyond the boundaries covered by my examples?
6. Do my examples contain reasonable predictive force?

Deductive reasoning, in its earliest form, attempts to replace experience with logic. Where induction relies on multiple experiences to support a generalization about those experiences, deduction uses a pattern of statements to defend a conclusion. Perhaps the best-known early example is the following:

All humans are mortal. (major proposition)

Socrates is a human. (minor proposition)

Therefore, Socrates is mortal. (conclusion)

Each statement here is called a **proposition**; the last one is the **conclusion**, and it is supported by the first two, called, in turn, the major proposition and minor proposition. As you can see, the first statement is a generalization and the second is a particular example. Essentially, this three-part form places a general subject in a class, then places a particular subject in a class, then concludes by observing that the particular subject must have the same property as the general because they belong to the same class (mortal humans). We have said, "All a's are b; c is an a; therefore, c is also a b." If we do this in the correct form and if the propositions are true, then the reasoning will be both sound and valid. The point to remember here is that we arrive at the general truth through the **operation of logic** rather than the enumeration of particular instances. If we wished to arrive at this conclusion inductively, we would have to **list many instances** of people we knew who had died before offering the "Socrates is mortal" conclusion.

This is necessarily a simplified description of the syllogism, the main feature of traditional reasoning. You can learn more about syllogistic logic by asking your instructor. What is important to grasp here is the fact that you can establish something about a particular subject by linking it to a general observation; you don't have to keep multiplying your examples.

If we apply deductive reasoning to the earlier subject of global warming, we could say, "Ice that is warmed will shrink; the arctic glaciers are shrinking; therefore, the glaciers have been warmed." This is, in fact, one of the means employed by the scientific community to back its point about global warming.

THE TOULMIN MODEL OF ARGUMENT

Stephen Toulmin, a British philosopher, felt that syllogistic logic was too difficult for the average writer to use comfortably in writing an argument. In his *The Uses of Argument* (Cambridge, 1958) Toulmin said,

> Ever since Aristotle it has been customary, when analysing the micro-structure of arguments, to set them out in a very simple manner: they have been presented three propositions at a time, "minor premiss; major premiss; *so* conclusion".... Can we properly classify all the elements in our arguments under the three headings, "major premiss", "minor premiss" and "conclusion", or are these categories misleadingly few in number? (96)

From this starting point, Toulmin goes on to suggest we would be better to copy the field of law and its practices in constructing arguments. He ends by explaining three major terms and three minor terms he believes would replace the Aristotelian terms and serve us better in the building of an argument.

Toulmin's three major terms are **data**, **claim**, and **warrant**.

- The **claim** is, of course, the central aim of the argument. However, the mass of the argument is devoted to support of that claim, whether through examples, reasoning, or counterargument.

- The **data** are the source of the reasoned appeal of an argument. We must offer our readers reasons why our **claim** is a valid one, one they can accept. And arguing differs from proclaiming in always stressing the reasons for acceptance in concrete, fact-based reasoning. Whether we use inductive or deductive means, we have to include data to support our claims. If we want to make the **claim** that coal-based generator stations are going to increase the carbon dioxide in the atmosphere, we need support. Simply saying that the air smells noxious when we are close to such a plant is not a fact but an impression. If, however, we can go to an expert witness and discover that, while coal accounts for only twenty-five percent of the electricity generated globally, it causes thirty-nine percent of "energy-related carbon dioxide emissions" (*The Vancouver Sun*, 24 March 2008, D8), we have a **fact-based support** for our claim.

- It is easiest to understand **warrant** by connecting it to another of its forms, "warranting" or even "warranty." We know a warranty guarantees the quality of a product by assuring the customer a replacement if the product breaks before the warranty expires. We understand the warrant issued by a court is a fact-based reason or reasons why a judge should grant the government the right to search premises or arrest somebody. In Toulmin's model, *warrant* means the logic or reasoning that guarantees the offered facts are a sufficient support of the claim's validity. What the writer has to decide, in each claim-based paragraph, is whether or not the warrant has to be explicitly stated or whether the reader can be trusted to infer the connection from the facts. In the example above, the fourteen percent discrepancy between the generation of electricity and the generation of carbon dioxide is an inferred warrant that the fuel used in this case is dirtier than other fossil fuels when burnt. In each paragraph you write in an argument using the Toulmin model, you therefore have to decide whether to trust your reader to infer the connection between claim and data or whether to supply it directly.

The three additional terms Toulmin suggested for use in constructing arguments are **backing**, **rebuttal**, and **qualifier**.

- The term **backing** is attached to the process of warranting. Suppose, in the above case, that we did not feel the simple numerical difference between twenty-five percent and thirty-nine percent was sufficient to make the case for coal's being the dirtiest of the fossil fuels; we would then attach more fact-based support to the warrant. In this case, if we knew that countries with heavy coal-based generation created more carbon dioxide per megawatt of electricity produced than countries generating electricity by other means, we could add that fact to our warrant as an additional guarantee that coal was indeed the culprit.

II ACADEMIC WRITING

- **Rebuttal** is really the same element as counterargument or refutation, but it is accomplished in a briefer way. It also can be an **exception** rather than a refutation. In the case we have been using—the "dirtiness" of coal as a fuel—we could establish an exception if all the coal-fired generating stations had the best current scrubbing and filtering elements included to reduce the release of carbon dioxide. That exception would not have much force, however, if the output of carbon dioxide still exceeded alternative forms of generating energy even after the scrubbing and filtering. More often, of course, we attempt to rebut the argument of the position that opposes our position.

- A **qualifier** is, like rebuttal, an element related to the warrant. It relates directly to the force of the warrant. There will be times when the warrant is absolute and cases where it is not. When we introduce qualifiers like "generally" and "probably," we are qualifying the force of our claim's truth, advising our readers that the truth we are stating is a provisional rather than an absolute truth.

One way of clarifying the structure proposed by Toulmin is to reproduce, in diagrammatic form, the argument we have been referring to about the "dirtiness" of coal-based energy.

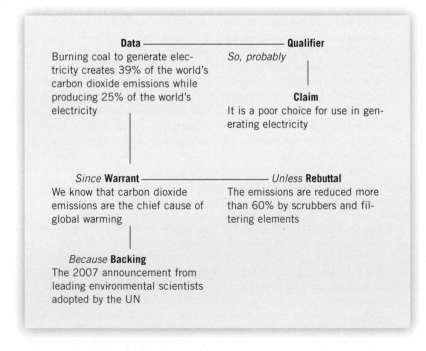

This example demonstrates the way the Toulmin model can be used to build an argument. Once you are familiar with the six terms and can hold them comfortably in your head while you write, you should be able to write an academic argument that is fact- and reason-based. Additionally, simply applying the three major terms as an **editing tool** when you revise your essay will ensure you have relevant facts supporting claims (and warrants where necessary) in each of your working paragraphs.

One further use for the Toulmin terms is to analyze an essay with them. If we look at the sample MLA essay included in Chapter 22, we can see how the use of data, claims, and warrants allows the author to build a convincing argument.

The introduction of the essay uses its opening sentences to establish a **context** for the argument to come, with the second sentence establishing the key terms, "observers" and "participants." The last two lines of the opening paragraph then state the **major claim** being advanced: "Both Wilson and Vanderhaeghe are unequivocal in their message: Reluctance to oppose obvious transgression is both irresponsible and immoral. No matter how many times one washes one's hands, a sin of omission remains a sin."

The succeeding paragraphs support this claim by detailing **specific instances** of "sins of omission" committed by each of the protagonists in the two novels that are the subject of the argument. These become the data that support the essay's leading claim. The second paragraph of the essay supplies a good example of this means of supporting and extending the essay's thesis.

The paragraph begins with a quote from a critic (expert witness) about the "political stance" of *The Englishman's Boy* and follows this up with a direct restatement of the essay's claim through introducing the subject of the protagonist's "vacillation." This supplies the **claim** and it is placed first in the paragraph. What is important for us to note is the way the writer immediately proceeds to offer **data** to support the claim. In this case, the proof is established by narrative details about Harry Vincent's refusals to commit or to act. The writer finds a direct quotation from Rachel to reinforce her claim about Harry's refusal to act: "Alright then, *do* something. Don't play helpless." This reminds us that direct speech from a character in the action provides one of the best kinds of data to support an interpretation.

The third paragraph continues the search through the novel's text to show how the action reinforces this theme of vacillation and refusal to act. The data offered include direct comments by Harry and Rachel and emphasize Harry's retreat to Canada and his withdrawal into watching rather than doing.

The fourth paragraph is devoted to **warranting**. The essay's writer understands the need to explain the link between **data** and **claim.** The first sentence of this paragraph focuses on the warrant behind the data, Harry's avoidance of responsibility for his actions and their results. The second sentence emphasizes the refusal as a moral failure, a "[refusal] to struggle against ... evil." This addition reminds us of the value of **backing.**

Paragraphs 5, 6, and 7 continue the use of the Toulmin model, with a **claim** given initially in the fifth paragraph about Rachel's contrasting character, a person who can act and does. This claim is then repeatedly supported by **data** and further explained by **warranting.** The essay's author even goes to the length of enlisting Vanderhaeghe's own words from an interview to aid in the warranting, the insistence that not acting, not accepting one's communal role, is a distinct moral failure. The author realizes the authority of the novel's writer commenting on the novel's action.

This detailed explanation of how the principal terms of Toulmin's model for argument—data, claim, and warrant—can be employed in a literary analysis should give you a sense of how you may adapt the model to the academic arguments you are assigned in different subjects. Even when you are editing, try using the model as an aid to that editing. Ensure that each of your paragraphs has a claim and support for that claim. Include warranting whenever you think it is not implicitly present. Check that your supporting claims are linked frequently enough to your **overall claim** or **thesis.**

8-c Common Errors in Writing Academic Essays

Years of experience dealing with academic papers at different levels have shown us that there are a relatively limited number of weaknesses that recur in student writing, particularly in the early years of a college/university program. If any of the following sound familiar to you, then you need to learn how to eliminate them from your academic writing.

- The use of unsupported claims in paragraphs
- The absence of specific development in paragraphs
- The general absence of definition from the analysis
- The absence of sufficient facts from the writing
- The inability to write effective rebuttals
- A weak or incomplete or poorly focused thesis

THE USE OF UNSUPPORTED CLAIMS IN PARAGRAPHS

Using unsupported claims is a frequent occurrence in first-year papers that stems from a misunderstanding of how the standard academic paragraph works. For some reason, the writer confuses claims and warrants (see the Toulmin model in 3-c and 8-b) and uses one generalization to support another. For instance, assume that the writer is making the claim in a paragraph that small-market teams in the NHL cannot compete successfully with large-market teams. The writer offers, as a defence, the statement that large-market teams have more financial resources. This is, however, simply another claim, and the paragraph now contains two unsupported claims instead of one. The instructor in this case has no evidence that the student understands how to make a point by supporting a claim, and a weak mark is the most likely result. At best, this reveals a vague thought process; at worst, it offers assertions that are undefended and therefore of little worth.

The writer of such a paragraph simply hasn't learned that a paragraph in academic writing can usually accommodate only one claim; the rest of the paragraph is devoted to supporting that claim and linking it to the overall analysis. And this fact is not limited to those assignments described as "arguments." The necessity for specific supports and warranting for a claim exists in all academic writing. The student could have established, through specific facts, that the small-market team has an arena seating 17,000 fans, while typical large-market teams have arenas that seat from 18,000 to 20,000 fans. The size of the ancillary revenues for broadcasting closed-circuit games to local fans would also favour the large market team. Oddly enough, even as minor a feature as the wife of a player preferring a city in California to one in Alberta can play a role. With a little thought, the writer can ensure that claims are backed by facts rather than by more claims.

Whatever the reason, nothing leads more certainly to failure in a paper than the inability to offer specific factual supports for general claims. When you are editing your paper, use one dedicated sweep to check how you supported your claims. Did you include facts? Did you connect the fact or facts to your claim through warranting where necessary? Did you ever support a claim with another claim? You may even want to use differently coloured highlighting, whether manual or electronic, to identify claims and supports as you go through your essay.

THE ABSENCE OF SPECIFIC DEVELOPMENT IN PARAGRAPHS

The lack of specific development is closely related to the lack of support for a claim and often reveals itself by the presence of many short paragraphs in a paper. While it is simplistic to suggest there should be some standard length for paragraphs in academic writing, it is fair to point out that three- and four-sentence paragraphs are likely to be successful only when they are used as transition paragraphs.

The general work of a paragraph in an academic paper is to establish a claim and to link that claim to the other claims in the analysis or argument. Usually, that will take five to ten sentences to accomplish. You need specific supports, a sentence or two warranting the connection between the supports and the general claim, and perhaps some definitional work. You can't do that in three or four sentences.

THE GENERAL ABSENCE OF DEFINITION FROM THE ANALYSIS

In academic writing, the exact meaning of a term is important, particularly if the success of the analysis depends on your reader having the same meaning in mind as you do. This is an important enough matter to require you to engage in more than denotative definition. It is a simple act to cite a definition provided by a dictionary, but it may not serve your purpose sufficiently. What if the crucial term in the essay on small- and large-market terms was "success"? How would you define such an abstract term? Is it success in monetary terms, or linkage with the community, or overall wins and losses? In a case like this, you need to provide a stipulative definition, one where you specify your intended meaning and link it to your larger purposes. Stipulative definitions use the history of a word, contrast, usage, and many other means to arrive at a complex and complete definition to be shared with the reader. Any time you are dealing with a subject where a term has significant and diverse meanings, offer a definition. You will impress your instructor by showing that you are attentive to specific meaning and know how to create a stipulated definition.

THE ABSENCE OF SUFFICIENT FACTS

The lack of sufficient facts is always a revealing deficiency. Generally, a paragraph needs only one claim but multiple facts. Remember that you need at least two facts just to construct an inference. The absence of facts or concrete support tells you most typically that you are not ready to write the analysis you had in mind. You need to gather more facts and concrete support before continuing. A quick way of checking the proportions of fact and generalization in your essay is to use high-lighting to isolate claims and supports for claims. That should tell you quickly if your proportions are reasonable. It will also let you know if you are using general-ized statements to support generalized statements, another flaw guaranteed to reduce the quality of your essay.

THE INABILITY TO WRITE EFFECTIVE REBUTTALS

The rebuttal or refutation or counterargument is a common feature in academic writing. It is, for instance, a standard element in the seven-part classical model of argument and also appears in the Toulmin model (see 3-c and 8-b). You may choose to exclude rebuttal from an analytic essay but not from other kinds. Rebuttal or refutation is essential in an argument and helps the credibility of your position by honestly responding to opposing positions. It is also frequently present in analytical essays when the analysis attempts to be persuasive.

You can construct a rebuttal very simply. First, write a neutral and complete account of the counterargument. Second, deal with any concessions you want to make to that position; remember that you don't have to dismiss it entirely. Third, identify the one or two or three most vulnerable premises in that position. With the aid of facts, state why you have problems with the counterargument. For instance, assume that you are opposing the argument that President Bush's emphasis on biofuels is the best long-term alternative to oil energy. You could concede the short-term contribution of ethanol manufactured from corn to show your fair-mindedness. Then you could point out that the price of corn has doubled since Bush's proclamation and provision of funding to increase corn production. If necessary, you could point out factually the amount of energy required to convert corn to ethanol and transport the product to the larger mar-kets where it has its greatest value. If you can factually show that converting corn to ethanol involves using significant energy, contributes to inflation by artificially raising the price of corn, and reduces global warming by only a small factor, you have effectively rebutted the thesis that the Bush policy is an intelligent option.

A WEAK OR INCOMPLETE OR POORLY FOCUSED THESIS

Many times, the real problem in an academic essay is the overall position that is supposed to drive it. The term "thesis" describes the overall position or purpose of a paper. Whether you prefer to use a term like "controlling claim" or some other term, you will agree that a weakness in this part of an essay will be quite damaging.

To understand the thesis more exactly, remember that it has two parts, not one. A thesis names a subject or issue and asserts a perspective on that subject/issue. Sometimes, the weakness in the thesis is simply the fact that the subject is named but no clear position is defined on that subject. A successful thesis is never general or fuzzy. Consider the following theses:

> A small-market team, because of its weaker financial base, cannot compete successfully with a large-market team.

> Although there are occasional exceptions, small-market teams in today's professional sports leagues cannot compete equally in the long term with teams whose markets and revenue bases are significantly larger.

What should be apparent to you is that the more successful theses are those that include necessary concessions, avoid universal or categorical positions, and offer reasonably exact terms. Before you become deeply immersed in drafting your paper, check to see if your thesis has sufficient depth and clarity to sustain your analysis or argument.

You should also be aware that a thesis may appear in different locations in an essay. An "Information" essay will probably offer its thesis at the end of a first paragraph. In a "Report," that thesis might even be contained in the Executive Summary that precedes the "Report." An "Argument" also normally offers its central position early—in the first paragraph of a short essay, or as late as the fourth paragraph in a longer essay. The classical model of argument actually uses its early paragraphs to provide background for the overall issue that has precipitated the argument and defines the opposing positions before any single position is announced. Finally, the "Analytical" essay has more freedom about where its thesis might appear. While it usually appears early, the "Inquiry" form of analysis reserves it for later, realizing that a number of provisional theses will first have to be tested and amended before a fully satisfactory final position emerges.

The qualities you must avoid in your positioning statement, however, are

- vagueness,
- lack of clarity in terms and position, and
- confusing a subject with a thesis.

Conclusion

The student entering first-year university who is asked to write six to ten essays in the first semester is challenged in two ways. The first is the simple mass of the writing requirement and the fact that major assignments are often not handed out until after the semester has commenced. Therefore, the time available for doing them has shrunk before the student has even commenced planning how to respond. The second challenge is just as often the cause of failure, however. The student may not have had much practice writing a reasoned essay and may be struggling to understand the forms of reasoning preferred by a particular discipline. For that reason, students should study the kinds of weaknesses covered above and edit their essays before submitting them. The penalties for weak or absent reasoning are often more severe, in academic essays, than the penalties for awkward or unclear expression.

9 SUMMARY

One essential skill for writing academic papers is the ability to summarize. Any research paper and many long papers or reports require you to read and understand many different sources. To capture your understanding of a particular text sufficiently so that you can refer to that understanding later, it is standard practice to summarize the parts of the text you find most significant. A summary is a condensed version of the text expressed in your own words (see Chapter 17). Ideally, your summary should occupy about thirty percent of the space taken up by the original. You would typically create a file for each major resource consulted and store your summaries there, along with paraphrases and direct quotations.

Given the time constraints you face if you are enrolled in a full program of studies, you need to make your notes quickly and accurately. Get into the habit of learning where the most important material in a text typically occurs: in introductory overviews, summaries, and at the beginning of paragraphs. Remember that you are typically interested in the claims or lead ideas and not in the supports offered for those ideas or claims. If you can master the art of summarizing quickly and efficiently, you will have a valuable ally in drafting major papers.

The following guidelines will help you develop a summary.

1. Read the passage. As you read, concentrate on gaining a comprehensive understanding of the author's intention. If the passage is in a book you own, you might want to highlight or underline key points as you read.

2. Re-read the passage.

3. Find the major claim in the first paragraph of the passage; write down the claim on a separate piece of paper. Do the same for the second and subsequent paragraphs.

4. Eliminate all illustrations or examples that may appear in these paragraphs, unless an illustration is an integral part of the claim.

5. Examine any definitions that appear in the paragraphs of the passage; decide if they are important enough to retain.

6. If you copy a phrase of the original passage, make sure you identify it as a quotation so that you will know to treat it as such if you subsequently use the phrase in your own work. Remember, too, that if you summarize a passage and use it in your work, you will need to give a reference for the material, so make sure that you copy down the page number for a citation.

7. Once you have assembled the raw materials for your summary (claims, essential definitions, illustrations, dates, facts), use them to help you write the first draft.

8. As you write your first draft, remember to express the main points of the passage in your own words. (You may find that there is no viable alternative way of expressing special terms and the like.) In addition, feel free to combine points as long as you do not change the author's intended meaning by doing so. Finally, use quotation marks to identify phrases copied from the original passage.

9. Check your first draft to see that it includes all the essential material and is written in your own words. Edit the draft for unnecessary repetition and wordy expression, and look for places where you can combine or condense statements.

10. Write a final draft in which you concentrate on clarity and effective sequencing.

You can practise your summarizing skills with another student. You could both write a summary of the same passage or paragraph and then compare your final drafts. (You may be surprised how different the two versions are.) If you practise and enhance your summarizing skills and combine them with your reading skills and other critical thinking skills, you will improve your ability to gather the informed resources you need as support for your essays.

WRITING A LITERARY ANALYSIS

10

A literary analysis requires you to present and defend an argument based on your interpretation of a text. Depending on the topic, a literary analysis will contain some or all of the elements associated with each of its three major parts: the introduction, the body paragraphs, and the concluding paragraph. For more information about each type of paragraph, see Chapter 39.

10-a Introduction

The opening paragraph (or paragraphs) of a literary analysis must name the topic, state the writer's position on that topic, and provide any background necessary to an understanding of that position. The introduction may also preview the argument to be presented and define any terms critical to the argument. The introduction of a literary analysis will include most of the following elements:

1. *General opening comment.* This comment names your topic and, if necessary, the context in which it appears.

2. *Focusing statement.* The focusing statement narrows the subject area named in your opening sentence and expresses your position on the topic.

3. *Explanatory statement(s).* This element provides any information that is necessary to clarify the opening comment or focusing statement. For example, an explanatory statement might provide a definition of a key term used in the opening comment or clarify the context in which the topic is being analyzed. Often more than one sentence is needed to communicate this information.

4. *Thesis statement.* The thesis statement expresses in specific terms the central point of your argument. A thesis statement typically appears at the end of the introductory paragraph(s).

5. *Overview of your argument.* Like the preview element in the introductory paragraph of an essay (see Chapter 39), this optional element provides readers with a sense of the direction your argument will take.

To sum up, the introductory elements outlined above involve the following activities:

Naming ➤ Narrowing ➤ Explaining ➤ Stating ➤ Previewing

10-b Body Paragraphs

The argument used to prove a thesis is presented in the body paragraphs of the literary analysis. To construct effective body paragraphs, you can apply what you have already learned about sequencing ideas (Chapter 34), paragraph purpose (Chapter 35), paragraph development (Chapter 36), paragraph transitions (Chapter 37), paragraph structure (Chapter 38), and special-purpose paragraphs (Chapter 39). Remember that the sentences that make up a body paragraph should follow a clear and logical sequence, and that each paragraph should advance your overall argument. The following model is one of many you could use to construct a body paragraph:

1. Use your first sentence as a *transition*, a bridge that connects one paragraph to the next.

2. The second sentence, called a *claim sentence,* is one in which you present the next claim you make in your argument.

3. The claim sentence is followed by the *definitional or background sentence,* in which you present all the background information necessary to your claim. You may require more than one sentence to accomplish this task.

4. The fourth task, called a *demonstrating position,* requires you to prove your claim. In this part of the paragraph, you write as many sentences as are needed to present the logic and evidence that supports your claim. Support may take the form of a simple illustration or example.

5. In this model, you conclude by specifying how the paragraph's claim relates to and advances the overall argument.

To sum up, the body-paragraph model outlined above involves the following activities:

Connecting ➤ Claiming ➤ Defining or Restricting ➤ Proving ➤ Relating

10-c Concluding Paragraph

The concluding paragraph of a literary analysis typically contains the following elements:

1. *Summary.* The summary encapsulates the main points of the argument. Unless your argument is unusually complex, your summary should generally not run longer than three sentences.

2. *Restatement.* The restatement is a concise and emphatic reiteration of your thesis.

3. *Indication of general significance.* This optional element provides some indication of the general significance of your thesis by pointing out its connection to a larger topic. For example, you might relate your thesis to a recurrent pattern in the writer's work or some general observation about human behaviour.

Whether it ends with a restatement or with an indication of general significance, your concluding paragraph should convey an impression of finality; readers should be left with the sense that nothing of importance remains to be said.

To sum up, the concluding-paragraph elements outlined above involve the following activities:

Summarizing ➤ Restating ➤ Signifying

To write an effective essay exam, you must be able to apply general skills such as *recall, interpretation, time management,* and *focused writing.* An essay exam also requires you to apply critical thinking skills such as *inference, causal analysis, summary, analysis, evaluation,* and *synthesis.*

Do not wait until the last moment to prepare for an exam. You should study throughout the term, and you should carry out your studies in a systematic fashion. Establish and follow a realistic schedule of study activities, such as summarizing key content, mastering new terms and concepts, and working on difficult topics. Let your understanding of the material dictate how much time you devote to studying. You might consider using a six-step weekly study schedule:

1. Read new material.

2. Take notes.

3. Relate new material to material you have already learned.

4. Review material from the preceding week.

5. Make a note of material you think you should review again the following week.

6. Review material you have not mastered in previous weeks.

As a complement to independent study, you can establish a study group that meets on a regular basis. Reviewing and discussing course material with your peers is a good way to test your grasp of that material.

Use the following lists of strategies as a general guide for all your exam preparations.

11-a Before the Exam

Review your study materials.

- Review your summary notes from the course.
- Combine your lecture and summary notes.
- Highlight or underline in your notes key ideas, key concepts, and terms for special study.
- Create a glossary (including definitions) of key terms introduced in the course.
- Select evidence to support each key idea.
- Note the connections among key ideas.
- Use your organized list of key ideas as a study guide.

11-b During the Exam

1. *Use the first five to ten minutes of the allotted exam time to read, plan, and organize.*

   - Read the instructions before you do anything else.

- Quickly write down any important facts, definitions, or formulas you think you will need and are afraid you will forget.

- Decide whether the questions ask for definitions, problem solving, application of knowledge, or explanations. Underline the key words and verbs employed in the questions. Remember that different verbs, such as *analyze* and *compare,* require you to do different things. See Chapter 13 for definitions of verbs you will encounter in both exam questions and research essay instructions.

- Develop a strategy for handling the exam in general and each question in particular. If the exam gives you choices, make your choices now. Decide where to start.

- Divide the exam time according to the marks awarded for each question, factoring in the time you allotted to planning and editing.

- Stick to the time you allot yourself for each answer. If you think one answer needs more time, you can always leave some blank space at the end of your answer and come back to that answer when you finish the rest of the exam.

- List relevant points for the question you want to answer first and arrange the points in an effective sequence.

- Use the points to develop a thesis or claim (or rephrase the question to formulate a thesis). Remember that your thesis must address the question you are asked. Some students like to incorporate the actual words of the question into their opening statement.

- Stick to the topic and use specific evidence to support your points.

- Remember that each paragraph should relate to your thesis and to the previous paragraph.

- Your conclusion should provide a restatement of the thesis, a summary of the main points, and a comment that synthesizes your argument.

2. *While writing, budget your time and try to write complete, well-organized answers.*

- Use only one side of the exam-book pages. Double-space essay and paragraph answers so that you leave yourself room to make additions and corrections when you read over your work. Use the other side of the exam-book pages for your rough work or corrections.

- Use vocabulary that is appropriate to the exam's discipline.

- Make use of theories or arguments that are relevant to the topic.

- Analyze: don't list or summarize unless the question asks you to do so.

- Make relevant connections between points and explain information clearly.

- Watch the time. If you find you have too much information and not enough time, you will have to edit your argument or use point form.

3. *Use the closing minutes of exam time to revise, edit, and proofread.*

- People who mark exams are primarily interested in the organization and content of your answers. Remember that a proofreading sweep (which eliminates errors in spelling, usage, and punctuation) is not as important as the content, coherence, and logic of your answer.
- Ask yourself these simple editing questions:
  - Have I supported each of my points?
  - Are my facts correct, clearly stated, and relevant?
  - Does each paragraph support and extend my argument? (If a paragraph is irrelevant, delete it.)

11-c Multiple-Choice and Short-Answer Exams

- Some examiners who use multiple-choice exams subtract the number of wrong answers from the number of right answers. If the exam instructions indicate that this is the case, be cautious about guessing. If you are not confident about your answer, you may be better off leaving a question unanswered.
- In a long exam with a large number of multiple-choice or short-answer questions, start at the beginning and work through the questions in the order in which they appear.
- On your first pass through an exam, respond only to questions whose answers you are sure of. Later, return to questions you have not answered.
- Be careful with multiple-choice questions that have two or more similar answers. If you are not sure of the answer, come back to the question later.
- Remember that short answers should be unified and to the point.
- Always leave enough time to review and revise your answers.

12 CONSTRUCTING AN ERRORS CHART

As early as possible in your academic career, you should learn how to analyze your writing in order to improve it. One simple aid to such analysis is the errors chart, which categorizes errors in your writing. The correction abbreviations listed in Table 12-1 are used by most instructors to note errors in essays. You can construct an errors chart using these and other correction abbreviations as headings. Whenever an essay is returned to you, record the number and type of errors you made by putting a check mark under the appropriate heading in your errors chart. The results will reveal the areas in your writing that need improvement.

Table 12-2 shows a sample errors chart for the sentence. You can use it to record your error patterns by putting a check mark under the appropriate headings in the chart. You may also construct errors charts for the word, paragraph, and essay levels.

TABLE 12-1 Correction Abbreviations

ugr faulty agreement between verb and subject (42-a) or between pronoun and antecedent (42-c)	does not qualify as a sentence (41-a) **fs** fused sentence: independent clauses joined with no punctuation or connecting word (41-b)	**red** redundant wording (44-a) **ref** faulty pronoun reference: vague, ambiguous, or misleading (43-a)
amb ambiguous pronoun references (43-a) or phrasing	**gen** weak generalization or unnecessarily general statement	**rpt** unnecessary repetition (44-a)
awk awkward construction or phrasing	**id** unidiomatic expression: faulty word combination (a common problem with prepositions) (44-h)	**shift** confusing or unnecessary shift in subject, person, number, tense, voice, or mood
chop too many short, simple sentences in succession; subordination required (33-b)	**jarg** inappropriate use of technical language; wordy, inflated writing (44-f)	**slang** inappropriate use of slang (44-c) **sp** misspelled word **sub** subordination required (33-a)
coh lack of coherence: sentence, paragraph, or essay is not consistent in structure, logic, and thought (Ch. 37, Ch. 40)	**log** error or weakness in logic; statement does not follow from what precedes it	**syn** faulty syntax, incorrect word order **t** error in verb tense (27-c, 42-b)
cs comma splice: independent clauses joined with only a comma (41-b)	**mixed** mixed construction; sentence contains elements that do not grammatically fit together	**thesis** absent, weak, or poorly defined and articulated thesis statement in essay (39-a, Ch. 14)
dev weak paragraph structure or development (Ch. 36)	**mm** misplaced modifier; modifies wrong word (43-b)	**tr** transposed letters **trans** missing, faulty, or weak transition (Ch. 37)
dm dangling modifier: a modifier with no word in the sentence for it to modify (43-c)	**nsw** no such word exists **obs** obscure meaning (44-d) **p** errors in punctuation (Part X)	**?** unclear **unity** paragraph or sequence of paragraphs lack unity
doc missing source or faulty documentation of source	**¶** faulty paragraph division: new paragraph needed or not needed	**v** incorrect verb form (27-c)
emph weak, absent, or inappropriate emphasis (33-c)	**//sm** faulty parallelism, or parallelism required (37-c, 43-d)	**var** lack of variety in sentence patterns (Ch. 33)
evid missing or weak evidence or support for statement	**pres** faulty presentation of quotation, paraphrase, summary, or other source material	**w** wordy (44-a) **wc** inappropriate word choice (Ch. 44) **wm** word(s) missing
form faulty manuscript form or essay format		
frag sentence fragment: group of words that		

TABLE 12-2 Errors Chart: Sentence

	ASSIGNMENT 1	ASSIGNMENT 2	ASSIGNMENT 3	ASSIGNMENT 4	ASSIGNMENT 5
Agreement					
Awkwardness					
Comma splice					
Fragment					
Fused sentence					
Mixed construction					
Punctuation					
Reference					
Shift					
Variety					
Verb tense					
Word order					

EXERCISES

EXERCISE II-1 PLAGIARISM

1. If you read a passage that contains specific information and you paraphrase the information by putting it in your own words, you

   a. do not have to acknowledge the source of the borrowing

   b. need only list the source text in your bibliography

   c. need a parenthetic reference and an entry in your bibliography for the source

2. If the passage is only five words long, you

   a. do not need to acknowledge the source of the borrowing

   b. need to acknowledge the source with both a parenthetic reference and an entry in your bibliography

   c. only need to list the source in your bibliography

3. If you can find the specific information in three different publicly available sources, you

   a. do not need to acknowledge the source of the information as it is considered to be common knowledge in the public domain

   b. need to acknowledge the first of the sources as your preliminary source in both a parenthetic reference and your bibliography

   c. need to acknowledge all three of your sources in your parenthetic reference and your bibliography

4. If you have someone help you with your essay, the individual's work need not be considered his or her property, and you will not risk being accused of plagiarism.

   a. True

   b. False

5. If two people work on different aspects of a written assignment and use each other's work, this is collaborative writing, not plagiarism.

   a. True

   b. It depends on whether the assignment allows for people to work together.

   c. False

6. Material on the Web is not owned by anyone. Often there is no author mentioned on a webpage; therefore, you do not have to treat quotations taken from the Web in the same way that you treat quotations taken from a book. You can treat the material as common knowledge. *Note: You will have to consult Part XI for the formatting of parenthetic references/notes and bibliography entries.*

    a. True

    b. False

7. First read the short passage from Thomas King's 2003 Massey Lectures *The Truth About Stories: A Native Narrative,* then examine the series of statements from students' essays. Examine each student's statement and decide how or if material from King's passage needs to be cited or in any other way documented so that the students will not be accused of plagiarism.

Thomas King's passage

It took my brother and me four days to drive to New Mexico. We could have made the trip in three days, but we kept getting sidetracked by interesting stops. My favourite was a McDonald's on the Will Rogers Turnpike near Claremore, Oklahoma. I generally avoid places like McDonald's but this one had a tiny Will Rogers Museum on the first floor of the restaurant, as well a statue of Rogers himself in the parking lot standing next to a flag-pole, twirling a rope.

Tourists pulling off the turnpike and seeing the statue for the first time would probably think Rogers was some kind of famous cowboy. In fact, he was a famous Indian, a sort of Indian/cowboy, a Cherokee to be exact.

But more importantly, he was what the political and literary theorist Antonio Gramsci called an "organic" intellectual, an individual who articulates the understandings of a community or a nation. During the 1930s Rogers was probably the most famous man in North America. He performed in circuses and Wild West shows. He starred in the Ziegfeld Follies, and from 1933 to 1935 he was the top male motion-picture box-office attraction. Over forty million people read his newspaper columns on everything from gun control to Congress, and even more listened to his weekly radio show. He did just about everything with the exception of running for office. "I ain't going to try that," he said. "I've got some pride left."

Rogers was born near Claremore, Oklahoma, and his family was prominent in the Cherokee Nation. But he didn't look Indian. Not in that constructed way. Certainly not in the way Curtis wanted Indians to look. And tourists pulling into the parking lot and seeing the statue for the first time would never know that this was an Indian as famous as Sitting Bull or Crazy Horse or Geronimo.

> —Thomas King, *The Truth About Stories: A Native Narrative,*
> *41–42*, published by Anansi in Toronto, 2003

Student statements

a. Thomas King discovered Will Rogers' complex history when he was driving through New Mexico with his brother.

Style I am using:
MLA   APA   Chicago   CSE

____ This sentence does not need a citation.

____ This sentence needs a citation.

If you think it needs a parenthetic reference, write what should be in that reference if there were only one book by King mentioned in the essay.

_____

If you think the information in this quotation needs a bibliography entry, provide one here.

_____

_____

b. King learned from the experience that the truth about people's lives is more complex than we think it is; Rogers was not only a famous cowboy, but his family was also prominent in the Cherokee Nation.

Style I am using:
MLA   APA   Chicago   CSE

____ This sentence does not need a citation.

____ This sentence needs a citation.

If you think it needs a parenthetic reference, write what should be in that reference if there were only one book by King mentioned in the essay.

_____

If you think the information in this quotation needs a bibliography entry, provide one here.

_____

_____

c. Besides being a famous cowboy, Will Rogers was also famous because he was a star in a number of movies in the 1930s.

Style I am using:
MLA   APA   Chicago   CSE

____ This sentence does not need a citation.

____ This sentence needs a citation.

If you think it needs a parenthetic reference, write what should be in that reference if there were only one book by King mentioned in the essay.

_____

If you think the information in this quotation needs a bibliography entry, provide one here.

_____

_____

d.   King notes that over forty million people read Rogers' newspaper columns on everything from gun control to Congress; he had an even larger following for his radio program.

Style I am using:
MLA   APA   Chicago   CSE

____ This sentence does not need a citation.

____ This sentence needs a citation.

If you think it needs a parenthetic reference, write what should be in that reference if there were only one book by King mentioned in the essay.

_____

If you think the information in this quotation needs a bibliography entry, provide one here.

_____

_____

EXERCISE II-2 USING THE TOULMIN MODEL

Choose three paragraphs from Kathleen Lenaghan's APA sample essay in Chapter 23. Do a Toulmin analysis of each paragraph that you select.

1.   Indicate whether any of the following appear in the paragraph you are analyzing: claim, fact, warrant, backing, qualifier, rebuttal.

2.   Indicate whether you think the paragraph is complete and sufficiently reasoned.

Research Essays

Whenever you write a research essay or report, you engage in the research process. The seven-step system described in this section is designed to smooth your progress through this complex process. Although the steps are presented as separate units, there is considerable overlap among the activities associated with them. Note-taking, for example, is something you are likely to do at both the research and reading stages of the research process. As you gain more research experience, you will learn to tailor the system to accommodate your particular research needs.

13 STEP 1: DEFINING THE ASSIGNMENT

Your first task in any research essay is to conduct an analysis of the research assignment. A fundamental part of that analysis is defining your audience, purpose, and scope; clarifying the assignment instructions; and determining your research requirements.

13-a Audience

The voice you adopt in your essay, the vocabulary you use, and the stance you take will depend on your understanding of your audience and its expectations. The assignment instructions may or may not specify an audience. If no audience is specified, you should not assume it is limited to your instructor. Ask yourself the following questions:

- If the audience is specified in the assignment, what are the expectations of that audience? How well informed is the audience about the assignment topic?
- If the audience is not specified, should I seek guidance from my instructor or should I address a generalized audience?
- If the audience is my instructor, what are his or her expectations?
- Is the audience likely to have a position on the topic?
- If the audience does have a position, what might it be?
- How interested in the topic is the audience likely to be?
- What response do I want to elicit from my audience?

13-b Purpose

Purpose refers to the aim or objective of your essay. You need to know *why* you are writing before you progress through the various stages of the research process. Like the audience, the purpose may or may not be specified in the assignment instructions. If it is not defined, try to determine the common purpose(s) to which the assignment seems to lend itself. In other words, does the topic provide opportunities for you to *describe, inform, recommend, evaluate, argue, interpret*, or some combination of these?

Before you complete the preliminary phase of your research project, you should know the answers to these questions:

- What is the purpose of the assignment? Is the purpose explicitly stated or is it implied?
- Am I being asked to write a demonstration essay? Am I to show I have mastered certain concepts in the specified field?
- Am I invited to define my own approach or is an approach assigned to me?
- If an argument is called for, are the terms of the argument given in the assignment?
- Is the language of the assignment prescriptive or open?

13-c Scope

Scope refers to the breadth or range of the assignment. To define the scope of an essay, ask yourself these questions:

- Does the assignment specify the extent or range of the research that will be required?
- Does the assignment specify how long (in terms of number of pages) my final essay draft should be?
- Are the terms supplied in the assignment general or specific?
- If the terms are general, does the assignment give me the option of defining them more precisely?
- Is the assignment "open" in the sense that it allows me to create my own topic or scope?

If you cannot answer some of these questions, or if you are having difficulty creating your own topic, you should see your instructor for guidance.

13-d The Instructions

One of the first things you should do when you get a research assignment is analyze the instructions. Consider the following sample assignments:

- *Review* criticism of the Young Offenders Act and *specify* the view of corrections theory held by each major type of criticism.
- *Analyze* the major choices in presentation software available to a mid-sized firm and *recommend* the package your firm should purchase.
- Although conflict over the issue of abolition is commonly regarded as the primary cause of the American Civil War, the North was motivated by economic rather than moral concerns. *Agree* or *disagree* and *discuss*.

III RESEARCH ESSAYS

- *Evaluate* the major features that caused large audiences to return faithfully to the episodes of the various *Survival* series.

The verbs that indicate the tasks you are being asked to perform as a writer are critical to these assignments. You should underline such verbs in the assignment instructions and, using the following glossary as a guide, specify the demands each verb makes.

- *Account for* asks you to perform causal analysis—that is, use supporting detail to demonstrate how and why a particular phenomenon occurred.
- *Analyze* means to take something apart to see how it works. If you are asked to analyze, you must clarify the grounds on which that analysis is conducted. In an analysis, you may examine the parts, steps, sections, or causes of your topic (compare to *synthesize*).
- *Assess* requires you to examine a topic critically to determine its value or significance.
- *Compare* asks you to examine two or more topics to find and explore similarities.
- *Contrast* requires you to examine two or more topics to find and explore differences.
- *Defend* asks you to express a particular position and defend it through the use of supporting detail.
- *Define* requires you to invent your definition by (1) drawing on your research, (2) using the classical defining mechanism of placing your topic in the class to which it belongs and then distinguishing it from all other members of that class, (3) employing an invented definition, or (4) using such definitional techniques as history and background, comparison and contrast, or context. The success of your essay depends on the thoroughness and wide applicability of your definition. Remember that a definitional essay does not mean defining a few terms; it asks you to make definition the entire focus of your essay.
- *Evaluate* asks you to judge a topic. You cannot evaluate without first creating and announcing the criteria or standards you employ in evaluating your topic. Is economy a sufficient criterion? What about flexibility or currency? It is up to you to establish and defend the criteria of your evaluation.
- *Review* requires you to present a summary of the topic and examine the summary for the purpose of evaluation.
- *Summarize* asks you to express briefly the main points of the topic.
- *Synthesize* requires you to merge, creatively, multiple perspectives (compare to *analyze*).
- *Trace* asks you to ascertain the sequence of, or account for, the stages in the development of the topic.

13-e Research Requirements

To determine what your research requirements are, you must first decide if you need to use primary sources or if you can complete the assignment using secondary sources alone. Primary sources are an integral part of the topic you are writing about, while secondary sources are interpretations of that topic. If you were writing an essay on the pioneer experience in nineteenth-century Ontario, you might draw upon such primary sources as the diaries and letters of immigrants who settled in the province; books and other materials that deal with those immigrants, whether directly or indirectly, would constitute your secondary sources.

What if you were trying to discover some of the reasons people drop out of high school? You would be engaging in primary research if you were to assemble a group of high-school dropouts and either interview them or have them fill out an online questionnaire you had devised. An interview or questionnaire would be a far more direct means of researching this subject than, say, reading an article in *Maclean's* about high-school dropout rates in Canada.

STEP 2: DEVELOPING A PRELIMINARY THESIS 14

If your topic is too broad, you will waste valuable time during the research process. You can narrow and focus a topic by developing a *preliminary thesis* (also called a *working thesis*). A preliminary thesis has two functions: (1) it names the topic, and (2) it indicates your anticipated position on that topic or the main point you expect to make about the topic in your essay. One of the easiest ways to arrive at a preliminary thesis is to use the looping technique (see 2-c). The statement you write about can be as simple as *When I think of X, I feel. . . .* Review what you have written to see if a focal point emerges. Here are three other techniques you can use to narrow and focus a topic:

1. *Limit the time frame.* If the topic encompasses a twenty-year period, change the time frame to a ten-year period. If the topic specifies no time period, specify one yourself. You should obtain your instructor's approval before narrowing an assigned time frame.

2. *Limit the geographical scope.* Instead of assessing the impact of the most recent recession on Canada as a whole, concentrate your assessment on a more specific region such as a province or a city. Instead of analyzing the causes of *all* earthquakes, analyze the causes of earthquakes in and around California. Often, you will find that narrowing your geographical scope helps you focus a topic.

---

3. *Reduce the number of topic elements.* A causal analysis that tries to deal with twelve isolated causes is probably too ambitious; concentrating on four to six causes would make the analysis easier to manage. If your topic has three parts, eliminating one of those parts will make it more manageable. If the topic calls for you to compare and contrast four subjects, see what happens when you reduce the number of subjects to two or three. Beyond making your topic more manageable, a reduction in the number of topic elements will tend to help you focus your purpose.

15 STEP 3: CONDUCTING RESEARCH

Once you are satisfied with your preliminary thesis, you can start creating a *working bibliography,* a list of works you want to consult or research you want to initiate. If you want to do primary research, you will need specific guidance from your instructor. Less challenging is secondary research, which involves building a working bibliography consisting of secondary sources. The place where you will most likely initiate your research for sources is the computer.

15-a Reference Sources: Internet

You can get a quick sense of the sources available to you online by activating a search engine such as Google and using key words for your search. Remember to evaluate the sources you find in your search as there are many unreliable sources on the Internet. For assistance in this evaluation, refer to the material on evaluating Internet sources in 15-d. Even if a source is affiliated with a postsecondary institution, you should check to see who the individual is and what that person's background and expertise are. You may find sites such as SparkNotes emerging as a resource, but that site will typically offer you generic information that does not go into the detail expected by your instructor.

When you find material online, select the portion you want for your research, highlight it, and then use the copy/paste commands to move it into a word-processing file. You will normally establish a folder in your computer and store separate files with information in that folder. Copy down the URL for your resource and the date you retrieved it.

15-b Accessing Your Library Catalogue Online

Besides doing a preliminary search on the Internet, you can also conduct a library search by topic through your library's online catalogue. As well as the books that surface in your search, you should also retrieve journal titles through your library's online journal index. Most academic libraries have subscriptions to a number of subject indexes that give you access to summaries of articles and, in fact, to whole articles. You can do this primary search from any location, as most libraries allow you to log in to their catalogue and indexes using your student identification and a password. Again, it is critical to note any access information you will need later when you retrieve any electronic sources to place in your computer file. (See also Academic Directories in 15-d.)

15-c Using the Library

Your college or university library gives you a second area to search for resources. It contains general works that will help you focus on the subject area that interests you or that forms the core of the assignment you have chosen. At this stage, you are compiling a working bibliography, a list of works you want to consult. For primary research, you should consult your instructor. For secondary sources, you can conduct your own search, and the library is one of your resources for that search.

- *Encyclopedias.* There are two types of encyclopedias: general and specialized. General encyclopedias, such as *The Canadian Encyclopedia* (edited by James H. Marsh), provide an overview of topics. Specialized encyclopedias, such as the *Encyclopedia of Music in Canada,* provide detailed articles that are usually written by a specialist in a particular field.

- *Dictionaries.* If you have trouble comprehending any term in your assignment, consult a dictionary. Like encyclopedias, dictionaries may be general or specialized. If your topic centres on a famous person, you should consult a biographical dictionary such as the *Canadian Who's Who* or the *Dictionary of Canadian Biography.* For more on dictionaries, see the online site for this text, at http://www.canadianwritersguide 4e .nelson.com.

- *Current fact books.* Yearbooks, almanacs, and other sources provide information about current events and statistical data. Current fact books such as *The Canadian Global Almanac* are updated annually, so be sure to check for updates.

- *Hansard.* If you are writing about a topic that requires you to examine an issue debated in the House of Commons or a provincial legislature, you can consult Hansard, the verbatim record of parliamentary and legislative debates in Canada. If the reference section of your library does not house the federal Hansard, you can access the debates through the Parliamentary Internet website (http://www.parl.gc.ca).

- *Periodical indexes.* If you are searching for sources of current information, you may wish to consult a periodical index. Periodical indexes, which may be general or specialized, list articles from newspapers, journals, or magazines. General indexes include the *Canadian Periodical Index, Reader's Guide to Periodical Literature, Canadian News Index, National News Index,* and *The New York Times Index.* Specialized indexes include the following: *Art Index, Business Periodicals Index, Education Index, General Science Index, Humanities Index, Index to Canadian Legal*

Literature, Philosopher's Index, and Social Sciences Index. You will also find that your library's periodical index includes online indexes and databases. You should become familiar with these indexes and databases, as they will give you electronic access to material that is not in the library (see Using Resources below for more on online resources).

USING RESOURCES

Many libraries subscribe to computerized databases—specialized electronic listings of books, articles, and essays—that are available in the sciences, humanities, and social sciences. These databases use key words to identify the topic or field of all the books, articles, and essays they list. To use a computer database, you merely enter your list of key words, and the computer conducts the search for you.

Computer databases have expanded in recent years to become essential aids to research. If your library subscribes to such resources, ask your librarian to help you learn to use them efficiently. Although your library may have resources on CD-ROM, online databases and subscription services are quickly replacing these resources. The advantage of online resources is obvious: they are continually updated with material during the year as opposed to CD-ROM databases, which are only updated annually. (For more details on using online databases and subscription services, see Research Utilizing Online Journals, page 76.)

15-d Research and the Internet

It takes considerable time and practice to become efficient at using the Internet as a research tool, but your task is greatly simplified if you use a search engine that supports Boolean terms. Named after the nineteenth-century mathematician George Boole, Boolean terms are words that help define a search. The three primary Boolean terms—AND, OR, and NOT—link topics in order to narrow or expand a search. The Boolean logic associated with each of these terms is described below.

- AND narrows a search by finding only documents containing all of the specified words or phrases. For example, if you search for *cats AND dogs,* only documents containing both words will be retrieved.

- OR expands a search by finding documents containing at least one of the specified words or phrases. For example, if you search for *cats OR dogs,* documents in which either word appears will be retrieved.

- NOT narrows a search by excluding documents containing specified words or phrases. For example, if you search for *cats AND NOT dogs,* all documents containing the word *cats* will be retrieved, except for those documents also containing the word *dogs.* (Note that most search engines will reject your search request if you use the Boolean term NOT alone; preface this term with AND.)

Other notes on Boolean searches:

- If you place an asterisk after a word—for example, French*—in most cases search engines will return any items with variants of the word: French, France, France's, etc.

- With some search engines, you can create groupings of terms by putting quotation marks around two or more series of words. When you do this, the search engine will look for each set of words you have set off in quotation marks: for example, "Newfoundland fisheries" AND "seasonal employment in Newfoundland."

Imagine that you are trying to write an essay on Guy Vanderhaeghe's *The Englishman's Boy*. You go to the Google site and, to start the search, type in the author's last name, Vanderhaeghe. When you click on the Search button, you are disappointed to find that the search returns 154,000 matches, an impossible number to work with. You then add "AND *The Englishman's Boy*" and your list of matches is reduced to 972—better, but still too many to be helpful. So you add a third narrowing addition, "AND Canadian criticism." That turns out to be a poor choice because you still get 815 matches. But you are really interested in what Canadian critics have written about the novel, so you go back to Google's main page and select the "pages from Canada" option. This gets you down to 270 matches, still too many to review. You expect to find the level of analysis you are looking for in an article from a peer-reviewed publication, so you add one more narrowing element, typing in "AND journals." Finally, you have drilled down sufficiently, and the response this time is 8 matches. When you look at your choices now, you are most interested in the journal *Essays in Canadian Literature*, and you check its title pages, finding an article by Daniela James from Volume 27.1 in 2002 titled "Truth and History; Representing the Aura in *The Englishman's Boy*" and another from Volume 25.2 in 2000 called "Unsettling the West: Nation and Genre in Guy Vanderhaeghe's *The Englishman's Boy*." You add these to your preliminary bibliography. For more efficient ways of accessing online material, see the section entitled Academic Directories below.

Like most other search engines, Google ranks its results according to the number of times the search words appear in a document. You will generally find the most useful matches near the top of the page.

SEARCH ENGINES

Try different search engines to see which works best for you, remembering that different search engines scan a different number of webpages. It is difficult to capture the activity of the search engines at a particular time. The following list reflects the report on searching published by SearchEngineWatch for December 2007.

RANKING OF SEARCH ENGINES BY PERCENTAGE OF TOTAL SEARCHES CONDUCTED	
Google	58.4%
Yahoo	22.9%
Microsoft	9.8%
Ask	4.6%
TimeWarner (AOL)	4.5%

If you want to focus on a Canadian topic, try http://www.Canada.com or http://www.canlinks.net.

III
RESEARCH ESSAYS

METASEARCH SITES

You might also want to use a metasearch site that allows you to search simultaneously on more than one search engine. The following sites check from six to fourteen search engines simultaneously for resources to assist you.

Ixquick	http://www.ixquick.com
Dogpile	http://www.dogpile.com
Webcrawler	http://www.webcrawler.com
Metacrawler	http://www.metacrawler.com
Clusty	http://clusty.com
SurfWax	http://www.surfwax.com
Copernic Agent	http://www.copernic.com

ACADEMIC DIRECTORIES

There are academic directories that you may find useful in searching for information in your field of study. The library at the State University of New York at Albany (http://library.albany.edu) lists the better academic directories currently available in the U.S. The University of California, Santa Barbara, lists a broad range of sites focused on literary studies (see http://vos.ucsb.edu/browse.asp?id=3). The Canadian Literary Archive at the University of Manitoba (http://www.umanitoba.ca/canlit) lists a number of sites related to Canadian literature.

You need to start by talking to a librarian to find out which online indexes and databases your library subscribes to. The Kwantlen library, for instance, has subscriptions to databases through Ebsco, ProQuest, Ovid, Wilson, Gale, and CSA Illumina. Your librarian will explain that these service providers simply give you access to the library's online database; it is the datebases themselves that you will be using. Kwantlen's library, for instance, through a service provider, gives students access to Academic Search Premiere, which links the researcher to material in the social sciences, the humanities, education, computer sciences, engineering, physics, chemistry, linguistics, fine arts, and literature from 1965 to the present. In research, as in so many other areas, your best friend is a librarian.

For instance, using Academic Search Premiere, if you placed "The Englishman's Boy" in the search box, indicated that it was a title, and hit the search button, you would come up with two full-text articles that you could consult. Compare that to the lengthy search necessary through Google to identify two research articles.

RESEARCH UTILIZING ONLINE JOURNALS

As libraries give students increased access to online journals and electronic copies of journal articles, students will make greater use of material available to them in this form in the process of writing academic papers. There are specific issues related to conducting this type of research efficiently.

ACCESS TO ONLINE JOURNALS THROUGH YOUR LIBRARY

You will have access to online materials through your college or university library. To use this material, you will need your PIN and a password. Electronic material does not take up limited library space, yet it allows students access to a variety of sources while at a computer connected to a server either in the library or elsewhere.

ADVANTAGES OF ONLINE RESEARCH THROUGH YOUR LIBRARY

The advantage of doing some of your research online should be obvious. It is quick and efficient. Even twenty years ago, for current information, students were limited to the journals local libraries subscribed to. Inter-library loans were and still are available for obtaining hard copies of articles only available at other institutions, but, to utilize such a loan, students have to ensure they have significant lead-time. Inter-library loans may not arrive immediately and do not allow a researcher the opportunity of previewing material to see if it is fully appropriate to the topic. With online library subscription services, more material is easily available. Some online sources will give you an abstract of an article, but others will give you access to its full text. In some cases, the full-text articles are e-mailed to you by a service the library subscribes to. Either way, via your library's online subscriptions, you will be able to access the full text of a number of articles easily and quickly at any location that offers you computer access to the library.

USING COPY AND PASTE TO COLLECT RESEARCH MATERIAL FOR ASSIGNMENTS

Online material is more easily collected, sorted, and stored than material from a book. When you are working with an online source that allows you to capture material electronically, you will be able to open individual files for each relevant article, write a short header for the file, and save the whole article in that file. If you later want to utilize this material, you can open a new file, give it a title, and then, using the copy and paste commands of your computer, move important passages from your article file to your new summary file. Make sure that, when you copy and paste material, you include the source of the material, the title of the article, the author's name, the relevant page number or numbers (if the pages are numbered), and the date of access. You also need to know that this procedure is one of the chief ways that students commit plagiarism because of failing to cite the original source; you will want to avoid that. Finally, be sure you evaluate the reliability of the source before deciding to use it.

PRINT A HARD COPY OF ARTICLES THAT MAY BE OF USE

You can print a hard copy of articles you believe will be particularly useful. Since it is hard to digest complex articles fully on a first reading, saving material to a file or printing a copy of it are good research behaviours. If you are printing an

III RESEARCH ESSAYS

article from a service provider, the date of access may not appear on the bottom of every page as it does when you download a page directly from the Internet. If this is the case, enter your date of access on the first page of the article. As well, be sure your hard copy includes all the information you will need to reference borrowings and to write a bibliographic entry.

TIPS FOR USING ONLINE MATERIAL

- Cut and paste quotations directly into the text of your essay. This will save you time and ensure that you do not introduce typographical or spelling errors.
- Check to see that the material you cut and paste is in the same font and font size as your essay when you use this technique. You do not want the argument of your essay to be marred by poor presentation.
- Treat material from an online source in the same way you would treat material obtained from any secondary source.
- Set off all direct quotations properly and make sure you also attribute your sources for paraphrased or summarized passages with a parenthetic reference and a bibliographic entry at the end of your essay.

INTEGRATING ONLINE MATERIAL USING PREWRITING TECHNIQUES

Organize data you have taken from an online source by topic or subject. If you have used an organized system to collect online, book, periodical, and primary source material in files, it will be easy for you to integrate quotations from your research into a final outline or any other prewriting structure by simply using copy and paste commands.

PLAGIARISM AND ONLINE MATERIAL: A WARNING

You must treat any material you gather online in the same manner you would treat material gathered from a book or a journal. More and more plagiarism cases involve students who think that, because they obtained their secondary sources online or electronically, it is not necessary to cite these sources. Make sure you treat any borrowing of material (direct quotation, paraphrase, or summary) the same. Whether the source is print or electronic, the source must be cited, and there must be an entry for the source in the bibliography at the end of your essay.

ASSESSING ONLINE RESOURCES

The Internet has given us an amazing resource, one that offers access to knowledge from diverse sources. The problem for a person writing a research essay, however, is to distinguish valid information from invalid information. As such, after ordering a search on the Internet about a particular subject and finding fifty or sixty or a hundred suggestions, how should you proceed?

The following offers a simple way to begin discriminating among the resources available.

1. The best resource for advice on how to separate the good resource from the bad is provided by *The Columbia Guide to Online Style*, pages 3–23 in particular.

2. When you do choose a particular site and author or authors, you should check for **reliability** first. The best guide to reliability is if the resource you want to use has been reviewed before it was posted on the Internet. Online books and journal articles rate the highest in this regard because they have been **peer-reviewed**. The next level of reliability would include magazines and newspapers, because they have been selected by an editor and are subject, to some degree, to public review. By the time you get to chat rooms, MUDs, blogs, and wikis, the reliability factor is low.

3. If **currency** is an important quality in your research, then the highest rating will go to material that has been posted on the Internet **quickly**, with the minimum separation between the event or issue that is your subject and the posting of the analysis or commentary. That means that individual sites have gained in importance, and material like online books have declined in importance, given the time gap caused by the need for peer review, publishing preparation, and allied features. The same holds true for journal articles, particularly for those that are published in print format first.

4. The **profile** of the writer or writers of an Internet article or study is also important. It is often the case that a profile of the author(s) is available at the Internet site. If not, you can check biographical and related sources for information. If the author has been published before, you should be able to enter his or her name in Google, Ask Jeeves, Dogpile, Yahoo, or a comparable search engine and get profile information. Remember to check for the **level of expertise** the author has in the area you are researching.

5. The Columbia Guide believes it is important to gauge the level of **stability** of your resource. As such, online books and articles will rate higher than individual sites. In the former case, you should be able to return to the site at a future time and find the material to be identical or nearly the same as it was when you first referenced it. On individual sites, that may not be the case. Remember that stability is a quality that is at least as important for your readers as for you.

6. Perhaps the final test you should conduct is the **bias** test. Can you tell, from the background you have received about your resource, whether it is **biased** in any way toward one feature or another of your subject? In an argument or inquiry essay, bias becomes an important issue. Bias can be as simple as a foundation's funding source or as complex as a previous employment history. You must ascertain whether your source has any predisposition toward the subject you are researching.

15-e The Working Bibliography

As you conduct your library and Internet searches, you should continue to build a working bibliography consisting of sources that are relevant to your topic and preliminary thesis. You can record sources in an electronic file or on index cards. Each book and periodical article citation in your working bibliography should include the following (applicable) information:

BOOK	ARTICLE
Call number	Author(s)
Author(s)	Title and subtitle
Title and subtitle	Title of journal, magazine, or newspaper
Edition	Date and page numbers
City of publication	Volume and issue numbers
Publisher's name	
Year of publication	

NOTE: For information about MLA, APA, and Chicago style requirements for the citation of electronic sources, see pages 124 (MLA), 151 (APA), and 171 (Chicago).

Before you leave this stage of the research process, test the adequacy of your working bibliography by answering these questions:

1. Are all the listed sources relevant to my topic?

2. Do the sources cover all facets of my topic?

3. Are my sources current or are they out of date? Is my subject one where currency is important?

4. Is my list sufficiently balanced? If my subject is one in which opposing positions are taken, have I included at least one reference hostile to my position?

5. Is my working bibliography too ambitious? How much time do I have to complete my research essay and what can I reasonably expect to accomplish within that time?

16 STEP 4: READING

Reading with a critical eye is not the same as reading for pleasure. Unlike general readers, researchers are concerned with understanding the strengths and weaknesses of their sources. To achieve that understanding, they read in a structured and systematic fashion and engage in the activities of previewing, note-taking, and taking stock.

16-a Previewing

You should begin the reading process by acquiring an overview of the material. If the source is a book, you can ascertain its general content by reading the preface (if there is one) and last chapter or final paragraphs, and by looking at the table of contents and the index. The table of contents in particular will help you ascertain those parts of the book that are most relevant to your topic. For more information about previewing (and the related techniques of skimming and scanning), see 3-a.

16-b Note-Taking

As you read, take careful, detailed notes. Your note-taking should be systematic. (For a discussion of the mechanics of note-taking, see Chapter 17.) Before you begin to read, you should have a fairly strong sense of the source's relevance to your topic. The kinds of notes you take during the reading process will depend on your topic and preliminary thesis; generally, they will include the following:

- ideas and facts that either support or contradict your preliminary thesis;
- your own questions and comments about the material;
- specific examples of the author's biases and assumptions; and
- any concepts or key terms that are relevant to your topic.

If you plan to read the source more than once, you may wish to refrain from note-taking until the second reading. Just as note-taking during a lecture can interfere with your ability to absorb information, note-taking during a first reading can interfere with your ability to follow an argument or analysis from start to finish.

16-c Taking Stock

At the conclusion of your reading and note-taking, compile a list of the research tasks that remain. If you are not sure what these tasks might be, ask yourself the following questions:

- Do I understand all the key terms relevant to my topic?
- What questions arising from my reading do I need to answer?
- Has my preliminary thesis changed as a result of my reading?
- Do I have a good understanding of the strengths and weaknesses of my sources?
- Do I have a good understanding of each author's assumptions or biases?
- Do I have all the sources I need to write about my topic, or do I need additional sources in my working bibliography?

Students and researchers typically take notes on paper or in electronic files. The older system of using note cards has largely given way to computer storage. You still need an efficient storage system and a comprehensive strategy for taking notes. Generally, you should set up a folder for each major written assignment and establish files for each of your significant resources and for your initial draft of your paper.

The first note for each resource should also be your bibliographic note and should record all the data you need for writing a bibliographic note, from author through to date of access if it is a note from an online resource. You do not want to be scrambling, after finishing your paper, to look up selected resources to retrieve bibliographic data. Your regular notes can follow the first bibliographic note.

Generally, the notes you are writing will be one of three kinds (aside from the bibliographic). They perform, respectively, the functions of *quoting, paraphrasing*, and *summarizing*.

1. *Quotation.* When you quote a passage, you copy it word for word; now, of course, that copying may be done electronically, but you should still place quotation marks around it to remind you that it is a quotation. If there is a page break in your quotation, it should show in the pagination; if not, show it by placing a slash between the word ending one page and the word starting the next.

2. *Paraphrase.* The paraphrase note is often the longest note you write. It is roughly the length of the source you are paraphrasing but is written in your own words. You should use this kind of note sparingly because of the time it takes to compose.

3. *Summary.* This is the most condensed kind of note you write and the basic workhorse of note-taking. A summary note is written in your own words and is no more than thirty percent of the length of the original passage you are working on. For more on summarizing, see Chapter 9.

Each of these three kinds of notes should record the pages or location of the original text from which you made the note. If you use any of these notes in your finished paper, you have to acknowledge their source in a citation.

To help you understand what is involved in each kind of note, imagine that you are writing an essay on the modernization of Japan after 1945, and you read the following two paragraphs in a book called *The Rise and Fall of the Great Powers*, by Paul Kennedy.

> There can be no doubt that the economic transformation of Japan after 1945 offered the most spectacular example of sustained modernization in these decades, outclassing all of the existing "advanced" countries as a commercial and technological competitor,

and providing a model for emulation by the other Asian "trading states." To be sure, Japan had already distinguished itself almost a century earlier by becoming the first Asian country to copy the West in both economic and—fatefully for itself—military and imperialist terms. Although badly damaged by the 1937–1945 war, and cut off from its traditional markets and suppliers, it possessed an industrial infrastructure which could be repaired and a talented, well-educated, and / socially cohesive population whose determination to improve themselves could now be channeled into peaceful commercial pursuits. For the few years after 1945, Japan was prostrate, an occupied territory, and dependent upon American aid. In 1950, the tide turned—ironically, to a large degree because of the heavy U.S. spending in the Korean War, which stimulated Japan's export-oriented companies. Toyota, for example, was in danger of foundering when it was rescued by the first of the U.S. Defense Department's orders for its trucks; and much the same happened to many other companies.

There was, of course, much more to the "Japanese miracle" than the stimulant of American spending during the Korean War and, again, during the Vietnam War; and the effort to explain exactly how the country transformed itself, and how others can imitate its success, has turned into a miniature growth industry itself. One major reason was its quite fanatical belief in achieving the highest levels of quality control, borrowing (and improving upon) sophisticated management techniques and production methods in the West. It benefited from the national commitment to vigorous, high-level standards of universal education, and from possessing vast numbers of engineers, of electronics and automobile buffs, and of small but entrepreneurial workshops as well as the giant zaibatsu. There was social ethos in favor of hard work, loyalty to the company, and the need to reconcile management–worker differences through a mixture of compromise and deference. The economy required enormous amounts of capital to achieve sustained growth, and it received just that—partly because there was so little expenditure upon defense by a "demilitarized" country sheltering under the American strategic umbrella, but perhaps even more because of fiscal and taxation policies which encouraged an unusually high degree of personal savings, which could then be used for investment purposes. Japan also benefited from the role played by MITI (its Ministry for International Trade and Industry) in "nursing new industrial and technological developments while at the same time coordinating the orderly run-down of aging, decaying industries," all this in a manner totally different from the American laissez-faire approach. (416–17)

The following are samples of notes you might produce while working on a research project about the Japanese recovery and reading Kennedy's book.

BIBLIOGRAPHY NOTE

D210	Kennedy, Paul. <u>The Rise</u>
K46	<u>and Fall of the Great Powers.</u>
1989	New York: Random House, 1989. Print.

SUMMARY NOTE

Kennedy   <u>Rise and Fall</u>

A motivated and well-educated work force, the use of Western management and production techniques, and government policies aimed at stimulating growth were the main engines driving Japan's post-1945 economic renewal. (417)

QUOTATION NOTE

Kennedy   <u>Rise and Fall</u>

"Although badly damaged by the 1937–1945 war, and cut off from its traditional markets and suppliers, [Japan] possessed an industrial infrastructure which could be repaired and a talented, well-educated, and / socially cohesive population whose determination to improve themselves could now be channeled into peaceful commercial pursuits." (416–17)

Note the word *Japan*, enclosed in brackets, in the sample quotation note. Remember that brackets are used to enclose material that you have inserted in the quotation (see Chapter 59). Remember as well that the slash indicates the point at which the quotation breaks between one page and the next.

The length of the Kennedy passage makes it obviously unsuitable for paraphrasing. You could, however, paraphrase the following excerpt from that passage:

ORIGINAL VERSION

> For the few years after 1945, Japan was prostrate, an occupied territory, and dependent upon American aid. In 1950, the tide turned—ironically, to a large degree because of the heavy U.S. spending in the Korean War, which stimulated Japan's export-oriented companies. Toyota, for example, was in danger of foundering when it was rescued by the first of the U.S. Defense Department's orders for its trucks; and much the same happened to many other companies.

PARAPHRASE NOTE

> Kennedy   Rise and Fall
>
> From 1945 to 1949, a defeated and weakened Japan relied on U.S. economic assistance. Things changed in 1950 when Japanese exporters became the beneficiaries of hefty U.S. expenditures related to the Korean War. Toyota was among the struggling Japanese companies kept afloat by purchase orders from the U.S. Defense Department. (417)

NOTE: If you include a paraphrase in your essay without documenting it, you are guilty of plagiarism. For information about avoiding plagiarism, see Chapters 7 and 21.

18-a Outlining

Research papers are extended essays. As such, formal prewriting activities such as outlining are useful in organizing your material before you start drafting. Once you have done the majority of your research, you will have a significant store of notes, thoughts, quotations, website references, and so on. Setting yourself the task of writing an outline for your paper will signal the end of the prewriting phase and the advent of the drafting stage.

You can decide if you want to attempt the most formal of outlines, the sentence outline, or whether a topical or phrasal outline will be sufficient. However, the discipline of writing this outline will force you to think about the different parts of your essay and how they interact. And that's a key step in the shift from amassing material to actually writing. For more information on outlining, refer to 1-e.

If time permits, you should write an initial draft of your research essay at least two weeks before the due date. Once you have completed your first draft, set it aside for a few days; imposing this distance will allow you to start the revising process with a fresh and critical eye. For general information about the drafting process, see Chapter 4. For more specific advice on writing an introductory paragraph, see 39-a.

18-b Segmenting

In this simple technique, also known as *sectioning*, you settle for a general map. You sketch only the major segments of your project. Once you do this, you assemble your notes under the appropriate segment headings and begin to write. In the sample assignment on Japan after World War II, there would be segments on initial recovery, expansion of productive capacity, consolidation, and government intervention and assistance.

One of the advantages of segmenting is that it allows you to tackle a manageable element immediately and not be intimidated by the size of your task. After you create your general map and assemble all your information under the appropriate headings, you can start writing about whichever segment you want. You may wish to start on the one you know best. It is always useful to begin with something you are confident about.

18-c Writing a Draft Introduction

Some writers like to tackle the introduction first; others write it last. If you prefer to start with your introduction, don't aim for a polished version at this stage. Writers who try to perfect their introduction before they move on to other drafting tasks often find themselves afflicted with writer's block. Remember that all you need is a base from which to start; just get the basics down—your topic, your proposed position on that topic, and (if appropriate) a preview of where your essay is going.

Keep the first draft of your introduction on hand as you proceed through the drafting stage. After you have finished your first draft, you can make any necessary revisions to the introduction.

18-d Integrating Quotations

SIGNAL PHRASES

Prose quotations of fewer than five typed lines in your essay (MLA style), fewer than forty words (APA style), or fewer than one hundred words (Chicago style) need to be worked skillfully into the text. A quotation that is dropped abruptly into the text will have a jarring effect.

Dropped Quotation

MLA

Cultural factors played a major role in Japan's post-1945 economic recovery: "There was social ethos in favor of hard work, loyalty to the company, and the need to reconcile management–worker differences through a mixture of compromise and deference" (Kennedy 417).

APA

Cultural factors played a major role in Japan's post-1945 economic recovery. "There was social ethos in favor of hard work, loyalty to the company, and the need to reconcile management-worker differences through a mixture of compromise and deference" (Kennedy, 1987, p. 417).

To smooth the transition between text and quotation, preface the quotation with a signal phrase or integrate the quotation fully with your text. A widely used signal phrase is the phrase *According to* followed by the author's name. The *According to* + *author* signal-phrase construction is set off with a comma.

In the following illustrations, you will see both MLA and APA citation styles given in the first example; they are then alternated in successive examples. The main difference between the two styles is the attachment of a date of publication to the author's name and the use of *p.* to signify page number in APA style.

Quotation with Signal Phrase

Cultural factors played a major role in Japan's post-1945 economic recovery. According to Kennedy, "There was social ethos in favor of hard work . . ." (417).

NOTE: Signal phrases should be used to introduce paraphrases and summaries as well.

Another common signal phrase consists of the author of the cited source and a verb that prepares readers for the quotation.

III

RESEARCH ESSAYS

Kennedy (1987) notes that "there was social ethos in favor of hard work ..." (p. 417).

NOTE: The preceding quotation begins with a lowercase letter (even though the original quotation begins with a capital letter) because a quotation introduced by the signal-phrase construction *Author + verb* is an essential syntactic part of the sentence.

The word *As*, the author's name, and an appropriate verb may also be used. This signal-phrase construction, like the *According to + author* construction, is set off with a comma.

As Kennedy points out, "There was social ethos in favor of hard work ..." (417).

NOTE: A quotation introduced by the signal-phrase constructions *According to + author* or *As + author + verb* retains the initial capital letter because it is modified by, but is not an essential syntactic part of, the rest of the sentence.

If the quotation is not an independent clause but is instead a word, phrase, or dependent clause, you need to weave the quotation into your own sentence.

Kennedy (1987) draws a vivid contrast between Japan's tradition of government intervention in the economy and "the American laissez-faire approach" (p. 417).

If there is a quotation within the quotation you wish to use, enclose the interior quotation in single quotation marks.

Kennedy offers a variety of explanations for the "'Japanese miracle'" that shaped the economy in the post-1945 period (417).

For more information about punctuation with quotations, see 55-a and 55-b.

VERBS IN SIGNAL PHRASES

The verb you use in an *Author + verb* or an *As + author + verb* signal-phrase construction provides readers with a sense of the source's purpose. For example, *reports* suggests an attempt to inform, while *argues* suggests an attempt to persuade. Following is a list of verbs commonly found in both *Author + verb* and *As + author + verb* signal-phrase constructions.

acknowledges	contends	points out
admits	declares	recommends
advises	explains	reflects
argues	implies	remarks
asserts	indicates	says
claims	maintains	states
comments	notes	suggests
confirms	observes	writes

SIGNAL STATEMENTS

If you wish to provide more information than can be accommodated in a signal phrase, you may instead use a signal statement. If the statement is an independent clause, it is separated from the quotation by a colon.

[MLA style] Cultural factors played a major role in Japan's post-1945 economic recovery. Kennedy (1987) comments on Japanese attitudes to work: "There was social ethos in favor of hard work . . ." (p. 417).

Signal statements are frequently used to introduce *long quotations,* prose quotations of more than four lines (MLA style), forty words or more (APA style), or one hundred words or more (Chicago style). A long quotation is not enclosed in quotation marks and is set off from the text by indenting ten spaces (MLA and Chicago) or five spaces (APA) from the left margin.

[MLA style] Kennedy identifies the economic challenges Japan faced and the principal factors that enabled it to stage its dramatic post-1945 economic recovery:

> Although badly damaged by the 1937–1945 war, and cut off from its traditional markets and suppliers, it possessed an industrial infrastructure which could be repaired and a talented, well-educated, and socially cohesive population whose determination to improve themselves could now be channeled into peaceful commercial pursuits. (416–17)

[APA style] Kennedy (1987) identifies the economic challenges Japan faced and the principal factors that enabled it to stage its dramatic post-1945 economic recovery:

> Although badly damaged by the 1937–1945 war, and cut off from its traditional markets and suppliers, it possessed an industrial infrastructure which could be repaired and a talented, well-educated, and socially cohesive population whose determination to improve themselves could now be channeled into peaceful commercial pursuits. (pp. 416–417)

BRACKETS AND ELLIPSES

You can use square brackets and/or ellipses to make a quotation fit grammatically into your own sentence. An excess of ellipsis dots and brackets in the same passage makes for difficult reading, so use these marks of punctuation sparingly.

[MLA style] According to Kennedy, Japan's "fanatical belief in achieving the highest levels of quality control . . . [and] the national commitment to vigorous, high-level standards of universal education" were driving forces in the country's economic transformation (417).

For further information about brackets and ellipses, see Chapters 59 and 61.

III RESEARCH ESSAYS

It is essential that you set your first draft aside for a few days before you try to edit it. Imposing this break allows you to gain a critical perspective on your essay. It also gives you an opportunity to review in your mind what you have written.

Revising an essay is a daunting task. You can make the revising process more manageable if you focus on one facet of your essay at a time. To achieve this focus, you can make use of the four editing sweeps introduced in Chapter 5 and revisited in this section.

19-a Structure Sweep

In a structure sweep, you check to ensure that there are logical connections between the various elements of your first draft. You may choose to highlight the main idea in each paragraph, together with the transitions between paragraphs. Regardless of the method you use to perform the sweep, you should ask yourself the following questions:

- Are the transitions between paragraphs clear?
- Does each paragraph have a focus and a purpose?
- Does each paragraph reflect and advance my thesis?
- Are all the parts of my argument logically developed?

As you do the structure sweep, add, strengthen, or clarify transitions as needed.

19-b Development Sweep

A development sweep is a way of ensuring that you have provided adequate support for the main claim in each paragraph. Using a pen, a highlighter, or a cursor, select the sentences within each paragraph that define, illustrate, offer factual support, or otherwise provide specific proof for the paragraph's general claim. You can use a specific colour to identify the support sentences. As you perform the sweep, ask yourself these questions:

- Is the supporting material clearly expressed?
- Is the supporting material persuasive?
- If there are only one or two supporting sentences within a paragraph, should other supporting sentences be added?
- Is my illustration complete? Is it clearly connected to my claim?
- Do I connect each claim to my essay's overall claim?

19-c Special-Paragraphs Sweep

In a special-paragraphs sweep, you concentrate on the introduction, the conclusion, and any other special paragraphs you have written. To begin, examine your introduction and answer these questions about it:

- Does it capture the reader's attention?
- Does it clearly establish my thesis or claim?

- Does it define difficult or challenging terms?
- Does it provide the background necessary to a successful argument?

Next, evaluate your conclusion in light of the following questions:

- Does it restate my thesis?
- Does it summarize the main points supporting my argument?
- Does it reiterate the general significance of my subject?
- Does the last sentence express an appropriate note of finality?

19-d Proofreading Sweep

While there is some flexibility in the order in which you do the above editing sweeps, you should perform the proofreading sweep last. This sweep is intended to uncover errors in spelling, punctuation, and usage. You can initiate a proof-reading sweep by using your spell checker; if yours is not activated, check the Help guide in your computer to find out how to activate it. Most word-processing programs have the spell check set by default to American English. To change this, go to the language selection area of your word-processing program and select Canadian English from the list. Guidelines relating to the proofreading sweep are provided in 5-d. You can use the errors chart (Chapter 12) to guide your revision of usage errors.

You should also use the proofreading sweep as an opportunity to check for formatting errors. Specifically, check the following basic format requirements:

- separate title page or necessary information on the first page
- pagination in top right-hand corner of each page except a separate title page
- indented paragraphs
- aligned left margin
- double-spacing throughout, except for Chicago-style block quotations (single-space)
- correct parenthetic referencing
- correct quotation formats
- correct documentation style in Works Cited, References list, or Bibliography

EXERCISES

EXERCISE III-1   USING LIBRARY RESOURCES

The following exercise will help you learn about your library's resources. Complete the exercise by using any one of the suggested topics or by using a topic you have been assigned to do research on.

III RESEARCH ESSAYS

1. East Coast or West Coast offshore fisheries

2. the cost of health care in a Canadian province

3. computer technology and the changing workplace

4. single-parent families

5. sexually transmitted diseases

6. the rights of smokers

7. student loans / student debt

8. the governing party (either federally or provincially)

9. Louis Riel

10. the Parti Québécois

11. unemployment

12. a Canadian writer: Alice Munro, W. O. Mitchell, David Adams Richards, Roch Carrier, Marie-Claire Blais, Alistair MacLeod, Dionne Brand, Michael Ondaatje, Margaret Atwood, Guy Vanderhaeghe

13. the CBC or the NFB

14. multiculturalism

PART 1

1. Search the reference section of your library for books that will give you an overview of your topic. To find information about a topic of general interest in Canada, consult an encyclopedia such as *The Canadian Encyclopedia,* a periodicals index such as *Canadian Periodical Index,* or an online index such as *Canadian Newsstand.*

2. When you find an article in a periodicals index that is clearly relevant to your topic, write down the necessary bibliographical information in your working bibliography (see 15-e).

3. Locate the source in your library's periodical room. Scan the article and write down one interesting piece of information about your topic. Do not forget to record the page number(s) where you found the information. Alternatively, use your library's online indexes to find an article for this purpose.

4. Use electronic access to accomplish the tasks outlined in #2 and #3 above. Use Academic Search Premiere to find an article relevant to a research task you are working on in your field.

1. Using your library's electronic catalogue, conduct a subject search of your topic. If your search turns up an unmanageable number of titles, you may need to narrow and focus your topic (see Chapter 14). Conversely, you may find you have to broaden your topic. If your library does not carry any titles by or about Marie-Claire Blais, for example, search a related subject such as Quebec writers.

2. When you find a relevant source, write down the necessary bibliographical information (see 15-e).

3. Locate the title in the library. If the title is a book, look at the table of contents and the index to ascertain which parts of the book are most relevant to your topic. Check the bibliography and record bibliographical information sources that are of particular relevance.

4. Conduct an Internet search to discover sources for the topic you are researching. Use your library's databases as much as possible for this search. Write down the five best sources you find.

EXERCISE III-2 BUILDING NOTE-TAKING SKILLS

The notes you take during the reading stage of the research process are critical to the success of your first draft. In this exercise, you practise the note-taking skills of summarizing, quoting, and paraphrasing.

Use the excerpt from Reinhold Kramer's "Nationalism, the West, and The Englishman's Boy" *(see pages 15 and 16) to do the following note-taking activities:*

1. Create a separate document for a bibliography note to record the information given in the footnote in Chapter 3 on page 14.

2. Write a summary of Kramer's three paragraphs in eight sentences or fewer and place it in the document.

3. Write a quotation note complete with page information for your document.

4. Create a file note that paraphrases the third paragraph of Kramer's excerpt.

Documentation

Different academic disciplines use different systems of documentation. The Modern Language Association (MLA) style, presented in the *MLA Handbook for Writers of Research Papers,* is used throughout the humanities. The American Psychological Association (APA) style, contained in the *Publication Manual of the American Psychological Association,* is followed by writers and students in the social sciences. The *Chicago Manual of Style* is the format recommended for history papers and is sometimes employed in other disciplines. The Council of Science Editors (CSE) style, presented in *Scientific Style and Format,* is the standard reference style for those in the scientific community. (Bibliographical information for the MLA, APA, Chicago, and CSE titles, and for style manuals used in a variety of disciplines, is provided in Table 20-1.)

TABLE 20-1   Style Manuals: Selected Disciplines

CHEMISTRY

Coghill, Anne M., and Lorrin R. Garson., ed. *The ACS Style Guide: Effective Communication of Scientific Information*. 3rd ed. Washington, DC: American Chemical Society, 2006.

GOVERNMENT

Canada. Public Works and Government Services Canada. Translation Bureau. *The Canadian Style: A Guide to Writing and Editing*. 2nd ed. Toronto: Dundurn Press, 1997.

HUMANITIES

Modern Language Association of America. *MLA Handbook for Writers of Research Papers*. 7th ed. New York: Modern Language Association of America, 2009.

HUMANITIES, NATURAL AND SOCIAL SCIENCES

The Chicago Manual of Style. 15th ed. Chicago: University of Chicago Press, 2003.

HUMANITIES AND SCIENCES: ONLINE STYLE

Walker, Janice R., and Todd Taylor. *Columbia Guide to Online Style*. 2nd ed. New York: Columbia University Press, 2006.

JOURNALISM

Tsko, Patti, ed. *The Canadian Press Stylebook: A Guide for Writers and Editors*. 14th ed. Toronto: Canadian Press, 2006.

McFarlane, J. A., and Warren Clements. *The Globe and Mail Style Book: A Guide to Language and Usage*. 9th ed. Toronto: McClelland and Stewart, 2003.

LAW

Canadian Guide to Uniform Legal Citation. 6th ed. Toronto: Carswell, 2006.

Yogis, John A., et al. *Legal Writing and Research Manual*. 6th ed. Markham, ON: Butterworths, 2004.

MEDICINE

Iverson, Cheryl, et al. *AMA Manual of Style: A Guide for Authors and Editors*. 10th ed. New York: Oxford University Press, 2007.

MUSIC

Holomon, D. Kern. *Writing about Music: A Style Sheet from the Editors of 19th-Century Music*. Berkeley: University of California Press, 1988.

TABLE 20-1 Style Manuals: Selected Disciplines *(continued)*

PHYSICS

American Institute of Physics. *AIP Style Manual*. 4th ed. New York: AIP, 1990.

SCIENCE

Style Manual Committee, Council of Science Editors. *Scientific Style and Format: The CSE Manual for Authors, Editors, and Publishers*. 7th ed. Reston, VA: Council of Science Editors with Rockefeller University Press, 2006.

SOCIAL SCIENCES

American Psychological Association. *Publication Manual of the American Psychological Association*. 5th ed. Washington, DC: APA, 2001.

The following examples of book, journal, and newspaper reference entries illustrate the basic differences among MLA, APA, Chicago, and CSE styles of documentation.

BOOK

Chao, Lien, and Jim Wong-Chu, eds. *Strike the Wok: An Anthology of Contemporary Chinese Canadian Fiction*. Toronto: TSAR, 2003. Print. [MLA]

Chao, L., & Wong-Chu J. (Eds.). (2003). *Strike the wok: An anthology of contemporary Chinese Canadian fiction*. Toronto: TSAR. [APA]

Chao, Lien, and Jim Wong-Chu, eds. *Strike the Wok: An Anthology of Contemporary Chinese Canadian Fiction*. Toronto: TSAR, 2003. [Chicago]

Chao C, Wong-Chu J, editors. 2003. Strike the wok: an anthology of contemporary Chinese Canadian fiction. Toronto: TSAR. [CSE]

JOURNAL

Hoben, Allan, and Robert William Hefner. "The Integrative Revolution Revisited." *World Development* 19.1 (1991): 17-30. Print. [MLA]

Hoben, A., & Hefner, R.W. (1991). The integrative revolution revisited. *World Development, 19* (1), 17–30. [APA]

Hoben, Allan, and Robert William Hefner. "The Integrative Revolution Revisited." *World Development 19*, 1 (1991): 17–30. [Chicago]

Hoben A, Hefner RW. 1991. The integrative revolution revisited. World Dev 19(1):17-30. [CSE]

NEWSPAPER

Rasbach, Noreen. "Investor Stereotypes: Do Women Really Do It Better?" *Globe and Mail* 16 Feb. 2008, BC ed.: B8. Print. [MLA]

Rasbach, N. (2008, February 16). Investor stereotypes: Do women really do it better? *The Globe and Mail*, p. B8. [APA]

Rasbach, Noreen. "Investor Stereotypes: Do Women Really Do It Better?" *Globe and Mail*, February 16, 2008, sec. B. [Chicago]

Rasbach, N. 2008 Feb 16. Investor stereotypes: do women really do it better? Globe and Mail (BC Ed.) Sect. B:8 (col. 1-6). [CSE]

Chapters 22–26 describe the various styles of documentation in detail.

21 AVOIDING PLAGIARISM

The most significant difference between the research essay and other forms of expository writing is the demand placed on writers of a research essay to find authoritative sources to support their arguments or analysis. In doing so, writers also assume the ethical responsibility of formally acknowledging all borrowings made from these sources, whether they be quotations, paraphrases, summaries, facts, or perspectives. Any failure to do so constitutes plagiarism. You are not required to document common knowledge, information that is widely known and accessible from multiple public sources. Every other borrowing, however, must be formally cited.

Suppose that you want to borrow material from the following sentence, which appears on page 417 of a book by Paul Kennedy entitled *The Rise and Fall of the Great Powers.*

> For the few years after 1945, Japan was prostrate, an occupied territory, and dependent upon American aid.

If you were to include the following sentence in your essay without documentation, you would be guilty of plagiarism.

> From 1945 to 1949, a defeated and weakened Japan relied on U.S. economic assistance.

To avoid plagiarism, you need to cite your source.

> As Paul Kennedy notes, a defeated and weakened Japan relied on U.S. economic assistance from 1945 to 1949 (417).

Instead of using a paraphrase, you could quote the original source. (For information about integrating quotations into the text of an essay, see 18-d.)

> Paul Kennedy notes, "For the few years after 1945, Japan was prostrate, an occupied territory, and dependent upon American aid" (417).

The parenthetical references shown in the preceding examples reflect MLA style, the subject of Chapter 22.

For more information on plagiarism, see Chapter 7.

MLA STYLE

Be aware of the following changes in the 2009 seventh edition of the *MLA Handbook for Writers of Research Papers*:

- Titles of works such as books, paintings, plays, films, or any other work that was underlined previously in MLA style, are now italicized.
- MLA does not give guidance for the presentation, in handwritten copy in an exam or time-limited test, of titles of works such as books or other complete works. In these situations, the MLA convention of underlining should apply.
- URLs for online material are generally omitted in works-cited entries.
- Each works-cited entry now requires that its medium be provided: Print, Web, CD, LP, Television, Radio, Film, DVD, Videocassette.

22-a Parenthetical References

In MLA style, a parenthetical reference identifies a source and refers readers to the full description of the source in the list of works cited. Following are some sample MLA-style parenthetical references.

Author and page (short quotation)   Prose quotations that run no more than four lines in your essay and poetry quotations that contain no more than three lines of poetry are integrated into the text and enclosed in double quotation marks. The author's name need not appear in the parenthetical reference if it is included in the signal phrase. (For information about signal phrases, see Chapter 18.)

Mark Kingwell defines happiness as "the possession of virtuous character and the performance of virtuous action" (327).

Japan's post-1945 economic renewal was driven in part by a "national commitment to vigorous, high-level standards of universal education" (Kennedy 417).

For an example of a short poetry quotation see *Contemporary poem* on page 105.

Author and page (long quotation)   Poetry quotations that include more than three lines of poetry and prose quotations that run more than four lines are set off from the text by indenting one inch (2.5 cm) from the left margin. Block quotations are not enclosed in quotation marks.

LONG PROSE QUOTATION

Swift's ironic "A Modest Proposal" paints a devastating portrait of Ireland's poor:

> Some persons of a desponding spirit are in great concern
> about that vast number of poor people, who are aged,

diseased, or maimed, and I have been desired to employ my thoughts what course may be taken to ease the nation of so grievous an encumbrance. But I am not in the least pain upon that matter, because it is very well known that they are every day dying, and rotting, by cold, and famine, and filth, and vermin, as fast as can be reasonably expected. (58)

LONG POETRY QUOTATION

In her glosas, P. K. Page honours writers who have had an impact on her thinking and writing. For example, in "A Grain of Sand," Page starts her poem with the first four lines of William Blake's "Auguries of Innocence":

> To See the World in a Grain of Sand
> And a Heaven in a Wild Flower,
> Hold Infinity in the palm of your hand,
> And Eternity in an hour. (1–4)

Author of more than one source　If the list of works cited contains more than one work by the same author, name the title in the parenthetical reference or in the text.

In *Larry's Party*, the central metaphor for human existence is the maze, "a circling, exquisite puzzle of pain, and pain's consolation" (Shields 160).

The central metaphor for human existence is the maze, "a circling, exquisite puzzle of pain, and pain's consolation" (Shields, *Larry's Party* 160).

If the title of the work is long, use a shortened version in the parenthetical reference.

In "Canadian Monsters: Some Aspects of the Supernatural in Canadian Fiction," Atwood describes the *wendigo* and Coyote as "supernatural forces in the environment . . . against which the human characters measure themselves" (235).

The *wendigo* and Coyote are "supernatural forces in the environment . . . against which the human characters measure themselves" (Atwood, "Canadian Monsters" 235).

Two or three authors   If the source has two or three authors, include them in the parenthetical reference or name them in the text.

Between 1933 and 1945, Canada opened its doors to fewer than 5000 Jews (Abella and Troper xxii).

As Abella and Troper point out, between 1933 and 1945 Canada opened its doors to fewer than 5000 Jews (xxii).

More than three authors   If the source has more than three authors, include in the text or parenthetical reference only the name of the first author followed by *et al.* ("and others").

According to Simpson et al., depression among stroke victims tends to deepen with time (45).

A recent study found that depression among stroke victims tends to deepen with time (Simpson et al. 45).

Unidentified author   If the name of the author is unknown, either use the source's full title in the text or use the first two or three words of the title in the parenthetical reference.

> According to a recent article entitled "The Poverty Trap in Ontario," there is a direct link between welfare reform and increased levels of homelessness (28).
>
> There is a direct link between welfare reform and increased levels of homelessness ("Poverty Trap" 28).

Corporate author   Place the names of corporate bodies in the parenthetical reference or in the text. (The preferred placement for long names is in the text.) In the parenthetical reference, shorten words that are commonly abbreviated.

> In the mid-1980s, the Women's Legal Education and Action Fund sought to force positive changes in family benefits law in Ontario (174).
>
> A diatom was identified as the cause of the mysterious outbreak of food poisoning (Natl. Research Council 36).

Authors with the same last name   If the works-cited list contains works by two or more authors with the same last name, include the first initial in the parenthetical reference.

> (J. Smith 13)
>
> (D. Smith 45-49)

If the initial is shared, write the first name in full.

(Alan Greenfeld 167)

(Abe Greenfeld 22)

Multi-volume work If your essay cites more than one volume of a multi-volume work, include the volume number in the parenthetical reference. Note that a space separates the colon and the page number.

In her diary, Virginia Woolf expressed her reservations about *Ulysses* (2: 199-200).

Literary works For most contemporary literary works, the treatment of references is simple, with the page number being the minimum information you need in a parenthetical citation for a prose work and the line number or numbers for a poem.

CONTEMPORARY NOVEL [page number]

In *The English Patient*, Michael Ondaatje's Almasy shows his contempt for the European view of civilization when he narrates of the war in North Africa: "The Barbarians versus the Barbarians. Both armies would come through the desert with no sense of what it was" (257).

CONTEMPORARY PLAY

Contemporary plays do not, as a rule, use the convention of listing the line numbers for an act. Some also do not break acts down into scenes in the way that classical plays do. If you are faced with a play that does not use the conventions of act/scene/line, use a page number for your reference.

> **CONTEMPORARY POEM [line number or numbers]**
>
> In her poem "Audubon," Anne Carson is cryptic in her comment on the much lauded naturalist: "On the bottom of each watercolor he put 'drawn from nature' / which meant he shot the birds" (2-3).

MLA suggests that you include either the word *line* or *lines* before the number reference the first time you make a parenthetical line reference, so your reader knows the reference is to line numbers (*lines 4-5*). Subsequent references need only include the line numbers (*7-8*).

When citing literary works that are available in several editions, help readers locate the passage by providing more than just the page number.

For a classic prose work, follow the page number with the chapter or part number.

> In *Women in Love*, Gerald's death in the Tyrolese mountains is observed by "a small bright moon" (Lawrence 532; ch. 30).

For a classic verse play, include the act, scene, and line numbers in the parenthetical reference. Use arabic numerals unless roman numerals (V.iii.244–45) are preferred by your instructor.

> In *King Lear*, the dying Edmund reveals a touch of humanity when he asserts, "Some good I mean to do / Despite of mine own nature" (Shakespeare 5.3.244-45).

NOTE: If you are using an edition of a play that numbers the lines by page, ask your instructor if he or she wants you to include page numbers in the citations.

Some longer poems such as Milton's *Paradise Lost,* Pope's *An Essay on Criticism,* and Tennyson's *In Memoriam* are divided into sections. When you are citing a passage from such a work, cite the section and follow that with the line number or numbers.

The most famous, yet cryptic line in Pope's *An Essay on Criticism* is a remark that everyone knows only too well: "A little learning is a dangerous thing" (2.15).

Indirect quotation Use the abbreviation *qtd. in* to indicate that you are using someone else's report of a writer's or speaker's words.

Voltaire once said, "As for the obvious, leave it to the philosophers" (qtd. in Kingwell 14).

NOTE: MLA prefers that material be taken from an original source rather than quoted indirectly.

Parenthetic references for online material MLA states that parenthetic references for material from the Web should follow the same format as references for any other material. You should cite the page number of a Web source if it has page numbers. If the source does not have page numbers but numbers the paragraphs, you may cite the paragraph number. Otherwise, you should cite the title and list the source in your works-cited list at the end of your paper.

ONLINE DICTIONARY DEFINITION
If you use a specific definition from an online dictionary, place the word you have defined in a parenthetic reference and follow it with the abbreviation "def." and the number or letter the dictionary placed beside that specific definition. As well, write an entry for the dictionary in your works-cited list.

Two bits, an expression used to designate 25¢ or a quarter of a dollar, dates back to 1730 and is connected to Spanish coins that were at that time cut into eight parts ("Two Bits," def. 1).

22-b Content and Bibliographical Notes

MLA allows the use of content and bibliographical notes with parenthetical documentation. These optional elements add to the information provided in the text. *Content notes* offer explanation, comment, or information that would interrupt the flow of the essay if it were included in the text. *Bibliographical notes* either comment on sources or refer readers to sources relevant to the topic under discussion.

Both kinds of notes are formed the same way. Insert a superscript arabic numeral at the appropriate place in the text and then write the note, prefacing it with a matching numeral. Indent the first line of the note like the first line of a paragraph. Position the note either as a footnote at the foot of the page or as an endnote at the end of your essay.

CONTENT NOTE

TEXT

Atwood's re-creation of the life and times of Grace Marks--a sixteen-year-old domestic servant sentenced to life imprisonment in 1843 for her perceived role in the murders of her employer and his housekeeper--is concerned with the process by which the case became a cause célèbre, not with the thorny question of Marks's actual guilt or innocence.[1]

NOTE

[1] The many contradictions, gaps, distortions, ambiguities, and political agendas she uncovered during her research into the Marks case led Atwood to conclude that the answer to this particular question is "unknowable" (37).

BIBLIOGRAPHICAL NOTE

TEXT

In writing about Canadian literature, one is immediately faced with the fact that Canada is beset with problems that originate in colonial attitudes.[1]

NOTE

[1] For an in-depth discussion of the effect of colonialism on post-colonial societies, see Edward Said's *Culture and Imperialism* (New York: Knopf, 1994).

22-c List of Works Cited

The list of works cited, which starts on a separate page at the end of the essay, contains complete bibliographical information for all the sources cited in the text. When constructing a works-cited list, follow these guidelines:

- Start the list on a separate page and title the list *Works Cited*.
- Centre the title an inch (2.5 cm) from the top of the page.
- Arrange the list *alphabetically* by the surnames of the authors or editors.
- If a work has no author or editor, alphabetize it according to the first word of its title. If the title's first word is *a, an,* or *the,* use the second word to determine placement.
- Do not indent the first line of each entry in the works-cited list. Indent subsequent lines a half-inch (or 1.25 cm). This format, called a *hanging indent,* makes the authors' surnames stand out for easy reference. (If your word processor has one, use the hanging-indent feature to format entries.)
- Double-space between the title and the first entry, and between and within entries throughout the list.
- Italicize the title of a work unless it is part of a whole.

For a sample list of works cited, see page 138. Following are some sample works-cited entries.

BOOKS AND OTHER NON-PERIODICAL WORKS

One author You will find in a book's title and copyright pages the three basic units of a book entry: (1) author; (2) title; and (3) place of publication, publisher, year of publication. Use a shortened form of the publisher's name (for example, *Scribner's* for *Charles Scribner's Sons; Norton* for *W.W. Norton and Co., Inc.; Oxford UP* for *Oxford University Press; or Simon* for *Simon and Schuster, Inc.*).

Sakamoto, Kerri. *The Electrical Field.* Toronto: Knopf, 1998. Print.

Two or three authors Name the authors according to the order in which they appear on the title page. Invert the name of the first author so that the surname comes first. Separate the authors' names with commas.

McNaught, Kenneth, and David Bercuson. *The Winnipeg General Strike.*

Don Mills, ON: Longman, 1974. Print.

Nader, Ralph, Nadia Milleron, and Duff Conacher. *Canada Firsts: Ralph*

Nader's Salute to Canada and Canadian Achievement. Toronto:

McClelland, 1992. Print.

More than three authors Name only the first author listed on the title page, and follow the name with a comma and *et al.* ("and others").

Betcherman, G., et al. *The Canadian Workplace in Transition.* Kingston,

ON: IRC, 1994. Print.

IV DOCUMENTATION

Author with an editor   After the author and the title, write the abbreviation *Ed.* ("Edited by") followed by the name of the editor.

> McClelland, Jack. *Imagining Canadian Literature: The Selected Letters of*
>
> *Jack McClelland.* Ed. Sam Solecki. Toronto: Key Porter, 1998. Print.

Corporate author   Begin the entry with the corporate author's name, even if it is the name of the publisher as well.

> Canadian Authors Association. *Canadian Writer's Guide.* Markham, ON:
>
> Fitzhenry, 1997. Print.
>
> Canadian Museum of Civilization. *In the Shadow of the Sun: Perspectives*
>
> *on Contemporary Native Art.* Hull, QC: Canadian Museum of
>
> Civilization, 1993. Print.

Unidentified author   Begin the entry with the title. Remember that titles are alphabetized by the first word other than *a, an,* or *the.*

> *The International Guide to English Language Programs,* 1998. Victoria: EI
>
> Educ. Intl., 1997. Print.

More than one work by the same author   If your works-cited list contains two or more works by the same author, name the author only in the first entry. Begin subsequent entries with three hyphens followed by a period. List the entries alphabetically by title.

> Mistry, Rohinton. *A Fine Balance.* Toronto: McClelland, 1995. Print.
>
> ---. *Such a Long Journey.* Toronto: McClelland, 1993. Print.

Editor   Follow the name or names with the abbreviations *ed.* ("editor") or *eds.* ("editors").

> Heron, Craig, ed. *The Worker's Revolt in Canada, 1917-1925.* Toronto: U
>
> of Toronto P, 1998. Print.

Translation   Begin the entry with the author's name. After the title, write the abbreviation *Trans.* ("Translated by") and follow the abbreviation with the name of the translator.

> Gravel, François. *Miss September.* Trans. Sheila Fischman. Dunvegan,
>
> ON: Cormorant, 1998. Print.

Edition other than the first   If a book's title page indicates a later edition of the book, name the edition, in abbreviated form, after the title in your entry. An edition may be identified by number (*2nd ed., 3rd ed.,* etc.), by year (e.g., *2009 ed.*), or by name (*Rev. ed.* for "Revised Edition").

> Siegel, Arthur. *Politics and the Media in Canada.* 2nd ed. Whitby, ON:
>
> McGraw, 1996. Print.

Multi-volume work   If you are citing two or more volumes of a multi-volume work, indicate (using the abbreviation *vols.*) the total number of volumes before the publication information.

> Bell, Quentin. *Virginia Woolf: A Biography*, 2 vols. London: Hogarth, 1972.
>
>   Print.

If your essay cites only one volume, write the volume number before the publication information and provide publication information only for that volume.

> Bloom, Harold, ed. *The Art of the Critic: Literary Theory and Criticism*
>
>   *from the Greeks to the Present*. Vol. 9. New York: Chelsea, 1989. Print.

Book in a series   If the book is part of a series, name the series (and any series number) after the medium of publication.

> Rogers, Edward S., and Donald B. Smith, eds. *Aboriginal Ontario:*
>
>   *Historical Perspectives on the First Nations*. Toronto: Dundurn, 1994.
>
>   Print. Ontario Historical Studies Ser.

Anthology or compilation   Follow the name of the editor or compiler with a comma and the abbreviation *ed.* or *comp.*

> Downie, Mary Alice, and Barbara Robertson, comps. *The New Wind Has*
>
>   *Wings: Poems from Canada*. Toronto: Oxford UP, 1984. Print.
>
> Glover, Douglas, ed. *Best Canadian Stories 99*. Ottawa: Oberon, 1999.
>
>   Print.

Selection in an anthology or compilation Name the author of the selection, the selection title, and the title of the book. If the book has an editor or compiler, write the abbreviation *Ed.* ("Edited by") or *Comp.* ("Compiled by") after the title, followed by the person's name. Give the inclusive page numbers of the selection between the publication information and the medium of publication.

Klein, A. M. "Haunted House." *The Collected Poems of A. M. Klein.*

Comp. Miriam Waddington. Toronto: McGraw, 1974. 22-25. Print.

Richler, Mordecai. "The Summer My Grandmother Was Supposed to

Die." *The New Canadian Anthology: Poetry and Short Fiction in*

English. Ed. Robert Lecker and Jack David. Scarborough, ON:

Nelson, 1988. 374-83. Print.

Multiple selections in an anthology or compilation If you are citing two or more selections from the same collection, create an entry for the collection and cross-reference individual selections to the entry. For each selection, write the name or names of the author or authors and the title, the last name of the collection's editor or editors, and the inclusive page numbers.

Blaise, Clark. "The Bridge." Lecker and David 443-48.

Di Michele, Mary. "Poem for My Daughter." Lecker and David 270-71.

Lecker, Robert, and Jack David, eds. *The New Canadian Anthology: Poetry*

and Short Fiction in English. Scarborough, ON: Nelson, 1988. Print.

Ondaatje, Michael. "King Kong Meets Wallace Stevens." Lecker and

David 250-51.

Thomas, Audrey. "Déjeuner sur l'Herbe." Lecker and David 411-22.

Article in a dictionary or an encyclopedia Entries for information from dictionaries and encyclopedias are treated in the same way that you treat a poem or essay in an anthology. An entry for a word from a dictionary, however, does not need a reference to the dictionary's editor. An entry for an article in an encyclopedia will name the author of the article (if there is one), the article's title, the title of the encyclopedia, the edition number, the year of publication, and the medium of publication. Full publication information is not necessary if the reference book is well known. In this case, list the edition number and/or the year the edition was published.

Doucett, Leonard E. "Drama in French." *The Canadian Encyclopedia.*

2000 ed. Print.

"Zeugma." *The Oxford Encyclopedic English Dictionary.* 1991. Print.

Introduction, preface, foreword, or afterword Name the author of the element, identify the element, and then give the title of the book, the author (after the word *By*), and the editor (if there is one). Capitalize the name of the element but do not italicize it or enclose it in quotation marks. After the publication information, give the inclusive page numbers of the element and the medium of publication.

Vernon, Lorraine. Afterword. *Time Capsule: New and Selected Poems.* By

Pat Lowther. Victoria: Polestar, 1996. 247-51. Print.

Book published before 1900 If the book you are citing was published before 1900, omit the name of the publisher. Use a comma, rather than a colon, between the place of publication and the date.

James, William. *The Principles of Psychology.* New York, 1890. Print.

Republished book Add the original publication date after the title of the book. Then give the publication information for the edition you are citing.

> Mitchell, W. O. *The Vanishing Point.* 1973. Toronto: Macmillan, 1992. Print.

New material contained in the republication, such as an introduction or after-word, should be added after the original publication date.

> Austen, Jane. *Mansfield Park.* 1814. Introd. Tony Tanner.
>
> Harmondsworth, Eng.: Penguin, 1966. Print.

Publisher's imprint   Imprints are special names under which publishers group their books. If the title page of a book you are citing includes the name of an imprint along with the name of the publisher, cite the imprint name followed by a hyphen and the publisher's name. NOTE: The publisher's name is the most critical element.

> Shields, Carol. *Small Ceremonies.* Toronto: Vintage-Random, 1976. Print.

Pamphlet   Treat a pamphlet entry as you would a book entry.

> Leduc, Paul. *A Walking Tour of Old Montreal.* Montreal: City of
>
> Montreal, 1973. Print.

Government publication   If the name of the document's author is not identified, begin with the name of the government that issued the document, followed by the name of the government agency.

> Canada. Federal Cultural Policy Review Committee. *Report of the Federal*
>
> *Cultural Policy Review Committee.* Ottawa: Dept. of
>
> Communications, Information Services, 1982. Print.

Conference proceedings   List conference proceedings as you would books. After the title, add relevant information about the conference that is not included in the title.

> King, Karyn, and Rita M. Bean, eds. *Proceedings of the Annual Conference*
>
>   *and Course on Literacy: Literary Instruction: Practices, Problems,*
>
>   *Promises.* June 1990, U of Pittsburgh. Pittsburgh: U of Pittsburgh P,
>
>   1990. Print.

Unpublished dissertation   Enclose the title in quotation marks. After the title, write the abbreviation *Diss.* followed by the name of the degree-granting body, the date, and the work's medium.

> Campbell, Peter. "'Stalwarts of the Struggle': Canadian Marxists of the
>
>   Third Way, 1879–1939." Diss. Queen's U, 1991. Print.

Published dissertation   List published dissertations as you would books, but after the title add relevant information. If the dissertation was published privately, state *privately published* instead of a publisher's name.

> Ames, Barbara. *Dreams and Painting: A Case Study of the Relationship*
>
>   *between an Artist's Dreams and Paintings.* Diss. U of Virginia, 1978.
>
>   Ann Arbor: UMI, 1979. Print.

Abstract of a dissertation   Give the publication information for the dissertation, followed by the abbreviation *DA (Dissertation Abstracts)* or *DAI (Dissertation Abstracts International)*, the volume number, the date, the page number, and the medium of publication. If the *DA* or *DAI* is paginated by the series number *A, B,* or *C,* identify the appropriate series number at the end of the page number.

> Berkman, Anne Elizabeth. "The Quest for Authenticity: The Novels of Toni
>
> Morrison." Diss. Columbia U, 1988. *DAI* 48 (1988): 2059A. Print.

ARTICLES AND OTHER PUBLICATIONS IN PERIODICALS

A periodical is a publication, such as a scholarly journal, a magazine, or a news-paper, that appears at regular intervals. When citing a publication in a periodical, follow these general guidelines:

- If an article in a periodical is not printed on consecutive pages, write the first number and a plus sign; for example, to cite the page numbers of an article that appears on pages 34–41 and 78–79, write *34+* (not *34–79*).
- When a title appears as part of a larger title, treat it as you would if it were by itself: "The Role of Fate in *Macbeth*" (an article about a play). For information about the treatment of titles of works in general, see 62-a.
- Abbreviate the names of months except for May, June, and July.

Article in a journal   For a periodical that numbers pages continuously within each annual volume, write the volume number (in arabic numerals) after the journal's title, followed by a period and the issue number (if available).

> Woodcock, George. "Managing Hatred in Two Centuries." *Queen's*
>
> *Quarterly* 100.4 (1993): 827-31. Print.

Article in a journal that uses only issue numbers   For a periodical that does not use volume numbers, cite only the issue number.

> Powell, Martyn, and Malcolm Crook. "VII. Eighteenth Century." *Annual*
>
> *Bulletin of Historical Literature* 91 (2007): 83-103. Print.

Article in a monthly or bimonthly periodical For a periodical that appears every month or every two months, give the month(s), year, and page numbers.

> Le Guin, Ursula K. "Staying Awake: Notes on the Alleged Decline of
>
> Reading." *Harper's* Feb. 2008: 33-38. Print.

Article in a weekly or biweekly periodical For a periodical that appears every week or every two weeks, list the day, month, and year.

> Parks, Tim. "Hell and Back: A New Translation of Dante's *Inferno*." *New*
>
> *Yorker* 15 Jan. 2001: 84-89. Print.

Article in a daily newspaper List the author (if there is one), the article's title, the title of the newspaper, the complete date, the page number (including the section letter), and the medium of publication. Omit any initial article in the newspaper's name *(Vancouver Sun,* not *The Vancouver Sun).* If an edition is identified on the masthead, add a comma after the date and name the edition (e.g., *metro ed.).*

> Walton, Dawn. "The Inuit Cultural Matrix Reloaded." *Globe and Mail* 15
>
> Feb. 2008, BC ed.: A3. Print.

Unidentified author in a periodical Begin with the title if no author's name is given.

> "Christine Day: A Woman's Place Is at the Helm." *Maclean's* 3 Mar.
>
> 2008: 65. Print.

Editorial or letter in a periodical   Add the word *Editorial* or *Letter* after the title (if any) or author's name.

> Nodelman, Barry. "The Precarious Life of Children's Literature Criticism."
>
>   Editorial. *Canadian Children's Literature* 33.2 (2007): 1-16. Print.
>
> Rachlis, Val. Letter. *Maclean's* 28 Jan. 2008: 3. Print.

Review   To cite a review, give the reviewer's name and (if there is one) the title of the review. Then write *Rev. of* followed by the title of the reviewed work, the name of the author (or editor, director, etc.), the name of the periodical, and the rest of the publication information. For a film or theatre review, add relevant information about the production.

> Andrew, Sheila. Rev. of *The Contexts of Acadian History, 1686-1784*, by
>
>   Naomi E. S. Griffiths. *Dalhousie Review* 72 (1992): 555-57. Print.
>
> Eisner, Ken. "Voyage of the Dammed." Rev. of *Up the Yangtze*, dir. Young
>
>   Chang. *Georgia Straight* 14-21 Feb. 2008: 57. Print.

OTHER SOURCES

Television or radio program   List the episode's title (if any), the title of the program or series (italicized), the network, the local station and city (if any), the broadcast date, and the medium of reception. Add other relevant information such as narrator, performers, or director.

> "Episode 15: Wheat Week." *Little Mosque on the Prairie.* CBC-TV.
>
>   30 July 2008. Television.
>
> "Marcel Proust: In Search of Lost Time." Narr. Barbara Nichol.
>
>   3 episodes. *Ideas.* CBC Radio One. 1-15 June 1998. Radio.

Sound recording   Arrange the information in an entry (for example, composer, performer, conductor) according to your research emphasis. Include relevant information such as manufacturer and year of issue. Indicate the medium after the date of publication: *Audiocassette, Audiotape* (reel-to-reel tape), *CD,* or *LP* (long-playing record).

> Fleming, Renée. *Strauss Heroines.* Weiner Philharmoniker. Cond.
>
> Christoph Eschenbach. Decca, 1999. CD.
>
> Hansard, Glen, and Markéta Irglová. "Falling Slowly." *Once: Music from the*
>
> *Motion Picture.* Sony, 2007. CD.

Enclose the title of a specific song in quotation marks.

> Krall, Diana. "Devil May Care." By Bob Dorough. *When I Look in Your*
>
> *Eyes.* Verve, 1999. CD.

Treat a spoken-word recording as you would a musical recording.

> Thomas, Dylan. "A Child's Christmas in Wales." *Dylan Thomas: Volume*
>
> *1.* Caedmon, 1952. LP.

Film, videocassette, or DVD   List the title, the director, the distributor, the year of release, and the medium consulted. Other relevant information, such as the writer, producer, or performers, may be added. If you are citing a videocassette or DVD, cite the year of original release, the distributor, the year of release in that medium, and the medium.

> *No Country for Old Men.* Dir. Ethan Coen and Joel Coen. Perf. Javier
>
> Bardem. 2007. Paramount Vantage, 2008. DVD.

> *Henry V.* Dir. Kenneth Branagh. Perf. Kenneth Branagh, Paul Scofield,
> Derek Jacobi, Ian Holm, and Emma Thompson. 1989. CBS/Fox
> Video, 1990. Videocassette.

If you wish to focus on a particular individual's work on the production, begin the entry with that person' name.

> Damon, Matt, perf. *The Bourne Ultimatum.* Dir. Paul Greengrass. 2007.
> Universal, 2007. DVD.

Live performance Begin with the title of the play, concert, ballet, or opera. Add relevant information, such as director, conductor, or performers, and conclude the entry with the location and date of the performance and an indication that you are citing a performance.

> *Coming Up for Air.* By George Orwell. Adapt. and dir. Leslie Mildiner.
> Perf. Bernard Cuffling. Dorothy Somerset Studio Theatre,
> Vancouver. 10 Nov. 2007. Performance.
>
> *Transit of Venus.* By Victor Davies. Libretto by Maureen Hunter. Dir.
> Larry Desrochers. Cond. James Meena. Perf. Russell Braun, Judith
> Forst, Jean Stilwell, Monica Huisman, and Colin Ainsworth.
> Centennial Concert Hall, Winnipeg. 24 Nov. 2007. Performance.

Work of art State the artist's name, the title of the work, the date and medium of composition, the name of the organization in which the work is housed, and the city. If the work is part of a private collection, follow the title with the name of the individual who owns it.

> Colville, Alex. *Hound in Field*. 1958. Casein tempera. National Gallery of
>
> Canada, Ottawa.

Map or chart   Treat a map or chart as you would a book with an unidentified author, but add the word *Map* or *Chart* after the title.

> *Newfoundland and Labrador*. Map. Ottawa: Natural Resources Canada,
>
> 2001. Print.

Cartoon   Begin with the cartoonist's name and (if there is one) the title of the cartoon. Then write the word *Cartoon* and conclude the entry with the rest of the publication information and the medium of publication.

> Chast, Roz. "The N.R.A.'s Written Test for a Gun License." Cartoon. *New*
>
> *Yorker* 2 Aug. 1999: 90. Print.

Interview   To cite a published interview or an interview broadcast on television or radio, begin with the name of the person interviewed and the title of the interview, if any, in quotation marks. Conclude with the appropriate bibliographical information and the medium of publication.

If the interview is untitled or has a title that does not indicate the nature of the source, use the descriptive identifier *Interview*. Add the interviewer's name if known and relevant.

> Shields, Carol. Interview. *Globe and Mail* 26 Feb. 2000: D2-3. Print.

> Garneau, Marc. Interview by Shelagh Rogers. *Sounds Like Canada.* CBC
>
> Radio One. 5 Oct. 2004. Radio.

If you conducted the interview, state the type of interview (*Personal interview, Telephone interview*).

> Marchand, Benoit. Personal interview. 9 May 2000.

Lecture, speech, address, or reading   State the speaker's name, the title of the oral presentation (if known) in quotation marks, the sponsoring body (if any), and the location and date of the presentation. Conclude with an appropriate description (*Lecture, Address, Reading, Keynote speech,* etc.) to show the form of delivery.

> Carey, Peter. Harbourfront Reading Series. Brigantine Room, York Quay
>
> Centre, Toronto. 28 Feb. 2001. Reading.
>
> Yee, Paul. "Becoming a Writer." The Helen E. Stubbs Memorial Lectures.
>
> Osborne Collection of Early Children's Books, Lillian H. Smith
>
> Branch, Toronto Public Library, Toronto. 19 Oct. 2006. Lecture.

Personal communication   To cite a letter you have received, begin with the sender's name. Then write the phrase *Letter to the author* followed by the date.

> Page, P. K. Letter to the author. 16 Apr. 1994.

ELECTRONIC SOURCES

Electronic sources include CD-ROMs, e-mail, software programs, websites, online databases, and information available using telnet, gopher, file transfer protocol (FTP), and other access modes. This section deals specifically with e-mail, CD-ROMs and DVD-ROMs, and websites.

CAUTION: Be aware that sources on the World Wide Web lack the stability of their print counterparts; an online document may be revised, or it may even disappear altogether. In addition, there is no guarantee that the information contained on a website is of good quality and error-free. For these reasons, you should evaluate online sources carefully and obtain your instructor's approval before using them in an essay.

Electronic communication   To cite electronic mail you have received, begin with the sender's name and, if there is one, the title (taken from the subject line). Then write the phrase *Message to the author* followed by the date and the medium of delivery (*E-mail*). If the e-mail was to someone other than you, instead of writing *Message to the author*, write *Message to* plus the name of the recipient of the e-mail.

> Chiang, Valerie. "Re: Archetypes." Message to the author. 7 Mar. 2001.
>
> E-mail.

CD-ROM or DVD-ROM   Treat a publication on CD-ROM or DVD-ROM as you would a book, but indicate the medium (CD-ROM or DVD-ROM) after the publication information.

> *The 1999 Canadian Encyclopedia World Edition.* Toronto: McClelland,
>
> 1998. CD-ROM.

If you are citing only part of the CD-ROM or DVD-ROM, state the author of the part and/or the title of the part before the CD-ROM's or DVD-ROM's title.

Vastokas, Joan M. "Native Art." *The 1999 Canadian Encyclopedia World*

Edition. Toronto: McClelland, 1998. CD-ROM.

WEB SOURCES

In its seventh edition (2009), the *MLA Handbook* stresses that the referencing of electronic material should have the same goal as the referencing of printed texts—the accurate identification of a text and how it may be located. However, electronic texts have not arrived at a standard format and are also less stable than printed texts. Therefore, that suggests that more information should be given for electronic than for printed texts. Specifically, MLA requires that a citation or bibliographic entry for an electronic text should include information about electronic publication and access details.

By "access details," MLA now means the date (or dates) you read the electronic text. The sixth edition of the *MLA Handbook* required the inclusion of the URL for the text; the seventh edition now recommends that the URL not be included unless your instructor requires it or you are certain that your readers could not locate your resource without having the URL. Of course, if you do include a URL, it must be enclosed in angle brackets (< >) and appear as the last element in the citation, and the URL cannot be split between two lines unless you do so following a slash. Generally, however, MLA has concluded that URLs have become too cumbersome and unstable to be a useful part of works-cited list entries.

In summary, a works-cited reference for an electronic source will add two areas of detail: the type of medium (*Web*) where the source appears, and the date of access (the date or dates when you read or downloaded the source).

AUTHOR

Include the name or names of the author(s) of the text. Use the name of a site if no individual author is identified; if neither an author nor a site is named, use the name of the site's sponsor. The name of a single author is stated with the surname first and the given name second; the names of a second and third author are listed in standard order. If there are more than three authors, simply name the first and then add a comma and "et al."

TITLE

Include the title of the work, italicized. If it is a title of part of a whole, present the title of the part in quotation marks and italicize the title of the whole. If there is an editor, compiler, or translator, his or her name follows the title.

PUBLICATION DETAILS WHEN PRINTED VERSION AVAILABLE
If there is a printed version of the text, give the publication information for that version first. This is quite common with articles in periodicals or newspapers.

PUBLICATION DETAILS FOR ELECTRONIC SOURCE
The publication details for the electronic source of the text follow the publication information for the printed version. These may include the title of the site, the name of an editor for the site (if one exists), the volume or issue number or other identifying details for an article from a journal, the date of the electronic publication or update (if one is given), the name of the service from which the text was taken, the name of the list or forum (if the text is drawn from such a source), the number of units in the text (if individual units such as pages or paragraphs are identified), and the name of any institution or organization acting as the site's publisher or sponsor (if not available, use *N.p.*).

Chao, Lien. "Anthologizing the Collective: The Epic Struggles to Establish Chinese Canadian Literature in English." *Essays on Canadian Writing* 57 (1995): 145-61. *ProQuest.* Web. 20 Apr. 2009.

The last two publication details required in the citation of an electronic source are

- the medium of publication (*Web*), and
- the date that you visited the site and read or downloaded the text.

Please consult the MLA site for updates on documenting electronic sources. The URL for the site is http://www.mla.org

The following examples provide an overview of the more common electronic sources and how they would be cited on a works-cited page.

Scholarly project

Godwin-Jones, Robert, ed. *Nineteenth-Century German Stories.* Foreign Lang. Dept., Virginia Commonwealth U, 1994. Web. 12 Jan. 2004.

Jokinen, Anniina, ed. *Anthology of Middle English Literature (1350–1485).*

N.p., 5 Sept. 2000. Web. 13 Nov. 2004.

Document within a scholarly project

Schiller, Friedrich. "The Sport of Destiny." Trans. Marian Klopfer. 1786.

Nineteenth-Century German Stories. Ed. Robert Godwin-Jones.

Foreign Lang. Dept., Virginia Commonwealth U, 1994. Web. 12 Jan.

2004.

Professional site

Professional Writers Association of Canada. Home page. Professional

Writers Association of Canada, 2006. Web. 30 Oct. 2004.

Personal site

Atwood, Margaret. *O.W.Toad: Margaret Atwood Information Site.*

Margaret Atwood, 2008. Web. 6 Sept. 2008.

Lancashire, Ian. Home page. University of Toronto, 23 Jan. 2005. Web. 1

Mar. 2005.

Book

> Montgomery, Lucy Maud. *Anne of Green Gables.* 1908. *Literature.org: The*
>
> *Online Literature Library.* Knowledge Matters Ltd., n.d. Web. 14
>
> Nov. 2004.

The above example is from a website that reproduces a book but does not give its original publication information. MLA suggests that if the site does give that information, it may be important to include it in your works-cited entry. If you do, you should include the information in this order: author's name, title of work, city of publication, publisher (if published after 1900), date of publication, title of website or database, medium of publication consulted (*Web*), and date of access.

> Babbage, Charles. *Passages from the Life of a Philosopher.* London, 1864.
>
> *Online Books Page.* Web. 24 Apr. 2009.

Article in an information database

> "Canadian Literature: 1960 and Beyond." *Encyclopedia Britannica Online.*
>
> Encyclopedia Britannica, Inc., 2009. Web. 18 Jan. 2009.

Article in a journal

> Ward, Ian. "Shakespeare and the Politics of Community." *Early Modern*
>
> *Literary Studies* 4.3 (1999): n. pag. Web. 3 Jan. 2004.

Article in a magazine

Bemrose, John. "Finding Reality in Fiction." *Macleans.ca*. Maclean's

Magazine, 17 July 2000. Web. 8 Aug. 2000.

Article in a newspaper

Richler, Mordecai. "Fighting Words." *New York Times*. New York Times, 1

June 1997. Web. 31 Aug. 1999.

Material from a library subscription service As libraries move from subscribing to hard copies of periodicals to utilizing library subscription services that allow users to access periodical articles electronically, works-cited entries for online service articles will become more prevalent. Although it is convenient for students to access articles electronically, citing the source of an article acquired online can be challenging.

The new MLA guidelines for articles from databases simplify what was a complex issue. As MLA does not recommend that you include URLs with works cited entries unless your instructor wants you to, after the information that would be needed for a print periodical, you need only add the title of the database (in italics), the fact that the material is from the Web (*Web*), and the date of access (day, month, and year).

Here is an example of a works-cited entry for an article from a database:

Kramer, Reinhold. "Nationalism, the West and *The Englishman's Boy*."

Essays on Canadian Writing 67 (Spring 1999): 1-22. *ProQuest*. Web.

20 Apr. 2009.

In summary, an entry for an article you obtained through a subscription service will include the following elements:

- Author
- Title of essay
- Title of periodical
- Publishing details
- Pages (if not available, use *n. pag.*)
- Database
- Medium of publication
- Access date

Non-periodical publications: Wikis, blogs, course webpages, and other electronic sources   MLA describes how to set up an entry for material from a "non-periodical publication," and these guidelines can be adapted for citing material from a wiki, blog, or course webpage. The main elements are

- the author's name (or compiler, director, editor);
- the title of the work (in italics if the work stands alone, or in quotation marks if it is a part of a larger element);
- the title of the site, wiki, blog, or course webpage (in italics), if there is such a name;
- the version or edition, if known;
- the publisher or sponsor if there is one, or *N.p.* if one is not listed;
- the date of publication, if known, or *n.d.* if not;
- the medium (*Web*); and
- the date of access.

Buirs, Betty Anne. "The Thesis Statement—Narrowing the Topic." *Virtual Learning Centre.* The Learning Centre, Kwantlen Polytechnic University, 2009. Web. 17 Apr 2009.

In most examples in the *MLA Handbook* itself, the elements that are listed are author, title, title of site, publisher or sponsor, date of publication, medium, and date of access. Many of MLA's examples exclude version or edition, publisher, sponsor or *N.p.*, and date of publication or *n.d.* If you are unsure of the format for an individual entry, see your instructor. You might also want to look at Columbia Online style, as it covers numerous online possibilities that MLA, APA, or CSE do not comment on.

22-d MLA-Style Sample Essay

In MLA style, a title page is not required in an essay. (If a title page is required by your instructor, you can create one based on the guidelines provided in 23-d.) Use double-spacing between all lines in the essay, including the works-cited list. Number all pages consecutively throughout the essay (write your surname before the page number). For information about setting up a works-cited list, see 22-c.

On the following pages you will find an MLA-style essay.[1] Format specifications are pointed out in the marginal notes.

---

[1] Adapted from an essay by Daryl Kroell, a student in an English literature class.

Kroell 1

Daryl Kroell

Mr. Al Valleau ← Author's name, instructor's name, course's name and section number, and date typed 1" (2.5 cm) from top of first page and flush with left margin

English 1201, Section 11

26 Mar. 2004

Title centred on page → See No Evil, Hear No Evil

In recent years, a profound apathy has settled over the true north strong and free. Yes, average Canadian citizens are still relatively well informed, still willing to collaborate and negotiate; yet, perhaps because of these qualities, they more often resign themselves to the status of observers, rather than participants, in rituals of world power and prestige. To mollify their egos, Canadians then affect a pose of smug self-righteousness toward those they behold—a façade at once haughty yet redolent of envy. For, in their secret hearts, they long to be players. Unable to resolve this delicate predicament, modern Canadians, like sulky children, quite often do … nothing. Ethel Wilson, in *Swamp Angel*, and Guy Vanderhaeghe, in *The Englishman's Boy*, keenly expose this schizophrenic national tendency and its effect on the individual Canadian psyche. They unflinchingly deplore the futility and even depravity of perpetual fence sitting. Both Wilson and Vanderhaeghe are unequivocal in their message: Reluctance to oppose obvious transgression is both irresponsible and immoral. No matter how many times one washes one's hands, a sin of omission remains a sin.

Paragraphs indented 1/2" (1.25 cm) → As Reinhold Kramer points out, "*The Englishman's Boy* harbours a number of complexities that make its political stance less than innocent" (6). The complexity of Vanderhaeghe's novel is evident in particular in the narrator and chief protagonist, Harry Vincent, who personifies vacillation and, with that vacillation, competing points of view. Harry, a Canadian expatriate employed as a junior scenarist in 1920s Hollywood, is a man who steadily follows the line of least resistance in all his affairs. He tumbles into his job by the sheer fortune of a lunch-counter conversation with Rachel Gold, a beautiful, clever, and ambitious woman. Yet, even though he harbours ambitious aspirations, both with his career and his emotional attraction to Rachel, his fear of rejection stops him from expressing any reservations he has about his job and his feelings for

Rachel; even when she challenges Harry: "All right then, *do* something. Don't play helpless," he chooses to only "half-believ[e] she want[s] to be touched" (Vanderhaeghe 271).

The wretched Harry is hesitant even in hesitation; as narrator, he forlornly reiterates Rachel's criticism without realizing its implication: "Do something, she said. But what? Ambiguous. Wasn't it?" (271). He is equally pathetic in his dealings with his employer, Damon Ira Chance, a man who came to Hollywood to "assist Mr. Griffith in his great work . . . mak[ing] American movies" (16). Griffith's "great work" includes the infamous film *The Birth of a Nation*, which glorifies the Ku Klux Klan while denigrating African Americans. Chance offers Harry a covert assignment at double his previous salary; all Harry must do is find, interrogate, and then betray a reclusive old cowboy, Shorty McAdoo. Harry achieves this dubious goal, to the ultimate ruination of the cowboy, and the deaths of Chance and his assistant, Fitzsimmons. Underpinning Vanderhaeghe's complex portrait of his Canadian narrator is the fact that although Harry ultimately realizes the devastation he has wrought, he still shirks responsibility, and slinks back to the safe neutrality of Canada.

There he hides, a literal as well as figurative spectator, standing "each night . . . at the back of [his] theatre, watch[ing] spectres and phantoms slide across the screen" (326). Harry Vincent is the epitome of Canadian indifference at its worst: a spineless tragic figure who, by refusing to struggle against—or even acknowledge—encroaching evil, loses his career, the woman he loves, and, most of all, his soul.

In contrast, Rachel Gold, a "respected . . . and . . . sought after" scriptwriter for Best Chance Pictures, is a woman who encounters life boldly and valiantly (35). She neatly divides males into two categories: *mensches,* men "you could talk to but wouldn't sleep with," and gigolos, men "you could sleep with but wouldn't want to talk to" (36). She intuits that Harry has purchased his new-found prosperity with some betrayal, initially accusing him of accepting "snitch money" for providing Chance with "the names of anybody who talks union talk" at the studio (130). Rachel decries the rise of European fascism and its echoes in America, having experienced first-hand the brutality of racism. Thus, when Harry divulges Chance's desire to emulate Griffith, Rachel disparagingly exclaims, "What a great public-relations job [Griffith] did for the [Ku Klux] Klan and the lynching industry" (133). She astutely points out to Harry his "lack [of] . . . courage to take responsibility for [his] intelligence," and his infantile refusal to ask the difficult questions of Chance and of himself (180).

Yet her staunch integrity does not make her cold or unsympathetic; on the contrary, she emanates a brand of practical goodwill that extends to supporting Harry's invalid mother both financially and emotionally. When Harry finally alerts Rachel to the truth regarding Chance's bigotry, she stoically remarks, "When I hand the son of a bitch my resignation, I'll be free to write that novel I've been threatening the public with" (310). In stark contrast to Harry, Rachel willingly pays the price for taking decisive action; not for a moment does she consider betraying her ideals for mere economic expediency. In fact, she lands on her feet, finds a position at another movie studio, and even offers to help Harry yet again. Rachel personifies the vital, healthy, active essence of humanity: someone who has made a conscious attempt to determine what she believes in and has lived accordingly.

In Rachel, Vanderhaeghe presents the type of persona that Canadians once believed themselves to be; how ironic that this kind-hearted, generous citizen of the world should be, of all things, that Canadian nemesis: an American. Vanderhaeghe himself alludes to the dangers and ironies of national myth building that he presents with the characters of Rachel and Harry when, in an interview, he comments,

> "You can have a monolithic myth that excludes people, but, on the other hand, how do you arrive at healthy myths that give people a feeling of commonality? The more you include, the harder it gets. If all people were from the same community, it's easier, but it makes it insular and exclusive" (qtd. in Chan).

Block quotation set off and indented 1" (2.5 cm)

Thus, at its conclusion, *The Englishman's Boy*, rather than generating feelings that Harry has come to terms with his involvement with Chance and Shorty and Rachel, and become sensitive to the pitfalls of myth building, leaves the reader faced with a character that could have and should have made a difference, a Canadian who remains on the fringe of the action, afraid to act.

Ethel Wilson's *personae* are all Canadians, though (with apologies to George Orwell) some are more Canadian than others: specifically, Maggie Lloyd, *Swamp Angel*'s lead character. The story begins with Maggie leaving her overbearing husband, Eddie Vardoe; lacking the nerve or the will to confront him, she carries out a long-premeditated scheme and sneaks away without so much as a goodbye. Having "once lived through three deaths, and—it really seemed—her own," Maggie had married Eddie from pity, endeavouring "to save herself by an act of compassion and fatal stupidity" (Wilson, *Swamp Angel* 11). Although the deaths of a husband, child, and father are undeniably agonizing events to survive, and Eddie turns out to be a self-important prig, Maggie still feels remorse—not for the fact, but the manner, of her departure. Yet, in time, she finds herself happily living and working for a couple in a wilderness lodge, until she becomes the focus of the wife's jealous resentment. Ironically, Maggie feels compassion for Vera, the jealous wife, just as she once did for Eddie; however, in this new relationship she decides "to serve Vera Gunnarsen . . . expecting neither praise nor thanks" (Wilson, *Swamp Angel* 115). In contrast to her past behaviour with Eddie, Maggie determines to set down roots at Three Loon Lake, to remain at the lodge and "appl[y] herself to the matters in hand" (Wilson, *Swamp Angel* 209). Having accessed inner reserves, Maggie finds therein the spiritual comfort and ease to weather the storms of her life, neither forsaking her employers nor attempting to save them from themselves. In effect, she has forged an identity that nurtures her strengths. Donna E. Smyth reminds us that

Block quotation set off and indented 1" (2.5 cm) →

> We . . . realize that this was the way many women of the forties and fifties identified themselves to themselves. Generations of women have valued their social identity in the role of

IV DOCUMENTATION

wife/mother more than a unique personal identity. Wilson does
not question these conventions any more than do her characters,
but develops her fiction within the framework of a sharply
observed social reality. (88-89)

Though initially lacking the moral strength to function with integrity,
Maggie Lloyd, unlike Harry Vincent, changes and grows with her new life
experiences. In this sense, Maggie succeeds where Harry fails, arriving at a
"personal identity" reflective of her strengths and needs.

Nell Severance is Maggie's former neighbour and still her friend. An
eccentric one-time circus juggler of small revolvers, she still possesses her
favourite: a Swamp Angel, a name that had its origins in Wilson's husband
inheriting a very old "nickel and mother of pearl revolver . . . inscribed in
a flowing script [with] the words Swamp Angel (Wilson, "To Desmond
Pacey" 233). Nell's philosophy is the Christian Humanism of John Donne.
To Maggie, she affectionately preaches, "I see God everywhere. . . . We are
all in it together. 'No man is an Island, I am involved in Mankinde,' and
we have no immunity and we may as well realize it" (Wilson, *Swamp
Angel* 200). She is further possessed of the wisdom that "You cannot not
know what you do know" (MacLeod 761). Squarely shouldering the
responsibility imposed upon those who have undergone such an
epiphany, Nell makes peace with her daughter Hilda and with Hilda's
fiancé, thus clearing the way for her daughter's marriage and happiness.
She even instructs the obnoxious Eddie Vardoe in how to achieve a mod-
icum of contentment without Maggie. It is to Nell that Eddie vents his
humiliation and rage when he finds Maggie gone; it is Nell who confronts
him with his responsibility toward himself, commanding, "Sit . . . down
. . . [. . .] Compose yourself, Mr. Vardoe, and I will do you good, but if
you don't . . . listen, I shall spend no time on you" (Wilson, *Swamp Angel*
53).

Like Rachel Gold, Nell does not merely spout rhetoric; she acts
according to her own experience and inner lights, not those of any outside force. It is by virtue of this ethical strength that Nell achieves her
status as the moral heart of *Swamp Angel*.

These characters exist on a continuum. From the almost total lassi-
tude of Harry Vincent to the absolute vigour of Nell Severance, each
chooses a course of action and must pay the price accordingly—like all
members of the human race. The question is, at what point does tolerance become apathy? Matthew Henry's adaptation of Jeremiah 5:21,
"There are none so blind as those who will not see" (437), has seldom
applied more than today. Guy Vanderhaeghe and Ethel Wilson are clear in
their entreaty to all citizens: The price of ignoring ethics in favour of
comfort, of running away from a daunting confrontation, is far too high.
Like it or not, each human being is answerable for the life of all. People
must choose—and be willing to defend their choices; otherwise, their
freedom will be forfeited. And in that event, those making the decisions
will be the most powerful, the most ruthless, and the most brutal: in other
words, the victors. Bearing this in mind, nobody—not even Canadians—
can afford the luxury of remaining neutral.

Works Cited typed, centred, 1" (2.5 cm) from ⟶ Works Cited top of page

Kroell 7

Chan, Suzette C. "Two Views of the Old West." N.p., n.d. Web. 27 Apr. 2004.

Henry, Matthew. *Commentary on the Whole Bible.* Vol. 4. NY: Revell, n.d. Print.

Kramer, Reinhold. "Nationalism, the West and *The Englishman's Boy.*" *Essays on*

First line flush left; subsequent lines indented 1/2" (1.25 cm) ⟶ *Canadian Writing* 67 (Spring 1999): 1-22. *ProQuest.* Web. 27 Apr. 2004.

MacLeod, Alistair. "As Birds Bring Forth the Sun." *A New Anthology of*

Canadian Literature in English. Ed. Donna Bennett and Russell Brown.

Don Mills, ON: Oxford UP, 2002. 757-62. Print.

Smyth, Donna E. "Strong Women in the Web: Women's Work and Community

in Ethel Wilson's Fiction." *The Ethel Wilson Symposium.* Ed. Lorraine

McMullen. Ottawa: U of Ottawa P, 1982. Print.

Vanderhaeghe, Guy. *The Englishman's Boy.* Toronto: McClelland & Stewart,

1997. Print.

Wilson, Ethel. *Swamp Angel.* Toronto: McClelland & Stewart, 1990. Print.

---. "To Desmond Pacey." *Ethel Wilson: Stories, Essays, and Letters.* Ed. David

Stouck. Vancouver: U of British Columbia P, 1987. 232-35. Print.

23-a Parenthetical Citations

In APA style, a parenthetical citation in the text identifies the source of a borrowing and enables readers to locate the source in a list of references at the end of the essay. A typical parenthetical citation includes the author's name and the year of publication. (The inclusion of the date reflects the importance of currency of research in the social sciences.) Page numbers are usually provided only for direct quotations. Following are some sample APA citations.

Author and date Place a comma between the author and the date in the parenthetical citation. If the author is named in the text, place the date immediately after the name.

> People with Type 0 blood are more likely to develop duodenal ulcers
>
> than people with Type A, B, or AB blood (Eisenberg, 1978).
>
> Eisenberg (1978) found that people with Type 0 blood are more likely to
>
> develop duodenal ulcers than people with Type A, B, or AB blood.

Author, date, and page (short quotation) Quotations of fewer than forty words are integrated into the text and enclosed in double quotation marks. Note the use of the past tense *(reported)* in the text and the inclusion of the abbreviation *p.* before the page number in the parenthetical citation.

> As Schulsinger (1992) reported, "The greatest workplace stress occurs
>
> when jobs are high in stressors and low in controllability" (p. 56).

If the author's name does not appear in the signal phrase, place it in the parenthetical citation at the end of the quotation.

> According to one report, "The greatest workplace stress occurs when jobs
>
> are high in stressors and low in controllability" (Schulsinger, 1978, p. 56).

IV DOCUMENTATION

Author, date, and page (long quotation)   Quotations of more than forty words are set off from the text by indenting five spaces from the left margin. Quotation marks are omitted. The parenthetical citation follows the period at the end of the quotation.

Moos and Finney (1983) found the following:

> Relapse rates during the year after the completion of treatment may be as high as 60% or more. . . . Moreover, researchers have not been very successful in identifying superior treatment methods or in finding treatment approaches that are particularly effective for specific types of patients. Even the idea that more treatment (longer treatment of greater intensity) is better than less treatment has not received much support. (p. 1037)

Two authors   If a work has two authors, use both names in all citations. Note the use of the ampersand (&) in the parenthetical citation and the spelled-out *and* in the text.

The outcome measures used in the study have been criticized (Campbell & Tsuang, 2001).

Campbell and Tsuang (2001) have criticized the outcome measures used in the study.

Three to five authors   If a work has three to five authors, list all their names in the text or the parenthetical citation the first time you cite the work.

Interactions between heredity and environment can either facilitate or retard the manifestation of disorders (Rosenthal, Kelly, Allen, & Santos, 1995).

In subsequent citations, use only the name of the first author followed by *et al.* ("and others").

> Rosenthal et al. (1995) found that biochemical changes are often the
>
> result of environmental forces.

Six or more authors If a work has six or more authors, use only the first author's name followed by *et al.* in all citations, including the first.

> The threat of legal sanction has less impact on corporate crime than
>
> does the market environment in which companies operate (Samahin et
>
> al., 1998).

Unidentified author If the author's name is unknown, include in the parenthetical citation the work's title and the year of publication, placing the titles of books, periodicals, or reports in italics, and the titles of articles and chapters in double quotation marks.

> The discharge rates for treated and untreated clients were similar
>
> ("Treatment Evaluation," 1997).

Corporate author Spell out the name of a corporate body in the text.

> The Consensus Development Panel (1982) concluded that "the cluster of
>
> symptoms does not represent a single disease" (p. 627).

IV DOCUMENTATION

If the corporate body has a long and cumbersome name, spell out the name in the first parenthetical citation, followed by an abbreviation in brackets. In subsequent citations, use only the abbreviation.

FIRST CITATION

(Canadian Association of Schools of Social Work [CASSW], 2000)

SUBSEQUENT CITATIONS

(CASSW, 2000)

Authors with the same surname If your reference list contains works by two or more authors with the same last name, include the first author's initials in all citations.

D. L. Abrams (1998) found that individuals with effective support networks tend to have fewer symptoms of physical disorders in the face of stress than those without such support.

More than one work in parentheses Works by different authors who appear in the same parenthetical citation are listed in alphabetical order by the first author's surname and separated by semicolons.

(Braun, 1991; Langer et al., 1986; Wilkinson, 2000)

Two or more works by the same author are arranged by date of publication and separated by commas.

(Kamani, 1994, 1999, 2001)

Personal communication Identify published personal communications, such as letters and memos, in the text rather than in the list of references. Cite the sender's initials and surname, the words *personal communication*, and the date.

(C. Misaka, personal communication, February 26, 2001)

Online references to specific parts of a source Parenthetical citations for specific material from online sources present unique challenges in that much online material does not provide page numbers. When you are citing a specific part of a book, you need to refer to the page number. With an online source, if there is no page number, APA suggests you indicate the paragraph number for the source, using either "para." or the symbol "¶." If neither the page number nor the paragraph number is supplied, you should cite the heading as in the examples below.

(Statistics Canada, 2001, para. 2)

(Public Health Agency of Canada, 2004, Reported AIDS cases and eth-

nicity: A balance of changing proportions)

23-b Content Footnotes

Like the content note in MLA style, a content footnote is an optional element that expands on substantive information in the text. Content footnotes should not be repositories for complex or unnecessary information. APA style recommends that a content footnote convey no more than one idea.

A superscript Arabic numeral indicates the content footnote's position in the text. The first line of a footnote is indented like the first line of a paragraph. Footnotes are typed (double-spaced) on a separate page in the order of their appearance in the essay.

IV DOCUMENTATION

TEXT

Others have attempted to elucidate the interaction of biology and culture in the production of psychosomatic symptoms through examination of such variables as social class, gender, ethnicity, and age.[1]

FOOTNOTE

[1]Shorter (1994), for example, traces the evolution of various disorders--in particular, depression and anorexia nervosa--to show how patients in their quest for medical validation subconsciously develop symptoms that constitute legitimate disease in their particular cultures.

23-c List of References

In APA style, the list of references provides bibliographical information for an essay's parenthetical citations. The reference list, titled *References*, starts on a separate page at the end of the essay. Entries in a reference list are alphabetically arranged by the surnames of the authors or editors. Reference entries that lack authors or editors are alphabetized by the first word of the title, excluding *a, an,* or *the*. Double-spacing is used between and within entries throughout the list.

For individual reference entries, APA requires the use of a hanging-indent style.

American Psychological Association. (2001). *Publication manual of the American Psychological Association.* 5th ed. Washington, DC: Author.

Listed below are APA guidelines for creating reference entries, followed by sample entries for various types of sources. For a sample APA reference list, see page 161.

1. Invert authors' names that precede titles; do not invert authors' names that follow titles. Use initials instead of first and middle names in all authors' names. To cite a work by two authors, cite both names in the

first reference and in all subsequent references. For three to five authors, cite all in the first reference and, in subsequent references, the first followed by *et al.* For six or more authors, cite the first author plus *et al.* for all references except in the list of references, where you provide the surnames and initials of the first six authors and shorten any remaining authors to *et al.* In all cases, authors' names are separated with commas; an ampersand appears before the final author's name.

2. Follow the last author's name with the date of publication (in parentheses). If no date is available, write in its place *n.d.* (in parentheses).

3. Italicize titles and subtitles of books (include the period following the title in italics). Capitalize only the first word of the title and any subtitle, along with all proper nouns.

4. Italicize titles and volume numbers of periodicals (include in the italicizing the comma following the title or volume number). For journal titles, capitalize the first word and all other words except articles and prepositions.

5. Do not enclose titles of articles in quotation marks. Capitalize only the first word of the article's title and any subtitle, along with all proper nouns.

6. Include any initial article in the names of newspapers *(The Globe and Mail,* not *Globe and Mail).*

7. Use the abbreviation *p.* or *pp.* before page numbers of newspaper articles and selections in edited books. Do not use the abbreviation before page numbers in journals, magazines, and newsletters.

8. Omit from the names of publishers words that are not required to identify the publisher *(Wiley,* not *John Wiley & Sons).* However, retain the words *Books* and *Press* and spell out the names of university presses. Omit business abbreviations such as *Co., Ltd.,* and *Inc.* If the author named at the start of the entry is the publisher as well, write the word *Author,* not the author/publisher's name, in the publication information element.

ITALICS/UNDERLINING AND DASHES

APA style uses italics for titles of works; for periodicals, the title includes the volume number.

In APA-style essays, two hyphens (--) can be used to indicate a dash. There is no space before, between, or after the hyphens.

BOOKS AND OTHER NON-PERIODICAL WORKS

One author

Morrison, D. R. (1998). *Aid and ebb tide: A history of CIDA and Canadian development assistance.* Waterloo, ON: Wilfrid Laurier University Press.

Two or more authors

Burtch, B., & Larsen, N. (2006). *Law in society: Canadian readings.* Toronto: Nelson.

Corporate author

Canadian Pharmaceutical Association. (2008). *Compendium of pharmaceuticals and specialties (Canada).* Ottawa: Author.

Unidentified author

Encyclopedia of African peoples. (2000). New York: Facts On File.

Order of two or more works by the same author

Sacks, O. (1983). *Awakenings.* New York: Dutton.

Sacks, O. (1995). *An anthropologist on Mars.* New York: Knopf.

If the works are published in the same year, order the works alphabetically by title, adding a lowercase letter to the year: (2007a) *Problem at work* . . . (2007b) *Work as therapy.*

Order, same author with same publication date

Eichler, M. (1988a.) *Families in Canada today: Recent changes and their policy consequences.* Toronto: Gage.

Eichler, M. (1988b.) *Nonsexist research methods: A practical guide.* Boston: Allen & Unwin.

Editor

Caruth, C. (Ed.). (1995). *Trauma: Explorations in memory.* Baltimore: Johns Hopkins University Press.

Translation

Lévi-Strauss, C. (2000). *Structural anthropology* (C. Jackson & B. Schoepf, Trans.). New York: Basic Books. (Original work published 1958)

Edition other than the first

Morrison, K. (2006). *Marx, Durkheim, Weber: Formations of modern social thought* (2nd ed.). Thousand Oaks, CA: Sage.

Selection in an edited book

Christie, G. (2007). Police-government relations in the context of state-Aboriginal relations. In M. Beare & T. Murray (Eds.), *Police and government relations: Who's calling the shots?* (pp. 147–172, 176–182). Toronto: University of Toronto Press.

Entry in an encyclopedia or dictionary

Swanson. P. (2006). Habitat for humanity. In *Encyclopedia of world poverty* (Vol. 2, pp. 455–456). Thousand Oaks, CA: Sage.

Government publication

Abbott, K. (2003). *Urban Aboriginal women in British Columbia and the impacts of the matrimonial real property regime.* (Catalogue No. R2-271/2003E). Ottawa: Indian and Northern Affairs.

Canadian Centre for Justice Statistics. (1992). *The future of crime statistics from the UCR survey.* Ottawa: Statistics Canada.

Published contribution to a symposium

Wheeler, D. (1991). Creating culturally specific AIDS interventions: An example of the ethnographic approach to program evaluation. In K. J. Jaros & G. C. St. Denis (Eds.), *Proceedings of the 1991 Public Health Social Work Institute* (pp. 36–54). Pittsburgh: University of Pittsburgh.

Unpublished paper presented at a meeting

Bowman, E. (1995, May). *The reality of repressed memories: A review of the research.* Paper presented at the Fifth International Spring Conference of the International Society for the Study of Dissociation, Amsterdam.

Dissertation abstracted in DAI

Gaar, S. J. (1989). Environmental factors associated with emergent literacy in deaf and hearing children (Doctoral dissertation, Boston University, 1989). *Dissertation Abstracts International, 50,* 18007A.

Pendar, J. E. (1982). Undergraduate psychology majors: Factors influencing decisions about college, curriculum and career. *Dissertation Abstracts International, 42,* 4370A-4371A (University Microfilms No. 82 06, 181)

Unpublished dissertation

Reimer, M. A. (1987). *The social organization of the labour process: A case study of the documentary management of clerical labour in the public service.* Unpublished doctoral dissertation, Ontario Institute for Studies in Education, Toronto.

Unpublished manuscript

Wahlsten, D. (1991). *Heredity and the mind.* Unpublished manuscript, University of Alberta, Edmonton.

IV DOCUMENTATION

PERIODICALS

For standard models of periodical references, see 4.07, General Forms, on p. 223 of the APA *Publication Manual*, 5th ed.

Article in a journal paginated by volume

Hinduja S., & Patchin J. (2008). Cyberbullying: An exploratory analysis of factors related to offending and victimization. *Deviant Behavior, 29*(2), 129–156.

Article in a journal paginated by issue

Atkins. C. (2006). A cripple at a rich man's gate: A comparison of disability. *Canadian Journal of Law and Society, 21*(2), 87–111.

Article in a magazine

Casey, A. (2008, January–February). Carbon cemetery. *Canadian Geographic,* 56–66.

For a biweekly or weekly magazine, add the correct day after the month.

Article in a daily newspaper

Carmichael, K. (2008, March 11). Kill RESP bill or go to polls, Liberals told. *The Globe and Mail,* pp. A1, A9.

Letter to the editor

Shams, Z. (2001, January 11). Women in Iran [Letter to the editor]. *The Globe and Mail*, p. A12.

Review

Platt, J. (2008, Winter). [Review of the book *Family and community in Ireland*]. *Journal of the History of the Behavioural Sciences, 41*(1), 77.

ELECTRONIC SOURCES

The fifth edition of the *Publication Manual of the American Psychological Association* reminds writers of papers to do two things when citing an electronic work:

- send readers to the direct source rather than to a home page or more remote source
- take special pains to provide accurate and reliable addresses (URLs)

The fifth edition has also withdrawn the previous APA requirement that URLs be written on a single line to avoid confusion, using a reduced font, if necessary, to provide that address. Writers can now run an address into a second or even a third line, as long as they ensure that the break between lines only occurs "after a slash or before a period" (*Manual,* 5th ed., p. 271).

Finally, the fifth edition recommends certain other details for the citation of electronic texts, including the following:

- If you have viewed only the electronic version of an article that is also available in a print version, place the words "Electronic Version," in brackets, after the title of the article, as in Author/Title of article [Electronic Version]/Title of journal/Access date and URL.
- If you are referring to an article or publication that you think may have been changed or altered or that has data that are time-sensitive, include the date when you read or downloaded the article. Note that the APA recommends that you record this as the last part of a citation, the format of the following example: Retrieved August 4, 2008, from http://biology.mcgill.ca.
- Check your URLs three times: when you draft a paper, when you are doing the last draft, and when you are editing your proofs.

- APA also cautions writers about using electronic discussion groups of any kind as formal references in a paper. Because these sources are not peer-reviewed and not, in the judgment of APA, "scholarly content," you are best to leave them out as references in a formal paper.

- When referring to an aggregated database, APA now asks that you add only the date of your retrieval of the material and the formal name of the database. You do not have to include the URL.

Please consult the APA website for current information and instruction about the citation of electronic references. That website is located at http://www.apastyle.org/elecsource.html.

Listed below are sample APA-style entries for various types of electronic sources.

Book

Gray, H. (1918 edition). *Anatomy of the human body*. Retrieved January

17, 2008, from http://www.bartleby.com/107/

Article in a journal

A REFERENCE TO AN ARTICLE ALSO FOUND IN A PRINT SOURCE

Charles, S. T., Reynolds, C. A., & Gatz, M. (2001, January). Age-related

differences and change in positive and negative affect over 23 years.

Journal of Personality and Social Psychology, 80, 136–151. Retrieved

July 9, 2008, from http://www.apa.org/journals/features/

psp801136.pdf

A REFERENCE TO AN ARTICLE FOUND ONLY IN AN ONLINE SOURCE

Spillman, B. C., & Pezzin, L. E. (2000). Potential and active family care-

givers: Changing networks and the "sandwich generation." *The*

Milbank Quarterly, 78. Retrieved January 19, 2008, from

http://www.milbank.org/quarterly/7803feat.html

Journal abstract

Hurtz, G. M., & Donovan, J. J. (2000). Personality and job performance:
The Big Five revisited [Abstract]. *Journal of Applied Psychology, 85*,
869-879. Retrieved July 15, 2004, from http://
content.apa.org/journals/apl/85/6/869.html

Article in a magazine

Millar, A. (2008, March 18). Facebook cheating scandal nothing new.
Macleans. Retrieved March 19, 2008, from
http://oncampus.macleans.ca/education/2008/03/18/
facebook-cheating-scandal-nothing-new/

Article with no author and no date Begin the reference with the title if there
is no author. Place the date of retrieval after the notation for no date (n.d.).
Follow the date of retrieval with the URL.

Sociology in the higher education of women. (n.d.). Retrieved March 25,
2008, from http://www.theatlantic.com/doc/189211/
womens-education9bg

Article in a newspaper

York, G. (2008, March 18). Photo evidence of Tibet horror comes to
light. *The Globe and Mail*. Retrieved March 20, 2008, from
http://www.theglobeandmail.com/servlet/story/RTGAM.20080318
.wtibet19/BNStory/International/home

Review

> Kenneally, C. (2000, August 9). [Review of the book *The making of intel-*
>
> *ligence*]. *Salon.* Retrieved September 14, 2008, from http://salon
>
> .com/books/review/2000/08/09/richardson/index.html

Entry in an encyclopedia

> Differential psychology. *Encyclopedia Britannica Online.* Retrieved
>
> October 31, 2008, from http://members.eb.com/bol/
>
> topic?eu=30910&sctn=1

Independent document (unidentified author)

> *Electronic references* (2001, January 10). Washington, DC: American
>
> Psychological Association. Retrieved July 16, 2008, from
>
> http://www.apastyle.org/elecref.html

Database

> Statistics Canada. (n.d.). *Crimes by type of offence.* Retrieved January 22,
>
> 2008, from the CANSIM database.

23-d APA-Style Sample Essay

The three main components of an APA essay are the title page, the text or body of the essay, and the list of references. Your title page should include the following elements:

- the first two or three words of the title, followed by the page number, in the upper right-hand corner;
- a shortened version of the title of the essay, set flush left;
- the full title of the essay, centred; and
- identifying information (author's name, course name and section number, instructor's name, and date), centred.

Start the body of the essay on a separate page and include a running head (APA refers to this as a "page header") and page number in the upper right-hand corner of all pages of the essay. Begin the reference list on a separate page. (For information about setting up a reference list, see 23-c.) Use double-spacing between all lines in the essay and the reference list.

Your instructor may ask that you prepare an *abstract*, a one-paragraph summary of the contents of your essay. The abstract, which should not exceed 120 words, is placed on a separate page between the title page and the text. Your essay may also include one or more appendixes. Appendixes follow the reference list, with each appendix beginning on a separate page.

On the following pages are excerpts from an APA-style essay.[2] Format specifications are pointed out in the marginal notes.

---

[2] Adapted from an essay by Kathleen Lenaghan, a student in a sociology class.

Running head (first two or three words of title and page number) in upper right-hand corner

Discussing *Quiet Rage* 1

Page header (short title) set flush left

DISCUSSING *QUIET RAGE: THE STANFORD PRISON EXPERIMENT*

Discussing *Quiet Rage: The Stanford Prison Experiment* in

Sociological Terms

Full title, author's name, course name and section number, instructor's name, and date centred on page

Kathleen Lenaghan

Sociology 1125, Section L16

Professor Ogden

April 10, 2008

Note: This sample title page includes the course name and number, the date, and the instructor's name. Check with your instructor as to whether you should include this information on your title page.

Philip Zimbardo conducted The Stanford Prison Experiment in 1971 to test the validity of his "dispositional hypothesis." The experiment that followed has become one of the most controversial sociological studies ever performed and one of the most referenced studies in sociology classrooms. This essay uses the sociological imagination to describe *Quiet Rage: The Stanford Prison Experiment* (1992), the film documenting the study, by relating the concepts of personal troubles to public issues. Additionally, this essay will discuss research methodology and ethics, concepts of statuses and roles, and the Thomas Theorem.

Background Information

Paragraphs indented five spaces →

Zimbardo proposed, in the dispositional hypothesis, that people who seek careers as corrections officers are predisposed to the sadistic intimidation and degradation tactics seen in penitentiaries and thus enjoy work that allows them to express these tendencies, contrary to the generally accepted idea that guards become "hardened" after exposure to inmates over time. Zimbardo further asserted that prisoners were imprisoned because they lacked the ability to function in normal society. Therefore, the negative and violent conditions of prison are a result of the dispositions of the guards and inmates. To test this hypothesis, Zimbardo created a prison setting where "normal" people filled the roles of both prisoners and guards. He recruited 24 volunteers and randomly assigned them the role of guard or prisoner. To make the experiment realistic, police removed the prisoners from their homes and charged them with a false offence. After the police had fingerprinted and booked the prisoners, the guards blindfolded and transported the prisoners to the prison that had been set up in the basement of a building on campus. The initial timeline for the experiment was two weeks, but, as the behaviour of the guards became increasingly aggressive and the mental state of the prisoners deteriorated, Zimbardo halted the study after just six days. This experiment is both one of the most studied sociological experiments and one of the most controversial, due to the extreme behaviours of the participants and the debate over the ethics of the research method.

An important part of Zimbardo's research is the aspect of authority. The lengths that the guards were willing to go to in order to terrorize the prisoners were shocking, but, ultimately, they were following Zimbardo's instructions. One guard, "John Wayne," asserted that he took it as far as possible in order to perform his own experiment on the prisoners, but the vast majority of guards believed they were simply doing what Zimbardo wanted them to do. Stanley Milgram explored this trust in authority in his 1960 study where he found Americans to be "an obedient people: not blindly obedient, not blissfully obedient, just obedient" (Meyer, 1970, p. 58).

Research Method: Was It Ethical?

In evaluating the ethics of the Stanford Prison Experiment, a relevant set of standards is the 1949 Nuremberg Code (National Institutes of Health, 1949). The experiment adheres to the majority of the 10 requirements of the code, but deviates in some important areas. The participants in the study were voluntary and informed participants, which is the cornerstone of ethical research in experiments such as this one. Zimbardo designed the experiment to prove something that would benefit society; by using the findings of the study, he theorized that it would be possible to create prisons that were not so prone to violence.

Zimbardo breached the Nuremburg Code by refusing to allow Prisoner 8126 to leave. According to the Code, "the human subject should be at liberty to bring the research to an end if he has reached the physical or mental state when continuation of the research seems to him to be impossible" (McIntyre, 2006, p. 52).

The Sociological Imagination

According to C. Wright Mills in *The Sociological Imagination* (1959), the sociological imagination is "a quality of mind that will help [sociologists] to use information and to develop reason in order to achieve lucid summations of what is going on in the world and of what may be happening within themselves" (p. 5). He goes on to outline the three questions to ask when using the sociological imagination to evaluate a society: "What is the structure of this particular society as a whole? Where does this society stand in human history? What varieties of men and women . . . prevail in this society" (pp. 6, 7)? These sociological questions can be applied to *Quiet Rage* as a means of understanding the behaviours of the prisoners and guards.

The social structure within the prison system was set up with the prisoners at the bottom of the hierarchy, with the guards holding authority over them. Above the guards was Zimbardo, who identified himself as the prison warden. This social structure is different from a "normal" social structure, where the interactions between the classes are dictated by social norms and folkways, because there are concrete rules that define the relationships betweens guards and prisoners. The *status quo* is maintained by regulating the behaviour of the prisoners and empowering the guards to exert their authority and control over them.

When examining where the prison society in *Quiet Rage* stands historically, it is important to recognize that the environment is artificial and its intended period of existence was only two weeks. Its historical significance comes from the information drawn from the study, rather than any growth and change that occurred within the prison society.

Ultimately, the person who prevailed in this constructed society was Zimbardo, who placed himself at the top of the social hierarchy. The guards also prevailed because Zimbardo gave them the power and authority to run the prison. This was appropriate as it mirrored the structure of real prisons in that period with white men generally in power.

Social Status, Roles, and Stigma

Status, role, and stigma are essential concepts for understanding the social relationships and identities of the participants in the Zimbardo study. A status is a social position held by a person within a society. In the Stanford Prison Experiment, Zimbardo divided the group into three statuses: the prisoners, the guards, and the warden. Zimbardo appointed himself as warden and then arbitrarily assigned statuses to student participants. The new statuses of "guard" or "prisoner" are the ascribed statuses of the participants. An important part of the prisoners' transition from their civilian status to their prisoner status was the degradation ceremony where they were stripped naked, hosed down, and then dressed in their uniforms. This helped to detach the prisoners from their pre-prison identity in order for them to accept their new status fully. This was an important process for the guards to go through as well because it reinforced their authority over the inmates, which was crucial for the social stratification within the prison setting. After a few days, the prisoners began to demonstrate their total internalization of their new roles by referring to themselves by their assigned numbers rather than their names. At this point in the study, prisoner status had replaced the individual pre-prison status as their master status. This kind of identity shift is evident in real prisoners as they replace their pre-prison self-image with a prison identity (Schmid & Jones, 1991).

References typed, centred, at top of page ──────▶

References

Dyer, G. (2006). Anybody's son will do. In L. J. McIntyre (Ed.), *The practical skeptic: Readings in Sociology* (pp. 212–223). New York: McGraw Hill.

Goffman, E. (2006). Presentation of self in everyday life. In L. J. McIntyre (Ed.), *The practical skeptic: Readings in Sociology* (pp. 58–68). New York: McGraw Hill.

Hanging indent for reference entries ──────▶ McIntyre, L. J. (2006) Doing the right thing: Ethics in research. In L. J. McIntyre (Ed.), *The practical skeptic: Readings in Sociology* (pp. 48–57). New York: McGraw Hill.

Meyer, P. (1970, February). If Hitler asked you to execute a stranger, would you? Probably. *Esquire, 74*, 72–73, 128–132.

Mills, C. W. (1959). *The sociological imagination.* Oxford: Oxford University Press.

National Institute of Health. (1949). Nuremberg code. Retrieved April 2, 2008, from http://ohsr.od.nih.gov/guidelines/nuremberg.html

Schmid, T. J., & Jones, R. S. (2006). Suspended identity: Identity transformation in a maximum security prison. In L. J. McIntyre (Ed.), *The practical skeptic: Readings in Sociology* (pp. 224–235). New York: McGraw Hill.

Zimbardo, Philip G. (Director). (1992). *Quiet rage: The Stanford prison experiment* [Motion picture]. United States: Stanford University.

Note: At present, APA style has only set up a style for citing a motion picture; it does not, as yet, make a distinction between a motion picture and a documentary produced only on DVD or on video. Check with your instructor to see if he or she wants you to be more specific when you utilize work from a video or DVD.

IV DOCUMENTATION

The style generally known as Chicago style or CM (for Chicago Manual) style is easy to learn because it uses the same basic approach as MLA, combining a minimal textual citation with a concluding list of sources consulted. What differs in the Chicago style is the means used to convey the textual citation. The only complicated element in the Chicago formula is that there are two citation styles recommended in *The Chicago Manual of Style,* one that reflects APA practice and one that reflects the MLA approach. The first uses the author–date system, while the second, the "humanities" version, uses superscript numbers in the body of the essay with a set of notes, either at the bottom of the page (footnotes) or on a separate page (endnotes) preceding the bibliography. We will focus on the number–note system and recommend that students check the *Manual* if they wish to use the other system.

There is one other variant in Chicago style that you should know about when writing an essay using this documentation format. Chicago style distinguishes a block or extended quotation from an integrated, short quotation on the basis of either one hundred words or eight lines of text. Therefore, once your quotation reaches either of those limits, you need to present it as an extended or block quotation by

- separating the quotation from your text by indenting it one tab;
- not using quotation marks to segregate it from your own text;
- adding the appropriate superscript number after the period that concludes your block quotation to signal the location of your endnote on the quotation's source.

Chicago style does discuss the use of smaller fonts for notes, but you do not need to follow that example unless your instructor asks you to. Check with your instructor to ensure that there are no other formatting instructions he or she prefers beyond those covered here.

24-a The Citation

Assume that you are writing an essay on film production trends and you want to quote from the following paragraph:

> During the past twenty-five years, there have been numerous shifts and developments in Hollywood filmmaking—so much so that to claim that one could describe all the shifts and changes in one general category misses some important nuances. Nevertheless, the dominant idea and ideal since the breakout success of *Jaws* and *Star Wars* is captured in the idea of the "blockbuster": films that shatter the barrier between market segments and draw crowds who line up around the block. Blockbuster films are crafted as events or spectacles—they are highly anticipated and carefully controlled. (Susie O'Brien and Imre Szeman, *Popular Culture*, 2004)

Your actual reference occurs in the following manner:

If "blockbuster[s]: films that shatter the barrier between market segments"[1] is the appropriate category for the *Lord of the Rings* trilogy, it is clear that the mix of the fantasy, moral quest, and action genres accomplished in these films appeals to a wide range of market segments.

If you were using the author–date system of Chicago style, you would insert (O'Brien and Szeman 2004) after "market segments"; this would lead your reader to the correct entry in the references list at the end of your paper.

However, the humanities format is different. Note that there is a superscript (raised) number following the quotation marks that complete the quote. (In your word-processing program, go to the "Format" menu, select "Font" from the choices listed, and select the superscript option; this will create the superscript version of the number for your note.) For an indirect borrowing, the note number could follow the period that concludes the sentence in which the borrowing appears. But the *Manual* recommends that the superscript number denoting an endnote immediately follow a direct quotation. This number alerts the reader to a citation reflecting a direct or indirect borrowing. In Chicago style, that citation always used to be presented at the foot of the page in what was called, logically, a footnote. Now, you have a choice of placing the note either at the foot of the page on which the citation is made or on a separate page immediately preceding the bibliography page. It is demonstrably easier to use the "endnotes" model because you don't have to plan each of your pages in advance to accommodate footnotes.

In the case above, your endnote would be

1. Susie O'Brien and Imre Szeman, *Popular Culture: A User's Guide* (Toronto: Thomson Nelson, 2004), 120.

Every superscript number in the text of your essay corresponds to a note under the same number on a notes page (or pages) following the text of your essay and preceding the bibliography page(s).

Please note the following features of the number–note system recommended by *The Chicago Manual of Style* for humanities disciplines:

1. The superscript number is placed at the end of a direct quotation or at the end of the sentence in which an indirect borrowing occurs.

2. The numbering of the notes is cumulative, whether you are using footnotes or endnotes; we recommend that you use endnotes.

3. The notes page is set up by centring the title, *Notes,* on the page, followed by consecutively numbered notes conveying the essential information

for the sources of your citations; leave two lines between the title and your first note.

4. Present the endnotes in a double-spaced format, the same format Chicago style recommends for your whole paper.

5. Each note is indented three spaces for its first line and left-aligned for any other lines.

6. A second or subsequent note to a particular source should be done in a shortened form; for instance, a subsequent reference to the source cited above would take the following form:

> 3. O'Brien and Szeman, 33.

(If you were using more than one source by O'Brien and Szeman, you would also have to add the title *Popular Culture* here before the page reference.)

7. You may also use the shortened form of the note if you are including full information on each source in your concluding bibliography; most instructors, however, prefer to have the full information given in the first note where the source is cited.

24-b The Bibliography

Chicago style for the humanities stipulates that the list of sources consulted for a paper should be called the bibliography. Although "bibliography" suggests printed texts, Chicago style uses the word to include all texts, including online and visual/aural texts. The following list of examples is intended to cover only basic sources. Please note the double-spacing of all examples here; you should also carefully observe the ways in which a note and a bibliography entry differ in format and use of internal punctuation.

For a complete listing, consult *The Chicago Manual of Style* in the reference section of your library or go to the following website: http://www.press.uchicago .edu/Misc/Chicago/cmosfaq.

BOOKS

The *Manual* specifies the following elements are "included, where applicable," in notes and bibliographic entries. The bolded entries indicate the most commonly included elements:

- **author/editor/translator/institutional author, with full name in standard order for notes and surname first for bibliographic entries**
- **title, including subtitle**

- editor, translator, compiler, if one appears on the title page
- edition, if the second or subsequent edition
- volume, if applicable
- series title, if applicable
- **facts of publication—city, publisher, date of publication**
- page number(s), if the reference is to part of a larger whole
- URL and other information for online books

In each of the following examples, "NOTE" stands for the format to be used in a footnote or endnote and "BIBLIO" stands for the format required in a bibliographic entry.

Book by one author

NOTE

1. Kay J. Anderson, *Vancouver's Chinatown: Racial Discourse in Canada, 1875–1980* (Montreal: McGill-Queen's Press, 1995), 34.

BIBLIO

Anderson, Kay J. *Vancouver's Chinatown: Racial Discourse in Canada, 1875–1980.* Montreal: McGill-Queen's Press, 1995.

Book by two or three authors

NOTE

2. John Frederick Nims and David Mason, *An Introduction to Poetry,* 4th ed. (Toronto: McGraw-Hill, 2000), 6.

BIBLIO

Nims, John Frederick, and David Mason. *An Introduction to Poetry.* 4th ed. Toronto: McGraw-Hill, 2000.

Book by more than three authors

NOTE

3. James Reinking et al., *Strategies for Successful Writing: A Rhetoric, Research Guide, Reader, and Handbook,* 2nd Canadian ed. (Scarborough, ON: Pearson Prentice Hall, 2004), 81.

BIBLIO

Reinking, James, Andrew Hart, Robert van der Osten, Sue Ann Cairns, and Robert Fleming. *Strategies for Successful Writing: A Rhetoric, Research Guide, Reader, and Handbook.* 2nd Canadian ed. Scarborough, ON: Pearson Prentice Hall, 2004.

Book with a corporate or institutional author

NOTE

4. American Psychological Association, *Publication Manual of the American Psychological Association,* 5th ed. (Washington, DC: American Psychological Association, 2001), 105.

BIBLIO

American Psychological Association. *Publication Manual of the American Psychological Association.* 5th ed. Washington, DC: American Psychological Association, 2001.

Selection from an anthology or similar collection

NOTE

5. Irving Layton, "The Way the World Ends," in *The Norton Introduction to Literature,* 6th ed., ed. Carl Bain, Jerome Beaty, and J. Paul Hunter (New York: W. W. Norton, 1995), 833.

BIBLIO

Layton, Irving. "The Way the World Ends." In *The Norton Introduction to Literature,* 6th ed., edited by Carl Bain, Jerome Beaty, and J. Paul Hunter, 833. New York: W. W. Norton, 1995.

Anthology or edited book

NOTE

6. R. S. Gwynn, ed., *Literature: A Pocket Anthology* (Toronto: Addison-Wesley Educational Publishers, 2002).

BIBLIO

Gwynn, R. S., ed. *Literature: A Pocket Anthology.* Toronto: Addison-Wesley Educational Publishers, 2002.

Government publication Format a note and a bibliographic entry for a publication by a government department or agency in the same way you would for a corporate author. The name of the government department or agency responsible for the publication becomes the author entry and the name of the publication is the title. In recording the publication data, look first for the city of publication and second for the government printer. Finally, record the year of publication, and, for the note form only, the page reference for your quotation or borrowing.

PERIODICALS

The Chicago Manual of Style uses the term "periodical" for scholarly and professional journals, magazines, and newspapers. The elements to be included are

- author's or authors' names
- title and subtitle of article or column
- title of periodical, magazine, or newspaper
- issue information (volume, issue, number, date)
- page reference (use a single page reference for a direct reference to a sentence or paragraph and an inclusive page reference for a general reference to an article)

Journals

NOTE

7. Larry T. Sieber and Kenneth L. Davis, "The Pathophysiology of Schizophrenia Disorder: Perspectives from the Spectrum," *American Journal of Psychiatry* 161, no. 2 (2004): 338–413.

8. Lorraine York, "Letters in Canada 2002: Fiction," *University of Toronto Quarterly* 23, no. 1 (2003-4): 4–14.

BIBLIO

Sieber, Larry T., and Kenneth L. Davis. "The Pathophysiology of Schizophrenia Disorder: Perspectives from the Spectrum." *American Journal of Psychiatry* 161, no. 2 (2004): 338–413.

York, Lorraine. "Letters in Canada 2002: Fiction." *University of Toronto Quarterly* 23, no. 1 (2003–2004): 4–14.

The Chicago Manual of Style states that the issue number does not need to be given for journals that use continuous pagination throughout the year or for journals that list the month or season before the year.

Article from a monthly magazine   For magazine citations, you may cite either a specific page number, or, if you are referring to the whole article, the range of page numbers for the article.

NOTE

9. Thomas Frank, "Lie Down for America: How the Republican Party Sows Ruin on the Great Plains," *Harper's*, April 2004, 33–48.

BIBLIO

Frank, Thomas. "Lie Down for America: How the Republican Party Sows Ruin on the Great Plains." *Harper's*, April 2004, 33–48.

Article from a weekly magazine

NOTE

10. James Deacon, "In Defence of the Masters," *Maclean's*, April 12, 2004, 38–39.

BIBLIO

Deacon, James. "In Defence of the Masters." *Maclean's*, April 12, 2004, 38–39.

Unsigned article from a weekly or monthly magazine

NOTE

11. "Urban Adventures," *TV Guide*, May 1–7, 2004, 37.

IV DOCUMENTATION

The bibliographic entry is written the same as the note but without a number.

BIBLIO

"Urban Adventures." *TV Guide,* May 1–7, 2004, 37.

Signed article from a daily newspaper   Chicago style suggests you include either the edition name (e.g., "final edition") or the section number the article appears in, but not the page number.

NOTE

12. Steven Edwards, "Rwandan Victims Not Just Tutsis, Study

Suggests," *Vancouver Sun,* April 8, 2004, sec. A.

BIBLIO

Edwards, Steven. "Rwandan Victims Not Just Tutsis, Study Suggests."

Vancouver Sun, April 8, 2004, sec. A.

Unsigned article from a daily newspaper   Basically, you write the note for an unsigned article in a newspaper the same way as for a signed article. The one adjustment you have to make is to move the article's title into the place normally reserved for the author's name. Using the example above, the correct note would now look like this:

NOTE

13. "Rwandan Victims Not Just Tutsis, Study Suggests," *Vancouver*

Sun, April 8, 2004, sec. A.

You would write the bibliographic note with the name of the newspaper where the author's name would normally appear.

BIBLIO

Vancouver Sun. "Rwandan Victims Not Just Tutsis, Study Suggests."

April 8, 2004, sec. A.

ELECTRONIC SOURCES

In its comments on electronic sources, *The Chicago Manual of Style* initially stresses the fact that electronic texts are subject to change in a way that printed texts are not—changes in address and changes in content. Electronic articles are also not necessarily subject to the review by publishers and peers that is part of academic publishing in other media. As such, the *Manual* stresses that writers must take special pains to ensure their borrowing is current, accurate, and accessible. Additionally, writers are asked to select the most permanent version if multiple versions exist.

In citing an electronic source, writers are asked to add two elements not present in the citation of a printed text: the URL or address of the source, and the date the source was accessed. Aside from these two additional elements, the citation takes the same format recommended for a printed text, whether a book, an article, or another genre. Simply add to the format recommended by the *Manual* two concluding elements:

- the address (URL) of your source
- the date (day, month, and year) that you found this source; the *Manual* calls this the access date

Note that it is not necessary to add your date of access if the data and information in the document you read is not time-sensitive and you believe the address is stable. If an access date *is* required because of the nature of the resource, leave a space after the URL and then add, for example, "(accessed April 15, 2009)" followed by a period.

Instead of having an extra segment on electronic sources, therefore, the *Manual* adds a guide on citing an electronic version at the end of its instructions on how to cite books, articles, and multimedia.

The one additional piece of advice provided is the instruction to break a URL that runs more than one line in length at a point where no confusion is possible on how it is to be read. Place the break after a slash or before any punctuation mark. Nothing (such as a hyphen) should be added to the address to signify that it continues to another line.

BOOKS

For a book, therefore, simply add the URL and the date of access at the end of a normally formatted citation. If the citation is for a book that is published conventionally as well as online, add the URL at the end of the citation as in the example that follows. If it is published only online, construct the citation according to the information you have following the Chicago guidelines for what information needs to be included (see pp. 164–65).

NOTE

14. Hilary Stead, *Guelph: A People's Heritage, 1827–2002,*

http://www.electricscotland.com/canada/guelph/articles/guelph.htm

(accessed July 7, 2008).

BIBLIO

Stead, Hilary. *Guelph: A People's Heritage, 1827–2002.* http://www

.electricscotland.com/canada/guelph/articles/guelph.htm (accessed

July 7, 2008).

PERIODICALS

The same general guideline applies to articles in periodicals. Simply add, at the end of the list of identifying details, the URL and, if necessary, because of time-sensitive data or content, the date you accessed the resource. The examples below illustrate the citations for four different kinds of periodicals. Only the note format is included here because the differences between note and bibliography format are slight, and you should be familiar with them by this point.

Journal article also published conventionally

NOTE

15. Mark Warr and Christopher G. Ellison, "Rethinking Social

Reactions to Crime: Personal and Altruistic Fear in Family Households,"

American Journal of Sociology 106, no. 3 (2000), under "The Consequences

of Fear," http://www.journals.uchicago.edu/AJS/journal/issues/v106n3/

050125/050125.html.

Article published in a magazine in both conventional and online formats

> **NOTE**
>
> 16. Katherine Macklem, "The Death Watch: Should Unloved and Perennially Broke Air Canada Be Put Out of Its Misery?" *Maclean's*, April 26, 2004, http://www.macleans.ca/topstories/business/article .jsp?content=20040426_79219_79219 (accessed April 15, 2009).

Article published in a magazine in online format only

> **NOTE**
>
> 17. Greg Palast, "Florida's Flawed 'Voter-Cleansing' Program," *Salon*, June 29, 2004, http:www.salon.com/politics/featurc/2000/12/04/voter (accessed June 9, 2009).

Article in an online newspaper

> **NOTE**
>
> 18. David Kravets, "Language a Battleground in Abortion Suits," *Yahoo! News*, April 20, 2004, http://dailynews.yahoo.com/.

Follow the same format for articles from online newspapers, but add the access date only if your discipline requires you to do so. Check with your instructor.

The University of Chicago Press, which publishes *The Chicago Manual of Style*, believes that a superior mechanism for identifying the source of an online text will emerge shortly. In 2003, they reported that "digital object identifiers" were one such alternative to be examined and that these were already in use in one setting. As such, you should check the website identified earlier for updates on this attempt to replace URLs.

The Columbia Online style originated in 1994 when Janice Walker developed a style for citing electronic sources that was adopted by the Alliance for Computers and Writing, named the Walker/ACW Style Sheet, and published on the Web.

Columbia Online utilizes five principles for citation style. They are the principles of

- access
- intellectual property
- economy
- standardization
- transparency

The format of an essay using Columbia Online style depends on whether you are going to print your essay or submit it electronically for print publication. If your essay is to be printed in hard copy, double-space the body of the essay, block quotations, and bibliography, using hanging indents for bibliography (works cited, references). If you are submitting an essay electronically, also double-space the entire bibliography but do not indent any of the lines of the entries. Separate each entry with two blank lines to create extra white space.

In Columbia Online style, a work directly referenced in an essay is called either a "work cited" or "reference." One that is consulted but not referenced can be listed separately in a list entitled "Works Consulted."

When preparing an essay in Columbia Online style, use a standard font such as Times New Roman, Palatino, Arial, or Courier 12.

25-a Summary of the Two Styles: Humanities Style and Scientific Style

HUMANITIES STYLE

Author's surname, first name. [if no author, corporation, or organization, start with the title] "Title of Document." *Title of Complete Work.* Version or Edition. Document date or date of last revision or modification. URL or name of database and publisher (access path, directory, keywords, or file numbers [if applicable]) (date of access).

SCIENTIFIC STYLE

> Author's surname, initial(s). (Date of document). Title of document.
>
> *Title of source work* [if there is one]. (Edition or revision [if there is
>
> either]). Name of database and database publisher, or URL, or
>
> directory, document, or file number (date of access).

25-b Humanities Style

Use italics for book, magazine, or journal titles. Include the designation or description for specific parts of a work (preface, abstract) immediately before the title of the work.

IN-TEXT CITATIONS

Unless the author has supplied page numbers or paragraph or section numbers, there is no set pagination. In this situation, cite the author's last name only in the text of your essay.

> A post-multicultural society will have different attributes than a melting
>
> pot or a mosaic (Bal).

If you make several references to the same online source in a paragraph, place your reference at the end of the paragraph. If you have placed the author's name in the text of your essay, you can omit the parenthetical reference.

> According to a 2003 study on obesity in Canadian children between the
>
> ages of seven and thirteen, thirty-three percent of boys and twenty-six
>
> percent of girls are overweight. The study also discovered that ten per-
>
> cent of boys and nine percent of girls in this age range are obese
>
> (Willms, Tremblay, and Katzmarzyk).

IV DOCUMENTATION

If there are no page numbers, you may use file names, section names, or paragraph or line numbers (if they are given) in a citation. The following example uses a section name.

> In "Does the Aging of the Population Really Drive the Demand for Health Care?" Uwe E. Reinhardt notes that patients' files in the U.S. are still paper-based, a problem that creates a large administrative overhead for hospitals ("Aging and the Supply Side of the Health System").

Citing multiple works by the same author If you are citing more than one work by an author, you may shorten the works' titles in the text of your essay or in your parenthetic reference.

Site with no author, moderator, or editor: cite the organization In the body of the text, cite the name of the organization or news service in the parenthetic note.

> The British Columbia Teachers' Federation (BCTF) reports that standardized tests have helped perpetuate negative self-images in Aboriginal students in B.C.
>
> The Government of Newfoundland and Labrador admitted that 108 patients whose breast cancer tests were misread have now died (globeandmail).

Site with no author or organization named: Start with the title Start your parenthetic note with the document's title or a shortened version of it enclosed in quotation marks or italicized, depending on whether it is an entity in itself or a part of a larger entity.

If there is no title, cite the file name in your parenthetical reference To add such a reference to your Works Cited, simply enter the whole website address and follow it with the date of access in parentheses.

Credits of images or graphics   Include credits for images or graphics underneath the image or on a credits page. Unless you have taken a graphic or other
visual from a site that offers free graphics or images, you may need to obtain permission for its use.

Personal communications, e-mails, chat-room material   Personal communication, including e-mails, chat-room messages, telephone calls, or even face-to-
face conversations need to be noted in the text, either in the lead-in to the
information or in a parenthetic citation.

> In a chat-room conversation with the students of Crim 2312 . . .

WORKS CITED

More than one entry by the same author   In a works-cited list, when you have
more than one entry by the same author, after the first entry use three dashes to
indicate the author's name.

> Owen. Wilfred. "Mental Cases." *War Poems & Manuscripts of Wilfred*
>
> *Owen.* http://www.hcu.ox.ac.uk/jtap/warpoems.htm#21 (18 Mar.
>
> 2008).
>
> ———. "Strange Meeting." *War Poems & Manuscripts of Wilfred Owen.*
>
> http://www.hcu.ox.ac.uk/jtap/warpoems.htm#1 (18 Mar. 2008).

If the material has no author, no title, and does not list an organization, start
with the webpage or website address.

Webpage

> Downes, Stephen. "OLDaily." 18 Mar. 2008. *Stephen's Web.* http://
>
> www.downes.ca/news/OLDaily.htm (18 Mar. 2008).

HUMANITIES STYLE | 177

Author or moderator of a site Include the author or moderator or person responsible for the site if one is listed. Next, list the name of the site, presenting the site title in the same way you would present the title of a book, in italics.

> Ballantyne, P. (2008). Home page. http://www.comnet.ca/~pballan/
>
> Index.html (29 Nov. 2008).

A maintained or compiled site If the webpage or website is maintained or compiled, and your main focus is the site, list the name of the individual responsible for maintenance after the title of the site or page. If your focus is the person who maintains the site, list the entry under the person's name and place his or her name at the beginning of the entry. Place the abbreviation "maint." or "comp." (for *maintained* or *compiled*) after the individual's name: "Webb, A. maint."

Links from main pages If a site will not allow you to go directly to a page without going through the home page, cite the home page and, after the URL for that page, specify the links to access specific material: (Links: Archives/Browse the Archives/5 May 2006) (30 Dec. 2007).

Website or article with no author Start with name of the organization or, if there is no organization, the title of the article.

> **WEBSITE**
>
> *Timesonline.* 2008. http://www.timesonline.co.uk/tol/news/ (30 May 2008).
>
> **ARTICLE**
>
> Name of author/organization. "Title of Article." *Website Title.* (date
>
> posted or) Last updated 21 Feb. 2008. Website address (date of
>
> access).

Home page If you are citing the opening page of a website that has no title, place the descriptor "Home Page" after the name of the website's organization.

Council of Science Educators of Canada (CSEC). Home Page. 2008.

http://csec.ca/index.html (11 June 2008).

Article in an online journal   Cite the URL for the main page of the journal unless the article can be accessed by a unique URL. If it can, cite the specific URL for the article.

Surname, first name. "Title of Article." *Title of Journal*. 7.2 (2007). URL

(4 Mar. 2008).

An article that was previously published in hard copy   Cite the print publication information, including the volume, issue, date of publication, and original page numbers before you cite the electronic address.

Author's Name. "Title." *Journal Name*. 12.3 (2002): 212-28. *Online*

Journal Title. URL (18 Mar. 2008).

Article in an online newspaper

Author's name. "Title of Article." Onlinepaper.com. 24 Mar. 2008. URL

[direct URL if possible; if not, site URL] (3 Apr. 2008).

Akkad, Omar El. "Judge Sides with Khadr Defence Team."

Globeandmail.com. Mar 15 2008. http://www.theglobeandmail.com/

servlet/story/RTGAM.20080314.wkhadr0314/BNStory/International/

home (16 Mar. 2008).

Conference papers online   These are listed following the same standard model: Author, "Title." Conference name. City and dates of conference. Online location of conference papers. Date document posted or last revised. URL (date of access).

> Author. "Title of Paper." Name of Conference. Winnipeg 12-14 Oct.
>
> 2008. Conference Storage for Manitoba Universities. 30 Nov. 2008.
>
> URL (5 Dec. 2008).

Revisions, modifications, editions, or versions   After the title of an article, include " Rev." or "Mod." followed by the date of revision or modification using day, month, year presentation. Similarly, include the version or edition number after a title by writing "Vers." followed by the version number: "Vers. 2.3."

Part of the page (graphic, image, or audio or video file) that does not have its own URL   When citing a graphic, an image, or an audio or video file from a webpage, you may wish to make a reference to the file type in square brackets (e.g., [Image]) immediately after the title of the work. Place a period after the file type before the URL. Unless you have taken a graphic or other visual from a site that offers free graphics or images, you may need to obtain permission for its use.

> Caravaggio, Michelangelo. *The Taking of Christ* [Image]. In National
>
> Gallery of Ireland. http://www.nationalgallery.ie/html/
>
> paintings.html (26 Mar. 2008).

Mailing lists, newsgroups, blogs, wikis, chats, MOOs, MUDs, and online games
All of these online possibilities can contain material that you may want to cite. You can do so using the standards that Columbia Online has established for other online material.

> Author. "Title." Date of posting. *Title of List/Group/Blog/Chat/Moo/.*
>
> (*online mailing address* if applicable for a mailing list/*Name of news-*
>
> *group* if applicable. URL (date of access).

WebCT Blackboard and online course materials   References to online material from a course website should, normally, include the name of the instructor, the course title (place "Home Page" after the course title), the date of the course, and the name of the institution. Include the URL if the course site is on the Web. When referencing online handouts, e-mails, discussion boards, or chat rooms for a course, cite the author of the material, its title and the date of posting or publication, the name of the course, the date, the instructor's name, the courseware the material was in, if applicable (e.g., WebCT, Blackboard, Moodle), the name of the institution and the URL, if applicable, and the date of access.

25-c Scientific Style

IN-TEXT CITATIONS

The *Columbia Guide*'s second set of guidelines, for the sciences, follows the *Publication Manual of the American Psychological Association.* In-text parenthetic citations follow APA style and include the author's name, if not in the text, and the year of publication. Include pagination if the source utilizes pagination.

With page number   The page number is preceded by the abbreviation *p.*, as in this citation: (MacDonald, 2005, p. 22).

With no page number   If there is no page number, cite the name and the date (MacDonald, 2005). Subsequent references need cite only the name (MacDonald) unless the site lists line numbers, section numbers, or paragraphs. If it does, you should include them in lieu of page numbers: (MacDonald, 2005, line 59), (MacDonald, 2005, sec 2.3), (MacDonald, 2005, para. 11), or (MacDonald, 2005, ¶ 11).

No date   If there is no date for the online material, use the date of access with your citation: (Lim, 8 Aug. 2008).

No author   Cite the organization and the date: (IBM, 2007).

No author, no organization as author   Cite the webpage title or a shortened version of it, followed by the document date, if given, or the date of access if there is no document date: (*Health*, June 2006), (*Women's Health Matters*, 15 Mar. 2008).

You can sidestep problems caused by citations that do not have authors or titles by including the source information in the text of your essay: "According to the Grisoft website (2008) ..."

Citing graphics, images, or audio or video files   Cite by author if known and not included in the body of your essay, or the file name, followed by the year of publication or date of access: (187991main_Brian-Karczewski-full.jpg, 2008). If you incorporate a graphic or other visual file into your paper, simply place the URL for the source under the image or diagram. Unless you have taken a graphic or other visual from a site that offers free graphics or images, you may need to obtain permission for its use.

Personal communication   You should include citations for personal communication including e-mails, chat-room messages, telephone calls, and conversations, even though you will not include entries for them in your list of references at the end of your essay. You parenthetic note should include the date that your communication occurred: (Dromana, personal communication, September 12, 2006).

REFERENCES

In the Columbia scientific style for bibliography entries, the date of publication gives the name of the month written in full and is ordered year-month-day. In contrast, the date of access at the end of an entry uses abbreviations for all months except May, June, and July, and is ordered month-day-year.

In most cases, scientific style entries are very similar to humanities style entries except for the positioning and presentation of the date of the document, the title of the document, and the type of document (e.g., "Home page" in scientific style; "Home Page" in humanities style).

The designation or description for specific parts of a work (preface, abstract) is placed immediately after the title, enclosed in square brackets, prior to the end punctuation.

Webpage or website with no title

Mookerjea, S. Home page. http://www.uofaweb.ualberta.ca/

   sociology/mookerjea.cfm (17 Mar. 2008).

Opening page of an entire site

American Psychological Association (APA). (2008). Home page.

   http://www.apa.org/ (26 Mar. 2008).

Webpage or website maintained or compiled   Similar to the practice in the humanities style, the scientific style credits someone with maintaining or compiling a site. In the scientific style, though, the person who is doing this task is listed after the title of the site, or, if there is no site name, after the date. The information is placed in parentheses: (A. Macpherson, Comp.), (A. Macpherson, Maint.).

Article in an online journal   An article in an online journal follows the format for a standard scientific entry, with the author's name and initial(s) coming first, followed by the date of publication. The title of the article has no quotation marks around it and uses a capital for only the first word and proper nouns. The only other difference between a scientific entry and a humanities entry occurs in the presentation of the volume and issue numbers for a journal. In the scientific style, the volume is followed by the issue, which is placed in parentheses: 7(1). In the humanities style, the volume number is separated from the issue number by a period: 7.1, and the information is followed by the date of publication in parentheses.

Article in an online magazine   Make sure that, in listing the date of publication after the author or authors' names, you include the complete date. Note that the month is written out in full. The date of access should be placed at the end of the entry, but this date uses the abbreviated form for all months except May, June, and July.

Millar, L. Blind willow, sleeping woman. (2006, September 14).

Salon.com. http://search.salon.com/results/?query=

murakami&breadth=archive&page=1 (26 Mar. 2008).

Article in online newspaper or news service, and links and search path information   Besides the usual information, include any links or search terms after the URL and before the date of access. Use this model when you are citing an article or a website or webpage from another source and need to show links or search path information.

Bailey, I. (2008, March 17). Residential schools protest interrupts

morning mass. globeandmail.com. http://www.theglobeandmail

.com (Links: Search Archives) (17 Mar. 2008).

If there is no author named, cite the news service, group, or agency. If there is no group or agency named, start with the article title.

NOTE: If an article can be accessed from a unique URL, list that in your entry; if it cannot, list the URL for the publication and supply the links as above.

Conferences   Conference papers are often available online. To cite a paper follow this format:

Surname, Initial. *Title of the paper*. Paper presented at [name of confer-

ence and city where it took place]. URL (date of access).

Government website

Name of government and agency. (Date of publication if known). *Title*

of website. URL (date of access).

Online book

Surname, Initial. (Date of publication). *Title of book*. (Rev. date if there is

one). URL (date of access).

Online book previously published

Surname, Initial. (Date of print publication). *Title of book*. City of publi-

cation: Publisher. URL (date of access).

Webpage or website, revised or modified or in an edition or version   Include "Mod." or "Rev." and the date after the title.

> Surname, Initial. (Date of publication). Title (Mod. year, month day).
>
>   *Title of site.* Organization. URL (date of access).

If you need to cite a website with both a modification and an edition or version, indicate the modification after the author's name and the version after the title.

> Surname, Initial. (Mod. year, month day). Full title. (Vers. 2.1). URL
>
>   (date of access).

Graphics, images, and audio and video files   Treat the title of a work of art, motion picture, CD, video, and DVD the way you would treat the title of a book.

> Surname, Initial. Title of work. [Audio]. (2008, August 14). *Site name.*
>
>   URL (date of access).

After the title, add a descriptor for the type of material it is, set in brackets.

Article, abstract, or review from a library database   In citing this type of information, notice that both the title of the source journal and the title of the database are in italics, but the name of the database publisher is not. Before the access date, include the file or document number if the database includes one.

IV DOCUMENTATION

> Surname, Initial. (Date of publication). Title of article. *Journal name,*
>
> 2(1), 23-31. *Academic Search Premier.* EBscoHost. (access number if
>
> given). (date of access).

Mailing lists, newsgroups, blogs, wikis, chats, MOOS, and MUDS   If you are citing someone's comments in a chat, cite the individual as the author before the title of the chat or discussion group. Then indicate the coordinator's name, if there is one, the chat room/group name and its location name in the following manner: "In A. B. Cliff (Coordin.), Studies in rocks. *Earth Sciences* 2." Use the elements of the following model as your guide:

> Surname, Initial or alias. (Date of publication). Title of work. In coordi-
>
> nator's name, title of group, blog, or MOO. *Title of the collection of*
>
> *groups if there is one.* URL for the group (date of access).

WebCT Blackboard and online course materials   Online material from a course website should, normally, include the name of the instructor, the date of the material, "Home page," the course title, and the name of the institution. Include the URL if the course site is on the Web, and the date of access.

> Surname, Initial. (2008, Fall). Home page. Crim. 2340. Concordia
>
> University, Montreal. URL (date of access).

When citing a handout, e-mail, discussion board, chat room, or any other material for a course, cite the author of the material first, the date of posting or the course date, the title of the document, the name of the course, the instructor's name, and the name of the institution. Although e-mail messages, discussion boards, and chat-room conversations may be cited in the body of your paper, they do not need a reference in scientific style.

Whereas earlier editions of the CSE style manual, *Scientific Style and Format,* focused on biology and medicine, the seventh edition covers all scientific disciplines.[3] Revisions to the seventh edition will be posted in the document "Corrections to Publications" at the Council of Science Editors website (http://www.councilscienceeditors.org/) as updates become available.

26-a In-Text Citations

The CSE style manual presents two systems of in-text citation: the name-year system and the citation-sequence system.

NAME-YEAR SYSTEM

The name-year system is similar to APA style (see 23-a). In this system, text citations refer to an alphabetically arranged list of references at the end of the document.

AUTHOR NAMED IN TEXT

Gould (1991) found that . . .

SAME AUTHOR, DIFFERENT YEARS

Gould (1985, 1987a, 1987b, 1989) found that . . .

TWO AUTHORS

(Gould and Vrba 1982)

THREE OR MORE AUTHORS

(Alberts and others 1994)

MULTIPLE CITATIONS

A number of studies (Gould and Calloway 1980; Gould and Vrba 1982; Erlich and others 1984; Garrett and Gould 1984; Crosland and Crozier 1986) found that . . .

---

[3] To more accurately reflect its expanding membership, the Council of Biology Editors changed its name to the Council of Science Editors in 2000. The seventh edition of *Scientific Style and Format* reflects this change in its subtitle: *The CSE Manual for Authors, Editors, and Publishers.*

CITATION-SEQUENCE SYSTEM

In the citation-sequence system, superscript numbers identify in-text citations and correspond to the sequence of numbers in the list of references. The superscript note number is placed immediately after the reference and before punctuation (if any).

> Scientists are not only attempting to synthesize self-replicating molecules, they are also persuading existing biological molecules to evolve artificially in the laboratory. The initial groundbreaking work in this area began in the 1960s and 1970s, with work by Sol Spiegelman's group on RNA evolution in vitro[1]. Over the following decade their research was extended by Manfred Eigen, Christof Biebricher[2], and others in Göttingen.

Here are the reference entries for these two sources:

> 1. Mills DR, Peterson RL, Spiegelman S. Proc Nat Acad Sci USA 1967;58:217.
>
> 2. Biebricher CK. Cold Spring Harbor Symp Quant Biol 1987;52:299.

NOTE: If you cite a reference more than once, use the same superscript number to identify it in the text.

If a single reference points to more than one source, list the source numbers in a series. Use commas to separate numbers that do not form a sequence[1,6,7,13] and a hyphen to separate more than two numbers in a continuous sequence[1,6,7,13-15].

26-b List of References

Start the list of references on a separate page at the end of your essay. In CSE style, you can use one of the following for your reference list title: References, End References, Reference List, Literature Cited, or Bibliography. Ask your instructor for guidance on choosing a title. If you are using the name-year system, arrange the reference entries alphabetically by author name; if you are using the citation-sequence system, organize the entries in numerical sequence.

Regardless of the system of in-text citation you use, the CSE recommends a flush-left style for reference entries. All entries are single spaced. Individual entries are separated by a single blank line space.

Listed below are general guidelines for creating CSE-style reference entries.

1. *Authors' names.* List authors by surname, followed by a space and initials without spacing or punctuation. If there are two to ten authors, separate the names with commas; do not use *and* or *&* before the name of the last author. If there are more than ten authors, list the first ten, followed by the phrase *et al.* or *and others.*

2. *Book entries.* Do not underline or italicize book titles. Capitalize only the first word of the main title and all proper nouns. Use a short version of the publisher's name *(Cambridge Univ Pr, not Cambridge University Press; Harcourt, not Harcourt Brace and Company).* For the place of publication, if a city is well known and cannot be confused with another city, use the name of the city by itself. If there is the chance of confusion, add the province, state, or country after the city's name: London (ON) or London (UK). Use a short version of the publisher's name if the publisher is well known; Nelson Education Ltd. becomes Nelson, for instance. Note, however, that CSE writes out the names of university presses in full: Cambridge University Press. Follow the publisher's name with the number of pages in the book (if you are citing the entire book) followed by the abbreviation *p.* as in "245 p." If you referred to only select pages of the book in your essay, conclude the entry with the abbreviation *p.* followed by the page numbers you referred to: "p. 23-30."

3. *Periodical entries.* Do not enclose titles of articles in quotation marks. Capitalize only the first word of the article's main title and all proper nouns. Do not underline or italicize periodical titles. If a journal title is longer than one word, abbreviate it: omit articles, conjunctions, and prepositions that are not part of a scientific term and shorten all remaining words. (For a selected list of abbreviations of journal titles in CSE style, see Table 26-1.) Capitalize the first letter of each word in the abbreviated journal title. Do not use spaces to separate (a) the volume/issue numbers and the page numbers in a journal entry; (b) the periodical title and the page numbers in a magazine entry; and (c) the periodical title, section number, and page numbers in a newspaper entry. Abbreviate all months except May; do not use a period with month abbreviations.

TABLE 26-1 CSE Style: Abbreviation of Journal Titles

WORD	ABBREVIATION	WORD	ABBREVIATION
Abstracts	Abstr	International	Int
American	Am	Journal	J
Annual	Annu	Laboratory	Lab
Association	Assoc	Mathematical	Math
Biochemistry	Biochem	Microbiology	Microbiol
Biology	Biol	National	Nat
Bulletin	Bull	Neurology	Neurol
Canadian	Can	Nuclear	Nucl
Chemistry	Chem	Organic	Org
College	Coll	Physics	Phy
Environmental	Environ	Science/Scientific	Sci
European	Eur	University	Univ

4. *Inclusive page numbers.* To indicate a range of pages for a chapter in a book, use the abbreviation *p.* followed by the range of numbers (p. 5-12, p. 96-97, p. 294-316, p. 1005-1006.). To indicate pages in a journal article in a reference list, indicate the page numbers if they are continuous without a *p.* (334-339). If the pagination is discontinuous, your citation for the article should reflect that by listing the page numbers that the article can be found on (342-348, 359, 361-362).

Placement of dates The reference-entry examples that follow reflect the use of the name-year system. In references based on the name-year system, the date appears after the author(s) name(s). If you are using the citation-sequence system, place the date as shown below:

BOOK
1. Gould S. The flamingo's smile: reflections in natural history. New York: Norton; 1985.

JOURNAL
2. Hawking SW. Arrow of time in cosmology. Phy Rev D 1985;32:2489.

NEWSPAPER
3. Ingram J. Genome shows 'junk' DNA may have role to play. Sunday Star 2001 Feb 18;Sect F:8.

BOOKS, ARTICLES IN PERIODICALS, AND OTHER SOURCES

Book by one author

> Gould S. 1985. The flamingo's smile: reflections in natural history. New York: Norton.

Book by two or more authors

> Alberts B, Bray D, Lewis J, Raff M, Roberts K, Watson JD. 1994. Molecular biology of the cell. New York: Garland.

Book with editor(s)

> Broadbent D, editor. 1993. The simulation of human intelligence. Oxford: Blackwell; 1993.

Book by corporate author

> [CSE] Council of Science Editors. 2006. Scientific style and format: the CSE manual for authors, editors, and publishers. 7th ed. Reston, VA p. 680

NOTE: Adding the number of pages as a final element is optional.

Book published in a new edition

> Dawkins R. 1989. The selfish gene. 2nd ed. Oxford: Oxford University Press.

Article in an edited book

Smith M. 1983. Current controversies in evolutionary biology. In: Grene, M, editor. Dimensions of Darwinism. Cambridge: Cambridge University Press p. 273-286.

Article in a journal paginated by volume

Hawking SW. 1985. Arrow of time in cosmology. Phy Rev D 32:2489.

Article in a journal paginated by issue

Dyson FJ. 1979. Time without end: physics and biology in an open universe. Rev Mod Phy 51(3):447-460.

Article in a monthly or bimonthly periodical

Holland JH. 1992 July. Genetic algorithms. Sci Am. 44-50.

Article without an author

What will happen to geology? 1969. Nature 221:903.

Article in a newspaper

Ingram J. 2001 Feb 18. Genome shows 'junk' DNA may have role to play. Sunday Star;Sect F:8 (col. 1).

Letter to the editor

Leyton E. 2001 Feb 22. Protecting patients from harm is the issue facing society. [letter to the editor]. Kingston Whig-Standard;Sect 1:6 (col. 1).

Editorial in a periodical

Smith KY. 1991. New dangers in our field [editorial]. Am J Nucl Eng 12:15-16.

Thesis or dissertation

Rothman GA. 1989. Learning style, vocational interest, and choice of major for a population of hearing-impaired college students [dissertation]. Buffalo: State Univ of New York. 113 p. Available from: University Microfilms, Ann Arbor, MI, GAX89-13546.

Personal communication

Cheung KF. 2001 Jan 16. Documentation style in science and mathematics.

WEB SOURCES

To document Web sources in a manner consistent with the principles of CSE style, use the following basic model:

Author's name (last name, first and any middle initials). Date of publication. Document title [Internet]. [cited Date of access] Available from: URL

IV DOCUMENTATION

Listed below are sample CSE-style entries for various types of Web sources.

Professional site

> Council of Science Editors. 2000. [Internet]. CSE home page. [cited 2008 Aug 18]. Available from: http://www.councilscienceeditors.org

Book

> Woolfram S. 2002. A new kind of science [Internet]. Champaign, IL: Wolfram Media. [cited 2008 June 7]. Available from: http://www .wolframscience.com/nksonline/toc.html

Article in a Journal

> Wood R. 2008. Climate change: Natural ups and downs. Nature [Internet]. [cited 2008 June 12]; 453. Available from: http://www .nature.com/nature/journal/v453/n7191/ full/453043a.html

Database

> Hydrographic Climate Database. 2007. [Internet]. Ottawa: Department of Fisheries and Oceans. [updated 2007 Feb 14; cited 2008 Oct 7]. Available from: http://www.mar.dfo-mpo.gc.ca/science/ocean/database/ doc2006/clim2006app.html

Article in a magazine

> Stabb M. 2000 Win. Citizens for science. Seasons [Internet]. [cited 2000 Feb 28]. Available from: http://www.ontarionature.org/seasons/article .php3?current_key=4

Article in a newspaper

> Glanz J. 2001 Jan 16. Experiments on dense matter evoke big bang. New York Times on the Web [Internet]. [cited 2001 Jan 16]. Available from: http://www.nytimes.com/2001/01/16/science/16QUAR.html

EXERCISES

IV-1 PARENTHETICAL CITATIONS

Work through the following questions using MLA, APA, or Chicago styles where indicated.

1. In MLA, APA, and Chicago styles, a parenthetical citation for a short quotation (i.e., a quotation integrated into the text) is placed (check one)
    (a) between the closing quotation mark and the period _____

    (b) after the period and the closing quotation mark _____

    (c) before the period and the closing quotation mark _____

2. Reproduce the sentence below, with MLA-, APA-, and Chicago-style parenthetical citations added. Base your citations on the following information: Smith is the author of *one* source in the essay; the source, a book entitled *The Comma*, was published in 2003; the quotation is from page 45.

    Smith contends that "there are only four major rules for the use of the comma."

MLA

_____

_____

APA

_____

_____

Chicago

_____

_____

IV DOCUMENTATION

3.   Reproduce the sentence below, with MLA-, APA-, and Chicago-style parenthetical citations added. The bibliographical information is the same as that given in question 2 but Smith is the author of *two* sources in the essay.

Smith contends that "there are only four major rules for the use of the comma."

MLA

_____

_____

APA

_____

_____

Chicago

_____

_____

4.   Reproduce the sentence below, with MLA-, APA-, and Chicago-style parenthetical citations added. The author, who is not named in the text, is Smith and the rest of the bibliographical information is the same as that given in question 2.

It has been said that "there are only four major rules for the use of the comma."

MLA

_____

_____

APA

_____

_____

Chicago

_____

_____

5.   Reproduce the sentence on the next page, with MLA-, APA-, and Chicago-style parenthetical citations added. The quotation is from page 93 of a book by Adams and Smith that was published in 1995.

According to one authority, "The semicolon is easy to use once you have mastered the comma."

MLA

_____

_____

APA

_____

_____

Chicago

_____

_____

6.   Reproduce the sentence below, with MLA-, APA-, and Chicago-style parenthetical citations added. The quotation is from page 576 of a 1998 book by Adams, Jones, Smith, and Thomas. Assume you are citing the source for the first time.

The authors assert that "no one has problems with the period."

MLA

_____

_____

APA

_____

_____

Chicago

_____

_____

7.   Reproduce the sentence below, with MLA-, APA-, and Chicago-style parenthetical citations added. The idea for the sentence comes from page 72 of an article entitled "Punctuation Problems." The article was published in 2000 and its author is not known.

A common error associated with independent clauses is the comma splice.

MLA

_____

_____

APA

_____

_____

Chicago

_____

_____

_____

8. Write an MLA-style parenthetical citation for the sentence below. The quotation is from Shakespeare's *Hamlet* (Act 3, Scene 1, line 56). Shakespeare's indecisive protagonist asks, "To be, or not to be: that is the question."

MLA

_____

_____

9. In MLA, APA, and Chicago styles, a parenthetical citation for a long quotation (i.e., a quotation set off from the text) is placed: (check one)

(a) inside the final quotation mark _____

(b) before the final period _____

(c) after the final period _____

10. Use Chicago's humanities style to write an endnote for the following quotations:

(a) The quotation is from pages 3–4 of *The Journals of Mary O'Brien 1828–1838*, edited by Audrey Saunders Miller and published by Macmillan Canada in 1968.

In an early journal entry, O'Brien writes of her voyage across the Atlantic: "Found my way to my berth after some difficulty and after sleeping soundly found my way out again. Neither gout nor prudence could prevent my first taking a twilight and then a starlight view of the scene."[1]

_____

_____

(b) The quotation is from p. 23 of David Macfarlane's *The Danger Tree*, published by Macfarlane Walter & Ross in Toronto in 1991.

To give his readers a sense of how many Newfoundlanders felt about the referendum votes that resulted in Newfoundland joining Canada, Macfarlane writes, "On the day that the results of the 1948 referendum were announced, my grandfather rose from his armchair in Grand Falls and turned off the radio. 'Oh my poor country,' he said. Nothing he saw of confederation ever changed his opinion."

_____

_____

IV-2 BIBLIOGRAPHY ENTRIES

1. According to MLA and Columbia humanities styles, how should entries in a works-cited list be formatted? (Check one.)

   (a) first line of the entry indented five spaces and subsequent lines flush left _____

   (b) all lines in the entry indented five spaces _____

   (c) first line of the entry flush left and subsequent lines indented five spaces _____

   (d) all lines in the entry flush left _____

   (e) b or c _____

2. According to APA and Columbia scientific styles, how should entries in a reference list be formatted? (Check one.)

   (a) first line of the entry indented five to seven spaces and subsequent lines flush left _____

   (b) all lines in the entry indented five to seven spaces _____

   (c) first line of the entry flush left and subsequent lines indented five to seven spaces _____

   (d) all lines in the entry flush left _____

   (e) a or c _____

3a. Entries in an MLA- or APA-style bibliography should be (check one)

   (a) single-spaced with a space between entries _____

   (b) single-spaced with no space between entries _____

   (c) double-spaced throughout _____

3b. Entries in a CSE-style bibliography should be (check one)

  (a) single-spaced with a space between entries _____

  (b) single-spaced with no space between entries _____

  (c) double-spaced throughout _____

4. Create MLA-, APA-, CSE, and Chicago-style entries using the following bibliographical information: Beth Ginsburg; New York; Harper and Row Ltd.; 2001; *A Guide to Punctuation.*

MLA

_____

_____

APA

_____

_____

Chicago

_____

_____

CSE

_____

_____

5. Create MLA-, APA-, CSE-, and Chicago-style entries using the following bibliographical information: *Business Communication: Strategies and Skills*; second edition; Richard Huseman, Dixie Stockmayer, John Hatfield, James Lahiff, John Penrose; Holt, Rinehart and Winston; Toronto; 1988.

MLA

_____

_____

APA

_____

_____

Chicago

_____

_____

CSE

_____

_____

6. Assume that your bibliography includes two sources by John Hagan: a book entitled *Structural Criminology* (Rutgers University Press, New Brunswick, New Jersey, 1989) and an article entitled "Comparing Crime and Criminalization in Canada and the U.S.A." *(Canadian Journal of Criminology,* volume 14, issue 3, 1989, pages 361–71). Create MLA- and APA-style entries for each Hagan source and show how the entries would be ordered in each bibliography.

MLA

_____

_____

APA

_____

_____

7. Use the following bibliographical information to create MLA- and APA-style entries for an article in an anthology: article—George Orwell's "Shooting an Elephant"; anthology—*Great Short Essays*, edited by James Cooke (Nelson Canada, Scarborough, Ontario, 1993).

MLA

_____

_____

APA

_____

_____

8. Create MLA-, APA-, and Chicago-style entries using the following bibliographical information: Judith Fitzgerald; "McLuhan, Not Atwood!"; *Books in Canada;* volume 24, issue 9; December 1995; pages 3–5.

MLA

_____

_____

APA

_____

_____

Chicago

_____

_____

9. On Wednesday, July 30, 2003, on CBC Radio One's program *Ideas,* Michael Ignatieff gave the first of five lectures, "The Lesser Evil," from the 2003 *Gifford Lectures* at the University of Edinburgh. Using this information, create an MLA-style radio program entry.

MLA

_____

_____

10. Create an MLA-style film entry using the following bibliographical information: *Margaret's Museum;* directed by Mort Ransen; starring Helena Bonham Carter, Kate Nelligan, Clive Russell, and Kenneth Welsh; released by Malofilm International in 1995.

MLA

_____

_____

11. Create an MLA-style sound-recording entry for "Sensory Deprivation," from Sloan's 1999 CD *Between the Bridges,* manufactured by murderecords.

MLA

_____

_____

12. Create an APA-style reference listing for one of the following website references:

(a) "The Budget Speech 2004" delivered by the Honourable Ralph Goodale, Minister of Finance, on Tuesday, March 23, 2004, in Parliament. The text of the speech was downloaded from the website http://www.fin.gc.ca/budget04/speech/speeche.htm on May 27, 2004.

(b) "The Budget Address for the Fiscal Year 2004–2005" delivered in the Nova Scotia House of Assembly on April 22, 2004, by the Honourable Peter Christie, Minister of Finance. The text of the speech was downloaded from the website http://www.gov.ns.ca/finance/budget04/budget_address.asp on May 28, 2004.

13. Create an MLA- or Columbia humanities-style works-cited entry for one of the following website references:

(a) A lecture delivered by John Ralston Saul at the University of New South Wales in Sydney, Australia, in January 1999 and broadcast on ABC TV. The full text of the address was downloaded on May 29, 2004, from the website http://www.abc.net.au/specials/saul/default.htm. The URL where the printable transcript of his address can be found is http://www.abc.net.au/specials/saul/fulltext.htm.

(b) Wilfred Owen's original manuscript for "Dulce et Decorum Est," which was downloaded from The Wilfred Owen Multimedia Digital Archive at http://www.hcu.ox.ac.uk/jtap/ on May 29, 2004. The actual page of the manuscript was at http://www.hcu.ox.ac.uk/jtap/images/mss/oefl/FascS/f316r.jpg.

14. Create a Chicago- or CSE-style bibliography entry for one of the following website references:

(a) An unsigned article entitled "Joseph R. Smallwood" in *TheFreeDictionary* at http://www.thefreedictionary.com/. The URL for the article is http://encyclopedia.thefreedictionary.com/Joseph+R+Smallwood. The site was accessed on June 1, 2004.

(b) The online reproduction of volume one of the first edition of *A Voyage to the Pacific Ocean* by James Cook and James King, originally published in four volumes in London for John Fielding in 1785. The online facsimile of the first edition starts on the webpage http://www.canadiana.org/ECO/PageView/17639/0003?id=557e512f784b27a2. The page from which different pages in the manuscript can be accessed is http://www.canadiana.org/ECO/mtq?doc=17639. The site where the facsimiles were located was accessed on May 30, 2004.

(c) The late-17th-century commentaries of William Dampier on the Galapagos Islands in his two books *Adventures of William Dampier* and *A New Voyage Round the World.* Dampier's commentary on the Galapagos Islands was accessed on January 7, 2005, at http://www .galapagos.to/TEXTS/DAMPIERW.HTM.

Basic Grammar

The parts of speech are a system used by grammarians to help explain the function and relationship of the words in sentences. Words can be divided into nine parts of speech: noun, pronoun, verb, adjective, adverb, conjunction, preposition, article, and interjection.

27-a Nouns

Nouns are words that name persons, places, things, or ideas.

> *Trudeau* remained a mysterious and reclusive *figure* for many *Canadians.*

> The *Prius hybrid is Toyota's entry* in the *competition* among *automakers* to sell fuel-efficient *cars.*

> The *focus group* was startled by the *revelation* that the *popcorn* sold in *theatres* contains more *fat* than a *hot dog.*

From these examples and others you can study for yourself, certain properties of the noun should become clear.

1. Nouns are frequently preceded by words like *the, a, an, my, your, some, each, every, his, this,* and *that.*

2. Nouns are often found in certain positions in a typical sentence. The most traditional positions are before the verb, after the verb, and after a preposition.

3. Nouns may be singular or plural in number. The plural form of a noun is most frequently formed by adding *-s* or *-es* to the singular form. Some nouns have only one form for both the singular and the plural (*moose, moose*). Other nouns are irregular in the way the singular form differs from the plural form (*wife, wives*).

4. Nouns tend to have certain endings that distinguish them from verbs or adjectives: *-ness, -ism, -ance, -ment.*

5. Nouns may function as subjects (and therefore appear in the subjective case) or objects (and therefore appear in the objective case). In the sentence *Shelley took the book from the shelf,* the noun *Shelley* is the subject, the noun *book* is the object, and the noun *shelf* is the object of the preposition *from.*

6. The apostrophe is used to form the possessive case of nouns (*Simpson's* lawn). The possessive case of singular nouns, including those that end in *-s,* is formed by adding *-'s* (*needle's* point, *Jones's* boat). The possessive case of plural nouns that end in *-s* is formed by adding only an apostrophe (*needles'* points).

7. Nouns can be classified into four categories according to the kind of entity they represent: a *common* noun names a general entity (*car*); a *proper* noun names a particular member of a class (*Chevrolet*); an

abstract noun names a quality or idea that is not tangible *(beauty)*; a *concrete* noun names something that is tangible *(grass)*. For more on proper nouns see page 369, Chapter 63.

8. A collective noun names a group of entities. Though it refers to more than one entity, its form is singular *(crowd, jury, team, committee)*. A singular pronoun is used to replace a collective noun (a *team* and *its* record) unless that noun refers to individual members of the group (a *team* and *their* paycheques).

ESL Focus   COUNTABLE AND NONCOUNTABLE NOUNS

There are two classes of nouns in English: countable and noncountable. Countable nouns name things that may be counted. They can be used with *one, a or an, the, many, several, some, few,* and numbers:

> five girls, the tree, several rocks, a few cities, many ideas

Singular countable nouns cannot appear alone. They must follow an article or a demonstrative or possessive adjective:

> a book, the pen, his ear, their project, this feeling, that rock

Plural countable nouns can appear alone, with *the,* or with numbers:

> teachers, the teachers, ten teachers

Noncountable nouns—which are sometimes called uncountable nouns or mass nouns—name things that are measured by their mass. They include some nouns that express abstraction:

> water, oxygen, butter, gold

> advice, anger, honesty, integrity

Noncountable nouns cannot be used with the indefinite articles *a* and *an.*

> a water, an oxygen, an advice, an integrity

Noncountable nouns can be used with *some, any,* or *more* to express quantity. They can also be connected to a countable noun to specify an amount:

> any water, ten litres of water

> some honesty, five examples of honesty

Most noncountable nouns do not have a plural form:

> advice, equipment, furniture, garbage, information, jewellery, luggage, machinery, money, scenery, traffic, vocabulary, water

continued

Nouns such as *candy, cereal, cheese, chicken, chocolate, fish, paper,* and *wine* can be countable or noncountable depending on their function in the sentence.

COUNT

Two wines that are good with dinner are Beaune and Volnay. [countable types of wine]

COUNT

I ate *two* candies. [countable pieces of candy]

NONCOUNT

It is nice to have *some wine* with dinner. [volume]

NONCOUNT

I like to eat *candy*. [general food type]

27-b Pronouns

A **pronoun** is a word that takes the place of a noun. The noun that the pronoun replaces is known as the pronoun's *antecedent*.

Although the *country* is rich in natural resources, *it* has a high unemployment rate.

Pronouns fall into nine categories: personal, possessive, reflexive, intensive, demonstrative, relative, interrogative, indefinite, and reciprocal.

PERSONAL PRONOUNS

A personal pronoun refers to specific persons or things. Personal pronouns agree with their antecedents in number and gender, but their case depends on their function in a sentence. Table 27-1 lists the 30 case forms of the personal pronoun. For more information about pronoun case, see Chapter 45.

POSSESSIVE PRONOUNS

A possessive pronoun indicates ownership.

John lost *his* wallet.

The employees are preparing *their* response to the layoffs.

TABLE 27-1 Personal Pronouns

SINGULAR

	SUBJECTIVE CASE	OBJECTIVE CASE	POSSESSIVE CASE
First person	I	me	my, mine
Second person	you	you	your, yours
Third person (masculine)	he	him	his
Third person (feminine)	she	her	her, hers
Third person (neuter)	it	it	its

PLURAL

First person	we	us	our, ours
Second person	you	you	your, yours
Third person (all genders)	they	them	their, theirs

ESL Focus   PERSONAL PRONOUNS AND CASE

In English, *case* refers to the form a noun or pronoun takes to indicate its grammatical function in a sentence. The following example sentences show singular personal pronouns in the subjective case (where they function as subjects), the objective case (where they function as objects), and the possessive case (where they function as possessives).

CASE	FIRST PERSON SINGULAR
SUBJECTIVE	*I* wrote my paper on Friday.
OBJECTIVE	The instructor told *me* I should have studied more.
POSSESSIVE	*My* paper did not receive a good mark.

CASE	SECOND PERSON SINGULAR
SUBJECTIVE	*You* got your paper back.
OBJECTIVE	The instructor gave *you* a good grade.
POSSESSIVE	*Your* grade in the course should be high.

CASE	THIRD PERSON SINGULAR
SUBJECTIVE	*He* said the exam would be difficult.
OBJECTIVE	The instructor told *him* to prepare for the exam.
POSSESSIVE	*His* grade will improve if he does well on the exam.

The case forms of plural personal pronouns are listed in Table 27-1.

REFLEXIVE PRONOUNS

Reflexive pronouns, which refer back to the subject of the sentence or clause in which they appear, are used to denote an action where the recipient and the doer are the same person or thing. A reflexive pronoun is formed by adding -*self* or -*selves* to a personal pronoun.

Did you hurt *yourself*?

She appointed *herself* to the board of directors.

The students treated *themselves* to a night on the town.

INTENSIVE PRONOUNS

Intensive pronouns are used to emphasize a noun (or its equivalent). They have the same form as reflexive pronouns.

The professor decided to conduct the seminar *herself.*

They *themselves* are responsible for the company's downfall.

The voters spoke to the prime minister *himself.*

DEMONSTRATIVE PRONOUNS

A demonstrative pronoun identifies or points to a noun.

That is my main objective.

These are Mary's belongings.

This is our finest china.

RELATIVE PRONOUNS

A relative pronoun introduces an adjective clause (see 28-f) and refers back to the noun or pronoun that the clause modifies.

The candidate *who* won the debate lost the election.

I sold my old Civic, *which* was in sad shape, for $1500.

Tomas found the keys *that* he had misplaced.

The relative pronouns *who, whose,* and *whom* refer to people; *which* refers to inanimate objects, animals, and groups of persons; and *that* refers to either things or persons. For more information about *that* and *which*, see 46-b.

INTERROGATIVE PRONOUNS

An interrogative pronoun introduces a question. Interrogative pronouns include *who, whom, whose, which,* and *what.*

Who was responsible for the Air India bombing?

Which book won the Giller Prize?

Whose car is parked in the reserved space?

INDEFINITE PRONOUNS

An indefinite pronoun makes a reference to a non-specific person or thing. Indefinite pronouns include *all, another, any, anyone, anything, each, everybody, everyone, everything, few, many, nobody, none, one, several, some,* and *somebody.* Many of these words may function as either pronouns or adjectives.

Does *anyone* know the solution to the problem? [pronoun]

Each client must pay a service fee. [adjective]

Indefinite pronouns often present problems in number and gender. (See 42-d.)

RECIPROCAL PRONOUNS

A reciprocal pronoun expresses a mutual relationship. There are only two reciprocal pronouns: *one another* and *each other.*

The classmates smiled tentatively at *one another* on the first day of the semester.

The two men complimented *each other* on their ties.

27-c Verbs

A **verb** is a word that expresses an action or a state of being. All verbs except *be* have four principal parts.

BASE FORM	I *open* the door.
PAST TENSE	I *opened* the door.
PAST PARTICIPLE	I have *opened* the door.
PRESENT PARTICIPLE	I am *opening* the door.

The principal parts are used to form tenses. There are four forms for each of the past, present, and future tenses of a verb (see Table 27-2).

TRANSITIVE AND INTRANSITIVE VERBS

A *transitive* verb takes an object, while an *intransitive* verb does not. An object is needed to complete the meaning of a transitive verb.

TABLE 27-2 Verb Tenses

PRESENT TENSE

SIMPLE PRESENT

The simple present indicates actions or conditions that are occurring now.

I stand	we stand
you stand	you stand
he, she, it stands	they stand

PRESENT PROGRESSIVE

The present progressive indicates actions or conditions that are ongoing.

I am standing	we are standing
you are standing	you are standing
he, she, it is standing	they are standing

PRESENT PERFECT

The present perfect indicates actions or conditions that began in the past and continue into the present.

I have stood	we have stood
you have stood	you have stood
he, she, it has stood	they have stood

PRESENT PERFECT PROGRESSIVE

The present perfect progressive indicates actions or conditions that began in the past, continue into the present, and may extend into the future.

I have been standing	we have been standing
you have been standing	you have been standing
he, she, it has been standing	they have been standing

PAST TENSE

SIMPLE PAST

The simple past indicates actions or conditions that occurred in the past.

I stood	we stood
you stood	you stood
he, she, it stood	they stood

PAST PROGRESSIVE

The past progressive indicates ongoing actions or conditions that occurred in the past.

I was standing	we were standing
you were standing	you were standing
he, she, it was standing	they were standing

TABLE 27-2 Verb Tenses (continued)

PAST PERFECT	The past perfect indicates actions or conditions that occurred in the past and were completed before some other past actions or conditions occurred.

I had stood	we had stood
you had stood	you had stood
he, she, it had stood	they had stood

PAST PERFECT PROGRESSIVE	The past perfect progressive indicates ongoing actions or conditions in the past that began before some other past actions or conditions began.

I had been standing	we had been standing
you had been standing	you had been standing
he, she, it had been standing	they had been standing

FUTURE TENSE

SIMPLE FUTURE	The simple future indicates actions or conditions that have yet to occur.

I will stand	we will stand
you will stand	you will stand
he, she, it will stand	they will stand

FUTURE PROGRESSIVE	The future progressive indicates ongoing actions or conditions that will occur in the future.

I will be standing	we will be standing
you will be standing	you will be standing
he, she, it will be standing	they will be standing

FUTURE PERFECT	The future perfect indicates actions or conditions that will be completed by some definite time in the future.

I will have stood	we will have stood
you will have stood	you will have stood
she, it will have stood	they will have stood

FUTURE PERFECT PROGRESSIVE	The future perfect progressive indicates ongoing actions or conditions that will be completed by some definite time in the future.

I will have been standing	we will have been standing
you will have been standing	you will have been standing
he, she, it will have been standing	they will have been standing

TRANSITIVE	The protester *threw* a pie at the politician. [The object *pie* completes the meaning of the verb.]
TRANSITIVE	I *varnished* the table this afternoon. [The object *table* completes the meaning of the verb.]
INTRANSITIVE	The villagers *gathered* in the square. [The verb has no receiver.]
INTRANSITIVE	The tourists *strolled* through Stanley Park. [The verb has no receiver.]

LINKING VERBS

A linking verb (V) connects the subject (S) with a *subject complement* (SC), a word or word group that identifies or describes the subject.

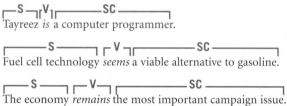

The most common linking verbs are *appear, become, feel, look, remain, seem, smell, sound, taste,* and forms of *be.*

ESL Focus   HELPING VERBS

Helping verbs (also known as *auxiliary* verbs) combine with main verbs to indicate tense. The most common helping verbs are forms of *be, have,* and *do.*

The forms of *be (am, is, are, was, were,* and *will be)* combine with the present-participle form of a verb (the *-ing* form) to create the progressive tense (see Table 27-2). The tense of the helping verb determines whether the past, present, or future progressive tense is formed.

I *am* writing a letter to confirm our agreement.

I *was* writing the letter when the phone call interrupted me.

I *will be* waiting in the lobby at noon.

The past-tense form of *be* combines with the past-participle form of a verb (the form ending in *-d, -ed, -n, -en,* or *-t*) to create the passive voice (see Chapter 50).

The letter *was* not *written* because of that interruption.

continued

The forms of *do* are used to establish questions, emphasis, and negation.

QUESTION   *Do* you want to finish the letter?

EMPHASIS   I *did* want to finish that letter.

NEGATION   I *don't* know when I will finish the letter.

NOTE: For questions, use forms of *do* when forms of *be* are not part of the answer. (*Do* you know what he said? Yes, I *do*.) Use forms of *be* when forms of that verb are part of the answer. (*Are* you going to the party? Yes, I *am*.)

The forms of *have* combine with the past-participle form to create the perfect tense.

PRESENT PERFECT   I *have* finished the letter confirming our agreement.

PAST PERFECT   I *had* finished the letter before you arrived.

FUTURE PERFECT   I *will have* finished the letter before you arrive.

Modal auxiliaries are helping verbs that express obligation, necessity, probability, and ability. Unlike the forms of *be, have,* and *do,* modals do not change form to indicate tense. There are nine modals: *can, could, will, would, may, might, must, shall,* and *should.*

OBLIGATION   My brother *should* wash the car.

NECESSITY   My brother *must* wash the car.

PROBABILITY   My brother *may* wash the car.

ABILITY   My brother *can* wash the car.

IRREGULAR VERBS

Although most verbs in English follow a regular pattern (I *talk* in the simple present tense, I *talked* in the simple past tense, I will be *talking* in the future progressive tense, and so forth), there are some two hundred irregular verbs. To learn how irregular verbs are conjugated, consult a dictionary or the list of common irregular verbs on page 216.

VERBALS

A verbal is a verb form that does not function as a verb in a sentence. There are three kinds of verbals: infinitives, participles, and gerunds. *Infinitives* can function as nouns, adjectives, or adverbs.

COMMON IRREGULAR VERBS

INFINITIVE FORM	PRESENT TENSE	PAST TENSE	PAST PARTICIPLE	FUTURE TENSE
to be	am, is, are	was, were	been	will be
to begin	begin(s)	began	begun	will begin
to break	break(s)	broke	broken	will break
to bring	bring(s)	brought	brought	will bring
to buy	buy(s)	bought	bought	will buy
to choose	choose(s)	chose	chosen	will choose
to come	come(s)	came	come	will come
to do	do(es)	did	done	will do
to drink	drink(s)	drank	drunk	will drink
to eat	eat(s)	ate	eaten	will eat
to feel	feel(s)	felt	felt	will feel
to find	find(s)	found	found	will find
to forget	forget(s)	forgot	forgotten forgot	will forget
to get	get(s)	got	gotten, got	will get
to give	give(s)	gave	given	will give
to go	go(es)	went	gone	will go
to have	have, has	had	had	will have
to hear	hear(s)	heard	heard	will hear
to hold	hold(s)	held	held	will hold
to keep	keep(s)	kept	kept	will keep
to know	know(s)	knew	known	will know
to lay	lay(s)	laid	laid	will lay
to lead	lead(s)	led	led	will lead
to let	let(s)	let	let	will let
to lie	lie(s)	lay	lain	will lie
to make	make(s)	made	made	will make
to mean	mean(s)	meant	meant	will mean
to prove	prove(s)	proved	proven, proved	will prove
to put	put(s)	put	put	will put
to read	read(s)	read	read	will read
to ride	ride(s)	rode	ridden	will ride
to say	say(s)	said	said	will say
to see	see(s)	saw	seen	will see
to send	send(s)	sent	sent	will send
to set	set(s)	set	set	will set
to sing	sing(s)	sang	sung	will sing
to sit	sit(s)	sat	sat	will sit
to speak	speak(s)	spoke	spoken	will speak
to swim	swim(s)	swam	swum	will swim
to take	take(s)	took	taken	will take
to tell	tell(s)	told	told	will tell
to think	think(s)	thought	thought	will think
to understand	understand(s)	understood	understood	will understand
to write	write(s)	wrote	written	will write

NOUN	*To win* is gratifying.
ADJECTIVE	They had little opportunity *to respond*.
ADVERB	He waited *to see* the replay.

Participles, whether present or past, function as adjectives.

| PRESENT PARTICIPLE | The *speeding* car was pulled over by the police. |
| PAST PARTICIPLE | The job required a *skilled* carpenter. |

Gerunds have the same form as present participles, but they function in sentences as nouns.

| GERUND | *Eating* is a necessity of life. |

ESL Focus GERUNDS AND INFINITIVES AFTER VERBS

A gerund is a verbal ending in *-ing (running, creating)*. An infinitive is a verbal consisting of the base form of a verb preceded by *to (to run, to create)*. Gerunds and infinitives that follow verbs function as direct objects (words or word groups that name the person or thing acted upon by the subject).

| GERUND AS OBJECT | He enjoyed *winning* the race. |
| INFINITIVE AS OBJECT | She agreed *to run* for office. |

Whether a gerund or an infinitive functions as the object in a sentence depends on the verb. Some verbs can be followed by a gerund but not by an infinitive. Other verbs can be followed by an infinitive but not by a gerund. Still other verbs can be followed by either a gerund or an infinitive.

VERBS FOLLOWED BY GERUND ONLY

admit	discuss	keep	recall
appreciate	enjoy	miss	regret
avoid	escape	postpone	risk
consider	finish	practise	stop
deny	imagine	quit	spend

• I regretted *spending* the money.

continued

VERBS FOLLOWED BY INFINITIVE ONLY

agree	expect	mean	promise
ask	have	need	refuse
beg	hope	offer	wait
claim	intend	plan	want
decide	manage	pretend	wish

- They need to *lower* their expectations.

VERBS FOLLOWED BY EITHER GERUND OR INFINITIVE

| begin | hate | love | start |
| continue | like | prefer | try |

- We began *counting* the votes. [gerund]

- We began to *count* the votes. [infinitive]

VOICE

The voice of a verb depends on whether the grammatical subject of the verb *acts* or *is acted upon*. If the subject acts, the verb is in the *active voice;* if it is acted upon, the verb is in the *passive voice.*

ACTIVE VOICE   The quarterback *threw* the ball downfield. [The quarterback *acts.*]

PASSIVE VOICE   The ball *was thrown* downfield by the quarterback. [The ball is *acted upon.*]

CHANGING PASSIVE VOICE INTO ACTIVE VOICE

1.   *Transitive verbs and passive voice:*

Some passive structures use a transitive verb (an action verb), which takes an object. In these sentences, the receiver of the action is the subject of the sentence, and the doer of the action is the object of the preposition *by.*

Passive voice

```
                  ┌─object of─┐
     ┌S┐ ┌─V─┐    │ prep by   │
The ball was kicked by Beckham.
```

To change this structure into active voice, give the sentence a subject that commits the action.

Active voice

┌─ S ─┐┌─ V ─┐┌─ DO ─┐
Beckham kicked the ball.

2.   *Passive structures that do not name anything that commits the action:*

In some passive structures, we are not told who or what is doing the action.

Passive voice

┌ S ┐┌─ V ──┐┌──────────── DO ────────────┐
It is suggested that students buy a good Canadian dictionary.

To turn this kind of passive structure into active voice, you need to supply the sentence with a subject committing the action.

Active voice

┌── S ──┐┌─ V ─┐┌──────────── DO ────────────┐
Instructors suggest that students buy a good Canadian dictionary.

Although writing is generally stronger when it is in the active voice, there are occasions when the passive voice is a more appropriate choice. Learn to distinguish one voice from the other, and be conscious of which voice you are using and why you are using it. For more information about active and passive voice, see Chapter 50. For problems with passive voice, see Chapter 13.

MOOD

Verbs may be cast in different moods depending on whether the writer wishes to make a factual statement (*indicative mood*), give a command (*imperative mood*), or express possibility rather than actuality (*subjunctive mood*). Generally, writers do not have difficulty distinguishing between the indicative and the imperative moods.

INDICATIVE	Toronto is in many respects the Chicago of Canada. [statement]
IMPERATIVE	Get me the evening newspaper. [command]

The subjunctive mood is more challenging. In the present subjunctive, the base form of the verb is used.

SUBJUNCTIVE	They proposed that she ∧ ~~leaves~~ *leave* as soon as possible.
SUBJUNCTIVE	It is essential that you ∧ ~~are~~ *be* appointed to the committee.

In the past subjunctive, the form of *be* is *were*.

were
SUBJUNCTIVE   If I ~~was~~ you, I'd follow his advice.

FORMS OF THE SUBJUNCTIVE

Formal writing requires the use of the subjunctive mood in statements about hypothetical conditions; *that* clauses following verbs that request, order, or recommend; and dependent clauses (see 28-f) beginning with *as if* or *as though*.

Hypothetical conditions   The subjunctive mood is used to express a condition that is wished for or imagined.

were
I wish he ~~was~~ here.

were
If I ~~was~~ wealthy, I'd quit this stupid job.

were
We could advance to the playoffs if our team ~~was~~ stronger.

That *clauses*   The subjunctive mood is used in *that* clauses following verbs such as *ask, command, insist, order, request, recommend,* and *suggest.*

accept
We recommend that the company ~~accepts~~ the deal.

quit
Sasha insists that her boyfriend ~~quits~~ smoking.

be
The lawyers ask that the verdict ~~is~~ overturned.

As if, as though *clauses*   The subjunctive is used in *as if* and *as though* clauses, which express a hypothetical comparison.

were
The rookie politician delivered his speech as if he ~~was~~ a contestant in a speed-speaking event.

were
The woman who anchors the local newscast acts as though she ~~was~~ a big star.

27-d Adjectives and Adverbs

Adjectives and adverbs are words used to modify other words. **Adjectives** are easier to understand than adverbs, since they modify only nouns or pronouns.

The *gifted* pianist won the *international* competition. [modify the nouns *pianist* and *competition*]

Dishevelled and *out of breath*, she boarded the plane. [modify the pronoun *she*]

The *confident* investor purchased *one thousand* shares. [modify the nouns *investor* and *shares*]

Adverbs modify verbs (or verbals), adjectives, other adverbs, or even entire clauses. Whereas adjectives answer the questions *which? what kind?* and *how many?* adverbs specify *in what manner, where, when, why,* and *how much.*

We drove *slowly* around the block. [modifies the verb *drove*]

The prime minister will convene a meeting *soon.* [modifies the verb *will convene*]

Antibiotics have proven to be an *extremely* important medical advance. [modifies the adjective *important*]

He plays the game *very* well. [modifies the adverb *well*]

Ironically, the spokesperson for Mothers Against Drunk Drivers was charged with impaired driving. [modifies the entire clause]

COMPARATIVES AND SUPERLATIVES

When comparing two items, use the comparative form of the appropriate adjectives and adverbs.

Chocolate is *better* than licorice.

When comparing more than two items, use the superlative form of the appropriate adjectives and adverbs.

Of all candy, chocolate is *best.*

The comparative of one-syllable and some two-syllable adjectives is formed by adding *-er* and the superlative by adding *-est (large, larger, largest).* The comparative of many adjectives of two or more syllables is formed by adding *more* and the superlative by adding *most (careful, more careful, most careful; interesting, more interesting, most interesting).*

The comparative of adjectives ending in *-y* is formed by replacing the *-y* with *-ier* and the superlative by replacing the *-y* with *-iest.* Do not form double comparatives or double superlatives by adding *more* or *most* to these forms of the comparative and superlative.

He was the *happiest* [not the *most happiest*] person there.

The following adjectives and adverbs have irregular comparative and superlative forms.

BASE FORM	COMPARATIVE	SUPERLATIVE
bad	worse	worst
badly	worse	worst
good	better	best
well	better	best
little	less	least
many	more	most
much	more	most
some	more	most

ESL Focus   INFINITIVES AND PARTICIPLES AS ADJECTIVES

In English, it is possible to use an infinitive or participle after certain verbs. When using *-ing* and *-ed* verbals as adjectives, be aware that your choice between the two endings will have a profound effect on the meaning of your statement.

The audience is *bored*. [The audience does not find the performance interesting.]

The audience is *boring*. [The audience does not stimulate the performer.]

The *exhausting* man made Manjinder uncomfortable. [The man was tiring to be with.]

The *exhausted* man made Manjinder uncomfortable. [The man was tired.]

Be sure to use the participle form that conveys your intended meaning.

CUMULATIVE AND COORDINATE ADJECTIVES

A series of adjectives can be cumulative or coordinate. A *cumulative* series is a sequence of adjectives in which each adjective modifies its successor *(light blue tweed material)*. Note that the adjectives in a cumulative series are not separated by commas.

In a *coordinate* series, the adjectives all modify the same noun and are therefore separated by commas *(talented, industrious, ambitious entrepreneurs)*. When coordinate adjectives are similar in nature, their order is unimportant *(smelly, overheated, humid room* and *overheated, smelly, humid room* are both acceptable). Order becomes an issue, however, when adjectives of different kinds occur in a series. You cannot say, for instance, *Norwegian, ten, fat, older gentlemen.* The following list will help you determine the correct order for your coordinate adjectives.

1. *Number or comparative or superlative form:* the, second, larger, smallest

2. *Evaluative adjective:* sour, dedicated, handsome

3. *Size:* huge, tiny, long

4. *Shape:* rectangular, round, ovoid

5. *Age:* old, young, eighteenth-century

6. *Colour:* magenta, green, scarlet

7. *Nationality:* Swedish, Canadian, Filipino

8. *Religion:* Muslim, Protestant, Jewish

9. *Material:* ceramic, pewter, wood

10. *Noun as adjective:* faculty lounge, student centre, economics curriculum

NOTE: You will rarely use more than three adjectives at a time to modify a particular noun.

ESL Focus   PLACEMENT OF ADVERBS

The placement of adverbs can cause ESL writers difficulty. By mastering a few rules, however, you can overcome that difficulty.

1. The position of an adverb is determined by what kind of adverb it is.

   a. Adverbs of *manner* (how a task is done) appear in the middle or at the end of the sentence.

      I *quickly* bent my mind to the task.

      I bent my mind to the task *quickly.*

   b. Adverbs of *time* are placed at the beginning or end of the sentence.

      In the morning, I eat lightly.

      I eat lightly *in the morning.*

continued

c. Adverbs of *place* appear at the end of the sentence.

He opened the door and went *into the room.*

d. Adverbs of *degree or emphasis* are placed directly in front of the word they modify.

He is *almost* ready to go to the game.

e. Adverbs of *frequency* are placed in the middle if they modify the verb and at the beginning if they modify the sentence.

She *always* likes to play golf.

Usually, she is early for her tee time.

2. An adverb that modifies an adjective or another adverb is placed before the word it modifies.

Tuition is *extremely* high today. [modifies the adjective *high*]

I was running *too* slowly to place well in the marathon. [modifies the adverb *slowly*]

EXCEPTION: The adverb *enough* always follows the adjective or adverb it modifies.

She dances well *enough.*

Do not place an adverb between a transitive verb and its direct object.

INCORRECT   He threw *quickly* the ball to the catcher.

REVISED   He *quickly* threw the ball to the catcher.

27-e Conjunctions

Conjunctions link words or word groups to one another and show the relationship between the elements connected.

COORDINATING CONJUNCTIONS

Coordinating conjunctions *(and, but, yet, or, for, nor, so)* join grammatically equal words, phrases, or clauses.

Shirley *and* Joseph have never got past their initial dislike of each other. [joins the words *Shirley* and *Joseph*]

You can park the scooter on the street *or* in the garage. [joins the phrases *on the street* and *in the garage*]

He didn't like the play, *so* he left at intermission. [joins the clauses *He didn't like the play* and *he left at intermission*]

SUBORDINATING CONJUNCTIONS

Subordinating conjunctions introduce dependent, or subordinate, clauses (see 28-f) and show the relationship between those clauses and independent clauses (see 28-e).

I couldn't risk leaving him alone *because* his despair seemed bottomless.

Unless the economy slows down, signs of inflation are bound to appear.

The investigators returned to the restaurant *where* the suspicious fire had occurred.

Following is a list of common subordinating conjunctions:

after	even though	so that	when
although	if	than	whenever
as	in order that	that	where
as if	once	though	whereas
because	rather than	unless	wherever
before	since	until	while

CORRELATIVE CONJUNCTIONS

Correlative conjunctions are pairs of conjunctions that join equal words or word groups.

both/and	neither/nor	not only/but also
either/or	not/but	whether/or

The joined words or word groups should be parallel grammatical elements.

We have *neither* the time *nor* the inclination to respond to your complaint.

The team resolved *not only* to reach the playoffs *but also* to win the Stanley Cup.

Either the newspaper prints a retraction *or* it faces a lawsuit.

For information about faulty parallel structure, see 43-d.

27-f Prepositions

Prepositions are connecting words that show the relationships between nouns or pronouns and other words in a sentence. A preposition can signal space and time *(above, below, near, after, before, until)* or exclusion *(except, but)*.

SPACE	The smokestack is *near* the river.
TIME	They went home *after* the show.
EXCLUSION	Everyone *but* Mr. Kwan signed the petition.

There are fewer than one hundred prepositions in English. Some common prepositions are listed below.

about	before	during	off
above	behind	except	on
across	below	for	onto
after	beside	from	out
against	between	in	over
among	beyond	inside	past
around	by	into	toward
as	concerning	near	under
at	down	of	within

ESL NOTE: The frequently idiomatic use of prepositions presents special challenges for ESL learners. Depending on where you live in Canada, you may talk about going *into* town, *down*town, *up*town, or even *over* town.

27-g Articles

There are three **articles** in English—*a, an,* and *the.* An article works like an adjective in that it appears before a noun and indicates either a specific version or a generic version of that noun.

SPECIFIC   The children set *the* table.

GENERIC   We want to purchase *a* table.

The correct use of *a* and *an* depends on the initial sound, not letter, of the word that follows. *A* should be used before all words beginning with a consonant sound and a sounded *h*. *An* appears before words beginning with a vowel sound or a silent *h*.

a computer	an apple
a European	an envelope
a historian	an hour
a hospital	an MP
a restaurant	an orange
a union	an uncle

ESL Focus   ARTICLES AND NOUNS

Articles can be a problem if your first language does not use articles before nouns. English uses articles in specific ways, some of which differ from how articles are used in other languages.

The article *the* precedes nouns that are specific; the articles *a* and *an* are used to mark nouns that are non-specific.

continued

SPECIFIC	He is *the first* person to win the game.
NON-SPECIFIC	He saw *a person* enter the house.
SPECIFIC	There is a tree in front of the house. *The tree* has become a local landmark. [The second *tree* is specific; it refers to something previously mentioned.]
NON-SPECIFIC	There is *a tree* in front of the house. There is also *a long, low hedge*. [Neither the tree nor the hedge is specific.]

WHEN TO USE *THE*	WHEN NOT TO USE AN ARTICLE
with names of countries that include such words as *kingdom, state, republic,* and union	with non-specific plural nouns and non-countable nouns
• the United Kingdom, the Republic of South Africa	• *Dogs* are good household pets; *rice* is a versatile staple food.
with plural proper nouns	with singular proper nouns
• the Rocky Mountains, the Toronto Maple Leafs, the United Nations, the Fungs	• John Smith, Dr. Mai Leung, Prime Minister Macdonald, Toronto, Quebec
with names of oceans, seas, rivers, gulfs, canals, and deserts	Exception
• the Atlantic, the Red River, the Sahara Desert	• My Canada is a Canada that is tolerant of cultural diversity.
with names of languages and proper names that include *of* in their title	with fields of study, names of diseases, and names of newspapers, magazines, and periodicals that do not have an article in the title
• the English language, the University of Manitoba	• geography, measles, *Maclean's* magazine

27-h Interjections

Interjections are isolated words or phrases that express emotion. They can stand alone as complete sentences or they can be connected to another sentence. If connected to another sentence, they are usually set off by punctuation marks. Exclamation marks set off intense interjections, while commas are used for mild interjections.

Hey! What do you think you're doing?

Oh! you startled me!

Ah, what an adorable puppy.

Oh well, at least you tried.

When you build a sentence, you draw on two sources. You have in your memory a large stock of words that you have gathered from your experience—reading, listening, speaking, consulting a dictionary. You also have in your mind a grammar, an implicit understanding of what words do what jobs in a sentence.

Your understanding of how to arrange words to say what you wish to say is known as *syntax,* the basic grammar from which you can build a wide variety of sentences. It is useful to remember that the parts of speech may be classified by function in that syntax: nouns and pronouns are *naming* words, verbs *assert* or *describe*, adjectives and adverbs *modify*, while prepositions, conjunctions, and articles *connect* or *link* sentence units together. That leaves *interjections* to do their unique job, as described above.

Once you are familiar with the parts of speech, you need to understand how they combine to make phrases and clauses, and how these phrases and clauses work to build sentences. A **phrase** is a group of words that functions as a noun, verb, or modifier; phrases cannot stand alone because they do not include both a subject (see 29-a) and a predicate (see 29-b). A **clause** is a group of words that contains both a subject and a predicate. There are two types of clauses: *dependent clauses*, which do not make a complete statement, and *independent clauses*, which do.

28-a Prepositional Phrases

The simplest building block in the English language beyond individual words is the **prepositional phrase**. A prepositional phrase consists of a preposition, its object, and any modifiers of the object. Although prepositional phrases usually function as adjectives or adverbs, they can function as subjects as well.

ADJECTIVE I hear the sparrows *in the trees.*

ADVERB *From their perches* they sing.

SUBJECT *In the trees* seems a happy place to be.

28-b Verbal Phrases

Verb forms that function as modifiers and nouns rather than verbs are called verbals; they include present participles (the *-ing* form of a verb), past participles (the form of the verb ending in *-ed, -d, -en, -n,* or *-t*), and infinitives (the base form of a verb preceded by *to*). A **verbal phrase** consists of a verbal with any modifiers, objects, or complements. There are three kinds of verbal phrases: participial, gerund, and infinitive.

PARTICIPIAL PHRASES

Participial phrases contain either present participles or past participles, and always function as adjectives.

Canadians *travelling abroad* need a valid Canadian passport.

Drenched to the skin, Mai admitted she should have carried an umbrella.

GERUND PHRASES

Present participles (verbals ending in *-ing*) that function as nouns are called gerunds. A gerund phrase is made up of a gerund with any modifier, object, or complement.

> *Being a good student* is difficult. [subject of the verb]

> John likes *being a good student.* [object of the verb]

INFINITIVE PHRASES

Infinitive phrases consist of an infinitive *(to see, to think, to kick, to be)* with any modifiers, objects, or complements. They can function as nouns, adjectives, or adverbs.

> *To be old* is a challenge. [subject of the verb]

> When he received a lifetime achievement award, the controversial director began *to feel vindicated.* [object of the verb]

> Travelling *to observe other cultures* can be an edifying experience. [adjective modifying *Travelling*]

> I laughed *to relieve my tension.* [adverb modifying *laughed*]

28-c Appositive Phrases

Appositives and appositive phrases identify or describe the nouns or pronouns that immediately precede them. The two types of appositives—restrictive and nonrestrictive—differ in their use of commas. A *restrictive appositive* is not set off with commas because it defines or limits the meaning of the noun or pronoun it names; it contains essential information and therefore could not be removed from the sentence. A *nonrestrictive appositive* is set off with commas because the information it contains is nonessential— that is, it expands on the meaning of the noun or pronoun but could be removed from the sentence without changing the basic meaning. (For more on commas and nonrestrictive elements, see 52-b.)

RESTRICTIVE	My sister *Tracy* is often afflicted with migraine. [The speaker has more than one sister.]
NONRESTRICTIVE	My sister, *Tracy,* is often afflicted with migraine. [Tracy is the speaker's only sister.]
RESTRICTIVE	The car *that is parked in the space with the expired meter* is about to be ticketed.
NONRESTRICTIVE	Haruki Murakami, *Japan's foremost contemporary novelist,* is becoming better known in Canada and other countries.

28-d Absolute Phrases

Absolute phrases are made up of nouns and participles, together with any modifiers or objects. An absolute phrase modifies an entire sentence or clause and is set off from the rest of the sentence with commas.

Her voice shaking with anger, she dismissed him from her office.

28-e Independent Clauses

An **independent clause** is a group of words that contains both a *subject* and a *predicate* and can stand alone as a complete sentence.

The door is closed.

The plane landed.

A *simple sentence,* one of the four sentence types (see 31-a), is made up of a single independent clause. It is possible to have a sentence that comprises only one or two words. The sentence *Sam yelled* or the command *Stop!* (*You* is understood) are examples of the simplest complete sentence type.

28-f Dependent Clauses

Dependent clauses (also known as *subordinate clauses*) contain both a *subject* and a *predicate* but cannot stand alone as complete sentences. A dependent clause functions within a sentence as an adverb, an adjective, or a noun.

ADVERB CLAUSES

Adverb clauses modify adjectives, adverbs, or words or groups of words that function as verbs. They begin with a subordinating conjunction and answer the questions *how, where, when,* or *why.*

When she reads the stock market report, Mel often finds new investment possibilities. [modifies a verb]

Upon learning that the winning lottery ticket was his, Tony looked happier *than he ever had.* [modifies an adjective]

The victims of the home invasion recounted the terrifying incident calmly, *as if they were still in shock.* [modifies another adverb]

ADJECTIVE CLAUSES

Adjective clauses (also known as *relative clauses*) modify nouns or pronouns. They begin with a relative pronoun *(who, whom, whose, whoever, whomever, that, which, whichever, what,* or *whatever)* or a relative adverb *(when, where, whether,* or *why)*.

The boy *who won the free tickets to the concert* was standing right in front of the stage when his name was called. [relative pronoun as subject of clause]

Jacques, *whom Kelly tackled,* had already gained fifteen yards on the play. [relative pronoun as object of clause]

The car *that was prominently featured in one of the early James Bond films* was an Aston Martin. [restrictive clause]

Henry Ford's Model T, *which remained in production for twenty years,* transformed Ford Motors into one of the world's leading automobile manufacturers. [nonrestrictive clause]

The reason *that Jack the Ripper committed his crimes* has eluded detectives for generations. [clause introduced by relative pronoun]

NOUN CLAUSES

Noun clauses function as subjects, direct objects, objects of prepositions, or subject complements. They begin with a relative pronoun *(who, whom, whose, whoever, whomever, that, which, whichever, what, whatever)* or with *when, where, whether, why,* or *how.* A noun clause can also function as an appositive and rename (identify or explain) a noun.

Whoever refuses to wear a seat belt courts disaster. [subject]

A business needs to know *what its customers want.* [direct object]

The mayoralty candidates scrambled for *whatever votes they could get.* [object of preposition]

You are *what you eat.* [subject complement]

The fact *that Mario had already seen the film* did not deter him from seeing it again. [appositive]

EXERCISES

EXERCISE V-1 PARTS OF SPEECH I

Underline the nouns, pronouns (excluding possessive pronouns), and verbs in each of the following sentences. Use numbers to identify the parts: 1 = noun, 2 = pronoun, 3 = verb.

1. Samuel Hearne's diary of his journeys leaves us an account of the rigours faced by the early explorers.

2. His account of the efforts he made to locate the Coppermine River is full of details about the Barren Lands he traversed.

3. Starvation was a constant companion on those journeys.

4. He writes of going five or six days without food, of his stomach shrinking, and of the intense pain he felt when he tried to force food into his stomach again.

5. Imagine how his civilized European audience would have reacted to Hearne's narrative of himself and his companions feasting on raw musk-ox meat.

6. Perhaps that is why he takes pains to explain how the absence of wood in the Barren Lands made fires an occasional luxury rather than a daily event.

7. No single story is more harrowing, however, than his account of the slaughter of a band of *Esquimeaux* by a war party of Athapaskans.

8. His use of *Esquimeaux* is interesting, revealing his belief that it is a French word.

9. The slaughter of this whole band of twenty—men, women, and children—is told in gory detail, including the writhing of a young girl against his legs as she dies.

10. Hearne then spends several paragraphs lamenting this barbarous act and reiterating his inability to avert it.

EXERCISE V-2 PARTS OF SPEECH II

In the paragraph below, underline, and identify using numbers, the following five parts of speech: 1 = adjective, 2 = adverb, 3= conjunction, 4 = preposition, 5 = article.

Example

  5   2   1   4 5

The mountain pine beetle that is rapidly destroying large areas of the

          4   3 2   4   4

forests of British Columbia and now Alberta came to North America in

   1   4   4

wooden crating used to transport goods from Asia to Canada.

How do we deal with our effect on the environment? The mere fact that we live and are active means we will have an impact on the environment. If we set aside land for parks, do we manage it actively, so that creeks run smoothly and the few roads we place in the parkland have a minimum impact upon the park? Or do we let nature take its course and limit our footprint upon the land? Do we, for instance, let the beaver build dams where they may, even if they flood some areas and starve others of water? Do we let forest fires started by lightning run their course, even though the fire will alter the landscape? How do we limit the effect of non-native pests that have no natural predators? The mountain pine beetle in western North America and the rabbit in Australia are examples of pests that have had a dramatic effect on an environment.

EXERCISE V-3 PHRASES

IDENTIFYING PHRASES

Underline and, using numbers, identify the type of phrase used in each of the following sentences: 1 = prepositional phrase, 2 = participial phrase, 3 = gerund phrase, 4 = infinitive phrase, 5 = appositive phrase, 6 = absolute phrase.

1. The mid-American plains, a vast landform straddling the Canadian border, have been described as boring.

2. The Canadian prairies form a horizontal world, unlike the vertical terrain of British Columbia.

3. A people assaulted by nature and by Eastern neglect, prairie dwellers concentrate on survival.

4. Amazed at the world's lack of interest in how it gets fed, they go stoically ahead with their sowing and reaping.

5. The elemental rhythms of their lives have provided a rich source of humour and faith for these people.

CONSTRUCTING PHRASES

For each of the following sentences, create the type of phrase named in the square brackets.

1. [absolute phrase] _____, the truck careened around the sharp curve.

2. *Pirates of the Caribbean: At the World's End,* [appositive phrase] _____, earned $140 million on the long weekend it was released.

3. In addition to [gerund phrase] _____, she was wet and shiv-
   ering from the evening's storm.

4. Having spent all his spare time grooving his golf swing, Anton wanted
   more than anything [infinitive phrase] _____.

5. The new laws will more or less outlaw smoking [prepositional phrase]
   _____.

EXERCISE V-4 CLAUSES

*Underline and, using numbers, identify each dependent and independent clause in
the following paragraph: 1= independent clause, 2 = dependent clause.*

As Canada matures as a country, its sense of what it means to be Canadian
changes. In the mid-twentieth century, the accepted view was that Canadians
were, for the main part, of European heritage, looking to western Europe, and in
particular, Great Britain and France, for a sense of identity and culture. The history taught in schools pointed to European exploration and focused on how the
fur trade was important to that exploration. It took for granted that the men of
the Hudson's Bay Company and the voyageurs of the North West Company were
the vanguard of those unearthing the riches of the land. Although much of the fur
trade depended upon Aboriginal peoples, their place was relegated to support for
exploration and exploitation, or opposition to European expansion and conquest.
Little in those school texts examined the immigration of peoples from other parts
of the world to Canada. The tone of mid-nineteenth-century newspaper articles
is reflected in Amor de Cosmos's remark about Chinese immigrants in his
Victoria paper *The Colonist*: "They may be inferior to Europeans and Americans
in energy and ability . . . and may remain among us a Pariah race; still they are
patient, easily governed and invariably industrious. . . . Hereafter, when the time

arrives that we can dispose with them, we will heartily second a check to their immigration. . . ." (qtd. in Morton 10). It is easy to see why status Indians did not get to vote federally until 1960, and Sikhs and people of Chinese and Japanese ancestry did not get the franchise until after World War II.

Sentence Elements

The sentence is the basic structure writers use to make the statements that form a paragraph. In order to write effective sentences, you need to understand the sentence's structure and the common sentence patterns writers employ. Similarly, you need to know the basic grammatical structure of the sentence and what each sentence's purpose is in order to create variety in your writing. The greater your knowledge of the sentence as a writing unit, the more likely you are to write clear and effective prose.

29 PARTS OF SENTENCES

The two main parts of a sentence are the subject and the predicate.

29-a Subjects

The *simple subject* (SS) of a sentence is a noun or pronoun that carries out an action, is acted upon, or has something said about it.

     SS
The *airplane* made an emergency landing.

A *complete subject* is made up of the simple subject and all the words that modify it.

The airplane with the damaged engine made an emergency landing.

A *compound subject* consists of two or more simple subjects joined by a coordinating conjunction or a correlative conjunction. (For information about coordinating and correlative conjunctions, see 27-e.)

    COMPOUND
 ┌ SUBJECT ┐
 SS   SS
Harper and Dion are political adversaries.

  ┌─COMPOUND SUBJECT─┐
      SS   SS
Neither the Oilers nor the Leafs advanced to the playoffs.

There are a variety of constructions in which the subject does not appear at the beginning of the sentence. In commands, the subject *you* is understood but not stated.

SS
[You] Get the ball!

SS
[You] Do your homework before watching TV!

In questions, the position of the subject changes.

SS
Why do *you* want to see that movie?

Sentences that begin with *there* can create confusion. *There* is not the subject of the sentence; it merely points to the subject that follows the verb.

SS
There is *Costa* over by the piano.

SS
There are *anchovies* on the pizza.

29-b Predicates

The *simple predicate* (SP) of a sentence is the main verb.

SP
Jeffrey Buttle *skated.*

A *complete predicate* consists of the main verb and its modifiers, together with any objects or complements and their modifiers.

┌──────────── COMPLETE PREDICATE ────────────┐
SP
Jeffrey Buttle *skated to a first-place finish at the 2008 World Championships.*

A *compound predicate* consists of two or more verbs that have the same subject and are joined by a coordinating conjunction or a correlative conjunction.

┌──────────── COMPOUND PREDICATE ────────────┐
SP   SP
Al *urged the company and advised the union to accept the deal.*

┌──────────── COMPOUND PREDICATE ────────────┐
SP   SP   SP
The forward *stole the puck, stickhandled down the ice, and scored.*

$$\overset{\displaystyle\overbrace{\qquad\qquad\qquad}^{\text{COMPOUND PRED}}}{\underset{\text{SP}}{}\quad\underset{\text{SP}}{}}$$

Mormons *neither drink nor smoke.*

$$\overset{\displaystyle\overbrace{\qquad\qquad\qquad\qquad\qquad}^{\text{COMPOUND PREDICATE}}}{\underset{\text{SP}}{}\qquad\qquad\qquad\underset{\text{SP}}{}}$$

The judge *not only found him guilty but also sentenced him.*

ESL Focus **RECOGNIZING SUBJECTS AND PREDICATES**

To express a complete thought, a sentence must include both a subject and a predicate. The subject consists of a noun or pronoun and the words surrounding that noun or pronoun. The predicate consists of the verb and the words surrounding that verb. The central element of a subject is the noun or pronoun, also known as the simple subject (SS). The central element of a predicate is the verb, also known as the simple predicate (SP).

   SS   SP
Dachshunds are unusual dogs. [*Dachshunds* is the noun; *are* is the verb.]

    SS   SP
That one chewed my shoes. [*One* is the pronoun; *chewed* is the verb.]

    SS SP
Then it jumped up on the sofa. [*It* is the pronoun; *jumped* is the verb.]

      SS   SP
My cousin's dachshund is virtually a member of the family. [*Dachshund* is the noun; *is* is the verb.]

29-c Direct and Indirect Objects

A *direct object* (DO) is a word or word group that names the person or thing acted upon by the subject (S). It answers the questions *what?* or *whom?* about the verb (V).

   S   V   DO
The dog bit *the man.*

In the preceding example, the direct object *the man* names the receiver of the verb *bit.* (*Whom* did the dog bite? *The man.*)

An *indirect object* (IO) is a noun or pronoun that answers the question *for whom?*, *to whom?*, *to what?*, or *for what?* about the verb.

```
S   V   IO ┌─ DO ┐
```
Sam gave *you* the tickets.

In the preceding example, the indirect object *you* is the receiver of the direct object *the tickets*.

When both objects are present in a sentence, the indirect object usually precedes the direct object.

```
        IO ┌── DO ──┐
```
Marie-Claire lent *me the dictionary*.

EXCEPTIONS: The direct object precedes the indirect object (1) when the indirect object is placed in a prepositional phrase;

```
   ┌─ DO ┐   ┌─ IO ┐
```
She sent *the package* to *her cousin*.

and (2) in sentences with the verbs *explain, describe, say, mention,* or *open*.

```
           IO ┌─ DO ┐
```
INCORRECT   Loa explained *Signe the concept*.

```
           ┌─ DO ┐   IO
```
REVISED   Loa explained *the concept to Signe*.

29-d Subject and Object Complements

A *subject complement* (SC) is a word or word group that follows a *linking verb* (forms of *be* and verbs such as *seem, appear, become, grow, remain, stay, prove, feel, look, smell, sound,* and *taste*) and identifies or describes the subject.

```
S  V ┌─SC ─┐
```
Guy is *our captain*.

```
┌── S ──┐  V  ┌──── SC ────┐
```
The company remains *a solid investment*.

An *object complement* is a word or group that follows a direct object and identifies or describes that object.

```
S     V   ┌─ DO ┐  OC
```
Natasha called Raj's project *superb*.

```
S       V      DO   ┌───── OC ─────┐
```
The reviewer pronounced the concert *an unmitigated disaster*.

One of the most important facts about English sentences is that, despite the endless variety in their shape and size, their rhythm and colour, they all fall into a limited number of structural patterns.

30-a Pattern 1: Subject–Verb

The simplest sentence pattern you can use is the subject–verb pattern. All that is necessary to complete this pattern is a subject and an *intransitive verb* (the kind of verb that takes no object).

   S   V
Birds fly.

   S   V
Fish swim.

Building on this pattern does not change the basic structure of subject–verb.

   S   V
Dogs bark frequently.

30-b Pattern 2: Subject–Verb–Direct Object

The verb in pattern 2 is the *transitive verb*, which transmits its action from a subject to an object.

     S   V   DO
The forward crosschecked the defenceman.

     S   V   DO
William and Mary drank a bottle of wine.

To better understand transitive verbs, think of the subject and transitive verb as asking the questions *who?* or *what?* and the direct object as answering either question.

Whom did the forward crosscheck? *The defenceman.*

What did William and Mary drink? *A bottle of wine.*

30-c Pattern 3: Subject–Verb–Subject Complement

Pattern 3 uses a linking verb (forms of *be* and verbs such as *appear, become, feel, grow, look, make, seem, smell,* and *sound*) to connect a subject to its complement. A *subject complement* is a word or word group that identifies or describes the subject.

   S   V   SC
That pie smells delicious.

```
S  V ┌─SC─┐
She is a lawyer.
```

```
S   V  ┌──── SC ────┐
He seems preoccupied today.
```

30-d Pattern 4: Subject–Verb–Indirect Object–Direct Object

Pattern 4 includes two objects: the direct object, which names the receiver of the action; and the indirect object, which identifies *to whom* or *to what* the action is done.

```
    S        V  ┌─IO─┐ ┌─DO─┐
The instructor assigns his students weekly tests.
```

```
 S  V ┌─DO─┐  ┌─IO─┐
She gave the bone to the dog.
```

```
┌── S ──┐  V  ┌── IO ──┐ ┌──DO──┐
Mrs. Scanlon bought her daughter a fax machine.
```

30-e Pattern 5: Subject–Verb–Direct Object–Object Complement

Pattern 5 includes an object complement, which identifies or describes the direct object named by the transitive verb.

```
┌── S ──┐  V     DO   ┌──── OC ────┐
Some people consider taxpayers an overburdened group.
```

```
┌──── S ──┐  V    DO  ┌── OC ──┐
The curling club named Gordon bonspiel chair.
```

SENTENCE TYPES

Another way to learn about sentences is to study their grammar. Grammatically, sentences are classified as *simple, compound, complex,* and *compound-complex.* You master sentence types over time, starting with the simplest types and progressing to the most complex.

31-a Simple Sentences

A simple sentence consists of one independent clause with no dependent clauses. The subject and/or predicate of the independent clause may be compound. A sentence may be long and complicated and still be a simple sentence as long as it connects only one subject or set of subjects to one action or set of actions.

Dick walked.

Dick and Jane walked to the store.

Until recently, Dick and Jane walked to the corner store and bought some candy every Saturday morning.

31-b Compound Sentences

A compound sentence consists of two or more independent clauses with no dependent clauses. It is therefore formed by coordination, with its two or more parts being equal. The clauses may be joined by a semicolon or by a comma and a coordinating conjunction *(and, but, or, nor, for, yet, so)*.

┌─INDEPENDENT CLAUSE─┐ ┌─INDEPENDENT CLAUSE─┐
The evidence is overwhelming; it cannot be denied or ignored.

┌─INDEPENDENT CLAUSE─┐   ┌─INDEPENDENT CLAUSE─┐
They want to go to Australia, but they can't afford the airfare.

31-c Complex Sentences

A complex sentence is composed of one independent clause (IC) with at least one dependent clause (DC). When a dependent clause precedes the independent clause, as in the first example below, it is set off with a comma.

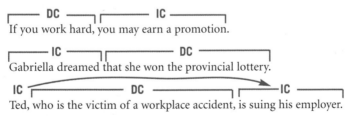

┌────── DC ──────┐┌────── IC ──────┐
If you work hard, you may earn a promotion.

┌────── IC ──────┐┌────── DC ──────┐
Gabriella dreamed that she won the provincial lottery.

IC ┌────────── DC ──────────┐┌──IC──────┐
Ted, who is the victim of a workplace accident, is suing his employer.

The complex sentence is formed through subordination, with one clause placed in a subordinate relationship to another clause. Complex sentences allow you to communicate more complex relationships than the coordinate or equal relationships conveyed by compound sentences. Subordinating conjunctions introduce the dependent clauses in complex sentences. (For a list of common subordinating conjunctions, see page 225.)

31-d Compound-Complex Sentences

A compound-complex sentence consists of two or more independent clauses and at least one dependent clause.

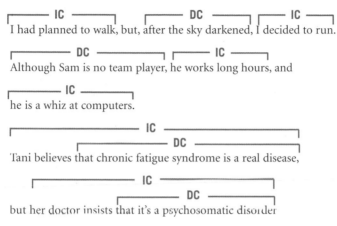

┌──── IC ────┐   ┌──── DC ────┐ ┌─ IC ─┐
I had planned to walk, but, after the sky darkened, I decided to run.

┌──── DC ────┐ ┌─ IC ─┐
Although Sam is no team player, he works long hours, and

┌──── IC ────┐
he is a whiz at computers.

┌──────── IC ────────┐
   ┌──── DC ────┐
Tani believes that chronic fatigue syndrome is a real disease,

┌──────── IC ────────┐
   ┌──── DC ────┐
but her doctor insists that it's a psychosomatic disorder

31-e The Tibbetts Model

An alternative approach to sentence grammar is presented by A. M. and Charlene Tibbetts.[1] The Tibbettses use the term BASE to denote the two elements essential to any independent clause—a subject and a predicate. A sentence's structure becomes more complex as additions are made to the BASE. There are three places where additions can be made:

1. An addition that is made before the BASE is called an *opener*.

2. An addition that comes between the BASE's subject part and its predicate part is called an *interrupter*.

3. An addition that follows the BASE is called a *closer*.

---

[1] See A. M. Tibbetts and Charlene Tibbetts, *Strategies of Rhetoric: With Handbook,* 5th ed. (Glenview, IL: Scott Foresman, 1987).

VI SENTENCE ELEMENTS

Here is the Tibbetts model applied to an example:

```
┌─────────── opener ───────────┐
Following the OPEC-imposed cuts in supply,

┌─ BA ─┐ ┌────── interrupter ──────┐
gas prices, always a leading economic indicator,

┌───── SE ─────┐ ┌────── closer ──────┐
increased rapidly, driving prices at the pump skyward.
```

NOTE: In addition to providing you with guidance as you learn to compose complex sentences, the Tibbetts model can help you use commas correctly. As you can see from the above example, the model's three sentence "joints"—the opener, the interrupter, and the closer—are not essential to the meaning of the sentence; they are nonrestrictive and thus have to be set off from the rest of the sentence with commas. When in doubt about whether a word, phrase, or clause is restrictive or nonrestrictive, you can apply the Tibbetts model to the problem.

32 SENTENCE PURPOSES

32-a Classification

Sentences can be classified in terms of the purposes they fulfill. *Declarative* sentences make a statement, *interrogative* sentences ask a question, *imperative* sentences convey a command, and *exclamatory* sentences express strong emotion.

DECLARATIVE	Mike Weir defeated Tiger Woods in match play at the 2007 President's Cup.
INTERROGATIVE	Did you see *Ratatouille*?
IMPERATIVE	Finish the report today.
EXCLAMATORY	What a sore loser she is!

32-b Formation of Interrogative Sentences

Interrogative sentences can be direct or indirect. A *direct question* asks a question directly and ends with a question mark. An *indirect question* is phrased differently: it reports rather than asks a question and is followed by a period.

DIRECT	Are the winters long in Winnipeg?
INDIRECT	She asked whether the winters were long in Winnipeg.

Declarative sentences with forms of the verb *to be (am, is, are, was,* and *were)* can be converted into direct questions by reversing the order of the subject and the verb.

DECLARATIVE	Increasing numbers of homeless people are sleeping on the street.
DIRECT	Are increasing numbers of homeless people sleeping on the street?

In direct questions that begin with *who, whom,* or *what,* the word order is determined by the case that is being used. If the subjective case is used, the subject *(who* or *what)* precedes the verb. If the objective case is used, the object *(whom* or *what)* appears before both the subject and the verb.

SUBJECTIVE	Who took the candy?
OBJECTIVE	Whom did the voters elect?

SENTENCE VARIETY

33

You can use your understanding of the sentence and its main components to inject some variety into your sentences. You can achieve variety in your writing by combining sentences, creating different sentence types, and making use of emphasis and contrast.

33-a Combining Sentence Elements

When you write, you are constantly creating relationships, assessing ideas, and determining priorities. In making these decisions, you are carrying out some of the basic planning and organizing of your work, but you are also determining whether an idea is coordinate (of equal value) or subordinate (of lesser value). This determination helps you to decide whether to combine particular sentence elements or leave them independent of each other.

Combining sentence elements can be as simple as joining subjects and predicates.

COMBINING SUBJECTS

Toronto has become a metropolis.

Montreal has become a metropolis.

Toronto and Montreal have become metropolises.

COMBINING PREDICATES

The football team runs the ball well.

The football team passes the ball well.

The football team runs and passes the ball well.

You can combine two independent clauses of equal importance by linking them with a comma and a coordinating conjunction *(and, but, so, for, or, nor, yet)*.

```
┌──────────────── INDEPENDENT CLAUSE ────────────────┐
Kim Campbell was Canada's first female prime minister,
```

```
        ┌─INDEPENDENT CLAUSE─┐
but she was in office very briefly.
```

If you were to decide that one independent clause is subordinate, you would rewrite it as a dependent clause.

```
┌──────────────── DEPENDENT CLAUSE ────────────────┐
Although Kim Campbell was Canada's first female prime minister,
```

```
    ┌─INDEPENDENT CLAUSE ─┐
she was in office very briefly.
```

The most important point in the preceding example is the brevity of Campbell's tenure, *not* the fact that she was Canada's first female prime minister. Making Campbell's prime ministership the most important point would reverse the emphasis.

```
    ┌──── DEPENDENT CLAUSE ────┐
Although she was in office very briefly,
```

```
┌──────── INDEPENDENT CLAUSE ────────┐
Kim Campbell was Canada's first female prime minister.
```

Instead of combining the two sentences about Campbell through either coordination or subordination, you could express the fact that Campbell was Canada's first female prime minister using an appositive phrase (see 28-c). The appositive phrase in the following example makes the brevity of Campbell's tenure the more important point.

```
    ┌──── APPOSITIVE PHRASE ────┐
Kim Campbell, Canada's first female prime minister, was in office very briefly.
```

33-b Combining Sentences

The following passage consists of simple sentences. As you read the passage, notice how choppy the flow of ideas is.

TOO CHOPPY Canada has many colourful place names. Some of them seem strange to us today. We do not remember the origin of those names. Baies de Ha Ha, Quebec, is a good example. Ha Ha comes from the old French word for dead end: *haha*. Other places are named after events. According to legend, Medicine Hat, Alberta, is such a place. A Cree medicine man lost his headdress at Medicine Hat. He was fleeing the Blackfoot.

To eliminate the choppiness in this passage, you could combine the second and third sentences to create a compound sentence and join the last three sentences to form a complex sentence.

REVISED Canada has many colourful place names. Some of them seem strange to us today, for we do not remember the origin of those names [*compound sentence*]. Baies de Ha Ha, Quebec, is a good example. Ha Ha comes from the old French word for dead end: *haha*. Other places are named after events. According to legend, Medicine Hat, Alberta, is the place where a Cree medicine man who was fleeing the Blackfoot lost his headdress [*complex sentence*].

You could transform the passage further by combining the first two sentences in the revised version to form a compound-complex sentence.

REVISED Although Canada has many colourful place names, some of them seem strange to us today, for we do not remember the origin of those names.

33-c Establishing Emphasis and Contrast

One way to keep your readers engaged is to introduce emphasis and contrast into your sentences. You can do so by *varying the lengths of your sentences, using periodic sentences where appropriate,* and *creating parallel structures.*

VARYING SENTENCE LENGTHS

The following passage consists of seven short sentences and a concluding long sentence. The long sentence derives much of its power from the contrast between its length and that of the sentences that precede it.

When he arrived in Ottawa, Stephen Harper puzzled veteran political observers. He was composed in personal presentation, conservative in dress, and careful in speech. He lacked the more immediately apparent magnetism of a Layton or a Chrétien. At press conferences, he stressed fact and precedent and detail rather than emotion. His common facial expression was limited to serious concern. He seemed a man born to wear a dark suit. He rarely joked or laughed aloud in public. *Behind this composed surface, however, lived the man who had succeeded in doing what more experienced political figures had failed to do—unite the conservative forces in Canada behind a single party.*

Equally effective is the next passage, in which the concluding short sentence is preceded by three long sentences.

Aside from a shared living space, what do the following species have in common—Atlantic cod, monkfish, bluefin tuna, rockfish, Atlantic salmon? If you answered that they are all on the list of fish we should avoid buying because their numbers are dangerously low, you are right. It is hard to get people to worry about a species as long as they keep appearing in stores for sale. It is also hard to get people to worry about fish when they are farmed in different areas of the world. But we are the people who virtually exterminated the most thriving species of fish ever known in Canada and made Newfoundlanders turn to fishing for oil instead of cod. *We need to start worrying.*

LOOSE AND PERIODIC SENTENCES

A loose or cumulative sentence begins with the subject and the predicate and then accumulates information as it progresses.

LOOSE *The ferry gently nosed into the dock,* the line of its journey still visible in its broadening wake.

In contrast, a periodic sentence builds to its main idea by not revealing the subject and predicate until the end.

PERIODIC The line of its journey still visible in its broadening wake, *the ferry gently nosed into the dock.*

You should use the periodic sentence sparingly. It is particularly effective in situations where you wish to place emphasis on the main idea in the independent clause. In the following pair of example sentences, the Dieppe facts gain significant additional power by being placed last rather than first in the sentence.

LOOSE *Nine hundred were killed and thirteen hundred were taken prisoner* of the five thousand Canadian troops who participated in the nine-hour battle at Dieppe.

PERIODIC Of the five thousand Canadian troops who participated in the nine-hour battle at Dieppe, *nine hundred were killed and thirteen hundred were taken prisoner.*

As these examples illustrate, a sentence element's position within a sentence determines the emphasis it receives.

PARALLELISM

Parallelism in a sentence is created by repeating grammatical elements, whether words, phrases, or entire clauses. Parallel structures give your writing a special kind of emphasis because they contain both repeating elements and changing elements. See how the phrase *They worried that* in the passage about the Calgary Flames establishes a repeating (or parallel) element and grants extra emphasis to the parts of the sentence that are different.

> In the 2004–2005 season, the Calgary Flames, after years of mediocre performance and consignment to the bottom half of the Western Conference, were worried heading into the post-Christmas part of the NHL season. *They worried that,* again, the opposition teams would score the timely and winning goals, get the quality of goaltending that single-handedly wins games, and generate the points necessary to qualify for the playoffs. *They worried that,* no matter how much effort they put into the last half of the season, they would be golfing while players on other teams excited their fans with playoff victories. They worried needlessly.

For more information about parallelism, see 37-c and 43-d.

EXERCISES

EXERCISE VI-1 IDENTIFYING SENTENCE PATTERNS

The five basic sentence patterns in English can be found in the following paragraph. For each of the seven numbered sentences, identify the sentence pattern—e.g., Pattern 2 (subject–verb–direct object).

(1) Ontario's huge population dwarfs that of all other provinces. (2) As a result, Ontario seems self-involved and narcissistic to the rest of us. (3) We consider it essential to our economy, essential to our international presence. (4) However, we fight its natural dominance with all our will. (5) Ontario offers us power, affluence, and culture. (6) Oddly, we resist that offering. (7) Like the mouse beside the elephant, we live quietly separate existences.

EXERCISE VI-2 IDENTIFYING SENTENCE TYPES

Identify the simple, compound, complex, and compound-complex sentences by placing the appropriate number at the beginning of each sentence: 1 = simple, 2 = compound, 3 = complex, 4 = compound-complex.

> Canada has a significant export business with China, but it pales in comparison with the mass of goods that Canada imports from China. Recently, this trade relationship has suffered in several key areas. The first challenge came from the tainted wheat gluten found in pet food that was exported to Canada from China. Menu Foods sold this food to Procter and Gamble, and they in turn marketed it in North American pet stores under names like Iams and Eukanuba. In both Canada and the United States, many pets died from the tainted food, and Menu Foods alone had to recall sixty million cans and pouches of pet food.

That recall received wide coverage in the media, and the reputation of Chinese exports suffered as a result. Shortly after, before the debate on pet food quality had ended, U.S. toy maker Mattel Inc. recalled millions of toys. It turned out that these toys, which had been imported from China, were covered in lead-based paints. Since the toys were intended for young children, and since children of this age like to put things in their mouth, there was a realistic fear that harm could come to these children as a result.

These incidents of pet food containing tainted wheat gluten and toys covered with lead-based paint highlight an important reality. The protections that Canadians assume exist to safeguard the quality of products made in Canada and sold to us don't necessarily exist in other countries. Since well over ninety percent of children's toys are manufactured in China, we have to rely on Chinese quality enforcement. In these two cases, that protection failed. China's announcement, in August, 2007, that it would improve its safety standards in food, drugs, agricultural, and other products may reassure some people.

However, it is hard to forget that the chief attraction of Chinese exported goods is their price point, and this low cost may be largely a product of lower wages and weak or nonexistent quality control. We should ask the companies importing from China to pay as much attention to the safety of their imported goods as they do to the price of those goods. We should also ask these companies to prepare their specifications for products from China with more diligence and to enforce these specifications at the point of production.

EXERCISE VI-3 COMBINING SENTENCES

The three sections below are made up of simple sentences. Where you think it would be advisable to do so, try to reduce the choppiness in these passages by combining simple sentences to form more complex sentence types. Remember, when you combine sentences, you may find you have to change the structure and arrangement of the phrases and clauses you are combining. You may even have to express the ideas differently. The objective is to maintain sentence variety while reducing the total number of sentences in the passage.

SECTION A

Much of the improvement in the Canadian economy beginning in 2004 was the result of our increased purchase of goods. This increase in retail purchasing was a result of two main influences. One influence was the rate of interest charged by banks. It was a very low rate. It was one of the lowest rates historically. The low interest rate translated into savings in some areas. People began paying less to carry their mortgages. It cost less to borrow money for purchases. Not surprisingly, our level of indebtedness grew. But that debt financed purchases. That spending kept money in circulation. The economy grew stronger. The second influence was a stronger Canadian dollar. This hurt exports. But it meant we paid less for imported goods. Many of our goods are imported. We pay more for such goods when our dollar is worth sixty-five cents based on an American dollar. When our dollar is worth more than an American dollar, imported goods are cheaper. So we purchase more. So our indebtedness increased. Basically, we bought more for less. Now we are finding out that can create its own kind of problem.

SECTION B

Reality programming on television has proven to have a wide appeal. It also has a continuing appeal. At one point, we might have expected that two or three maroonings of people on islands or in jungles would have been enough. But it hasn't been. Phony survivor plots have been joined by other versions of reality events we can spy on. One concerns travel. A group of people compete to get from one point to another in a limited time. Another places people in a house. Then the cameras roll. After those cameras start rolling, the people start acting. When they act or react, they show us something about themselves. Generally, it is far from being their good side. And the predictable elimination routine begins. The constant elements include the placing of people in an artificial situation. They also include a reason for those people to compete. They compete to stay there. They compete for money. More recently, they competed for fame. Young and generally untalented people lined up to compete for this potential fame. Generally, however, they competed for the right to embarrass themselves. The different element here was they got to embarrass themselves in front of strangers. And selected strangers got to say rude things to them to complete their humiliation. Reality programming is definitely strange. It is also a demeaning portrait of people.

SECTION C

Montreal is a community of communities. The city of Montreal is a distinct entity. So are St-Henri and Westmount. The two communities lie adjacent to each other. They are on the west side of downtown Montreal. Yet St-Henri is a working-class neighbourhood. Westmount is an affluent community. To the west of Westmount is Notre-Dame-de-Grâce. It is commonly called NDG. The locals fondly say that this initialism stands for No Damn Good. To the north of NDG lies Hampstead. It is a newer, wealthy neighbourhood. To the west of NDG lies Montreal West. It is a small, narrow community that was built in the first three decades of the twentieth century. To the north and east of the city of Montreal lies Outremont. It is one of the older, wealthy francophone communities. North of Outremont is the Town of Mount Royal. It is a newer, affluent community. To the south of the centre of downtown Montreal lies Pointe-St-Charles. It is the site of Victoria Bridge. Victoria Bridge was the first bridge to cross the St. Lawrence River. It was built by the Irish community of the Pointe. But Montreal is more than these communities. A fair list would have to include other communities. It would have to include Ville St. Pierre, Verdun, LaSalle, Lachine, Dorval, Pointe-Claire, Beaconsfield, Baie d'Urfé, Ste-Anne-de-Bellevue, Pierrefonds, Roxboro, Dollard des Ormeaux, St-Laurent, Côte St-Luc, Montréal-Nord, St-Léonard, Ville d'Anjou, Montreal Est, Pointe-aux-Trembles, Longueuil, St-Lambert, Greenfield Park, Brossard, Chomedey, and Laval. Even then, the list would not be complete.

Constructing Paragraphs

A paragraph can be simply defined as a set of sentences separated from other sets by the use of an indentation or line space preceding the initial sentence. It is important for the writer to realize that these sentences are grouped because all of them are about the same subject, sometimes called the paragraph's topic or claim. Typically, the paragraph addresses one subject; when writers introduce a new subject, they start a new paragraph.

The key qualities of a successful paragraph are *unity, coherence,* and *emphasis.* A unified paragraph focuses on a single subject or idea, while a coherent paragraph gains its unity from the linking of its sentences as they address that subject. Emphasis refers to the means the writer employs to engage and maintain the reader's interest, to make the paragraph not only informative but also clear and memorable. To write an effective paragraph, you need to know what the purpose of the paragraph is and how best to accomplish that purpose.

34 SEQUENCING IDEAS

Some of the most common ways to sequence the ideas in a paragraph are these:

- from general to specific
  - topic to illustration
  - problem to solution
  - claim to support for claim
- from specific to general
  - illustration to topic
- from least important or complex to most important or complex
- from most important or familiar to least important or familiar
- according to time
- according to space

Part of your understanding of sequencing may come from the sorting activities (listing, mind-mapping, branching, outlining, and so forth) that you engage in during the prewriting stage. When constructing a paragraph, you need to decide what the paragraph's *main claim* (or thesis) is and how it relates to the rest of the paragraph. You typically present the main claim in your paragraph's *lead* or *topic sentence.* Although the main claim may appear in the middle of your paragraph (as Figure 34-1 shows), it typically comes at the beginning or end.

Figure 34-1 Positioning the Main Claim

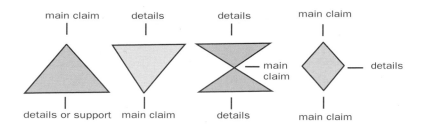

Ask yourself what the intent of your paragraph is. How does it relate to the paragraphs that precede and follow it? What transitions or links do you need to connect it to those paragraphs or to your topic? Your answers to these questions help you decide whether you want to start with your main claim and then support it with details or whether you want to start with one or more details and move to your main claim.

The following excerpt from Neil Bissoondath's *Selling Illusions* illustrates the relationship between the main claim (in italics) and the paragraph in which it appears.

> My own daughter will grow up knowing her families, seeing the photos of those now dead, hearing the stories of a distant past. She will know of her Québécois great-grandfather who went to war and returned damaged. She will know of her Trinidadian great-grandfather who began life in poverty and ended it in wealth. She will hear of the grandmothers she never knew. She will be acquainted with the varied streams of history that have come together to create her, at this particular time, in this particular place. *She will be acquainted, then, with her heritage: that body of knowledge that firmly plants the individual; the body of knowledge that requires no particular soil, no particular air; the body of knowledge that is like freedom because it can be carried safely through time and space in the capacious pocket of the mind, as orienting as a compass; the body of knowledge, then, that no one can ever steal or play with or manipulate into the service of social engineering.* Personal knowledge and sensitivities are media for growth. They are not the basis for public policy.
>
> — Neil Bissoondath, *Selling Illusions: The Cult of Multiculturalism in Canada*

Bissoondath's paragraph is complex. Its main claim, which appears near the end of the paragraph, is an extended and multi-layered idea. For that reason, Bissoondath sets it up carefully. He begins the paragraph with a statement about his daughter and her family history. In his next three statements, he provides illustrations of the knowledge his daughter will have of her family history. A second statement, which sums up the supporting details, leads into the author's main claim about the connection between family history and a person's roots. The paragraph concludes with a couple of transitional statements.

The structure of Bissoondath's paragraph, then, can be summed up as follows:

First statement

1. My own daughter will grow up knowing her families, seeing the photos of those now dead, hearing the stories of a distant past.

Details supporting the first statement

2. She will know of her Québécois great-grandfather who went to war and returned damaged.

3. She will know of her Trinidadian great-grandfather who began life in poverty and ended it in wealth.

4. She will hear of the grandmothers she never knew.

Second statement (sums up the supporting details)

5. She will be acquainted with the varied streams of history that have come together to create her, at this particular time, in this particular place.

Main claim (thesis)

6. She will be acquainted, then, with her heritage: that body of knowledge that firmly plants the individual; the body of knowledge that requires no particular soil, no particular air; the body of knowledge that is like freedom because it can be carried safely through time and space in the capacious pocket of the mind, as orienting as a compass; the body of knowledge, then, that no one can ever steal or play with or manipulate into the service of social engineering.

Transitional statements (prepare the reader for the next paragraph)

7. Personal knowledge and sensitivities are media for growth.

8. They are not the basis for public policy.

When you examine Bissoondath's last two statements, you can see how far he has travelled from his opening statement about his daughter and her family. The second of his transitional statements serves as a direct link to the topic of his book—the problems inherent in Canada's multicultural policy. In fact, the first word of his next paragraph is *multiculturalism.* Remember that your paragraphs must be more than just internally coherent, with individual parts supporting a main idea or claim; they must also relate logically to the paragraphs that precede and follow them.

PARAGRAPH PURPOSE

One of the keys to writing is to keep your purpose in mind. A paragraph's pattern of organization will largely depend on the paragraph's purpose. The following paragraph by Robertson Davies illustrates the relationship between sentences in a well-developed paragraph. The paragraph also illustrates how, with development, a paragraph will move through a series of levels of thought. As you read through the paragraph, note how each sentence relates to a specific element of the preceding sentence and how, as the paragraph develops, the focus of the development is controlled by this series of relationships and their link to the paragraph's purpose, which is the claim that Dickens's weakness is, in fact, a strength.

major claim	The powerful theatrical element in Dickens's writing has been deplored by critics. Edmund Wilson writes disparagingly of what he calls the ham element in Dickens. But what is ham? May not a great ham still be a great artist? Is it not an element of excess, of—no, not too much, but more than the rest of us are able to rise to in our lives and our creations? My dictionary gives as one definition of excess "over-stepping due limits." But whose due limits? Those of critics, who are always afraid of excess because they are at best classically restrained minds, and on the average crotch-bound, frightened people who fear that if they abandon themselves to the Dionysian excess of a great
example & transition	
question	
rhetorical question	
rhetorical question	
definition	
question & transition	
claim restated	

artist they may never again be able to retreat to their cosy nests? Do they not fear excess because it makes nonsense of their confined world? But the general public loves excess because it feeds upon the energy and invention of the great man, and thus it makes heroes of excessive characters, some worthy and many, it is to be feared, unworthy.

support

support

— Robertson Davies,
The Merry Heart

36 PARAGRAPH DEVELOPMENT

There are a variety of different patterns of organization you can use to develop your paragraphs. This section introduces eight developmental modes: *narration, description, exposition, example, explanation, classification and division, comparison and contrast,* and *definition.*

36-a Narration

A *narrative paragraph* tells you what happened or what is happening. To test the effectiveness of a narrative paragraph, ask the following questions:

- Is the illustration relevant or connected directly to the claim?
- Is the passage organized chronologically?
- Does the narrative show a cause-and-effect relationship between events?
- Is the lead or topic sentence the key to understanding the narrative?

The following paragraph, from Susanna Moodie's *Roughing It in the Bush,* recounts the events of a particular summer.

The summer of '35 was very wet; a circumstance so unusual in Canada that I have seen no season like it during my sojourn in the country. Our wheat crop promised to be both excellent and abundant; and the clearing and seeding sixteen acres, one way or the other, had cost us more than fifty pounds; still we hoped to realize something handsome by the sale of the product; and, as far as appearances went, all looked fair. The rain commenced about a week before the crop was fit for the sickle, and from that time until nearly the end of September was a mere succession of thunder showers; days of intense heat, succeeded by floods of rain . . .

— Susanna Moodie, *Roughing It in the Bush*

36-b Description

A *descriptive paragraph* sketches a portrait of a person, object, or event. To test the effectiveness of a descriptive paragraph, ask these questions:

- Are the description's various elements logically arranged?
- Do the primary elements of the description stand out?
- Does the description express a clear, dominant point of view?

A description does not have to be realistic to be effective. The following description of the Canadian prairies, from a book written in 1872, uses details that are more impressionistic than literal.

The great ocean itself does not present more infinite variety than does this prairie ocean of which we speak. In winter, a dazzling surface of purest snow; in early summer, a vast expanse of grass and pale pink roses; in autumn, too often a wild sea of raging fire. No ocean of water in the world can vie with its gorgeous sunsets; no solitude can equal the loneliness of a night-shadowed prairie: one feels the stillness and hears the silence, the wail of the prowling wolf makes the voice of solitude audible, the stars look down through infinite silence upon a silence almost as intense. This ocean has no past—time has been nought to it; and men have come and gone, leaving behind them no track, no vestige, of their presence.

— William Francis Butler, *The Great Lone Land*

36-c Exposition

Expository writing is writing that analyzes, that deals with ideas and engages the reader through its appeal to reason. The writing you do in postsecondary courses typically asks you to inform, persuade, or analyze in addressing a subject assigned to you. The most common structure of an *academic paragraph* is the stating of a claim and the use of reasoning to support that claim. The claim can be made early or late in the paragraph, but there must be reasoned support offered in defence of the claim. In the example that follows, the claim comes first.

> To readers brought up to respect "western" science, the most striking feature of Chinese civilization must be its technological pre-cocity. Huge libraries existed from early on. Printing by movable type had already appeared in eleventh-century China, and soon large numbers of books were in existence. Trade and industry, stimulated by the canal-building and population pressures, were equally sophisticated. Chinese cities were much larger than their equivalents in medieval Europe, and Chinese trade routes as extensive. Paper money had earlier expedited the flow of commerce and the growth of markets. By the later decades of the eleventh century, there existed an enormous iron industry in North China, producing around 125,000 tons per annum. . . . It is worth remarking that this production figure was far larger than the British iron output in the early stages of the Industrial Revolution, seven centuries later! The Chinese were also probably the first to invent true gunpowder; and cannons were used by the Ming to overthrow their Mongol rulers in the late fourteenth century.

> — Paul Kennedy, *The Rise and Fall of the Great Powers*

36-d Example or Illustration

An *example* or *illustration paragraph* uses a specific example to illustrate a point. In an example paragraph, the example should be clearly stated, and the point it is illustrating should be a valid one. The following excerpt, from a paragraph in Virginia Woolf's *A Room of One's Own*, uses the example of a fictitious sister to illustrate the unequal positions of men and women in Elizabethan England.

> . . . it would have been impossible . . . for any woman to have written the plays of Shakespeare in the age of Shakespeare. Let me imagine . . . what would have happened had Shakespeare had a wonderfully gifted sister, called Judith, let us say. Shakespeare himself went, very probably— his mother was an heiress—to the grammar school, where he may have learnt Latin . . . and the elements of grammar and logic. He was, it is well known, a wild boy who poached rabbits, perhaps shot a deer, and had, rather sooner than he should have done, to marry a woman in the neighbourhood, who bore him a child rather quicker than was right. That escapade sent him to seek his fortune in London. He had, it seemed, a taste for the theatre . . . became a successful actor, and lived at the hub of the universe. . . . Meanwhile his extraordinarily gifted sister . . . remained at home. She was as adventurous, as imaginative, as agog to see the world as he was. But she was not sent to school. She had no chance of learning grammar and logic. . . . She picked up a book now and then . . . and read a few pages. But then her parents came in and told her to mend the

stockings or mind the stew and not moon about with books and papers. . . . Soon . . . she was betrothed to the son of a neighbouring wool-stapler. She cried out that marriage was hateful to her, and for that she was severely beaten by her father. . . . She made up a small parcel of her belongings . . . and took the road to London. . . . She had the quickest fancy, a gift like her brother's, for the tune of words. Like him, she had a taste for the theatre. She stood at the stage door; she wanted to act, she said. Men laughed in her face. The manager—a fat, loose-lipped man—guffawed . . . no woman, he said, could possibly be an actress. He hinted—you can imagine what. . . .

— Virginia Woolf, *A Room of One's Own*

36-e Explanation

An *explanatory paragraph* explores its subject by breaking it into its constituent parts and describing those parts. The writer uses analysis to separate the whole into parts. Another way to write an explanation is to use *process* or *analogy*. A recipe is a common example of an explanation using process. Analogy uses a simpler or more familiar experience to help the reader understand an unfamiliar concept or process. The following paragraph, from Fred Hoyle's *The Nature of the Universe*, uses the metaphor of a balloon to explain how the universe is expanding.

> Short of using a lot of mathematics I cannot do better than use the analogy of a balloon with a large number of dots marked on its surface. If the balloon is blown up, the distances between the dots increase in the same way as the distances between galaxies. Here I should give a warning that this analogy must not be taken too strictly. There are several important respects in which it is definitely misleading. For example, the dots on the surface of a balloon would themselves increase in size as the balloon was being blown up. This is not the case for the galaxies, for their internal gravitational fields are sufficiently strong to prevent any such expansion. A further weakness of our analogy is that the surface of an ordinary balloon is two dimensional—that is to say, the points of its surface can be described by two co-ordinates; for example, by latitude and longitude. In the case of the universe we must think of the surface as possessing a third dimension. This is not as difficult as it may sound. We are all familiar with pictures in perspective—pictures in which artists have represented three-dimensional scenes on two-dimensional canvases. So it is not really a difficult conception to imagine the three dimensions of space as being confined to the surface of a balloon. But then what does the radius of the balloon represent, and what does it mean to say that the balloon is being blown up? The answer to this is that the radius of the balloon is a measure of time, and the passage of time has the effect of blowing up the balloon. . . .

— Fred Hoyle, *The Nature of the Universe*

VII CONSTRUCTING PARAGRAPHS

36-f Classification and Division

Classification groups items into categories on the basis of a unifying principle. The following paragraph classifies substances.

> Using the particle theory, we can understand two categories of substances: pure substances and mixtures. A pure substance contains only one kind of particle. For example, a piece of aluminum foil contains only aluminum particles. Sugar is a pure substance. It contains only sugar particles. A scoop of sugar made from Canadian sugar beets contains exactly the same kind of particles as a scoop of sugar made from Australian sugar cane. A mixture contains at least two different pure substances, or two different types of particles. When you drink a glass of milk or eat a cookie, you are consuming mixtures of different substances. Most common substances are mixtures.

> — Donald Plumb, *Science 9*

Division takes a single item and breaks it into parts. In the following paragraph, the topic—the listening process—is divided into three parts.

> We all listen to music according to our separate capacities. But for the sake of analysis, the whole listening process may become clearer if we break it up into its component parts, so to speak. In a certain sense we all listen to music on three separate planes. For lack of a better terminology, one might name these: (1) the sensuous plane, (2) the expressive plane, (3) the sheerly musical plane.

> — Aaron Copland, *What to Listen for in Music*

36-g Comparison and Contrast

When you *compare* two topics, you draw attention to their similarities. When you *contrast* two topics, you highlight their differences. A comparison and/or contrast paragraph may be structured in one of two ways. You may present information about one topic first and follow this with information about the other topic. The contrast paragraph below presents the two topics—small dinosaurs and large dinosaurs—one at a time.

> Dinosaurs may have been the biggest animals ever to walk the Earth, but not all of them were giants. One small, bipedal Late Jurassic dinosaur, Compsognathus, was no bigger than a rooster. This diminutive carnivore weighed just a few pounds and measured thirty-five inches at most from the tip of its snout to the end of its extremely long tail. At the opposite pole, bulky quadrupedal herbivores like Brachiosaurus (eighty-two feet long, sixty tons) come closer to what people picture as the classic dinosaur. But even this heavyweight has been outclassed. Discovered in 1972 and 1979 respectively, Supersaurus and, above all, Ultrasaurus smashed all records for sheer heft. Although

the identification of Ultrasaurus was based mostly on a shoulder blade, this creature probably measured more than ninety-eight feet in length and weighed an estimated 135 tons.

— Jean-Guy Michard, *The Reign of the Dinosaurs*

Alternatively, you may move back and forth between the two topics, focusing on particular aspects. The following paragraph uses this method to contrast the roles of leaders and managers.

The role of a leader is different from that of a manager. Good managers produce a degree of order and stability in employees. On the other hand, successful leaders bring about useful changes in an organization. An executive who discloses a new program for improving customer services is demonstrating leadership. An executive who answers questions about the new program and follows employee progress is demonstrating good management skills.

— Alan J. Auerbach and Shimon L. Dolan,
*Fundamentals of Organizational
Behaviour: The Canadian Context*

36-h Definition

A *definition paragraph* establishes the meaning of a word or a concept. Writers sometimes assume this simply means transferring a definition from a dictionary to the essay's page. But a definition paragraph deals with a stipulative definition, that is, what the writer takes a word or concept to mean. For a definition to occupy an entire paragraph, the subject is normally a complex one, as it is in the case of the westward advance of civilization in Canada. We write a definition paragraph when we have to explain clearly to our readers what a term or concept means. We may draw on example, history, contrast/comparison, even geography, for that definition, as the following example illustrates. For more on definition, see pages 51–52 and 70.

Civilization in Canada, as elsewhere, has advanced geometrically across the country, throwing down the long parallel lines of the railways, dividing up the farm lands into chess boards of square-mile sections and concession-line roads. There is little adaptation to nature: in both architecture and arrangement, Canadian cities and villages express rather an arrogant abstraction, the conquest of nature by an intelligence that does not love it. The word conquest suggests something military. . . . There are some features of this generally North American phenomenon that have a particular emphasis in Canada. It has been remarked . . . that Canadian expansion westward had a tight grip of authority over it that American expansion, with its outlaws and sheriffs and vigilantes and the like, did not have in the same measure. America moved from the back country to the wild west; Canada moved from a New France held down by British military occupation to a northwest patrolled by mounted police.

— Northrop Frye, "Conclusion," *Literary History of Canada*

36-i Causal Analysis

A *causal analysis* paragraph traces the reason why an event or process occurred. Often, the causal chain is longer than a single paragraph could cover, so an individual paragraph will trace only one constituent of that causal chain. For more on causal analysis, see pages 19–20. In the following paragraph, Richard Dawkins is considering the reasons why members of a species might choose to live together rather than separately. The entire causal argument runs several pages.

> If animals live together in groups their genes must get more benefit out of the association than they put in. A pack of hyenas can catch prey so much larger than a lone hyena can bring down that it pays each individual to hunt in a pack, even though this involves sharing food. It is probably for similar reasons that some spiders cooperate in building a huge communal web. Emperor penguins conserve heat by huddling together. Each one gains by presenting a smaller surface area to the elements than he would on his own. A fish who swims obliquely behind another fish may gain a hydrodynamic advantage from the turbulence produced by the fish in front. This could be partly why fish school. A related trick concerned with air turbulence is known to racing cyclists, and it may account for the V-formation of flying birds. There is probably competition to avoid the disadvantageous position at the head of the flock. Possibly the birds take turns as unwilling leader—a form of the delayed reciprocal-altruism to be discussed at the end of the chapter.

— Richard Dawkins, *The Selfish Gene*

37 PARAGRAPH TRANSITIONS

The connections between the sentences that make up a paragraph should be clear and logical. Transitions contribute to the coherence of a paragraph by indicating the precise relationships between sentences. Transitional devices include *transitional expressions, repetition,* and *parallel structure.*

37-a Transitional Expressions

Transitional expressions are words or phrases that signal the connections between sentences. As the following list indicates, transitional expressions perform a variety of functions.

TO ADD

additionally, also, and, as well, besides, further, furthermore, in addition, moreover, too

TO GIVE AN EXAMPLE

for example, for instance, indeed, in fact, namely, specifically, such as, to illustrate

TO INDICATE CLARIFICATION

in other words, simply put, that is, to clarify, to put it simply

TO INDICATE SEQUENCE

afterward, and then, before, finally, first (second, third), following, immediately, in the first place, last, next

TO EMPHASIZE OR FOCUS

above all, even, indeed, in fact, in particular, more importantly, obviously, of course, specifically, that is, truly

TO COMPARE

again, also, by the same token, in the same manner, in the same way, just as . . . so too, likewise, similarly

TO CONTRAST

although, but, conversely, despite, even though, however, in contrast, in spite of, instead, nevertheless, nonetheless, notwithstanding, on the contrary, on the other hand, rather, still, though, whereas, yet

TO INDICATE CONCESSION

admittedly, although it is true that, granted that, naturally, of course, to be sure

TO INDICATE TIME

after, after a while, afterward, as, as long as, as soon as, at last, at that time, at this point, before, currently, during, earlier, eventually, finally, formerly, immediately, in the future, in the meantime, in the past, lately, later, meanwhile, next, now, presently, recently, shortly, simultaneously, since, so far, soon, subsequently, temporarily, then, thereafter, until, when, while

TO INDICATE PLACE OR DIRECTION

above, adjacent to, around, behind, below, beyond, close to, elsewhere, farther on, here, inside, near, nearby, opposite, there, to the left, to the right, under, underneath

TO INDICATE CAUSE AND EFFECT

accordingly, as a result, because, consequently, due to, for this purpose, for this reason, hence, since, so, then, therefore, thereupon, thus, to this end

TO REPEAT, SUMMARIZE, OR CONCLUDE

after all, all in all, all told, altogether, as a result, as mentioned, as noted, finally, hence, in brief, in conclusion, in other words, in short, in summary, in the final analysis, on the whole, that is, therefore, thus, to conclude, to summarize, to sum up

37-b Repetition

Less common than the use of transitional expressions is the use of repetition to create transitions within paragraphs. The repeated element, which may be a word or phrase, functions as the paragraph's connective tissue. In Nellie McClung's novel *Purple Springs*, men petition a women's parliament for the right to vote. In her parody of the reasoning used by the premier of Manitoba, Sir Rodmond Roblin, to deny giving women the vote, McClung uses repetition (*unsettle, unsettled*) to unite the threads of an illogical argument for not giving men the vote:

> Would letting politics enter the home help matters? Ah no! Politics would unsettle our men. Unsettled men mean unsettled bills— unsettled bills mean broken homes—broken vows—and then divorce.

> — Nellie McClung, *Purple Springs*

37-c Parallel Structure

Parallel structures—a series of words, phrases, or clauses that have the same grammatical function—bring coherence to a paragraph by emphasizing the connections between ideas. In the first paragraph of *A Tale of Two Cities*, Dickens uses the parallel structures *it was the* and *we had/were* to link ideas that are diametrically opposed.

> It was the best of times, it was the worst of times, it was the age of wisdom, it was the age of foolishness, it was the epoch of belief, it was the epoch of incredulity, it was the season of Light, it was the season of Darkness, it was the spring of hope, it was the winter of despair, we had everything before us, we had nothing before us, we were all going direct to Heaven, we were all going direct the other way—in short, the period was so far like the present period, that some of its noisiest

authorities insisted on its being received, for good or for evil, in the superlative degree of comparison only.

— Charles Dickens, *A Tale of Two Cities*

For information about faulty parallel structure, see 43-d.

PARAGRAPH STRUCTURE

38

In the initial stages of constructing a paragraph, you are probably more concerned with clarifying your purpose and articulating your ideas than with deciding how your paragraph should be structured. You can increase the range of your composing choices, however, by becoming familiar with the structural patterns discussed in this section.

38-a The Levels Concept

The concept of *levels* in paragraphs was introduced by the American composition theorist Francis Christensen.[1] This concept issues from the fact that, in successful paragraphs, a sentence is a single unit of development. It cannot function on its own, however, and is necessarily connected to what comes before it and to what comes after. Christensen saw that a paragraph is created by combining sentences on different levels. The lead or topic sentence of a paragraph—the *level-one sentence* in Christensen's terms—contains the most general observation made in that paragraph about the paragraph's topic. A *level-two sentence* is a sentence that develops, in more detail, some part of what was said in the level-one sentence. A *level-three sentence* develops some aspect of what was conveyed in a level-two sentence. This feature of continuing subordination can lead, naturally, to further levels.

Christensen argued that every sentence in a paragraph is either subordinate or coordinate. A sentence that relates to the sentence immediately preceding it performs a *subordinate* function by developing more precisely some aspect of that sentence. A sentence that relates to the lead sentence is *coordinate* with the other sentences in the paragraph that relate to that lead sentence. When the first

VII CONSTRUCTING PARAGRAPHS

---

[1] See Francis Christensen, "A Generative Rhetoric of the Paragraph," in W. Ross Winterowd, ed., *Contemporary Rhetoric: A Conceptual Background with Readings* (New York: Harcourt Brace Jovanovich, 1975), 233–52.

sentence of a paragraph is the paragraph's lead sentence, the second sentence can be either subordinate or coordinate depending on its connection to the first sentence.

Christensen's model can be illustrated by identifying the level-one and level-two sentences in the passage that follows.

> British Columbia was one of the first provinces to escape the 1991–93 recession because of the extensive new markets it developed for its products over the previous decade. Of these new markets, none was more important than Southeast Asia.

LEVEL ONE   British Columbia was one of the first provinces to escape the 1991–93 recession because of the extensive new markets it developed for its products over the previous decade. [general observation]

LEVEL TWO   Of these new markets, none was more important than Southeast Asia. [more precise development of "new markets" aspect of preceding level-one sentence]

When you reason in your writing, Christensen observed, you do so principally by the methods of coordination and subordination. In coordination, a series of sentences develops a general observation; in subordination, each sentence represents a more detailed or exact development of an observation, image, or insight in the preceding sentence. Frequently, both coordination and subordination are used in a paragraph.

38-b Coordinate, Subordinate, and Mixed Structures

Christensen's analysis showed that it is possible to use three kinds of paragraph structures: *coordinate*, *subordinate*, and *mixed*. You can see how these structures work by examining the paragraphs that follow. In each paragraph, the number preceding each sentence denotes the level of that sentence.

COORDINATE STRUCTURE

(1) The paragraph, as a composing unit, has been affected by three principal influences in the last century. (2) First, it has been shortened by the advent of mass printing and publication and the commercial wish to please everyone. (2) Second, it has simplified its diction considerably, partly because of a shift in taste and style, partly because of an increasing uncertainty about the abilities of the mass reader. (2) Finally, it has increasingly resorted to artificial modes of emphasis in an attempt to sustain the reader's attention.

SUBORDINATE STRUCTURE

(1) The paragraph, a basic unit of composition, was severely influenced by the mass-production methods that came to dominate publishing in the last century. (2) Because the intended audience had increased tenfold and now included the barely literate as well as the rhetorically sophisticated, the paragraph grew shorter and shorter. (3) This condensing of average paragraph length was most notable in newspapers, where the narrow width of columns obscured the fact that most paragraphs had only a few sentences. (4) You should not be surprised, therefore, to learn that the average modern paragraph is less than half the length of a nineteenth-century paragraph.

MIXED STRUCTURE

(1) The paragraph, as a composing unit, has been affected by three principal influences in the last century. (2) It has been shortened by the advent of mass printing and publication and a wish to please everyone. (3) This shortening, gradual in the last part of the nineteenth century and the first quarter of the twentieth, was accelerated by Hemingway's example and the increasing influence of journalism. (2) The paragraph has also seen its diction simplified. (3) This can be attributed to shifts in both taste and style. (4) Certainly, the belief that plain speaking was honest speaking contributed to the dominance of a simpler vocabulary in the paragraph. (2) Finally, the paragraph came to cultivate increasingly artificial means of emphasis. (3) This is sharply evident in magazines appealing to teens where block letters, multiple exclamation marks, and direct, intimate address create a synthetically appealing style.

Christensen observed that the first sentence of a paragraph was frequently the lead or topic sentence, since the other sentences depended on it. He also discovered that the most common structure in paragraphs is the mixed sequence, in which both coordinate and subordinate patterns are used. Perhaps the most important truth demonstrated by Christensen's model is that all sentences in a paragraph must be connected in some way if your readers are to grasp your intentions. In practical terms, the model offers these benefits:

- *It helps you to edit your own work.* If you apply the levels analysis to your own writing, you quickly discover the paragraphs whose coherence is lacking or whose development is sketchy.
- *It helps you to compose paragraphs.* When you have a firm grasp of the structural options available to you, you write fuller and more convincing paragraphs.
- *It helps you to understand how published writers developed their own paragraphs.*

VII CONSTRUCTING PARAGRAPHS

In an essay, certain paragraphs perform unique tasks. The most important of these special-purpose paragraphs are introductory paragraphs, transitional paragraphs, and concluding paragraphs.

39-a Introductory Paragraphs

The first paragraph of an essay is probably the most demanding of all to write. In the opening paragraph, you must introduce your topic and at the same time capture the attention or interest of your readers. You have the option in this paragraph of giving your readers a clear sense of the direction of your essay. These three functions are fulfilled by means of the hook, the thesis statement (or claim), and the preview.

HOOK

The term *hook* comes from the world of television. Scriptwriters in that medium must establish a strong opening to discourage channel-surfing. As an essayist, you have a similar objective when composing your introductory paragraph. Techniques you can use to hook your readers include the following:

- a provocative quotation
- an engaging anecdote
- a powerful description
- a strong statement
- a memorable example
- a thought-provoking question
- an intriguing fact or statistic

All of these techniques or hooks must, of course, relate in some way to your topic.

THESIS STATEMENT

A key element of the opening paragraph is the thesis statement or claim, a single sentence that conveys your essay's central point or idea. Opening paragraphs typically move from the general to the specific, concluding with the most specific sentence in the paragraph—the thesis. In such a construction, general statements lead to more specific statements and all of these prepare readers for the thesis statement. For example, you could begin an introductory paragraph with a general statement about fisheries in Canada, follow this with increasingly specific statements about the industry, and conclude the paragraph with a thesis statement about the impact of federal fisheries policy on the Fraser River spring salmon runs over a four-year period.

PREVIEW

If you wish to give your readers a clear understanding of the direction your essay will take, you can include a preview in your opening paragraph. This element is optional. In an argument, for instance, you may elect not to present a preview because you may want your points, and the conclusion(s) you draw from them, to surprise the reader. A preview typically follows the thesis statement or claim.

In constructing a preview, you should avoid overused and stilted constructions such as *This essay will* . . . . See how naturally the author of the following opening paragraph previews her essay in the text following the thesis statement *Thin people need watching*. In the subsequent parts of her essay, Jordan writes about the different types of thin people who need watching.

> Caesar was right. Thin people need watching. I've been watching them for most of my adult life, and I don't like what I see. When these narrow fellows spring at me, I quiver to my toes. Thin people come in all personalities, most of them menacing. You've got your "together" thin person, your mechanical thin person, your condescending thin person, your tsk-tsk thin person, your efficiency expert thin person. All of them are dangerous.

> — Suzanne Jordan, "That Lean and Hungry Look"

39-b Transitional Paragraphs

Transitional paragraphs are used to signal a major transition between ideas. A transitional paragraph typically performs three tasks: summarizing, emphasizing, and previewing. It may also provide background on a subject.

The following excerpt from Sally Armstrong's essay "Veiled Threats: The Women of Afghanistan" illustrates how a transitional paragraph (shown here in italics) can knit together a narrative. When you read over the three paragraphs, you will see that, whereas the first paragraph focuses on the specific topic of the essay—the women of Afghanistan—the second paragraph shifts to an overview of the recent history of the country since 1972. In this paragraph, Armstrong provides background by describing how the Taliban came to power in Afghanistan and imposed its edicts on the women of the country. The third paragraph is a continuation of the general information that supports and explains the specific plight of the women of Afghanistan. One purpose of a transitional paragraph is to offer background on a subject being discussed.

> There are 30,000 widows in Kabul who are virtually destitute. When asked how they should cope, the Taliban reply again, "Let them die." In a particularly hateful response to the handicapped, some men have told their disabled wives that they'll no longer require prostheses as they no longer need to be seen outside.

Afghanistan is a country about the size of Manitoba. It has five major tribes that have warred endlessly throughout the centuries. It was a monarchy until 1972 and a republic until 1978 when the Soviets invaded. Then it became one of the last violent crucibles of the Cold War. The detested boot camp rule of the Soviets spawned the Mujahideen (Freedom Fighter) camps across the border in Northern Pakistan. Funded by the United States, Saudi Arabia and Pakistan itself, the Mujahideen were like folk heroes who represented a spiritual return to pre-communist Afghanistan. But within the camps, several factions jockeyed for power, each pretending to be more religious than the next to win the support of the people. In the process they planted the seeds for the fratricidal bloodbath that began with the defeat of the Communists. Life under the victorious Mujahideen proved to be as violent as it had been under the Communists and more religiously strict than the people had ever imagined. Enter the Taliban, young hoodlums who had never been to school and never known anything but war. Presently they control two-thirds of the country.

While the world has clearly grown weary of Afghanistan and its 18 years of war, the people trapped in that country and the 500,000 refugees who escaped to border towns in Northern Pakistan are hoping someone will "take up our quarrel with the foe." Although the Taliban have no official role in the Islamic Republic of Pakistan, their presence throughout the north is threatening. The steady rise in fundamentalism in Pakistan leaves many Afghan refugees and native Pakistanis in this northern region wary. Many women continue to wear burqas out of fear. Others are careful to cover up just to avoid attention from the extremists. There's an uneasy calm. It's like waiting for an intruder.

— Sally Armstrong, "Veiled Threats:
The Women of Afghanistan"

39-c Concluding Paragraphs

The final paragraph of an essay fulfills three basic functions:

(1) it summarizes the essay's key points;

(2) it restates the claim or thesis; and

(3) it indicates the general significance of the claim or thesis.

In addition, a concluding paragraph should strike a note of finality; it should leave readers with the impression that nothing of importance has been left unsaid.

Concluding paragraphs usually follow a specific-to-general pattern (the reverse of the general-to-specific pattern typical of introductory paragraphs). See how Geoffrey Bibby finishes his essay on the work of archaeologists:

Further we cannot go. We have been probing, with our picks and shovels and builder's trowels, not merely into the brains but perhaps also into the souls of men, and we must be content if our diagnosis is imprecise and inconclusive. But it does take us a little way beyond the conventional archaeological picture of the material lives of the simple peasants of barbarian Europe. Behind the material life, interleaved with it and perhaps dominating it, was the world of taboos and magic and superstition, the spirits of the earth and the heavens, who had to be bribed or placated or bought off. One of the occupational risks of Iron Age Europe, right up to the end of the Viking period scarcely a thousand years ago, was that of being chosen as victim, as the price to be paid for prosperity in the next harvest or victory in the next war. It was only with the coming of Christianity that human sacrifice ceased in Europe; looking on the bodies from the Danish bogs we should do well to realize that there, but for the grace of God, lie we.

— Geoffrey Bibby, "The Body in the Bog"

Bibby wants to lift the reader's mind beyond the facts he has recounted in his reconstruction of the events surrounding the discovery of bog bodies in Europe. His conclusion mentions his topic and the discovery it led to, thus fulfilling the basic need of a conclusion to summarize and restate. But Bibby's chief concern is to leave his readers with a sense of the general significance of his topic. He does this quite powerfully, employing echoes from his introductory paragraph, in which he wrote of archaeologists "probing into the workings of the human brain with picks, shovels, and builder's trowels." Now, in his conclusion, he evokes those tools again, giving the essay a rounded effect. He also designs his last sentence so that it carries an air of finality, with its concluding *lie we*. Remember that the ending of your essay should sound like the last word on the topic.

COMMON PARAGRAPH PROBLEMS

A number of factors can reduce the effectiveness of your paragraphs. Here are the most common pitfalls:

- undefined purpose or thesis
- lack of coherence
- wordy expression
- extraneous detail
- inappropriate example
- poor organization

- lack of unity
- confusing or missing transitions

The marginal notes that accompany the following paragraphs identify and comment on problems you should take care to avoid when constructing a paragraph.

POORLY ORGANIZED PARAGRAPH

Shift from settlement to expansion and authority.	In the "Conclusion" to his *Literary History of Canada*, Northrop Frye makes some interesting comments about the difference between how Canada and the United States were settled. He notes that, in Canada, the westward expansion had a "tight grip of authority over it" (829), and that it progressed geometrically.
No transition. New France relates only to half of first sentence. Vague transition.	New France was held by military rule, and the land was divided up into "chessboards of square mile sections." The United States had a historical imagination that
Related only marginally to first sentence.	embraced the image of "another redskin biting the dust" (830).
No transition. Undeveloped example. No link to opening claim or other statements.	John Brown and Vanzetti were in the American conscience, but Canada had Louis Riel. Other than these Canadian anomalies, he notes that the last two centuries had been a conquest of "the unconscious forces of nature" (830).

You cannot expect your readers to know how items in a passage are related to one another if you do not supply that information. You cannot assume that your readers have access to your sources to help them follow your analysis. Remember, it is easy to distort an argument when you leave out necessary information. Knowing how to summarize someone's commentary is a skill that needs practice.

Announced topic has two parts.	The debate about public transit quickly dissolves into two basic alignments of people, those who want to spend money on a public or collective purpose, and those who don't. The proponents of improved public transit naturally point to the environmental improvements that will follow from people leaving their cars at home. Our cities are increasingly unhealthy, violent, and expensive to run. This drives ever larger numbers of people to the sub-urban areas, where taxes are lower and the air is cleaner. Once settled, these people fight new development. They wonder what the lungs of our city will be if we cut down all the trees to build houses. Houses are, in fact, a double hit on the environment because they are made of wood. It follows, therefore, that people who oppose public transit are interested only in their right to have a car. Can we seriously defend such a right when we spend so much on streets and avenues and highways for cars to travel on? It's not clear to me that we can.
Writer shifts to new topic.	
Shift is even greater; by now, the reader has forgotten the initial claim.	
After three sentences on one topic, writer shifts again.	
Belatedly, writer remembers that original topic was public transit.	
At this point, nothing is clear to the reader; shifts from one topic to another create an incoherent paragraph.	

The author of this paragraph cannot seem to decide what the paragraph's purpose is. The lead or topic sentence that opens the paragraph is clear enough, but it is followed by a series of unrelated points.

If the writer had focused throughout on the main claim or thesis, the paragraph might have looked something like this:

The debate about public transit quickly resolves into two groups of people aligned against each other: those who want to spend money on a public or collective purpose, and those who do not. The proponents of public transit expansion cite the environmental improvements that follow when people leave their cars at home: cleaner air, reduced pollution of the upper atmosphere, even a decline in the global warming trend. Opponents of expanded public transit counter by stressing that transit systems never pay for themselves and require continual subsidy, cause deterioration in the neighbourhoods they traverse, and represent the many paying for the few. These arguments are all variations on a theme; the opponents see their immediate and short-term self-interest threatened by an expanded public transit system.

The revised paragraph exemplifies *unity* because it focuses on one topic only and *coherence* because the sentences within it relate to one another and follow a logical sequence.

EXERCISES

EXERCISE VII-1   PARAGRAPH BREAKS

The following passage, from Emily Carr's Klee Wyck, *has had its paragraph breaks removed. Insert the paragraph symbol (¶) where you think the original paragraph breaks might have been.*

I was down on the point watching a school of porpoises at play off Trail Island when a canoe came round the headland. She was steering straight for our beach. The Government allowed the Indians to use the beaches when they were travelling, so they made camp and slept wherever the night happened to fall. In the canoe were a man and woman, half a dozen children, a dog, a cat and a coop of fowls, besides all the Indians' things. She was a West Coast canoe—dug out of a great red cedar tree. She was long and slim, with a high prow shaped like a wolf's head. She was painted black with a line of blue running round the top of the inside. Her stern went straight down into the water. The Indian mother sat in the stern and steered the canoe with a paddle. When the canoe was near the shore, the man and the woman drove their paddles strong and hard, and the canoe shot high up on to the pebbles with a growling sound. The barefoot children swarmed over her side and waded ashore. The man and the woman got out and dragged the canoe high on-to the beach. There was a baby tucked into the woman's shawl; the shawl bound the child close to her body. She waddled slowly across the beach, her bare feet settling in the sand with every step, her fleshy body squared down on to her feet. All the movements of the man and the woman were slow and steady; their springless feet padded flatly; their backs and shoulders were straight. The few words they said to each other were guttural and low-pitched. The Indian children did not race up and down the beach, astonished at strange new things, as we always were. These children belonged to the beach, and were as much a part of it as the drift-logs and the stones. The man gathered a handful of sticks and lit a fire. They took a big iron pot and their food out of the canoe, and set them by the fire. The woman sat among the things with her baby—she managed the shawl and the baby so that she had her arms free, and her hands moved among the kettles and food.

— Emily Carr, *Klee Wyck*

EXERCISE VII-2 PARAGRAPH DEVELOPMENT

This exercise asks you to develop your paragraph development skills by using different methods of development to write paragraphs on the same topic—McJobs. Below are materials you can use in creating these paragraphs.

- Roslyn Kunin, a prominent economist, was one of the first to point out that the recovery after the recession of the early 1980s was different in kind from previous recoveries. She observed that the data on the recovery made it clear that, although the number of jobs had recovered to, and slightly surpassed, the number of pre-recession jobs, these jobs were different in kind from the jobs they had replaced.

- Generally, the new jobs paid less and were more subject to economic shifts.

- Perhaps the most notable shifts were toward the service sector and away from the industrial sector. Factory and production jobs were lost, and service jobs replaced them.

- It followed, therefore, that these new jobs were less frequently unionized, carried fewer benefits, offered a lower wage, and provided fewer hours in the week.

- Many of these jobs did not offer a sufficient number of hours per week to entitle the worker to a pension plan or other important security features.

- Some analysts saw the fast-food industry and the video-rental business as perfect models of this new phenomenon.

- In the 1990s, the phenomenon was sufficiently advanced that the labour projections of both the United States and Canada showed that only one of the top ten growth areas for jobs required any postsecondary education. Retail service and office cleaning began to show up as two of the highest-growth areas for work in the future.

- This development may also account for the fact that youths are remaining at home longer than they did historically. For many, the $8- or $9-an-hour job they hold does not let them run a car, rent an apartment, and pay for food also.

- The McJobs phenomenon finds its perfect symbol in the McDonald's service empire, where the majority of the workers receive pay rates close to minimum wage.

1. Write a paragraph on this phenomenon using either *definition* or *process* as your method of development.

2. Write a paragraph on this topic using either *example/illustration* or *causal analysis* as your method of development.

3. Write a paragraph on this topic using either *classification* or *comparison/ contrast* as your method of development.

EXERCISE VII-3   PARAGRAPH TRANSITIONS

Fill in the blanks in the following passages using the transitional expressions below.

1.	after all	13.	and	25.	at last
2.	as/as a result	14.	further	26.	finally
3.	hence	15.	still	27.	next
4.	however	16.	for example	28.	then
5.	in short	17.	in fact	29.	in addition
6.	thus	18.	indeed	30.	furthermore
7.	instead	19.	of course	31.	of course
8.	additionally	20.	thus	32.	also
9.	when	21.	but	33.	likewise
10.	furthermore	22.	besides	34.	similarly
11.	whereas	23.	although	35.	at this point
12.	if	24.	while	36.	simply put

SECTION A

When Adjutor Rivard wrote *Chez nous*, in 1914, he could not have known it would become a classic account of rural life in Quebec that would be translated by W. H. Blake and decorated with woodblock prints by A. Y. Jackson. _____, Rivard was simply writing about the life and language he loved and knew well.

_____ Blake notes in his Translator's Note, "Judge Rivard has made it a labour of love to seek out and embody in his graceful prose those forceful old words which ring so musically and 'mean just what they say'" (15). _____ the magic of *Chez nous* is not just the magic of the French it was originally written in; its interest _____ lies in the fact that it was lauded by the French Academy in 1920, and that it shows Rivard's love for and understanding of his native Quebec.

_____ writing sketches of the Quebec countryside, Rivard wrote two successful books on law: *De la liberté de la presse* and *Manuel de la Cour d'appel.* He was also one of the first people to study the relationship between the French spoken in Quebec and the French spoken in the parts of France the Quebecois emigrated from. _____ it is easy to forget those who laid the groundwork for an understanding of the past, we lose a part of ourselves when we ignore people like Adjutor Rivard. He speaks to us from our past.

_____ in Canada's social history, the media are telling Canadians that they are faced with a public debt that makes it very difficult for the Canadian government to continue governing the country in a traditional way. Canadians are being told that the effect the debt will have on health care and postsecondary education will be severe. _____, the doomsayers, as well as those who are transfixed by the public debt, are simply trying to strip the government of the control it has over social policies, and stress the values of competition and corporate and individual wealth. _____ John Ralston Saul points out in *The Doubter's Companion,* _____ there are no examples in the history of nations that have become wealthy because they paid their national debt, there are numerous examples of nations that have become wealthy because they have defaulted on their debts, renegotiated them, or simply refused to pay them. _____, the Athens that is thought of as the birthplace of Western civilization became the power that it was because it defaulted on its debts (89). _____, why is it that corporations are allowed to incur debts that they cannot pay and go bankrupt, _____ nations are expected to pay their debts? What is fair for a corporate entity should be fair for a social entity. _____ a society, Canada must think of the social consequences of its actions. _____ it thinks that unemployment, the stagnation of economic growth, and the further impoverishment of its citizens in the name of paying debt _____ allowing its corporate citizens the right to defer taxes and build up their debt is just, _____ the future for all Canadians is indeed bleak.

EXERCISE VII-4 PARAGRAPH STRUCTURE

Christensen argued that paragraphs are essentially built through the writer's use of coordination and subordination. In his model, each sentence in the paragraph relates either to the paragraph's central claim or to the sentence preceding it. To improve your understanding of this model, write three paragraphs that follow the suggested paragraph structures below. The first paragraph asks you to create a coordinate structure, the second a subordinate structure, and the third a mixed structure. In each case, the lead or topic sentence is given to you.

Coordinate Structure

(level-one sentence) The recent success of the Tim Hortons chain—a rapid move into second place among the fast-food franchises—is clearly a result of four major appeals they are able to make to their customers.

(level-two sentence)_____

_____.

(level-two sentence)_____

_____.

(level-two sentence)_____

_____.

(level-two sentence)_____

_____.

Subordinate Structure

(level one sentence) The rise in postsecondary tuition fees across the country over the last decade has had an enormous effect on the financial health of today's graduating students.

    (level-two sentence)_____

_____ .

    (level-three sentence) _____

_____ .

    (level-four sentence) _____

_____ .

Mixed Structure

(level-one sentence) Over the last five years, Canadians have become more and more aware of how threatened the five principles of the Canadian Health Care Act have become. Wait lists have increased in some areas, as underfunding and provincial–federal disagreements on a health accord have led the country closer and closer to losing universal, accessible, comprehensible, portable, and publicly administered health care.

    (level-two sentence)_____

_____ .

    (level-three sentence) _____

_____ .

    (level-four sentence) _____

_____ .

    (level-two sentence)_____

_____ .

    (level-three sentence) _____

_____ .

    (level-two sentence)_____

_____ .

    (level-three sentence) _____

_____ .

    (level-four sentence) _____

_____ .

    (level-one sentence, restatement) _____

_____ .

Grammatical Sentences

A sentence is an independent clause, a group of words that contains both a subject and a predicate. The subject names the thing or person that the sentence is about; it is acted upon by the verb. The predicate consists of the verb and any object, modifier, or complement of the verb. (For more information about subjects and predicates, see 29-a and 29-b.)

┌ SUBJECT ┐┌─────────── PREDICATE ───────────
Grey's Anatomy depicts the personal traumas of the staff of a metropolitan

─────┐
hospital.

┌── SUBJECT ──┐┌──────── PREDICATE ────────┐
Stephen King's fiction has influenced contemporary horror films.

Writers who lack a clear understanding of this formula run the risk of committing errors in sentence construction.

41-a Sentence Fragments

A sentence fragment is a word group that, for various reasons, fails to qualify as a sentence. For example, there may be no subject or no predicate.

NO SUBJECT Having crossed the Pacific. [Who crossed the Pacific?]

NO PREDICATE The first Chinese, who came to Canada from California in 1858. [What did the Chinese do?]

In a third kind of fragment, both a subject and a predicate are present, but they are preceded by a subordinating conjunction.

After Cirque du Soleil started to become popular in the United States. [What happened after it started to become popular?]

The preposition *after* makes the above a dependent clause. Dependent clauses cannot stand alone as complete sentences.

CORRECTING SENTENCE FRAGMENTS

A fragment that lacks a *subject* can be corrected by adding a subject or by combining the fragment with an independent clause.

FRAGMENT Having crossed the Pacific.

REVISED Having crossed the Pacific, the first known Japanese immigrant to Canada settled in Victoria in 1877. [combined with independent clause]

A fragment that lacks a *predicate* can be corrected by adding a predicate or by combining the fragment with an independent clause.

| FRAGMENT | The first Chinese, who came to Canada from California in 1858. |
| REVISED | The first Chinese, who came to Canada from California in 1858, were looking for gold on the Fraser River. [predicate added] |

ESL Focus MISSING SUBJECTS AND VERBS

You may be familiar with a language that allows the omission of an explicit subject or verb if the sentence is clear without it. Such an omission is not permitted in English, however. For that reason, the following examples are fragments, not sentences.

MISSING SUBJECT Has asked for plans for two new parks.

MISSING VERB The Grey Cup in Toronto in 2007.

MISSING VERB Winnipeggers very outgoing.

To revise these fragments, add the subjects and verbs required to complete the sentence.

City council
Has asked for plans for two new parks.
^

was held
The Grey Cup ^ in Toronto in 2007.

are
Winnipeggers ^ very outgoing.

EXCEPTION: The imperative sentence, which expresses a command, need not include a stated subject. For example, in the sentence *Clean up your room*, the subject *You* is assumed, not stated.

If the fragment is a phrase or a dependent clause, either combine it with an independent clause or turn it into an independent clause.

| FRAGMENT | In 1870 by the Icelandic community. |
| REVISED | In Manitoba, women's suffrage was first proposed in 1870 by the Icelandic community. [phrase combined with an independent clause] |

FRAGMENT	After Cirque du Soleil started to become popular in the United States.
REVISED	After Cirque du Soleil started to become popular in the United States, the company found itself undertaking more and more complex productions, especially in Las Vegas. [dependent clause combined with independent clause]
FRAGMENT	Although Quebec women who owned property could vote in municipal elections between 1809 and 1849.
REVISED	Although Quebec women who owned property could vote in municipal elections between 1809 and 1849, that right was taken away when politicians changed Quebec's Franchise Act. [dependent clause combined with independent clause]
FRAGMENT	The Women's Christian Temperance Union that saw votes for women meant votes for prohibition.
REVISED	The Women's Christian Temperance Union saw that votes for women meant votes for prohibition. [dependent clause turned into independent clause]

Most fragmented dependent clauses are partial thoughts that have been unintentionally separated from a nearby sentence where they belong. To correct such fragments, simply join the two parts.

FRAGMENT	Canadian women felt cheated. When the federal government extended voting rights in 1917 only to women in the armed services and to female relatives of men in the military.
REVISED	Canadian women felt cheated when, in 1917, the federal government extended voting rights only to women in the armed services and to female relatives of men in the military.

ESL Focus — VERBAL-PHRASE FRAGMENTS

A special type of fragment results when the writer assumes that a verbal phrase can function as a verb.

FRAGMENT	The candidate, *having learned* that he was trailing in the polls, and *knowing* that he would have a hard time catching up in the last week.

You may think the above example is a complete sentence because it contains words that sound like verbs. However, *having learned* and *knowing* are verbals, not verbs. The clause has a subject (*the candidate*) but no predicate because it has no verb; it does not tell its readers what the candidate *did* after learning he was trailing in the polls. Changing a verbal phrase to a verb or adding a predicate will correct the unintended fragment.

REVISED	*The candidate,* having learned that he was trailing in the polls, *knew* that he would have a hard time catching up in the last week.

REVISED	*The candidate,* having learned that he was trailing in the polls, and knowing that he would have a hard time catching up in the last week, *launched a series of hard-hitting television advertisements.*

41-b Run-On Sentences

One of the most common problems in writing is the run-on sentence. Run-on sentences consist of independent clauses that have not been joined correctly. They fall into two categories: the *fused sentence* and the *comma splice*.

FUSED SENTENCES

When two independent clauses are joined with no punctuation or connecting word between them, the result is a fused sentence.

FUSED SENTENCE	Constance loves to read she often falls asleep at night with a book pressed to her nose.

To correct a fused sentence, you have the following options:

1. Make the two independent clauses into separate sentences.

    Constance loves to read. She often falls asleep at night with a book pressed to her nose.

NOTE: To provide a link between the two sentences, you could add a transitional expression (*In fact, she often falls asleep at night with a book pressed to her nose*).

2. Link the clauses with a comma and a coordinating conjunction *(and, but, yet, or, for, nor, so)*.

   Constance loves to read, *and* she often falls asleep at night with a book pressed to her nose.

3. Link the clauses with a semicolon or with a semicolon followed by a conjunctive adverb.

   Constance loves to read; *consequently,* she often falls asleep at night with a book pressed to her nose.

4. Turn one of the independent clauses into a dependent clause.

   Because Constance loves to read, she often falls asleep at night with a book pressed to her nose.

5. Turn the two clauses into a single independent clause.

   Constance's passion for reading sometimes causes her to fall asleep at night with a book pressed to her nose.

COMMA SPLICES

A comma splice occurs when two independent clauses are joined with only a comma.

COMMA SPLICE   Michael Ondaatje's novel *The English Patient* was a critical and popular success, it was made into a movie.

The methods for eliminating comma splices are the same as those for correcting fused sentences.

SEPARATE SENTENCES

Michael Ondaatje's novel *The English Patient* was a critical and popular success. It was made into a movie.

COMMA AND COORDINATING CONJUNCTION

Michael Ondaatje's novel *The English Patient* was a critical and popular success, so it was made into a movie.

SEMICOLON AND TRANSITIONAL EXPRESSION

Michael Ondaatje's novel *The English Patient* was a critical and popular success; as a result, it was made into a movie.

SUBORDINATION OF CLAUSE

Because Michael Ondaatje's novel *The English Patient* was a critical and popular success, it was made into a movie.

TWO CLAUSES RECAST AS SINGLE INDEPENDENT CLAUSE

Michael Ondaatje's critically acclaimed and best-selling novel *The English Patient* was made into a movie.

AGREEMENT

42

The form of a word is determined by the word's association with another word. For example, a subject must agree with its verb and a pronoun must agree with its antecedent. Some words change their form depending on their number, person, gender, and tense.

42-a Subject–Verb Agreement

A verb must agree with its subject in number (singular or plural) and in person (first, second, or third).

	SINGULAR	PLURAL
FIRST PERSON	I see	we see
SECOND PERSON	you see	you see
THIRD PERSON	he/she/it sees	they see

SUBJECTS WITH *AND*

Most compound subjects joined by *and* are plural and therefore require a plural verb.

       live
Carlos and Sue ~~lives~~ in a one-bedroom apartment.

       are
Geneviève and Cloë ~~is~~ going to the dance next Saturday.

Two linked subjects that are viewed as a single unit take a singular verb.

       is
Strawberries and cream ~~are~~ Marsha's favourite dessert.

WORDS OR PHRASES BETWEEN SUBJECT AND VERB

Words or phrases that come between the subject and the verb can cause confusion.

> *was*
> *One* of the students ~~were~~ writing a report on the effectiveness of Canada's policy on multiculturalism.

In the preceding example, the subject is *one*, not *students*. *Students* is part of the phrase *of the students*, which modifies the noun (and subject) *one*. The verb must agree with *one*; only one student is writing the report.

When a singular subject is followed by a phrase beginning with *as well as, in addition to, together with,* or a similar construction, the verb should agree with the singular subject, not with the subject in the intervening phrase.

> *thinks*
> Gordon, together with his classmates, ~~think~~ Arnold Schwarzenegger's best acting has occurred during his time as the governor of California.

SUBJECTS JOINED BY *OR* OR *NOR*

When a compound subject is joined by *or* or *nor*, make the verb agree with the part of the subject closest to the verb.

> *Customs* or *tradition shapes* everyday behaviour.
>
> *Tradition* or *customs shape* everyday behaviour.

When a singular subject and a plural subject are joined by *either/or* or *neither/nor*, you can avoid awkwardness by placing the plural subject closest to the verb.

AWKWARD	Either the *passengers* or the *driver is* responsible for the accident.
REVISED	Either the *driver* or the *passengers are* responsible for the accident.
AWKWARD	Neither the *students* nor the *instructor is* happy that the classroom is too hot.
REVISED	Neither the *instructor* nor the *students are* happy that the classroom is too hot.

INDEFINITE PRONOUNS AS SUBJECTS

Indefinite pronouns such as *one, none, each, either, neither, another, anyone,* and *anything* refer to non-specific persons or things and are singular in meaning. The indefinite pronouns *everyone, everybody,* and *everything* are also singular even though they appear to be plural in meaning.

is
Everyone ~~are~~ disappointed that a Canadian team has not captured the Stanley Cup since Montreal won it in 1993.

Some indefinite pronouns, including *all, any,* and *some,* can be either singular or plural, depending on the noun they refer to.

SINGULAR   *Some* of the instructor's *lesson* is hard to understand.

PLURAL   *Some instructors* are hard to understand.

COLLECTIVE NOUNS AS SUBJECTS

Collective nouns such as *class, family, team, committee, audience, couple,* and *group* can take either a singular or a plural verb, depending on whether they function as a single unit or as individual members of a unit.

SINGULAR   The *jury has* returned a verdict of guilty. [functions as single unit]

PLURAL   The *jury are* debating the evidence. [function as individual members of unit]

The names of companies are collective nouns. Most company names with plural or compound forms take singular verbs.

Chapters *is* seeking to expand its customer base.

Smith and Sons *sells* a good line of linen.

For more information about collective nouns, see section 42-c and Chapter 47.

SUBJECT COMPLEMENTS

A verb should agree with the subject, not with the subject complement.

were
Excessive absences ~~was~~ the reason for the employee's dismissal.

In the preceding example sentence, the plural subject *absences* is linked to the singular complement *reason* by the plural verb *were.* If the subject and complement in this sentence were reversed, the verb would be singular.

was
The reason for the employee's dismissal ~~were~~ excessive absences.

For more information about subject complements, see 29-d.

INTRODUCTORY *THERE*

In sentences beginning with *There,* the number of the verb depends on the subject that follows *There.*

There *is* a *flaw* in Monique's design.

There *are* several *flaws* in Monique's design.

VIII GRAMMATICAL SENTENCES

ESL Focus NONCOUNTABLE NOUNS AND GERUNDS

Singular verbs are used with noncountable nouns and gerunds.

NONCOUNTABLE NOUN   The *information* is inaccurate.

GERUND   *Winning* is fun.

For more information about noncountable nouns, see the ESL Focus in 27-a.

WHO, THAT, WHICH

Verbs in dependent clauses introduced by the relative pronouns *who, that,* and *which* must agree with the antecedents of these relative pronouns.

The *Stoneys,* who *are* related to the Plains Assiniboine, traditionally lived along the foothills of the Rocky Mountains.

The *language* that *is* native to the Stoneys is a dialect of the Siouan language spoken by the Sioux.

PLURAL FORM, SINGULAR MEANING

Some nouns ending in -s are singular in meaning and therefore take singular verbs.

Mathematics ~~are~~ is an essential skill.

The *news* ~~are~~ is promising.

Some of these nouns may be either singular or plural depending on the context.

SINGULAR   Statistics *is* the most challenging course in the new curriculum.

PLURAL   His statistics *are* accurate.

In the singular example above, *statistics* denotes a field of study; in the plural example, it refers to a collection of specific information.

Words referred to as words or terms take singular verbs.

Councillors ~~are~~ is a term that is gender-neutral.

PHRASES OF MEASURE AND QUALITY

Units of money, time, volume, mass, length, and distance take singular verbs.

is
Two kilometres ~~are~~ the equivalent of a mile and a quarter.

is
Twelve dollars ~~are~~ too much to pay to see a movie that will soon be out on video.

TITLES OF WORKS

The title of a book, film, or other work of art takes a singular verb even if the title has a plural or compound form.

was
Tomson Highway's *The Rez Sisters* ~~were~~ first produced at the Native Canadian Centre of Toronto in 1986.

is
Romeo and Juliet ~~are~~ to be made into a film again.

42-b Tense Agreement

Verb tenses should clearly establish the time of the actions being described in a sentence or a passage. Tenses should be changed only when the context requires a shift.

The belief that Newfoundland *is* populated exclusively by fishers *is* patently

perpetuates
untrue. Yet this popular myth about Newfoundlanders ~~perpetuated~~ itself.

Problems with tenses can occur when quotations are used to support commentary.

Vanderhaeghe's *The Englishman's Boy* focuses in part on the battle that took place in the Cypress Hills in southwestern Saskatchewan in 1873. Vanderhaeghe comments specifically on the fact that those responsible for the massacre of Native people included both Americans and Canadians. Yet,

makes
Vanderhaeghe ~~made~~ another point at the end of his novel when he writes that, as a result of the incident, "The Canadian government formed the North West Mounted Police, sent it on a long, red-jacketed march into a vast territory, establishing claim to it. A mythic act of possession" (326).

VIII GRAMMATICAL SENTENCES

In the sentence leading into the quotation, *made* has been changed to *makes* because the present tense is used in the commentary that precedes the quotation. Besides making the verb tense consistent with the tense of the rest of the paragraph, it also follows the literary convention of utilizing the present tense in analyzing a literary work.

A sentence that combines commentary and quotation can create a more subtle problem.

AWKWARD   Dickens *observes* that Coke Town "*was* a triumph of
           fact; it *had* no greater taint of fancy in it than
           Mrs. Gradgrind." Dickens *had* no admiration for
           industrial Britain.

You could eliminate the awkward shift in tenses in the first sentence by changing the tenses of the verbs in the quotation from past to present. Changing the tense in the sentence following the quotation from past to present would eliminate a further awkward tense shift. When you alter a quotation in some way, you must enclose the added or changed words in brackets. (For information about brackets, see Chapter 59.)

REVISED   Dickens *observes* that Coke Town "[*is*] a triumph of
           fact; it [*has*] no greater taint of fancy in it than
           Mrs. Gradgrind." Dickens *has* no admiration for
           industrial Britain.

NOTE: Changing verb tenses in a quotation is permissible only if the change does not substantially alter the meaning of the quotation.

Some disciplines have specific tense preferences. For instance, the present tense is preferred in English and the humanities. If you are not sure which tense you should use, ask your instructor.

42-c Pronoun–Antecedent Agreement

Pronouns are words that replace nouns (see 27-b). A pronoun must agree with its antecedent——the word it replaces——in *number, gender,* and *person.*

The *soldiers* learned that *their* tour in Afghanistan would be more difficult and dangerous than had been anticipated.

Karima could not remember where *her* car was parked.

COMPOUND ANTECEDENTS

When the parts of a compound antecedent are joined by *and*, the matching pronoun is plural.

Britney Spears and Diana Krall have forged *their* individual careers in remarkably different ways.

A compound antecedent that is preceded by *each* or *every* requires a singular pronoun.

Each car and truck must meet stringent air-pollution standards before *it* is allowed on the road.

When a compound antecedent is joined by *or* or *nor*, the pronoun agrees with the nearest antecedent.

Neither the *manager* nor her *employees* are happy about *their* new assignment.

If the parts of the antecedent are of different genders, however, the sentence should be recast.

INCORRECT	Either Juan or Susan has an appointment with her dentist tomorrow.
REVISED	Either Juan or Susan has a dental appointment tomorrow.

INDEFINITE PRONOUNS

When the antecedent is an indefinite pronoun whose meaning is singular, the matching pronoun is singular.

One of the hockey players lost *his* temper.

When the antecedent is an indefinite pronoun whose meaning is plural, the matching pronoun is plural.

Many of the victorious teammates raised *their* arms in jubilation.

When the antecedent is an indefinite pronoun whose meaning can be singular or plural (e.g., *all, any, none,* and *some*), the matching pronoun is singular or plural depending on the noun it refers to.

SINGULAR	*Some* of the *art* appealed to *its* viewers.
PLURAL	*Some* of the *politicians* have broken *their* campaign promises.

Indefinite pronouns such as *one, anyone, someone, each, everybody, no one,* and *nobody* raise the problem of sexist bias when they are matched with a singular pronoun that is exclusionary and sexist.

EXCLUSIONARY   *Everybody* has to buy *his* own books.

To avoid exclusion, you can use both masculine and feminine pronouns.

REVISED   *Everyone* has to buy *his* or *her* own books.

Alternatively, you can replace the indefinite pronoun with a plural noun.

REVISED   *Students* have to buy *their* own books.

See Chapter 48 for a more detailed discussion of inclusive language.

ESL Focus   GENDER AND AGREEMENT

The gender of nouns and pronouns varies from language to language and from culture to culture. The two major languages in Canada, French and English, use gender in quite different ways. In French, pronouns and the nouns they replace are either masculine or feminine. In English, many constructions are gender-neutral.

- The *cat* rolled on *its* back.
- The *tree* shaded the cat with *its* branches.

Nouns that are gender-specific include *bull, cow, stag, doe, gander, goose, lady, lord, prince, princess, man,* and *woman*.

COLLECTIVE NOUNS

When an antecedent is a collective noun such as *committee, team,* or *audience,* the form of the matching pronoun depends on the context. A group that functions as a single unit requires a singular pronoun; a group that functions as individual members of a unit requires a plural pronoun. See also 27-a.

The environmental *committee* is conducting a review of *its* mandate. [functions as unit]

The environmental *committee* are divided on *their* understanding of global warming. [function as members of unit]

42-d Person Agreement

Do not shift among first, second, and third person unless meaning demands it. The following passage illustrates awkward and unnecessary shifts in person:

AWKWARD	If *people* go to a movie theatre on the weekend, *they* will probably encounter large lineups for the most popular films. *I* may even end up going to a film *I* did not intend, or want, to see. To ensure that *you* see the film of your choice, *you* should arrive early.

In the passage, the writer shifts from the third-person noun and pronoun (*people/they*), to the first-person pronoun (*I*), to the second-person pronoun (*you*). The problems of clarity and logic are easily solved by eliminating the person agreement problems.

REVISED	If *you* go to a movie theatre on the weekend, *you* will probably encounter large lineups for the most popular films. *You* may even end up going to a film *you* did not intend, or want, to see. To ensure that *you* see the film of your choice, *you* should arrive early.

COMMON SENTENCE PROBLEMS

43

43-a Unclear Pronoun Reference

Pronouns that do not refer clearly to their antecedents are common sources of confusion for readers. A pronoun reference is ambiguous when the pronoun could refer to more than one antecedent.

AMBIGUOUS	Roger told Samarjit that he was being transferred to Montreal.

As the following revisions indicate, there are two possible interpretations for this sentence.

CLEAR	Roger told Samarjit, "You are being transferred to Montreal."
CLEAR	Roger told Samarjit, "I am being transferred to Montreal."

Another kind of unclear pronoun reference occurs when there are too many intervening words between a pronoun and its antecedent.

CONFUSING	Economic recessions are the result of a multitude of factors that, in isolation, may be harmless; it is the confluence of these factors that triggers *them*.

A reader of this passage would have difficulty making the connection between the pronoun *them* and its antecedent *recessions*. To clarify, you could eliminate the pronoun by combining the two clauses.

CLEAR   Economic recessions are triggered by a confluence of factors that, in isolation, may be harmless.

The use of *it, this, that,* or *which* as a pronoun reference is another source of potential confusion. The problem arises when these pronouns are used to refer to whole sentences or ideas rather than to specific antecedents.

VAGUE   Each year during the holiday season, hundreds of bikers organize a drive to collect toys for disadvantaged children. They deposit the toys at a local donation centre on December 15. *This* is an unexpected and pleasing phenomenon.

In the preceding example, it is not clear what *This* refers to—the organized toy drive, the depositing of the toys at the donation centre, or perhaps both activities. To avoid confusion, you could revise so that *This* is eliminated.

CLEAR   Each year during the holiday season, hundreds of bikers organize a drive to collect toys for disadvantaged children. They deposit the toys at a local donation centre on December 15. *This charitable undertaking* is an unexpected and pleasing phenomenon.

Alternatively, you could replace *This* with a noun.

CLEAR   Each year during the holiday season, hundreds of bikers organize a drive to collect toys for disadvantaged children. They deposit the toys at a local donation centre on December 15. The bikers' *charitable undertaking* is an unexpected and pleasing phenomenon.

43-b Misplaced Modifiers

A misplaced modifier is a word, phrase, or clause that does not point clearly to the word or words it is intended to modify.

MISPLACED   Violence is a growing problem in modern society *which stems from fear and ignorance.*

In the preceding example, the dependent clause *which stems from fear and ignorance* follows *society* and therefore appears to modify it. It seems evident the writer intended the clause to modify *violence.*

REVISED   Violence, *which stems from fear and ignorance,* is a growing problem in modern society.

In general, a modifier should be placed either right before or right after the word or words it modifies.

Limiting modifiers such as *only, even, exactly, almost, nearly, hardly,* and *just* should be placed right before the words they modify. Note how changing the position of the limiting modifier alters the meaning of each of the following examples.

Only Ann Marie will receive $200 from her aunt.

Ann Marie will receive *only* $200 from her aunt.

Ann Marie will receive $200 from her *only* aunt.

A *squinting modifier* is a modifier that could refer to either the word(s) before it or the word(s) after it.

SQUINTING   Sonny said *in the morning* he would look for the missing dog.

You could avoid such ambiguity by revising the sentence in either of the following ways.

REVISED   *In the morning,* Sonny said he would look for the missing dog.

REVISED   Sonny said he would look for the missing dog *in the morning.*

43-c Dangling Modifiers

Dangling modifiers are words, phrases, or clauses that refer to something that is absent from the sentence. Frequently positioned at the beginnings of sentences, they appear to modify words they were never intended to modify. To revise a dangling modifier, you need to name the actor to which it properly refers.

DANGLING   After setting out on the trail to the mountain peak, fog rolled into the valley. [Fog can't hike.]

REVISED   After *we* set out on the trail to the mountain peak, fog rolled into the valley.

DANGLING   At the age of seven, her grandfather died. [There are no seven-year-old grandfathers.]

REVISED   At the age of seven, *she* learned that her grandfather had died.

DANGLING   Encouraged by the test results, English made sense as a major. [Who is encouraged by the test results?]

REVISED   Encouraged by the test results, *he* decided to major in English.

VIII GRAMMATICAL SENTENCES

PASSIVE VOICE AND DANGLING MODIFIERS

In the active voice, the agent of the action is also the subject. In the passive voice, the object acted upon becomes the subject.

ACTIVE   The man hit the ball. [*The man* is the subject/agent of the action; *hit* is the verb/action; *the ball* is the object acted upon.]

PASSIVE   The ball was hit by the man. [*The ball* is the subject/agent acted upon; *was hit* is the verb/action; *by the man* is a prepositional phrase.]

The following example illustrates how a dangling modifier can result from use of the passive voice.

PASSIVE/   ┌───── SUBJECT ─────┐
DANGLING   Having lost patience, the malfunctioning computer

┌─ VERB ─┐
was replaced.

Restoring the agent of the action and re-establishing the correct relationship between subject and action removes the dangling element.

              ┌ SUBJECT ┐┌ VERB ┐
ACTIVE   Having lost patience, the student replaced

┌───── OBJECT ─────┐
the malfunctioning computer.

For more information about the passive voice, see section 27-c and Chapter 50.

43-d Faulty Parallel Structure

When Shakespeare has Hamlet say "*To die, to sleep, to sleep, / perchance to dream*" (3.1.64–65), he is using parallel structure. Parallelism refers to a series of like grammatical elements—words, phrases, or clauses—that are expressed in repeating grammatical constructions.

WORDS   *Running, walking,* and *cycling* are all good forms of exercise.

PHRASES   To get to the market, you walk *across the street, through the park,* and *into the square.*

CLAUSES   To run for office, *you may have to join a party;* to join a party, *you may have to modify your controversial views.* [This example also includes parallel phrases—*to run for office, to join a party.*]

You violate parallel structure when you fail to use the same grammatical form for elements in a series.

NON-PARALLEL   An effective leader is capable of *inspiring* loyalty, *taking* risks, and the *acceptance* of responsibility.

PARALLEL   An effective leader is capable of *inspiring* loyalty, *taking* risks, and *accepting* responsibility.

For more information about parallel structure, see 37-c and 33-c.

EXERCISES

EXERCISE VIII-1 FRAGMENTS

Fix the sentence fragment errors in the following passage. Remember that a sentence fragment is always an incomplete sentence, one usually lacking either a subject or a verb. Rewrite the passage so that all the sentence fragments are eliminated.

A number of commentators have recently analyzed the curious phenomenon that sees more jobs existing in one year than in the preceding year but less gross income. This leads them inevitably to conclude that the net income attached to each job has declined. Or that the compensation for a significant proportion of the jobs has declined. A more likely scenario than the one that has every job declining in net value. No sector contributes more significantly to this phenomenon than the retail sector. In fact, Starbucks learns from McDonald's, and Safeway teaches Wal-Mart. The lesson of using hours and titles and myths to disguise the fact that the employer is not paying a living wage. The myth, of course, the disguise that makes the exploitation seem acceptable, a key ingredient in this whole decline in the net value to workers of jobs. The fiction is created by the employer that the job is only a temporary one, suitable for a young person hoping to earn enough to pay for her education. We are not supposed to notice that the person serving us at Wendy's is in her forties. An equally potent contributor to the net effect, the one mentioned above, the decline in value of jobs. Titles and competitions can also furnish a substitute for a reasonable pay level. McDonald's puts up pictures of their employee of April. Or May. Or September. A fifteen-dollar plaque or picture once a month is cheaper for an employer than paying fifteen dollars an hour. With benefits. And that leads us to the biggest deception of all. Here, Starbucks and Starbucks clones deserve special awards. The employee is asked to work three hours to cover the early morning rush. And then come back in for two hours at four o'clock to deal with the late afternoon push. What never happens for that employee is a simple forty-hour week, where benefits, security of income, Employment Standards protections, and other valuable rewards are earned. Including holiday pay. The employer who perpetrates this exploitation wants also to be seen as a contributor to the community. Pictures of sponsored teams on the wall. The twenty-six-year-old still living at home, however, knows better. These employment practices do not create a healthy economy, and these employers should not be admired. No plaques for them.

Total errors: 12

EXERCISE VIII-2 RUN-ON SENTENCES

Fix the run-on errors in the following passage.

Why is it that, when we are ready for another month of warm weather, it starts to turn cold at night and the mornings turn crisp and cool? Summer never seems to last long enough in our part of the world, just when we get used to having a summer tan and running around in lightweight clothes, autumn creeps up on us.

But autumn is still the most pleasant season its lingering, cool evenings, and its crisp afternoons certainly have more appeal than the minus-twenty days that are much too common to most Canadian winters. After all, in Canada autumn is the most memorable season; it is much more attractive than spring, which can be beautiful on the west coast, but which can also be only part of a short, swift transition from winter to summer in eastern Canada. Similarly, spring is nicer than winter or summer, when Canadians alternately freeze to death and roast.

When fall is approaching, there are many images that keep a Canadian heart warm and content, after all, there are many things to look forward to in the autumn. Yes, it is the harvest season, however, there are many festivals to keep Canadians busy too, especially in October. From the celebration of Thanksgiving, which comes a whole month earlier than the Thanksgiving of our neighbours to the south, to Halloween, October, with its Indian summer and bright, shiny days, is the centre of a Canadian autumn. It is the period when the leaves are most colourful, and there is a profusion of yellows, oranges, and browns in the woods; it is enough to lure anyone out into the country, even the most hardened urban dweller. Just a few kilometres from the cities, the glory of autumn awaits but it is necessary to pick a warm, dry day to get the most out of an outdoor adventure.

Nonetheless, in autumn, the days are growing shorter, the nights are getting longer soon it will start to get cloudy and snowy all across the nation; but right now the weather is fine, and it is time to be outdoors with a rake gathering up leaves and smelling the fresh scents of autumn.

Quicker than the first slapshot of another hockey season, October will be all but over and the witches and goblins of the dying days of autumn's most glorious month will be at everyone's door calling out for the last treats of harvest. Listen:

> *Trick or treat, smell my feet;*
> *Give me something good to eat.*
> *Not too big, not too small,*
> *Just the size of Montreal.*

Who was it that suggested that Canada didn't have its own culture? Who was it that thought we weren't unique people? Why do they think we have a red maple leaf on our flag?

Total errors: 8

EXERCISE VIII-3 FRAGMENTS AND RUN-ONS

Correct the fragment and run-on errors in the following passage.

My first memories of the Fraser Highway are cloudy, but certain images still are there when I think about it. Low fog on an early fall morning. This and an image of clear, blue mountains are strongest. But I remember how the towns looked too. When we drove through Langley at 6 a.m. on our way to fish up at Jones Lake. There was barely a soul moving about. And farther up the valley, around Chilliwack, the fields of hops were mixed with fields of corn, the traffic had started to move and the farmers were already moving their equipment into the fields for the day's work.

But the image of the morning sun as its first beams shone from behind the mountaintops out and across the valley. That was spectacular too. The clouds seemed to be sky-bound pieces of cotton candy that had escaped from the machines at the PNE and moved slowly up the valley to meet the morning light. Mount Baker was there in its glory, and Cheam Ridge was there too. Both looked higher and more special than they ever could in the full brightness of the sun. The light blue of morning across their back. The full majesty of the ragged peaks glowed, trees seemed to dissolve in the early-morning light as we ranged our eyes across the mountain slopes spreading out toward the valley floor below. The sunshine breaking across their topmost points.

But up the valley toward Hope, things still sat in a gloomy shadow so it was as if night refused to leave the area next to the mountains. Nonetheless, as we neared Bridal Falls, the first beams of sunlight shone down into the near reaches of the Fraser, the gloom was finally subsiding. That didn't mean that the day was warm yet, and, as we stepped out of the car at the roadside café at Laidlaw, a chill told us that winter was not that far away in these mountains that were physically so close yet geographically so distant from the nearby Pacific.

The journey wasn't over yet, as the slow ascent up the hanging valley of Jones Lake had surprises in store for us. The Fraser Valley stretching out before us at every bend. It was spectacular. It really was the perfect end view for a journey up the valley. There before us lay the valley, and, in the distance, Vedder Mountain marked off the area east of Abbotsford, similarly, to the north lay the mountains with Harrison Hot Springs nestled at their feet. A view worth remembering!

Total errors: 12

EXERCISE VIII-4 AGREEMENT I

Correct the errors in the following passages.

PERSON

Why do Canadians feel obsessed with their physical environment? Is it, as Northrop Frye suggested in 1965, that Canada's garrison mentality has become an "eternal frontier," "the first thing that the writer's imagination must deal with" in order to come to terms with Canada's legacy? Are Canadians forever stuck with images from the past that cut us off from alternative perspectives on the evolution of their cultural values and perspectives? Maybe we are faced with a situation where we have to reform our vision of ourselves, and recast the way we see ourselves and how we have evolved. The myth of the land is only one view of who Canadians are and what we are. Maybe, in recasting our self-image, as A. M. Klein said in "Portrait of the Past as Landscape," Canadians will have to "make a new thing / . . . perhaps by necessity and indirection bring / new forms to life."

(Continued below.)

Total errors: 10

SUBJECT–VERB

When Frye wrote his now famous "Conclusion" to *Literary History of Canada,* Canadians were content to see themselves in terms of a land that they felt was a dominant concern to them. Ironically, even while Frye was writing, the country was changing, and Canada, as well as Canadians, were changing too. Whereas, at the turn of the century, the majority of Canadians was rural, by the end of World War II Canada's majority were urban. The small village, with its handful of inhabitants, were on the decline, as was rural dwellers. Neither the villages nor the countryside were able to retain a young-adult population, which saw its future in fast-growing urban centres such as Halifax, Montreal, Toronto, Winnipeg, and Vancouver. No one in the country surrounding these growing cities were certain that there was a future in farming. The 80 kilometres separating these people from the cities were not a barrier to them any longer. Factory work, as well as jobs in all facets of secondary industry, were snapped up by eager young adults from the country who saw their future spelled out in urban terms. Neither friends and relatives back home in the country nor a country lifestyle were tempting once young adults had bought the bill of goods that the city had sold them.

Total errors: 10

SUBJECT–VERB, TENSE, PRONOUN–ANTECEDENT, AND VAGUE REFERENCE

Please review these kinds of errors in Chapters 41–43 before attempting this exercise. Correct all sentence errors of the types listed above in the following passage.

The 2006 election has given us a fractured Canada, one that is divided in their political loyalties. The Western provinces vote Conservative; Ontario splits its seats between the Conservatives and the Liberals; Quebec voted for the Bloc Québécois. In a year or two, will these divisions deepen, with a Conservative vote shifting again in Ontario, or will it strengthen? Canada's voting patterns suggest the presence of four distinct realities from one ocean to the other. There are a Liberal majority in Atlantic Canada, and forty-nine percent of the seats in Ontario are Liberal. The Conservative party holds thirty-nine percent of the seats in Ontario and seventy-two percent of the seats in the West. In Quebec, the Bloc holds nearly seventy percent of the seats. If these regional differences continue, it is possible that we will experience a succession of minority governments and lose the order that issues from having national governments in place for four to five years. The origins of the divisions across the country is probably due to the sense of distrust with which the West view the East and Quebec, and Quebec and Atlantic Canada views the rest of Canada. There is no escaping our need to deal with this split because we require a stronger sense of unity if we are to succeed in a generally fractured world. We should have a firmer sense of our common roots and history. It was that shared background we want to emphasize now as we are drifting into defensive camps. These can't provide the future we would prefer. At the same time, the two major parties felt great bitterness over the attacks each makes on the other. If these two are to have a campaign in the future based on policy rather than personality, this need more emphasis as the way back to a more dispersed and less regional division.

Total errors: 12

EXERCISE VIII-5   AGREEMENT II

Correct the agreement errors in the following passage. You might want to review 42-a and 42-b before doing this exercise.

The jury has returned their verdict. For the middle class at least, bigger is in. Neither burgers nor a vehicle are attractive to us if it doesn't have more size than ever before. What is the best-selling Ford line in Canada? If you answered "trucks," you would be right. Once we thought an Explorer was enough; now we want an Expedition. We even created a new language for the purpose of idiomatically capturing size. At the fast-food place, the server asks, "Do you want to biggie that combo?" Let me see. I'm already eating food groups that aren't good for me, so, if I answered "Naturally!" I'd be representing my class well.

We also live in homes that have both family rooms and living rooms; it might even have an entertainment room. When we move in, we think we need that size of a place because we are going to have 1.1 children, and he or she should have two bedrooms to choose from. Everybody knows they are entitled to a large house on a large lot in a small neighbourhood. If we have a density of four people per square foot downtown, the outer ring of suburbs should have their inalienable right to one person every three thousand square feet of space.

It's fair to ask if we caught this disease from our American neighbours. You have to wonder if the penchant of Americans for advertising every sight as "the world's largest dam or field of tomatoes or plane built of pine or garlic fields" is communicable. If everyone has to hype their world wonder, do we need to erect signs promoting the world's longest highway with nothing beside it? Some of the choices we have for promotion is natural material for inflation. The world's largest tidal bore actually is a bore. Size is not a synonym for quality or value, yet we act as if it were and choose based on this single criteria.

Not surprisingly, therefore, the carport yields to the attached single garage, and they give way for the double carport and then the capper—the triple carport with an added oversize dwelling for the motor home. We cannot build these houses without an appropriately sized lot and perhaps even acreage. We insist every car meet their assigned emission standards, and we build two-ton SUVs with three-hundred-horsepower engines to ferry us to the local Safeway. In the 1980s, we learned to love the four-cylinder engine and efficiency. In the twenty-first century's early years, we want excess in every item we own. A fridge once served a family; now we bought a freezer to complement the fridge, and the fridge has to have an icemaker capable of spitting out an endless chain of ice cubes made from filtered water. Anyone can have their barbecues but those of us living in the suburban ring want one that has a side burner to go with the H-ring burner and the mandatory rotisserie.

It's clear we have arrived at a new place with a new mantra. And that mantra is "Nothing succeeds like excess."

Total errors: 16

EXERCISE VIII-6 MISPLACED MODIFIERS

Correct the following passage by (a) underlining each misplaced modifier, and (b) indicating where that modifier—whether a word, a phrase, or a clause—should be located.

One of the most prevalent myths in circulation today is the myth of increased crime. The facts and statistics tell us there has been a decline in the incidence of crime generally, but politicians, editorials, and police authorities even continue to scare us with fearful accounts of increased criminal activity. It is easy to understand why a police representative would frighten us with assertions that violence and antisocial acts are increasing in both urban and rural areas, which are sparked by ignorance and poverty.

What informed people are less likely to discuss publicly is the reason for the decline in crime, actually. It is declining because the size of the cohort of young males in the population is falling, generally. It has been falling for some time. We may look for the cause by speaking of a rise in education or an increase of affluence in general or a fear of arrest and punishment growing. But the reason is simpler; the class of people responsible for criminal activity mostly is getting smaller. In the newspaper sometimes when we read of a particularly ugly crime, we are inclined to think it is increasing. But the facts say otherwise. The offending portion of the population has grown smaller and this leads to fewer crimes with former times compared.

The more interesting dimension of this shift is the prediction that it will continue, which has been advancing for some time, because the relative size of the young male cohort will continue to shrink. That is unlikely to reduce the general population's fear of crime and loathing, but it is true, unless other causes like poverty, lack of employment, and drug use primarily are sufficient to drive an increase by themselves. The future only will tell us if that is possible.

Total errors: 11

EXERCISE VIII-7 DANGLING MODIFIERS

Underline and then correct the dangling modifiers in the following passage.

Why is it that the old cliché asserts that in spring a young man's fancy turns to love? Is it that the male of the species is so gullible or beguiled by his opposite number that once a year he gives chase, or is this simply a way of retelling the story of the natural cycle of the seasons and mating? Whatever the case, in Canada there are other thoughts that accompany spring.

It would be easy to say that spring is a carefree time of the year in Canada, a time of the year when, instead of watching television, romance becomes paramount. However, when confronted with this idea, not a smile is smiled. The truth is much more complex. Disgruntled by a long winter, being romantic may not make sense. Indeed, April showers may bring May flowers in coastal B.C., but blizzards may kill May flowers in a large part of the rest of the country. Ready for the mild rains of spring, winter may still have a last say in the matter.

But even on the west coast, spring isn't meek and mild. Depressed by constant rain, moving to California may be what makes sense. Living in a rain forest, spring can pass right by. Instead of passing into the bright realm of a new season, the dreary days of an extended, wet winter can be felt.

Living on the prairies, even May can be a cruel month. After all, the seed catalogues recommend that people don't plant until after May 24, and even then there is danger of a freeze or a snowfall. Canada does not have the most forgiving climate. Discouraged by the weather, it is a wonder that emigrating didn't make sense. Although only a young country with promise, Canadians may well think of moving elsewhere.

Total errors: 10

EXERCISE VIII-8 PARALLEL STRUCTURE

Correct each error in parallel structure that you discover in the following passage.

Two of the most unlikely cultural heroes in recent times are Harry Potter and Frodo Baggins. Single-handedly, Harry's adventures made Raincoast Books a serious player in Canadian publishing rather than a local publisher headquartered in B.C. In fact, Raincoast had to rent large amounts of storage space just to house the Harry Potter books as they came out. Equally surprising is the rise to popular notice of Frodo the hobbit, unlikely hero, unexpected wanderer, and he wins over opponents that seem unbeatable. *The Lord of the Rings* trilogy, written by a specialist in medieval English literature, is not the raw material from which you would expect to construct a worldwide audience of fans.

Both Harry and Frodo share an urge for adventure, an apparently inexhaustible supply of courage for dangerous moments, an inventive and tricky mind, and enemies. Frodo's quest is more classically constructed than Harry's.

Frodo's quest has the call to take up an obligation, the mysterious adviser to aid in critical moments, friends, the unremitting threat from those forces who want the ring, and the essential suspense generated by one crisis immediately followed by another. Harry's world initially seems more akin to our own than Frodo's. There is a school to attend, a family to leave, new friends to make at the school, jousting. Of course, the jousting takes us off the path of familiarity. In a way, Harry's world depends more on mechanics, sorcery, a dark enemy is brought on stage, and atmosphere. But the draw for those who are fans of the two are the endlessly unfolding adventures and, of course, the fact each saga is available in movies. Today's younger generation has been raised in a visual world; even their typewriters have screens. It is natural that serial adventures presented with the most exotic of computer and generated-by-hand special effects would draw a vast and loyal crowd.

The final oddity of the two great successes is that they replicate the Saturday serials that once thrilled the parents and grandparents of those raptly watching Frodo and Harry. The linking element is not only the structure of crisis, resolution of crisis, slow build to new crisis, but also the odd beings that appear at moments to assist, and resolution of crisis and so on. There is the truth of the television series at work here, the truth that audiences get hooked to characters and feel compelled to watch each episode that these characters appear in, the truth that familiarity builds love—not contempt, and you can also build a fan base from the repetitions and use the same effects. Many critics have attempted to explain the unexpected drawing power of these odd heroes. But you can tell all you need to know by checking the dollars generated from the movies, the awards won by creators and directors and special effects technicians, the spinoffs of dolls and images for Christmas consumption, books sold. We don't know how long Harry and Frodo will ride the wave, but we do know it was an unexpected and unlikely ride.

   Total errors: 11

Usage and Diction

44-a Redundancy and Wordiness

A wordy sentence is one that contains more words than are necessary to convey the meaning of the sentence. For example, a sentence may contain a nonessential phrase such as *In my opinion* or a redundant phrase such as *at the present time* (when *now* would suffice). To achieve precision and economy in your writing, eliminate redundant and unnecessary words and phrases.

WORDY	In my opinion, I believe that we have never had it better than we do right now in the early years of the twenty-first century.
REVISED	We have never had it better than we do now.
WORDY	People who view themselves as inferior have a tendency to retreat from social occasions that force them to be outgoing and to interact with other people in a social situation.
REVISED	People who lack confidence tend to avoid social situations.
WORDY	It is a known fact that certain fans of rap stars, people who have devoted hundreds and hundreds of hours to learning everything possible about their idols, the stars they revere, make that the centre of their life and neglect everything else they might do or study.
REVISED	Obsessed rap-star fans make their idols the centre of their lives.
WORDY	My personal opinion on where the economy appears to be going, or at least appears to have gone, is based on the fact that more and more people are working additional hours for an increasingly shrinking pay envelope on paydays.
REVISED	Increasingly, people are working longer hours for less pay.

Combining sentence elements is one of the means by which you can achieve economy in your writing (see 33-a). A process that can help you identify redundancies is the proofreading sweep (see 5-d and 19-d).

In the course of your proofreading sweep, you should check for unnecessary *that*'s.

I hope ~~that~~ they stay.

Where is the computer ~~that~~ you bought?

Note, however, that the omission of *that* can lead to ambiguity or confusion.

The expectation is unrealistically high earnings will be reported.

As a result of the omitted *that*, the preceding example sentence could be inter-
preted in one of two ways: (1) *The expectation is that unrealistically high earnings
will be reported*; or (2) *The expectation is unrealistically high that earnings will be
reported.*

44-b Appropriate Connotations

Denotation is the exact, literal meaning of a word—the kind of meaning expressed
in a dictionary definition. *Connotation* refers to the values and associations attached
to a word. For example, the word *home* denotes "physical structure within which
one lives" and connotes such things as "refuge," "sanctuary," "haven," or "family." The
connotations you select will depend on your context—specifically, your audience,
purpose, and subject.

Our new line of swimwear is ideal for ~~overweight~~ full-figured customers. [A retailer
would not use the word *overweight* because it connotes obesity.]

As an employee, you need to be more ~~aggressive~~ assertive in your dealings with management. [The word *aggressive* is too strong for the context, a workplace.]

The celebrity was chased by ~~an assemblage~~ a crowd of reporters. [The word *assem-
blage* is too formal for the context.]

44-c Language Levels

Like speech, writing can be formal or informal. There are clear distinctions
between these two language levels. For example, *employer* and *They became angry*
are formal; *boss* and *They got mad* are informal. The following statements about
free trade provide a further illustration of the two language levels.

INFORMAL   Free trade is just a bunch of big shots who plan to
                  get rich at our expense.

FORMAL   Free trade is one of the mechanisms by which
                  powerful corporate interests exploit workers for
                  personal gain.

The language level you use will depend on your purpose, audience, and subject. More personal than formal writing, informal writing is appropriate when
your objective is to please or entertain (as in the case of a personal e-mail or
letter). A greater degree of formality is appropriate for academic, business, and
professional writing (reports, essays, and the like).

At the extreme end of informal writing is slang, exemplified by such terms as
geek and *nerd*. Slang expressions are usually acceptable only in very informal
writing such as personal correspondence. They pose the additional problem for
the writer of being current only briefly.

44-d Specific and Concrete Diction

Much of the cumulative effect of your diction has to do with the extent to which you choose words that are (1) specific rather than general and (2) concrete rather than abstract. *General* words identify a class of things (*book*); *specific* words name a particular member of the class (*Anil's Ghost*). *Abstract* terms are words or phrases that refer to ideas or qualities (*justice, beauty*); *concrete* terms are words or phrases referring to things that exist in the material world (*court, painting*). Although general and abstract words are sometimes necessary to convey your meaning, specific and concrete words are usually preferable because they make your prose more vivid and precise. The following sentences demonstrate the differences among the four types of words.

GENERAL   The child was upset over the incident.

SPECIFIC   The five-year-old girl screamed when the scoop of ice cream in her cone splattered on the pavement.

ABSTRACT   The struggle for market dominance in service industries is fierce.

CONCRETE   The war between Subway and McDonald's for the hearts and stomachs of North Americans now includes low-carb offerings.

GENERAL	LESS GENERAL	SPECIFIC	MORE SPECIFIC
car	American car	Pontiac	Pontiac TransAm
tree	deciduous tree	willow	weeping willow
furniture	chair	armchair	recliner

ABSTRACT	LESS ABSTRACT	CONCRETE	MORE CONCRETE
entertainment	visual entertainment	film	horror film
thoroughfare	route	street	Yonge Street
covering	cloth protection	jacket	brown leather jacket

Readers hunger for specific information, specific examples, and specific words. Wherever you have a choice, use the specific and concrete word instead of the general and abstract alternative. If you are still uncertain about the difference, examine the list above.

44-e Clichés

Clichés are expressions that were once fresh but have become tired and predictable through overuse. Here are some examples:

Raw hamburger is something you should avoid *like the plague.*

The mayor's comments are nothing but *smoke and mirrors.*

We should *leave no stone unturned* in our search for truth.

You look *as fresh as a daisy*.

He *roared like a lion,* but he was *as gentle as a lamb*.

The coat was *as light as a feather*.

The construction made traffic *grind to a halt*.

One problem with clichés is that they are not always understood. Most Canadians would not be familiar with the English expression *not by a long chalk*, which means *not in any way* and derives from the use of chalk to score points in games; more familiar is the Canadian version of this expression, *not by a long shot*. A more serious problem with the cliché is that it suggests a lack of original thinking on the part of the writer.

If a cliché offers an efficient way of expressing something, do not be afraid to use it. Expressions such as *tongue in cheek* and *rule of thumb* are probably preferable to unwieldy, invented alternatives. Generally, however, you should use your proofreading sweep as an opportunity to replace clichés with original and exact phrasing.

44-f Jargon

The *Concise Oxford Dictionary*'s definition of jargon may make you appreciate why you should avoid it: "Words or expressions used by a particular group or profession; barbarous or debased language; gibberish." Although the last two definitions are warnings, the first is the one that needs closer scrutiny. Sports, academic disciplines, business, government, the arts, and many professions build up specialized vocabularies. The problem occurs when members of a group using jargon try to communicate with people not familiar with that specialized usage. Communication breaks down almost immediately.

The computer industry, with its love of acronyms and initialisms, is particularly remote from the common language. How would you fare if someone used the following terms in writing or speaking to you?

- PDA
- KBPS
- USB II
- RAM
- LAN

- HTML
- URL
- XML
- MP3
- ISP

Academic discourse can be just as impenetrable to general readers, as the following passage from a book by the literary critic Philip Wheelwright demonstrates:

> A nodus of meaning is designated a universal when its specifiable references are related by virtue of some publicly verifiable similarity, of whatever degree of abstraction; it is designated a particular when its

specifiable references are related by virtue of some publicly verifiable space–time contiguity and continuity.

Use specialized language only if you are sure your audience will understand it. If you must use jargon in communicating with a non-specialist audience, be sure to provide the necessary definitions.

44-g Pretentious Language and Euphemisms

Just as jargon can befuddle readers, so too can *pretentious language*. Note how excessive formality and inflated language obscures the meaning of the first example sentence below:

PRETENTIOUS   If I were to manifest my most profound requital for your benefaction, I would have to use such words as extraordinary, consummate, unsurpassed, and ineffable.

REVISED   Thank you very much for your kind donation.

CAUTION: If you use a thesaurus to improve your vocabulary, make sure the words you choose are appropriate and that you understand their meaning. Do not get verbose. A wordy, pompous statement is no better than a weak, poorly expressed one.

Euphemisms are polite or socially acceptable words or phrases that writers use in order to avoid appearing blunt or tactless. The least acceptable euphemisms are those that are unnecessarily deceptive. Insidious euphemisms include *friendly fire* for gunfire coming from one's own side in a military conflict; *strategic misrepresentation* for lie; and *collateral damage* for civilian deaths resulting from a military action. Some common euphemisms are listed below.

EUPHEMISM	PLAIN ENGLISH
between jobs	out of work
chemical dependency	drug addiction
encore presentation	rerun
correctional institution	prison
disadvantaged	poor
downsize	lay off or fire
passed away	died
pre-owned automobile	used car
sanitary engineer	garbage collector

44-h Idioms

The word *idiom* is Greek in origin and means "a manifestation of the peculiar." Indeed, idioms—the peculiar expressions that every language adopts—can be confusing as well as frustrating to both native and non-native speakers. You cannot explain an idiom by logic. Nor do idioms follow predictable rules. On the other hand, idioms are proof that language is constantly changing, regional in nature, and far from simple or logical. Knowing this does not help you as a writer, but it will at least let you see there are structures in every language that you just have to memorize, for they follow no set rules. Idioms pose a special challenge to ESL learners because of this fact that they have to be individually learned and mastered.

Idiom often dictates which prepositions are used with which verbs. Here are some examples:

abide *by* (a decision)	in accordance *with*
abide *in* (a place or state)	independent *of*
according *to*	inferior *to*
accuse *of*	intend *to*
angry *with*	jealous *of*
averse *to*	preferable *to*
capable *of*	prior *to*
comply *with*	run *off* (not *off of*)
die *of*	superior *to*
different *from*	sure *of*
identical *with/to*	try *to*

In English, some verbs are followed by different prepositions depending on the object of the preposition.

adapt *to* (a situation); adapt *from* (a source)
agree *with* (a person); agree *to* (terms); agree *on* (a plan)
compare *to* (something in a different group); compare *with* (something in the same group)
conform *to*; conform *with*
differ *with* (a person); differ *over* (a question)
occupied *with* (a thing); occupied *by* (a person); occupied *in* (an act)
rewarded *by* (someone); rewarded *for* (something); rewarded *with* (an object)
wait *at* (a place); wait *for* (someone or something); wait *on* (a customer)

ESL Focus PREPOSITIONS USED TO INDICATE TIME AND PLACE

The following list demonstrates how to use *in*, *at*, and *on* to indicate time and place.

TO INDICATE TIME

IN   *Portion of time:* in the afternoon, in thirty seconds, in ten minutes, in two hours, in three days, in a month, in a year, in 1867, in January, in the spring

AT   *Specific time:* at 8:35, at noon, at lunch, at the start of the game

ON   *Specific day:* on Monday, on my birthday, on July 1, on St. Patrick's Day

continued

TO INDICATE PLACE

IN   *Enclosed area:* in the box, in the shower, in the living room, in the tunnel

      Location: in the street, in Hamilton, in Ontario, in Canada

AT   *Location:* at the corner, at the store, at the studio, at the computer, at the table

ON   *Surface:* on the page, on the book, on the table, on Yonge Street, on the prairies

ESL Focus   PHRASAL VERBS

A special type of idiom is the phrasal verb, which consists of a verb followed by one or two prepositions (called *particles* in this context). One of the difficulties of phrasal verbs for ESL learners is that their meaning as a unit is distinct from the meaning of the parts considered individually. The meaning of *look out* in "Look out for falling debris" (where *look out* is a phrasal verb) is different from the meaning of *look out* in "Look out the window" (where *look* and *out* are two independent words).

The following list of phrasal verbs does two things. First, it shows what preposition or adverb goes with the verb to make the phrasal verb. Second, it uses an intervening pronoun to demonstrate whether a word may come between the verb and its particle—as in *take (her/it) out.*

ask (her) out	fill (it) up	help out
break (it) down	get along	keep on
bring (her/it) out	get away	keep up
burn (it) down/up	get up	leave (it) out
call (her) up	give (it) away	look (it) over
call (it) off	give in	look (it) up
clean (it) up	give up	look into
clean up	go out	make (it) up
come across	go over	pick (it) out
cut (it) up	grow up	pick (it/her) up
do (it) over	hand (it) in	play around
drop (her/it) off	hand (it) out	point (it) out
drop in	hang (it) up	put (it) aside
drop out	hang on	put (it) away
fill (it) out	help (her) out	put (it) back

continued

put (it) off	speak up	try (it) on
put (it) on	stay away	try (it) out
put (it) out	stay up	turn (it) down
put (it) together	take (her/it) out	turn (it) on
put up	take (it) off	turn out
quiet down	take (it) over	turn up
run across	take care of	wake (her) up
run into	think (it) over	wake up
run out	throw (it) away	wear out
shut (it) off	throw (it) out	wrap (it) up

PRONOUN CASE

45

Pronoun case refers to the form of a pronoun that indicates the pronoun's function in a sentence. There are three cases in English: the *subjective* case, which is used for the subject of the sentence; the *objective* case, which is used for the object of the sentence or object of a preposition; and the *possessive* case, which indicates ownership. The pronoun forms for each of the three cases are listed below.

SUBJECTIVE CASE	OBJECTIVE CASE	POSSESSIVE CASE	
		AS AN ADJECTIVE	AS A NOUN
I	me	my	mine
we	us	our	ours
you	you	your	yours
he, she	him, her	his, her	his, hers
it, one	it, one	its, one's	its, one's
they	them	their	theirs

Seven common problems writers have in dealing with pronoun case are discussed below. For more information about pronoun case, see 27-b.

45-a *I* or *Me*

Some writers have difficulty deciding whether to use *I* or *me* in a sentence. You can avoid confusion by remembering that *I* functions as a subject, while *me* functions as an object of a verb or preposition.

SUBJECT	*I* like the mild winters in Vancouver.
OBJECT OF VERB	The mild winters in Vancouver surprised *me*.
OBJECT OF PREPOSITION	The mild winters in Vancouver appealed to *me*.

45-b Appositives

A pronoun that is used as an appositive (see 28-c) appears in the same case as the noun it renames.

      I

Two contestants, Ellen and ~~me~~, arrived early. [The appositive *Ellen and I* renames the subject *contestants*.]

The organizers congratulated the victorious teammates, Will, Diego,

    me

and ~~I~~. [The appositive *Will, Diego, and me* renames the direct object *teammates*.]

45-c *We* or *Us*

When the pronouns *we* or *us* are used with a noun, their case depends on whether they function as a subject or an object.

  We

~~Us~~ Manitobans are proud of our ethnically diverse culture. [*Manitobans* is the subject.]

       us

Parks Canada rewarded ~~we~~ volunteers with a trip to Pukaskwa National Park. [*Volunteers* is the object of the verb.]

Although the above constructions are grammatically correct, the revisions that follow would be less awkward.

As Manitobans, *we* are proud of our ethnically diverse culture.

Parks Canada rewarded volunteers like *us* with a trip to Pukaskwa National Park.

In the first revision, *we* is the subject of the verb and *As Manitobans* is its modifier. In the second revision, *us* is the object of the preposition *like*.

45-d Pronouns with *Than* or *As*

Using pronouns in comparisons beginning with *than* or *as* can be tricky. By mentally completing the sentence, you can determine which pronoun is appropriate.

I

Fazil is taller than ~~me~~.

I is the subject of the verb *am*, which is understood rather than stated. To mentally complete the sentence, add the verb: *Fazil is taller than I am.*

him

The voters distrusted no other politician as much as ~~he~~.

Him is the direct object of the understood but unstated verb *distrusted*. To mentally complete the sentence, add the verb: *The voters distrusted no other politician as much as they distrusted him.*

Changing the pronoun case in comparisons with *than* or *as* radically alters the meaning of the sentence.

> **SUBJECTIVE CASE**   Jean-Paul loves Maria more than *I*. [Jean-Paul loves Maria more than I do.]

> **OBJECTIVE CASE**   Jean-Paul loves Maria more than *me*. [Jean-Paul loves Maria more than he loves me.]

45-e Pronouns with Infinitives

Pronouns that act as the subject or object of an infinitive (the base form of the verb preceded by *to*) must appear in the objective case.

> **SUBJECT OF INFINITIVE**   He wanted *me* to see the play.

> **OBJECT OF INFINITIVE**   He wanted to take *me* to the play.

45-f Pronouns with Gerunds and Present Participles

When pronouns modify gerunds (verbals ending in *-ing* that act as nouns) or gerund phrases, they use the possessive case.

Our

The odds against ~~us~~ winning the lottery are ridiculously high. [*Our* modifies the gerund phrase *winning the lottery.*]

his

I envied ~~him~~ travelling to Spain. [His modifies the gerund *travelling.*]

For more information about gerunds and other verbals, see 28-b and the ESL Focus entitled "Gerunds and Infinitives after Verbs" in 27-c.

45-g Pronouns as Subject Complements

Pronouns that function as subject complements—words that follow linking verbs (see 27-c)—always appear in the subjective case.

I
The people most interested in spelunking are Jordan and ~~me~~.

she
It is ~~her~~ who approved the loan.

I
Superman looked the villain in the eye and declared, "Yes, it is ~~me~~, the Man of Steel!"

46 PRONOUN CHOICE

46-a *Who* or *Whom*

Like *I* and *me*, *who* and *whom* often cause problems for writers. In formal written English, the grammatical rule is straightforward. Use *who* (or *whoever*) when the pronoun is a subject or a subject complement. Use *whom* (or *whomever*) when the pronoun is the direct or indirect object of a verb or the object of a preposition.

The man *who* had been arrested called his lawyer. [relative pronoun as subject of the clause *who had been arrested*]

There are the firefighters *whom* we saw enter the burning building. [relative pronoun as object of the verb *saw* in the clause *whom we saw enter the burning building*]

The foundation grants scholarships to *whomever* it wants. [relative pronoun as object of the preposition *to*]

Who won the lacrosse game last night? [interrogative pronoun as subject]

Whom did she meet in Yellowknife? [interrogative pronoun as object]

With *whom* are you sitting? [interrogative pronoun as object of the preposition *with*]

46-b *That* or *Which*

That and *which* as relative pronouns introduce adjective clauses. Adjective clauses modify nouns or pronouns and may be restrictive or nonrestrictive. *That* is used to introduce a restrictive, or essential, clause. A restrictive clause limits the meaning of the noun it modifies and is essential to the meaning of the sentence.

Which is used to introduce a nonrestrictive, or nonessential, clause. A nonrestrictive clause, which is always set off by commas, merely adds information and therefore can be removed without changing the basic meaning of the sentence. (For more information about restrictive and nonrestrictive elements, see 52-b.)

RESTRICTIVE CLAUSE — The building ***that*** first caught my eye was the CN Tower.

In the above example sentence, the relative pronoun *that* introduces the restrictive clause *that first caught my eye*. The clause narrows or limits the identity of the building, so the information is essential.

NONRESTRICTIVE CLAUSE — Metal roofing, **which** is lightweight and inexpensive, is not suitable for this climate.

In the above example sentence, the relative pronoun *which* introduces the nonrestrictive clause *which is lightweight and inexpensive*. Because the clause does not narrow or limit the meaning of *Metal roofing*, the information is nonessential.

COLLECTIVE NOUNS 47

Collective nouns name groups. A collective noun takes a singular verb if the group functions as a unit and a plural verb if the group functions as individual members of a unit.

The *team is* playing well tonight.

The *team are* putting on their uniforms.

Some collective nouns, such as *linen, china, silver, hair, straw, timber, trout, fish, salmon, sheep*, and *grouse*, have identical singular and plural forms. The singular or plural nature of these collective nouns is determined by the number of the verb or pronoun that follows.

SINGULAR — The *trout jumps* high in the air, waving *its* tail as it *arches* its back.

PLURAL — Trout *are* not hard to catch on the Dean River if you know which parts of the river *they* tend to inhabit.

For more information about collective nouns and agreement, see 42-a and 42-c.

48-a Ethnicity and Race

Language can demean or exclude individuals or groups on the basis of ethnicity, race, and culture. For example, the word *Eskimo*, which may have come from the Abenaki word *esquimantsic* or the Chippewa word *ashkimequ* (meaning *eaters of raw meat*) has a pejorative connotation for the Inuit. Similarly, dividing the Canadian population into ethnic groups such as *Chinese-Canadians* or *Indo-Canadians* can exclude people from the mainstream. (Of course, it would be necessary to make such distinctions if you were writing about the cultures of Canada from a historical or sociological point of view.) As Rohinton Mistry points out in his short story "Squatter," even the idea of multiculturalism can be exclusionary:

> The Multicultural Department is a Canadian invention. It is supposed to ensure that ethnic cultures are able to flourish, so that Canadian society will consist of a mosaic of cultures—that's their favourite word, mosaic—instead of one uniform mix, like the American melting pot. If you ask me, mosaic and melting pot are both nonsense, and ethnic is a polite way of saying bloody foreigner.

48-b Gender

Sexist language also serves to exclude members of your audience. This kind of exclusionary language can reflect stereotypical thinking, such as the assumption that all nurses are women. A more concrete expression of sexist language is the traditional use of the generic personal pronoun *he*.

EXCLUSIONARY When a student enters college, *he* has to buy *his* own textbooks.

One solution to the generic *he* is to use a construction such as *she or he* or *her/him*. However, as the following revisions indicate, awkwardness can result if the usage is excessive.

AWKWARD When a student enters college, *he or she* has to buy *his or her* own textbooks.

AWKWARD When a student enters college, *he/she* has to buy *his/her* own textbooks.

A preferable solution in this instance is to make the pronouns and their antecedent plural.

INCLUSIVE When *students* enter college, *they* have to buy *their* own textbooks.

In some cases, you can address the problem of sexist language by substituting a gender-neutral term for a sexist term.

EXCLUSIONARY *Mankind* is in the midst of a technological revolution.

INCLUSIVE	*The human race* is in the midst of a technological revolution.
EXCLUSIONARY	The *chairman* is convening a meeting.
INCLUSIVE	The *chairperson* is convening a meeting.
EXCLUSIONARY	The *fishermen* worried about the depletion of fish stocks.
INCLUSIVE	The *fishers* worried about the depletion of fish stocks.

To avoid gender bias in your writing, you can refer to the following list of sexist terms and possible gender-inclusive replacements.

EXCLUSIONARY	INCLUSIVE
alderman	councillor
chairman	chairperson, chair, moderator
clergyman	cleric, minister, pastor
fireman	firefighter
fisherman	fisher, angler
foreman	supervisor
mailman	postal worker, mail carrier
man	person, individual
mankind	human beings, humankind, human race, people
man-made	synthetic, artificial, manufactured
manpower	personnel, human resources
man-sized	big
policeman	police, police officer
salesman	clerk, salesclerk, salesperson
steward, stewardess	flight attendant
to man	to operate, to staff
weatherman	meteorologist, weather forecaster
old wives' tale	superstition
workman	worker, labourer

REMOVING SEXUAL BIAS

APA style online recommends that writers use language that is inclusive rather than exclusive. They suggest the term *sexual orientation* be used rather than *sexual preference* and that *lesbian sexual orientation, heterosexual sexual orientation, gay male sexual orientation,* and *bisexual sexual orientation* be used rather than *lesbianism, heterosexuality, homosexuality,* and *bisexuality.* They also suggest that the terms *lesbian* and *gay male* are acceptable but *homosexual,* used as a noun or an adjective, is not, as it carries negative stereotypes. Similarly, *bisexual women and men, bisexual persons,* and *bisexual* should be terms included in a discussion of sexual orientation. Be aware that terms related to sexual orientation, like those related to gender, ethnicity, and race, can be exclusionary. In all your work, attempt to be inclusive. Ask your instructor for more specific guidance on terminology that is current in your field of study, or visit the APA site at http://www.apastyle.org/sexuality.html.

SALUTATIONS IN LETTERS

If the addressee is a woman, use *Ms.* rather than *Miss* or *Mrs.* in the salutation *(Dear Ms. Tsang)*. Alternatively, you may use the person's first and last names *(Dear Sandra Tsang)*.

If you do not know the gender of the addressee and wish to avoid the salutation *Dear Sir or Madam*, you can use an attention line that names the person's title *(Attention: Sales Manager)* in place of a salutation. Another option is to adopt as your letter style the simplified format (described in 67-b), which uses a subject line instead of a salutation.

49 COMPARATIVES AND SUPERLATIVES

All adjectives and adverbs have a positive or base form *(hard, slowly)*. In addition to their positive form, most adjectives and adverbs have a comparative form *(harder, more slowly)* and a superlative form *(hardest, most slowly)*. The comparative form is used to compare two things, while the superlative form is used to compare three or more things.

COMPARATIVE   Alberta is a *larger* province than Nova Scotia.

SUPERLATIVE   Quebec is the *largest* province in Canada.

The comparative of one-syllable and some two-syllable adjectives is formed by adding *-er* and the superlative by adding *-est*. The comparative of many adjectives of two or more syllables is formed by adding *more* and the superlative by adding *most*.

COMPARATIVE   Was Macdonald a *greater* prime minister than Laurier?

SUPERLATIVE   Was Macdonald our *greatest* prime minister?

COMPARATIVE   Day traders should be *more careful* with their savings.

SUPERLATIVE	As a group, retirees tend to be *most careful* with their savings.
COMPARATIVE	Real life is *more interesting* than fiction.
SUPERLATIVE	That was the *most interesting* book I've ever read.

The comparative of adjectives ending in *-y* is formed by replacing the *-y* with *-ier (lucky, luckier)* and the superlative by replacing the *-y* with *-iest (lucky, luck-iest)*. Do not add *more* or *most* to these forms of the comparative and superlative.

Last night she was the *luckiest* [not the *most luckiest*] gambler in the casino.

49-a Irregular Comparatives and Superlatives

Not all adjectives and adverbs follow a standard pattern when it comes to the formation of comparatives and superlatives. The three forms of some of these atypical adjectives and adverbs are listed below.

POSITIVE	COMPARATIVE	SUPERLATIVE
good	better	best
well	better	best
bad	worse	worst
badly	worse	worst
many	more	most
much	more	most
some	more	most
little	less	least
far	farther/further	farthest/furthest

49-b Absolute Terms

Absolute terms such as *equal, fatal, perfect, square,* and *unique* should not be given a comparative or superlative form. You cannot describe something as *more unique* or *most unique*, for example, because there cannot be degrees of uniqueness.

The skiing conditions couldn't be ~~more perfect~~ *better*.

Is arsenic more ~~fatal~~ *deadly* than strychnine?

The CN Tower is the most ~~unique~~ *unusual* building in Toronto.

The voice of a verb depends on whether the subject of the sentence is acting or being acted upon. In the active voice, the subject *does* the action; in the passive voice, the subject *receives* the action.

ACTIVE   The governor general *dissolved* Parliament.

PASSIVE   Parliament *was dissolved* by the governor general.

ACTIVE   The Trudeau government *imposed* the War Measures Act.

PASSIVE   The War Measures Act *was imposed* by the Trudeau government.

Writers are generally advised to use the active voice as much as possible because it results in prose that is not only crisper and clearer, but more dynamic.

The use of the passive voice is appropriate if the doer of the action is unknown or less important than the recipient of the action.

Their house *was broken into* last night. [doer unknown]

The conference *was held* in Charlottetown. [doer unknown]

Many people *were arrested* following the imposition of the War Measures Act. [doer less important than recipient]

In 1918, Canadian women *were given* the right to vote in federal elections. [doer less important than recipient]

For more on active and passive voice, see 27-c and 43-c.

51 SPLIT INFINITIVES

An infinitive consists of the base form of a verb preceded by *to (to walk, to believe, to represent)*. A split infinitive occurs when the two parts of the infinitive are separated by a modifier consisting of a word, phrase, or clause *(to fervently believe)*. A split infinitive that is awkward or potentially confusing to the reader should be eliminated.

AWKWARD   The politician was reluctant *to forcefully speak out* in opposition to welfare reform.

REVISED   The politician was reluctant *to speak out* forcefully in opposition to welfare reform.

AWKWARD	The defendant wants *to* as soon as possible *appeal* the guilty verdict.
REVISED	The defendant wants *to appeal* the guilty verdict as soon as possible.
AWKWARD	The newly created Conservative Party expects *to*, if public dissatisfaction with the Liberals persists, *increase* its support among voters.
REVISED	If public dissatisfaction with the Liberals persists, the newly created Conservative Party expects *to increase* its support among voters.

Although the split infinitive is still frowned on by some authorities, it is not an error. In some instances, a split infinitive is preferable to an awkward alternative construction. *I proceeded to slowly climb the stairs* is clearly less awkward than *I proceeded slowly to climb the stairs* or *I proceeded to climb slowly the stairs*. Similarly, *Few observers expect the Liberal candidate to actually lose* sounds better than *Few observers expect the Liberal candidate actually to lose* or *Few observers expect the Liberal candidate to lose actually*.

EXERCISES

EXERCISE IX-1   SLANG EXPRESSIONS

The following two passages contain slang expressions. Find these expressions and replace them with more formal language.

PART A

My buddies and I agree that it is mega fun to get together on a Saturday night to shoot the breeze and watch the boob tube. After all, Saturday night is *Hockey Night in Canada* on CBC, and nowadays the network is putting on a doubleheader every Saturday. It's a lot better than going out to see a stupid chick flick at the local multiplex, or going to the local pub and paying the same amount of money for one draft as it costs for a whole sack of suds at the beer store. That sucks. Besides, who needs to be pulled over by a jelly bean, made to puff, and hauled into the local cop shop? They slap a humongous fine on you, and your insurance rates go sky-high because you've been drinking and driving. It just ain't worth it. Yep, home is where the action is for me and my buddies. It's safe, it's sensible, and, if my buddies get to inhaling suds, we can always order out for a pizza and have some coffee long before they get behind the wheel and head on home. As that police officer said to me years ago, if you drink, don't drive, because accidents hurt people.

Number of expressions needing change: 24

Nine times out of ten it is easier to find a good DVD to watch than to find a good movie at a local theatre. Why is it that all the good movies are at cinemas on the opposite side of town? It seems the only movies that come to the local cinema are either for boppers or Echo Boomers. How interesting can a film be when it goes on and on about who is going to or wants to shag whom? Whatever! Even films that critics think are trendy are about bopping someone or are remakes of films that were successful ten to twenty years ago. Look at *The Bourne Identity's* Jason Bourne or the character of James Bond in the James Bond series. Take an old flick, put a new trendy hottie into the lead role, add sex interest, lots of action, and tons of bucks into the mix, and bing-bang-boom, you've got a blockbuster with mega-bucks pouring into the coffers. You've even got to wonder about Johnny Depp. Has he sold out by making the *Pirates of the Caribbean* trilogy, an overt plug for Disneyland balanced off with Depp's Keith Richards imitation? Add in younger heartthrob Orlando Bloom and Keira Knightley and you've got a license to print money.

Number of expressions needing change: 19

EXERCISE IX-2 PRETENTIOUS LANGUAGE

The pretentious language in the following sentences has obscured the meaning of the sentences. Examine each sentence until you think you understand what it is trying to say. Then rewrite the sentence in plain English.

1. An exhaustive, technologically assisted, projective analysis of the firm's human-resources profile in both short- and long-term eventualities has concluded that one short-term redundancy is the work currently assigned to your job category.

2. It is imperative that you circulate widely the conclusions reached in the testing cycle just completed on the O-ring that is the core of the secondary firing assembly; temperatures below 0° cause an unanticipated rigidity in the rubber comprising the ring so severe that its intended function is unfortunately compromised with utmost severity. Please inform those supervising the launch of this testing-cycle conclusion.

3. Profits in the calendar year just concluded were in proximate relation to the projections approved by the directors at last year's assembly except for the shift in interest incomes to a negative position, contradictory of the anticipated positive position and the aggressive actions of other firms in our sector, such that the leading result in the recent four quarters is similarly negative in our general accounting at this point in time, resulting in a loss that is minor in relation to our generally improved market profile.

4. The government's aggressive response to budget management in the past year has succeeded in addressing the debts incurred in the preceding

year so successfully that that same level of debt will not recur this year but has been, we are happy to report, virtually cut in half.

5. The GPA earned by your last semester's efforts is such that we will be pleased to entertain your application for courses at our institution two semesters from the date of your receipt of this letter.

EXERCISE IX-3   STUMP YOUR INSTRUCTOR

This simple exercise invites you to try your hand at pretentious and obscure writing.

Simply select a common aphorism—a short, memorable saying embodying common wisdom—and rewrite it in inflated language. You may, if your instructor agrees, work with another student on the exercise.

As you rewrite your chosen aphorism, play fair. Your rewritten version must include all of the sense of the original; at the same time, it must exclude any meanings not contained in the original. Here's an example:

APHORISM

All that glitters is not gold.

PRETENTIOUS VERSION

The discontinuous emissions of rays with a common spectrum is not an unvarying or compellingly reliable verification of an origin connected to auriferous material.

The rest of the work belongs to your instructor. She or he has to study what you have written and re-translate it into its original form. Decide collectively on your reward if you succeed in fooling your instructor.

EXERCISE IX-4   IDIOMATIC LANGUAGE

Choose the appropriate word from the idiom choices in brackets and find alternative expressions for the underlined words.

Although it may not be possible today to find prize antiques at a country auction, auctions are interesting cultural, economic, and social events. From the container of imported, European, turn-of-the-century furniture sold at auction in coastal British Columbia to the true country auctions of Ontario, Quebec, and Atlantic Canada, one can plan [1. *for/on*] finding a day's entertainment at an auction. The true country auction affords you an intimate view of local history and culture different [2. *from/to*] the one you would find in a book. As long as you are capable [3. *of/for*] waiting patiently, bidding in accordance [4. *to/with*] the local rules, and not 5. showing your hand, you may very well 6. lay your hands on a bargain. Someone else's 7. white elephant may be your 8. gem in the rough. Examine your purchase before you start to bid, though. You don't want to go home with what you think is a bargain only to find you have purchased a 9. lemon that is 10. not worth a dime. Even if you do not win a bid, you can always 11. chalk it up to experience. The more you know about people's bidding habits and the habits of the auctioneer, the more likely you are to be successful in the future.

At one of these gatherings, you are also sure to see the local people 12. first-hand and get some insights [13. *in/into/for*] their lives. What better way to get to know a neighbourhood independent [14. *to/of*] merchants or real-estate agents than by seeing what people's houses are like and what they contain? Besides, all sorts of goods lie [15. *on/in/around*] the gloom of an attic or the loft of a barn, stored [16. *away/up*] by a previous generation because they were thought no longer fashionable or useful. When indoor plumbing became common in rural Canada, the jugs, pitchers, and chamber pots of the last two hundred years suddenly became obsolete. What family wanted its neighbours to think they had not adapted [17. *to/for*] the new ways and still used a basin, a pitcher, and a chamber pot? No one wants to be seen as not conforming [18. *on/to*] social norms. These items, 19. hidden away for a time, become collectibles that people proudly display on their sideboards. I heard one shop owner comment that chamber pots made perfect containers for chips during a party. Now that would be the 20. acid test of the chamber pot's adaptability!

EXERCISE IX-5   PRONOUN CASE

In the following passage, correct all the errors in pronoun case that you discover. The pronouns in the first sentence indicate which pronoun case you should be using throughout the passage.

Although the odds against us winning a lottery are almost ludicrously high, we collectively invest millions in this new form of tax invented by revenue-hungry provincial governments, hospitals, and charities. No matter who we talk to, they will tell you that they just buy the tickets because the charity is a deserving one or because it's a cheap form of pleasure. We know, in fact, that whomever is telling us this fiction is disguising the truth that what they really enjoy is driving to work and thinking about the first use they're going to make of their $3.3 million windfall. The simple fact is that it is just fine in our culture to be greedy, to want more than we currently have. The wonderful appeal of the lottery is its instant reward. Us are the same in dreaming of the phone call or the television image of the balls dropping and forming the magical numbers that we have just purchased. We have seen the pictures in newspapers and on television of smiling winners beyond words, reduced to trite observations about continuing to work or paying off the mortgage or taking a trip. For all purposes, they are we, secretly knowing that the real reward is not having to ever worry again about the cost of things, whether houses or vehicles or a boat or whatever we secretly think will make us happy. The winner is whomever got lucky that day; it has nothing to do with earning something or saving something or investing prudently. Instead, it is the lightning bolt out of nowhere, an unearned, outright gift. Whomever gets it deserves it simply because there is no rationality to the contest at all. Instead it's a random confluence of a drawn number with a purchased number or a scratch card with the right image. My friends and me want to be the ones who get lucky. So do you and your friends. Yet we try and preserve our dignity by talking blandly of helping the hospital out, giving to a good cause, and all the other little excuses which disguise our desires even from we.

Total errors: 10

EXERCISE IX-6 *WHO, WHOM, THAT,* **AND** *WHICH*

Determine whether who, whom, that, *and* which *are used properly in the following passage. Make any necessary corrections.*

Although you would think that people would no longer embrace *Cinderella*—the story of a pretty young woman that is rescued from a life of poverty and servitude by a handsome, young, wealthy prince—the story remains popular. It may not be as popular as it once was when the storybooks which every child in Canada had included a rendition of the story. It was Walt Disney's animated film version of the story, of course, which embedded the story in the minds of the last three generations of North Americans. Whom does not remember the two small mice, Jacques and Gus, who help Cinderella escape the clutches of her ugly stepsisters and wicked stepmother? The story lives on as a part of the social fabric of our culture even though it reinforces sexual stereotypes which we should be trying to eliminate.

The movie *Pretty Woman* is one of Hollywood's modern versions of the Cinderella story. Here, the ugly stepsisters and stepmother are replaced by the ugly situation our young and beautiful but downtrodden heroine finds herself in—she is a prostitute. Our simple, uneducated beauty from Middle America, which has not had the means of opportunity to rise through the ranks of society, is down on her luck. In fact, when we first meet her, her beauty is hidden by the costumes and makeup she uses to ply her trade on the streets of Hollywood. Yet, since this is a fairy tale, she meets a charming prince, this time in the form of a handsome man that is looking for directions and whom, we learn, has also just lost his girlfriend. Who else did you expect her to meet? Of course, the prince, in the modern adaptation of the old tale, is a wealthy businessman, but the fundamental values of the story, though slightly altered, are intact. We are told to believe that a beautiful young woman which is almost destroyed by circumstance can still be rescued by a well-educated, wealthy, charming man.

The myth that every woman should look for her modern version of Prince Charming is frightening for a number of reasons. First, why is innate goodness always paralleled with beauty and wealth? Second, wouldn't it make for a more interesting, more realistic story if the downtrodden woman met a good man that was also down on his luck? It wouldn't even matter whom rescues who. But this is not likely in Hollywood, that is always loath to adopt more egalitarian, less traditional, less sexist values. We only encourage filmmakers by going to these movies and endorsing these values. As they say, if we didn't go, they would stop making them. Why are we our own worst enemies?

Total errors: 15

EXERCISE IX-7   AGREEMENT WITH COLLECTIVE NOUNS

The following sentences offer you a choice between using a singular or plural form of the pronoun or verb to agree with the collective noun that is the subject of the verb. In each case, study the context in which the noun is used and choose the correct pronoun or verb to agree with it.

1. The jury split, and, even after three days of argument, returned (*its, their*) verdict that (*it, they*) could not reach a consensus.

2. Our high-school group will be having (*its, their*) fourteenth reunion this year, and I plan to be there, if only to make fun of my friends as they age and settle into their thirties.

3. The troop of naval reserves (*assemble, assembles*) every year on Remembrance Day to add (*its, their*) presence to the ceremony.

4. The graduating class of 2009 can purchase leather holders for (*its, their*) degrees after the graduation exercises finish.

5. Coho salmon (*return, returns*) at the end of (*its, their*) life cycle to the same river or waterway to spawn.

EXERCISE IX-8   INCLUSIVE LANGUAGE

When writing, you must try to use language that is inclusive rather than exclusionary. The following paragraph includes examples of language that is offensive and exclusionary. Find each example, underline it, and suggest an alternative that is inclusive and not offensive.

A recent Zellers advertisement on "the law of the lowest price" depicted a judge banging his gavel on his bench top. Advertisements like this reveal their American origins unintentionally. No Canadian judge—whether he is trying Jamaicans in Toronto, Hell's Angels murderers in Montreal, or perhaps an Eskimo defendant at Pangnirtung—would be wielding a gavel. Only American judges do that. If anything underlines the more peaceable nature of Canadians with greater subtlety, I'm not sure what it might be. The Canadian judge follows the example of his British ancestors in this regard. The long line of men who have served the British judiciary have been content to let the gravity of the court keep order rather than employ a wooden hammer for that purpose. Perhaps the makers of the advertisement confused courts with municipal chambers, whether for school boards or municipal councils. There the chairman is usually supplied with a gavel. I feel certain the CEO of Zellers would be embarrassed if he understood the cultural gaffe implicit in the advertisement.

EXERCISE IX-9   INCLUSIVE LANGUAGE: GENDER AND SEXUAL BIAS

The following passage uses language that is not inclusive. Find and replace any words or phrases you think are not inclusive.

Sexual preference is a complex subject. Homosexuals are out of the closet. People's sexual preferences are more openly declared than they were twenty years ago. Lesbianism and homosexuality are topics that no one feels are taboo anymore. Today's homosexual no longer feels alienated from mainstream society. A look at television programs such as *Will and Grace* will show you how mainstream sexual orientation has become.

Just as mankind has become more sensitive to gender bias in language, people have become more sensitive to issues linked to sexual orientation. After all, it was not long ago that aldermen on a city council would not be aware of, or sensitive to, biases in the decisions they made. They might listen to a policeman's complaint about how the firemen were being given preferential treatment by city hall but be completely unaware of any gender bias in the hiring practices of both of these city departments. There were times, I am sure, when they just wanted to escape to a trout stream somewhere in the bush and become fishermen rather than politicians. But even trout streams are not neutral ground in an age when environmentalists question the ethics of the sport and when, still, the fisherman cannot rely on accurate weather forecasts from the weatherman. Is there a man-made sport or product that isn't free of close examination when people are challenging the norms of society? Even city hall, with all its resources, would not have sufficient manpower to check for all the possible biases that people are now sensitive to. It is enough to make a clergyman swear.

EXERCISE IX-10 COMPARATIVE AND SUPERLATIVE FORMS

Each of the sentences below offers a choice, in parentheses, between two words. Underline the right choice so that the sentence employs correct usage.

1. Of my two children, it is now clear that Adrienne is the *[greedier, greediest]*.

2. The 2007 movie *3:10 to Yuma* is a remake of a 1957 western that starred Glenn Ford as the bad guy with the good heart. The new film pays tribute to the original and to the story by Elmore Leonard, but some may think the original is the *[best, better]* film.

3. Of the many challenges students face when moving from the secondary to the postsecondary level, understanding the subject matter may be the *[less, least]* difficult.

4. Charles did badly in the LSATs, but Ivar did *[worse, worst]*.

5. When selecting avocados for guacamole, try to pick the *[softer, softest]* ones, especially if you're planning to make it that day.

6. Of the two breeds that originated in Newfoundland, the Labrador retriever is the *[smaller, smallest]*.

7. Surely, you are the *[more, most]* practised of the two of us when it comes to dealing with aggressive males.

8. The declining morale at many companies today can be traced to the fact that the *[larger, largest]* share of the profits and the *[lesser, least]* share of lay-offs are enjoyed by the senior managers.

9. He has agreed to be *[more, most]* responsible in looking after the family car from now on.

10. We asked you to come *[earlier, earliest]* than your supervisor tomorrow and to be the *[earlier, earliest]* of your whole crew at tomorrow's special sale.

EXERCISE IX-11 ACTIVE AND PASSIVE VOICE

SECTION A

Change any passive-voice clauses into the active voice.

When Newfoundland entered Confederation in 1949 after two referendums, the vote was very close: 78,323 people voted to join Canada and 71,334 voted for responsible government. The Confederation option won by the slim majority of 52.3 percent. Yet at the stroke of midnight on 31 March 1949, Newfoundland was led into the Canadian Confederation by Joseph R. Smallwood, its first premier. It is said that Newfoundland was abandoned by Britain. It is said that Newfoundland would have retained its distinctive lifestyle and customs more fully had it not joined Confederation, but there seem to be as many opinions about Newfoundland and Confederation as there are Newfoundlanders.

In fact, there are differing opinions about the nature of Confederation in every region of Canada. Human nature is such that, given any option, there will always be at least as many points of view as there are people. The fact that anything is decided is, in itself, a miracle. Native land claims should be settled by the government, says one group. Yet, in just as adamant a tone, another group is ready to suggest the land-claim settlement process should be abandoned entirely as cumbersome, unrealistic, and costly. Every cultural group should be given the same rights, says one point of view, but that point of view is countered with the position that the Canadian ideal of two founding peoples and Aboriginal rights would no longer mean anything if everyone were given the same rights. I suspect that if all important decisions were made by Canadian voters, we would not be able to make any important decisions at all.

Total changes: 11

SECTION B

The underlined passages are written in active voice. Transform these passages into passive voice. Some of the passages can be written in passive voice with or without a doer of the action. Note the effect that including or excluding the doer of the action has on each sentence and decide whether to include it.

In periods <u>when the government lays off people who work in the public sector</u>, <u>it handles the layoffs very carefully</u>. Although it may have to admit that <u>it is discharging a large number of civil servants and public-sector workers</u>, <u>it has to justify what it is doing</u>. Although the public does not like paying taxes, it does not want to be responsible for laying workers off. It wants <u>the government to do the dirty work</u>, and it wants to be divorced from the action.

Ironically, it is the same public that is outraged when <u>civil servants and public workers are unable to take care of its needs and desires</u>. Then <u>everyone wants to take responsibility</u> for finding funds to service society properly. Suddenly, <u>the newspapers see politicians</u> stating they know the needs of the people must be served. Suddenly, on radio programs, <u>listeners express their happiness at seeing services continued</u>.

Total changes: 10

Punctuation

Comma usage falls into two major divisions: commas used to *separate* and commas used to *set off*. If you think of the comma as doing one of these two tasks, you will understand when commas are needed and when they are not. For a less conventional approach to comma usage, see 31-e.

52-a Commas to Separate

1. Use a comma before a coordinating conjunction *(and, but, yet, so, or, nor, for)* joining independent clauses.

   > Canadian history is replete with examples of federal–
   >
   > provincial conflict, so the recent wrangling about transfer
   >
   > payments is hardly ^ surprising.

2. Use commas to separate three or more items—words, phrases, or clauses—in a series.

   > Carrots, beets, turnips, and potatoes were common winter
   >   ^   ^   ^
   > vegetables in nineteenth-century Canada.

   > Crosby swept across the blue line, pivoted around the defenceman,
   >   ^   ^
   > and barged into the slot.

   > When he was happy, when he ate well, and when he was paid
   >   ^   ^
   > well, Pavarotti sang like an angel.
   >   ^

   Although some writers prefer to omit the comma separating the last two items, most authorities recommend that this final comma—called a *series* or *serial comma*—be retained to avoid confusion.

3. Use commas with dates, addresses, and titles. Note the absence of the comma before the postal code in the address example.

   > On January 23, 2006, Canadians went to the polls to elect a
   >   ^   ^
   > new government.

   > Send the parcel to 2345 Willowbrook Crescent, Langley,
   >   ^   ^
   > British Columbia V3B 2K4.

   > Wendy Leung, M.D., has been appointed chair of the
   >   ^   ^
   > medical review committee.

NOTE: The newer date style of having the day precede the month removes the need for a comma, as in 28 June 2009.

52-b Commas to Set Off

1. Use commas to set off introductory elements.

> *Unfortunately,* many born politicians never enter politics. [adverb]

> The vocalist is hopeless; *however,* the new dancer shows promise. [conjunctive adverb]

> *In fact,* your theory is wrong. [transitional expression]

> *Before the election,* the candidates promised more than they could ever hope to deliver. [prepositional phrase]

> *Filled with apprehension,* Derek walked into the auditorium where the exam was being held. [participial phrase]

> *Marsha having arrived,* we began the meeting. [absolute phrase]

> *When the contestants are ready,* the game can begin. [adverb clause]

2. Use commas to set off nonrestrictive elements. An element is nonrestrictive if it adds information not essential to the meaning of the sentence; an element is restrictive if it defines or limits the noun in a way that is essential to the meaning of the sentence. (For more information about restrictive and nonrestrictive elements, see 46-b.)

> The 2006 film *Bon Cop, Bad Cop, which grossed more than any previous Canadian film,* was advertised as the first truly bilingual English-French film made in Canada. [nonrestrictive adjective clause]

> Marc Garneau, *who in 1984 became the first Canadian astronaut in space,* served as the mission specialist on his final shuttle operation. [nonrestrictive adjective clause]

> The stock market, *despite its risks,* remains the bedrock of retirement planning for many Canadians. [nonrestrictive prepositional phrase]

X PUNCTUATION

Peter Behrens's first novel, *The Law of Dreams*, was the winner

of the 2006 Governor General's Literary Award for fiction.

[nonrestrictive appositive]

3. Use commas to set off transitional expressions, parenthetical expressions, explanatory terms, and contrasted elements.

Whole wheat and vegetable oils, *for example*, are rich in

vitamin E. [transitional expression]

Environmental protection, *as far as I am concerned*, should

be the lead issue in the next federal election. [parenthetical expression]

A cerebrovascular incident, *or stroke*, is a sudden stoppage

of blood flow to a portion of the brain. [explanatory term]

Nurture, *not nature*, is the leading cause of criminal

behaviour. [contrasted element]

4. Use commas to set off forms of direct address, interrogative tags, the words *yes* and *no*, and interjections.

Ladies and gentlemen, kindly take your seats. [direct address]

You liked the film, *didn't you*? [interrogative tag]

Yes, it is raining. [word *yes*]

Oh, I wouldn't go that far. [interjection]

COMMAS TO SEPARATE

1. before a coordinating conjunction joining independent clauses
2. words, phrases, or clauses in a series
3. with dates, addresses, and titles

COMMAS TO SET OFF

1. introductory elements
2. nonrestrictive elements
3. transitional expressions, parenthetical expressions, explanatory terms, and contrasted elements
4. direct address, interrogative tags, the words *yes* and *no*, and interjections

52-c Misuses of the Comma

Do *not* use a comma in the following situations.

1. To set off restrictive elements

    The newspaper's entertainment reporter is interviewing the singer/ *Beyoncé.*

    The team/ *that wins the game*/ will proceed to the finals.

    Lionsgate's film/ *Crash*/ won the Academy Award for best picture in 2005.

    The woman/ *who lives in the corner unit*/ has filed another complaint against her noisy neighbours.

    The great schooners/ *that sailed out of Halifax for Atlantic and Pacific ports*/ were among the finest ships in the world during the age of sail.

2. Between a subject and a verb or a verb and an object (when there are no intervening phrases)

    Many businesspeople argue that the ability of Canadian companies to compete globally/ is undermined by our relatively high levels of corporate taxation.

    The governor of the Bank of Canada observed/ that the rapid rise in the Canadian dollar/ has caused problems for Canadian exports in the U.S.

3. After the last item in a series

    Political parties are always looking for talented, articulate, and ambitious/ people to run for office.

4. Between cumulative adjectives

    He is a dear/ old/ man.

    The suspect was wearing a soiled/ blue jacket.

5. Before or after a coordinating conjunction joining elements other than clauses.

    Neither Saul/ nor/ Judy is responsible for the company's problems.

    She worked for a newspaper/ and trained as a lawyer before entering politics.

6. With a question mark or an exclamation mark

"Are you coming?"/ Cynthia asked.

"Watch out!"/ James shouted.

7. To set off an indirect quotation

Sir Wilfrid Laurier forecast/ that the twentieth century would belong to Canada.

In 1966, John Lennon declared/that the Beatles were more popular than Jesus.

53 THE SEMICOLON

1. Use a semicolon to link closely related independent clauses.

The economy is up; interest in politics is down.
      ∧

The magazine article is not based on facts; it is based on
                                          ∧
rumour and speculation.

A number of Canadian comics have achieved stardom south of

the border; Jim Carrey and Mike Myers are notable examples.
          ∧

Reva has a reputation for diligence; indeed, her coworkers
                                    ∧
describe her as a perfectionist.

2. Use semicolons to separate items in a series when one or more of the items has internal punctuation.

The unlikely high-school clique consists of Mai, who loves to

party; Samantha, who loves to study; and Dave, who loves to
     ∧   ∧
sleep.

1. Use a colon after an independent clause to introduce a *list*, a *quotation*, an *appositive*, or an *explanation*.

> Visitors to foreign countries require the following: a foreign-language phrase book, traveller's cheques, health insurance, and a desire to experience different cultures. [list]
>
> The coach urged his struggling team to reflect on the immortal words of Yogi Berra: "It ain't over till it's over." [quotation]
>
> Mark's hypochondria is a response to his greatest fear: infection. [appositive]
>
> The reason for the company's success is plain: it is far more nimble than its competitors. [explanation]

2. Use a colon with the following: hours, minutes, and seconds; salutations, attention/subject lines, and copy notations in letters; elements in memo headings; titles and subtitles; biblical chapters and verses; and parts of bibliographical entries.

HOURS, MINUTES, AND SECONDS

The concert starts at 8:30 p.m.

He crossed the finish line at 10:34:23.

SALUTATIONS IN LETTERS

Dear Sir or Madam:

ATTENTION/SUBJECT LINES IN LETTERS

Attention: Kulwinder Singh

Subject: Board of directors meeting

COPY NOTATIONS IN LETTERS

cc: Thomas Ruffini

X PUNCTUATION

ELEMENTS IN MEMO HEADINGS

To: Sylvie Campeau

From: Heather Thomas

Date: April 2, 2009

Subject: Year-end report

TITLES AND SUBTITLES

Shadow Maker: The Life of Gwendolyn MacEwen

BIBLICAL CHAPTERS AND VERSES

Matthew 6:28

PARTS OF BIBLIOGRAPHICAL ENTRIES

Page, P. K. *Up on the Roof.* Erin, ON: Porcupine's Quill, 2007. [The colon separates the place of publication from the publisher.]

55 QUOTATION MARKS

55-a Direct Speech

1. Place double quotation marks around direct speech. (Direct speech may be accompanied by a speaker tag such as *he said* or *she wrote.*) Do not use quotation marks for *indirect speech*, speech that is reported or para-phrased rather than quoted directly.

    Northrop Frye once observed, "If a sculptor were to make a statue of a patriotic Canadian, he would depict somebody holding his breath and crossing his fingers." [direct speech]

    She said, "I'll meet you at the restaurant." [direct speech]

    She said she would meet us at the restaurant. [indirect speech]

2. Use commas to set off speaker tags from quotations.

    "The true character of the historical Grace Marks," writes Atwood, "remains an enigma."

EXCEPTION: Omit the comma when the speaker tag follows a quotation that ends with a question mark or an exclamation mark.

"Are you ready to go?" he asked.

"I'm more than just a rose in my husband's lapel!" declared Margaret Trudeau in 1976.

3. Use single quotation marks to enclose quotations within quotations.

> Alan Hustak's book *Titanic: The Canadian Story* tells of a British passenger, a woman named Esther Hart, who had a premonition of disaster. As Hart's daughter later recalled, "When she saw a headline in a newspaper that their new ship was unsinkable, she said, 'Now I know why I am frightened. This is flying in the face of God.'"

55-b Short and Long Quotations

1. Use quotation marks to enclose a prose quotation of four or fewer typed lines (MLA style), forty words (APA style), or eight lines/one hundred words (Chicago style) in your essay.

> Carol Shields has characterized Susanna Moodie, that most reluctant of Canada's early pioneers, as "a Crusoe baffled by her own heated imagination, the dislocated immigrant who never fully accepts or rejects her adopted country."

When the prose quotation runs longer than four typed lines (MLA), forty words (APA), or eight lines/one hundred words (Chicago), set it off from the text by indenting one inch (2.5 cm) (MLA and Chicago) or five spaces (APA) from the left margin. A quotation presented in this format, called a *block quotation,* is not enclosed in quotation marks. It can be either double-spaced (MLA and APA) or single-spaced (Chicago).

In *The Great Lone Land,* William Francis Butler captures the immensity of the Canadian prairie and the damage that Europeans did to it as they moved west across the country:

> Hundreds of thousands of skeletons dot the short scant grass; and when fire had laid barer still the level surface, the bleached ribs and skulls of long-killed bison whiten far and near the dark burnt prairie. There is something unspeakably melancholy in the aspect of this portion of the Northwest.
>
> [MLA style]

2. Use quotation marks to enclose a poetry quotation that runs no more than three lines. Note the use of slashes to indicate the separation of lines (see Chapter 57).

> In "Cypresses," D. H. Lawrence writes, "Evil, what is evil? / There is only one evil, to deny life."

A poetry quotation longer than three lines is set off line by line as a block quotation.

> The opening lines of "A Poison Tree" illustrate the deceptive simplicity of William Blake's language:

> > I was angry with my friend:

> > I told my wrath, my wrath did end.

> > I was angry with my foe:

> > I told it not, my wrath did grow.

55-c Titles

Use quotation marks to enclose the titles of essays and articles, short stories, poems, songs, speeches, parts of books, and episodes of radio and television programs.

An article entitled "Answering Systems from Hell" captures people's frustrations with corporate and governmental phone-answering trees. [article]

A similar note of melancholy is struck in Alice Munro's story "Jakarta." [short story]

This poem invites, and suffers from, comparison with Sylvia Plath's searing "Daddy." [poem]

My favourite Barenaked Ladies song is "If I Had $1000000." [song]

Martin Luther King, Jr., delivered his famous "I Have a Dream Speech" in 1963. [speech]

The authors of this computer guide discuss everything from mice to modems in a chapter entitled "Inside Out." [part of a book]

In "Forever Young," my favourite episode of *Grey's Anatomy*, a bus accident brings high-school students and a man Miranda had a crush on to the hospital. [episode of a television program]

NOTE: Italicize the titles of complete works such as books and periodicals (see 62-a).

55-d Other Uses for Quotation Marks

1. Quotation marks are sometimes used to set off words used ironically.

   > My "assets" consist of an Ikea bedroom suite and an overdrawn bank account.
   > The "therapy" psychiatry provides can be damaging to its recipients.

2. Quotation marks may be used to enclose words used as words or terms.

   > The word "skinny" has negative connotations.

   > The plural of "datum" is "data."

   > "Anomie" is a state of social breakdown.
   > NOTE: Italics may be used instead of quotation marks for this purpose (see 62-b).

3. Use quotation marks for words coined (invented) by a writer.

   > Interviews with "sexperts" are the backbone of Miller's irreverent study of sexual etiquette.

55-e Quotation Marks with Other Punctuation

1. Place commas and periods *inside* closing quotation marks.

   > "I'm studying for the chemistry exam," said Ahmed. "I expect to be up all night."

2. Place colons and semicolons *outside* quotation marks.

   > The narrator's intellectual curiosity about his mother's disease evolves into "lunatic devotion"; he neglects his wife and child to stay at his mother's side.

   > Here is the terrible truth about the "anorexia industry": it reinforces the very phenomenon it is designed to combat.

3. Put question marks and exclamation marks inside quotation marks if they belong to the quotation and outside if they apply to the sentence as a whole.

   > He said, "What's the matter?"

   > Has anyone read John Ralston Saul's essay "The Politics of Common Sense"?

Lisa said, "That's the dumbest thing I ever heard!"

On his résumé, our most uncooperative employee actually called himself a "team player"!

4. Place footnote numbers and page citations outside quotation marks.

As Abraham Maslow comments in his book *Motivation and Personality*, "It is quite true that man lives by bread alone when there is no bread."[1]

In *The Intelligence of Dogs*, Stanley Coren describes the Dandie Dinmont terrier as "a very distinctive little dog with deep soulful eyes" (13).

56 THE APOSTROPHE

The apostrophe has three main uses: to indicate the possessive case; to substitute for letters in contractions; and to form the plural of letters, numbers, and words used as words or terms.

56-a Possession

1. Add an apostrophe and -*s* (-*'s*) to form the possessive case of singular nouns (including those ending in -*s*) and indefinite pronouns.

The *teacher's* new car is a lemon.

Many of *Mavis Gallant's* short stories explore the dark repercussions of a world built on class differences.

The *witness's* testimony is full of contradictions.

It could have been *anyone's* book.

The reading list includes *Dickens's* most popular works.

EXCEPTIONS: To form the possessive of many Greek names and the names *Jesus* and *Moses*, add an apostrophe only (Jesus' teachings, Moses' leadership, Socrates' death, Euripides' plays, Ulysses' travels).

2. Add an apostrophe to form the possessive case of plural nouns ending in -*s*. If the plural does not end in -*s*, add an apostrophe and -*s*.

The *Joneses'* house has been sold.

The *students'* books were on the table.

We are raising money for the *children's* fund.

3. To indicate joint possession by two or more owners, make only the last noun possessive. To indicate individual possession, make all nouns possessive.

Nova and Seb's presentation was the most polished.

Candace's and *Todd's* political views differ greatly.

4. To form the possessive of compound nouns (a noun consisting of two or more words), add an apostrophe and -*s* to the last word.

Her *son-in-law's* play was panned by the critics.

Joan of Arc's battles against the English helped to revive French patriotism.

FORMING THE POSSESSIVE CASE WITH APOSTROPHES

Singular noun not ending in -*s*	add -'*s*
Singular noun ending in -*s*	add -'*s*
Indefinite pronoun	add -'*s*
Plural noun ending in -*s*	add apostrophe
Plural noun not ending in -*s*	add -'*s*
Two or more nouns	
joint possession	add -'*s* to last noun
individual possession	add -'*s* to all nouns
Compound noun	add -'*s* to last word in compound

56-b Contractions

Contractions are formed when certain letters are left out of words or phrases. As the following examples illustrate, an apostrophe is used to replace the missing letter or letters:

cannot/can't	rock and roll/rock 'n' roll
do not/don't	she is, she has/she's
does not/doesn't	she would, she had/she'd
I am/I'm	there is, there has/there's
I would/I'd	you will/you'll
is not/isn't	was not/wasn't
it is/it's	who is/who's
let us/let's	will not/won't
of the clock/o'clock	would not/wouldn't

Contractions are used frequently in conversation and informal writing, but they are usually avoided in formal writing.

56-c Plurals

Use apostrophes to form the plural of letters, numbers, and words used as words.

> Remember to dot your *i*'s and cross your *t*'s. [letters]

> At the 2002 Olympics, the judges awarded Canadian pairs skaters Salé and Pelletier *6.0*'s for their signature "Love Story" program. [number]

> The two *Incomplete*'s on Tim's transcript were a direct result of his illness earlier that year. [word used as a word]

NOTE: Styles change, and the current trend is to omit the apostrophe for many of these plurals (e.g., the three Rs, the 1990s, too many *if*s). Where there is the possibility of confusion or awkwardness, however, maintain the apostrophe.

57 THE SLASH

1. In a short quotation, use the slash to separate lines of a poem included within your text. Leave a space before and after each slash.

    > In "Low Tide on Grand Pre," Bliss Carman describes the aging process: "I deemed / That time was ripe, and years had done / Their wheeling underneath the sun."

2. Use a slash to separate the numerator and denominator in a fraction and the elements of an abbreviated date. Do not include a space before and after the slash in these situations.

    > $x/a + y/b = 1$.

    > 99/08/25

3. A slash is sometimes used instead of a hyphen to indicate a period overlapping two calendar years and to separate paired terms such as *student/teacher* and *producer/director*.

    > The Canadian Opera Company subscribers are looking forward to the 2009/10 season.

    > Union/management relations have deteriorated in recent years.

    > Avoid the use of *and/or* and *he/she* in formal writing.

1. Use parentheses to enclose supplementary information.

> Nellie McClung (1873–1951) fought for women's suffrage, factory safety legislation, and many other reforms.

> Tom Thomson's evocative paintings of northern Ontario's rugged landscapes (landscapes now threatened by logging interests) have lost none of their ability to captivate.

2. The material enclosed by parentheses may, among other things, identify, amplify, illustrate, clarify, or comment.

> A study of Ottawa politics would necessarily focus on the three P's (power, perks, and patronage) and the major players (MPs, deputy ministers, bureaucrats, lobbyists, and the press). [identifies]

> Alice Munro's eighth collection of short stories (all but one of which were originally published in *The New Yorker*) consolidated her reputation as a world-class storyteller. [amplifies]

> The drug guide's index lists a wide range of generic and brand-name drugs but only a smattering of subject entries ("refrigerating medicines" appears but not "ulcers" or "migraine"). [illustrates]

> Genetic (hereditary) information is organized into threadlike structures called chromosomes. [clarifies]

> The insidious partnership between politicians and lobbyists (a partnership virtually ignored by the media) runs counter to the values of a democratic society. [comments]

3. Parentheses are also used to enclose numbers or letters in a list.

> To conduct the experiment, you require the following materials: (1) safety goggles, (2) electrolysis apparatus, (3) water, (4) 5 g sodium sulfate, (5) power supply, (6) electrical leads, and (7) wooden splints.

PUNCTUATION X

BRACKETS   59

1. Use square brackets to enclose words or comments you have inserted into a quotation.

> Frank Newell, an embalmer from Yarmouth, "unexpectedly found [among the *Titanic*'s recovered dead] the body of a relative."

Timothy Findley described Glenn Gould as one of the "god-people, [who] are the truly, absolutely gifted, almost beyond human dimension or human comprehension."

The second of the preceding example sentences shows how brackets can be used to make a quotation grammatically consistent with the rest of the sentence.

2. If there is an error in the quotation, you can follow the error with a bracketed *sic*. Latin for "so" or "thus," *sic* is a way of telling readers that the mistake was in the original.

In a press release, the CEO said the company would "do everything possible to accompany [*sic*] the strikers' demands."

60 THE DASH

1. Like commas or parentheses, dashes may be used to set off parenthetical material. Dashes bring more emphasis to the added material than either commas or parentheses.

The biographer's account of Leonard Cohen's life—from his comfortable Westmount childhood, through his early days as a struggling poet, to his second career as a songwriter/performer— is meticulous and gracefully written.

2. Like colons, dashes may be used to introduce a list, an appositive, or an explanation.

The alternative bookstore offers seminars on three New Age topics— holistic medicine, Gaia theory, and reincarnation. [list]

David Cronenberg's twin passions—science and literature—are expressed in many of his films. [appositive]

Doctors who perform unnecessary surgical procedures have *furor therapeuticus*—the fury to treat—regardless of the potential costs to patients. [explanation]

3. A dash may also be used to signal an interruption or an abrupt shift in tone or thought.

"I don't understand what—" Liz broke off in confusion.

Julio Camargo's novel *Blindness* is tightly plotted, progressively disorienting, confusing in action—and surprisingly flat in its ending.

4. In MLA-, APA-, and Chicago-style essays, you can use either two hyphens (--) or a word-processing dash (—) to form a dash. There is no space before or after a dash.

ELLIPSES

1. The omission of words from a quotation is indicated by the use of ellipsis points. Use three points to indicate the omission of words within a sentence or the omission of a complete sentence or more within a quotation. (To indicate an omission that is preceded by a complete sentence, use four points, the first of which functions as a sentence period.)

> In their introduction to the *ITP Nelson Canadian Dictionary of the English Language,* the authors write, "We have . . . sought to show how the development of . . . Canadian English . . . mirrors our development as a nation."

Here is the original text of the quotation in the above example (omissions in italics):

> We have *also* sought to show how the development of *our own variety of English,* Canadian English, mirrors our development as a nation.

2. Use ellipsis points when you omit material from the middle or end of a quotation.

> Ben Okri writes, "we are living the stories planted in us early or along the way, or we are . . . living the stories we planted . . . in ourselves."

Do not use ellipsis points at the beginning of a quotation. You are entitled to start a quotation wherever you choose, as long as doing so does not change the original meaning of the quotation.

3. When your omission follows a period, include the period and then add the ellipsis. In the Calvert example below, you therefore have four points, the last three comprising the actual ellipsis. No space appears between the last letter and the first point because that point is the period of the quoted sentence and is not part of the ellipsis.

> In 1982, pre-tax bank profits were $1630.2 million, while taxes were $104.8 million. . . . an effective tax rate of 6.4% . . ." (Calvert 39).

4. MLA style requires that you place brackets around ellipsis points you have utilized to signal an omission from a quotation if the author of the quotation has already used ellipsis points in the passage.

> In "Just Rain, Racolet," Brand's narrator remarks, "So I did not mention the unnecessary clutter of tourists and cameras which had to be policed and . . . So I took this as a gift, this intimacy at Turtle Beach [. . .] and the lights and the hotel and the cigarette-smoking man Vi told to 'have a little respect.'"

5. The omission of one or more lines of poetry is indicated by a line of spaced periods running approximately the length of the preceding line.

> Turning and turning in the widening gyre
>
> The falcon cannot hear the falconer;
>
> Things fall apart; the centre cannot hold;
>
> . . . .
>
> Surely some revelation is at hand;
>
> Surely the Second Coming is at hand.
>
> – William Butler Yeats, "The Second Coming"

6. Ellipsis points may be used to mark a pause or hesitation.

> The oil companies are concerned above all with achieving . . . what? Profits at the expense of the environment.

> Sergio said, "It's just . . . I mean, if you want to know the truth . . . I'm not sure what caused the accident."

EXERCISES

EXERCISE X-1 COMMAS, SEMICOLONS, AND COLONS

Correct the errors in punctuation in the following passages. If you find errors of any other type, correct them too.

A. COMMAS TO SET OFF

Multinational corporations have had a larger effect on the way we live than we think. The most evident signs of their presence in our communities are the large malls and big box stores. It doesn't matter where you go in North America these days; the big box stores and the massive malls are everywhere.

At first we think of the large stores the so-called big box stores as having better prices than the small family run stores that used to dominate communities. We still use the term "mom and pop corner store" to describe these small community businesses. In most cases these small stores served a local community and knew their clients. When you entered a small business you could be assured of personal service by someone who knew what was in the store and would be able to help you if you were searching for a solution to a problem. Indeed personal service was one of the cornerstones of small businesses. If they were not able to keep their customers happy they knew they would lose that business.

Now people are enticed by the lower prices that large stores can offer them. They think they will be saving money if they buy at a large store. The selection is good, and the prices are good too. What more could people want? However there are hidden costs associated with buying goods at a big box store. Without a doubt these are not costs that such stores would be interested in you understanding.

Some of the large multinational corporations that run retail stores build their stores just outside of city limits to avoid higher taxes. Although this might be good for the corporation it is not necessarily good for anyone living within the city for two reasons. Large stores have a negative effect on small businesses. In a number of small towns where large stores have moved into facilities on the edge of town the downtown core starts to experience a decline in business. Stores close down, and people lose gainful employment. Although people are initially excited to go to the new store which has everything and look for bargains once the small stores in the downtown core have closed their doors the large store on the edge of town becomes the only centre where anyone can shop. When you are the only store in town you don't have to be as competitive and cut prices as you did before.

Besides having an effect on the downtown core of smaller centres the large store on the edge of town also has a negative impact on the city's tax base. Although the store may not be within the city's limits it as we have seen does have an impact on businesses that do reside within the city's limits and do pay taxes. Once those businesses close, however individual families may well find their property tax bill increasing or their municipal services declining.

Additionally the large store can also have a negative effect on those who work. Large stores like to have a small full-time staff and a large part-time staff. Having a large part-time staff means that they don't have to pay benefits and don't have to pay their staff more than the minimum wage. Sadly in this day and age as Naomi Klein points out in her book *No Logo* more and more large businesses treat their staff as if they are either students in need of part-time work to fund extras or old and retired and only working for pin money. Full-time work that pays a living wage is becoming harder and harder to find.

As you can see sometimes a bargain is not necessarily a bargain.

Total errors: 30 or 31 (one optional comma)

B. COMMAS TO SEPARATE AND COMMAS TO SET OFF

Newfoundland the last province in Canada to join Confederation joined on March 31 1949. Today, Newfoundlanders still comment on how distinct Newfoundland is and how mainlanders are different from them. This is not surprising, given Newfoundland's history, its unique cultural mix and the isolation that it has from the rest of Canada. Not surprisingly today Newfoundlanders are somewhat distrustful of the rest of Canada. Older Newfoundlanders still think of Newfoundland as a country not a province certainly not one of the Maritime Provinces. Yet the peoples of Newfoundland are distinct. In looking at Newfoundland, one must remember that St. John's the capital, is 687 kilometres from Corner Brook and 1,088 kilometres from St. Anthony which lies near the tip of the Northern Peninsula. The isolation of communities from one another before Newfoundland joined Confederation gave people in the outports a distinct sense of where they lived and who they were. Even today, the accents of some of the communities in Newfoundland speak to this isolation and the ethnicity of the people who settled in the communities. In the Avalon Peninsula near St. John's, Newfoundland's largest city, the place names reflect the colourful people who settled Newfoundland and made it their home: Pouch Cove, Witless Bay, Mistaken Point, Villa Marie, Chapel Arm, Dildo, Heart's Desire, Heart's Content and Gallows Cove.

A trip to Newfoundland is not complete without a journey to the west coast to Gros Morne National Park a UNESCO World Heritage Site, and to L'Anse aux Meadows in the north near St. Anthony. Gros Morne which contains spectacular examples of both continental drift and glacial erosion is home to over 230 species of birds. West Brook Pond a glacial trough, is surrounded by cliffs that rise 686 metres from its shoreline. Of interest also is Gros Morne Mountain the second highest peak in Newfoundland which rises 806 metres from sea level. The mountaintop is the most southern example of Arctic tundra and has been home to rock ptarmigan Arctic hare and woodland caribou. Like Gros Morne L'Anse aux Meadows is a UNESCO World Heritage Site. At L'Anse aux Meadows Parks Canada has erected replicas of the Norse settlement that was located here one thousand years ago. From the sod houses of the community you can look north and east toward a windswept bay. A change in climate that brought shorter and shorter summers and longer and longer winters affected the viability of the Viking settlement and eventually drove the Vikings back to Greenland.

Total errors: 22

C. THE SEMICOLON AND THE COLON

Note: This passage utilizes the MLA system for references.

In 2008: 150 years after the beginning of immigration from China to Canada; the complexity of the history of the Chinese in Canada is still unfolding. The titles of the books on the Chinese are in themselves an indication of some of the trials and tribulations the Chinese faced, *In the Sea of Sterile Mountains, A White Man's Province,* and *White Canada Forever: Popular Attitudes and Public Policy Toward Orientals in British Columbia* are evocative of the attitudes of the Euro-Canadian population toward immigration from China. The Opium Wars between the Chinese and Western powers from 1839 to 1869 not only was a sad period in China's history but also revealed, as James Morton points out in his book: *In the Sea of Sterile Mountains,* the attitude of major Western powers toward China. Morton notes that there is no small irony in the fact that the

Chinese had to: "be beaten senseless because they would not allow the importation of opium" (xiii). It is in this same period that the Chinese from the southern region of Guangdong province around the Pearl River basin started to immigrate to the west coast of North America. At first, they immigrated to California, as the 1849 gold rush in California held promise of relief from poverty, later, in 1858, their attention turned to gold discoveries on the Fraser River; an area that would eventually become a part of the province of British Columbia. As Wickberg points out in *From China to Canada*, three months into the Fraser River gold rush, the first Chinese purchased land in Esquimault, and Lee Chong: who came north from San Francisco, opened a business on Cormorant Street, the street destined to become the centre of Victoria's Chinatown. Wickberg writes: "He was the first Chinese to bring his wife and children to Victoria" (14). Wickberg also observes the 1871 census: "counted 1,548 Chinese, [but] there were only fifty-three women in the province, a ratio of only 35 per 1,000" (14). It is this fact that Patricia E. Roy seizes on in her book *A White Man's Province: British Columbia Politicians and Chinese and Japanese Immigrants, 1858–1914*. Roy calls the Chinese who came to the British crown colony at this point: "colonial sojourners." She writes that:

> The Chinese, however, set themselves apart in the Chinatowns that became a part of many British Columbia communities. This separation reduced opportunities for conflict and competition, but it also suggested that the Chinese were sojourners who did not want to mingle with the whites, settle permanently in British Columbia, or invest their earnings in its economy. (4)

Roy sees the Chinese as setting themselves apart from the rest of the community. She does not take into account the history of immigration patterns of other peoples who came to North America; nor does she examine the underlying sensibilities of the Chinese, many of whom were sponsored by villages in China and obliged, in a tradition common to a number of cultures around the world, to send money home to impoverished relatives.

As Kay Anderson points out in *Vancouver's Chinatown: Racial Discourse in Canada, 1875–1980*, "In an important and neglected sense, then, 'Chinatown' belongs as much to the society with the power to define and shape it as it does to its residents" (10). The exclusionary policies of Canada between 1871 and 1947 toward people of Chinese ancestry are a matter of public record.

In the article "Settling the Score: Hope for Redress in the Year of the Rooster," published in the online journal *Asian Canadian* on January 2, 2005, Sean Rossiter quotes Gim Wong as observing that the money paid by Chinese people immigrating to Canada starting in 1871: "'damn near $25 million'—was also the cost of building the Canadian Pacific Railway, not counting the lives of the 1,400 labourers who died doing the most hazardous work, such as blasting. The CPR was B.C.'s price for joining confederation."

Total errors: 14

EXERCISE X-2 PUNCTUATION

The following passage contains a variety of punctuation errors. Rewrite the passage so that it is correctly punctuated and all the errors are removed.

In his 2003 Massey Lectures *The Truth about Stories* Thomas King remarks repeatedly "The truth about stories is that that's all we are." King's assertion sounds like an oversimplification at first. How could we simply be stories. Aren't we more than that more than the sum of the parts more than the individual highlights more than the people we meet the places we visit the books we read the films we see the music we listen to. Are we just that. And if not what is it that we imagine we are. Like Denys Arcand's main character in his Academy Award winning *The Barbarian Invasions* we seem always to be questing for the something we did not do the something we did not say the somewhere we did not go we are afraid to be satisfied with the things we have done the people we have met and the stories we have told one another. In much of Canada we have forgotten how to tell stories of being. Instead we rely on the stories of others, films or books that tell us about what we think we would like to experience, where we would like to be. But that wish only negates our own experiences and trivializes them into ephemera, simple flotsam and jetsam tiresome and of no interest to others. Ironically it is in these ephemera, these so called flotsam and jetsam that the true stories lie, the ones that King writes of and the ones that are central to Arcand's film they are the substance of humanity the essence of who we are. It is these stories that we should be telling to others it is these stories that define us.

It is easy to miss the import of our stories, we too readily turn to the stories of others to define who we are what our culture is and where we live. But if we start to listen to our own stories to the personal histories we will arrive at a better understanding of our existence and the existence of those around us. It is no wonder that King ends each of his lectures, lectures filled with his own personal stories, and the stories of other writers with the remark:

> Take [this] story, for instance. It's yours. Do with it what you will. Cry over it. Get angry. Forget it. But don't say in the years to come that you would have lived your life differently if only you had heard this story.
>
> You've heard it now.

Truly we are the stories we tell, truly those stories are not fictions, they define us. They tell us what is important and what we care about and want to pass on to others. This is what Eliot is writing about when he observes in "Little Gidding": Here, the intersection of the timeless moment / is England and nowhere. Never and always." The next time you travel somewhere in your country listen to the stories you are told and the ones you tell. You will be the richer if you do.

Total errors: 45 or 47

EXERCISE X-3 QUOTATION MARKS, BRACKETS, ELLIPSES, AND SLASHES

The first three of the punctuation marks named above are associated primarily with handling quoted statements, especially in the writing of a formal report or essay. Even the slash has, as one of its uses, the separation of lines of quoted poetry. Read the following exercise as though it were part of a research essay. Read the excerpts that are quoted in Part 1 of the punctuation exercise first and become familiar with them. Then read the exercise itself, Part 2, and decide where the punctuation marks should go. Insert whatever punctuation is necessary to make the entire passage correctly punctuated.

NOTE: The slash that appears in the February 17 entry shows where page 51 ends and page 52 begins. For information about the use of the slash to indicate page breaks, see Chapter 17.

NOTE: For this exercise, use the conventions of MLA style.

PART 1

Excerpt 1

January 16

The cold is at this time so intense, that the ink freezes while I write, and my fingers stiffen round the pen; a glass of water at my bedside, within a few feet of the hearth, (heaped with logs of oak and maple kept burning all night long,) is a solid mass of ice in the morning. God help the poor emigrants who are yet unprepared against the rigours of the season!—yet this is nothing to the climate of the lower province, where, as we hear, the thermometer has been thirty degrees below zero. I lose all heart to write home, or to register a reflection or a feeling; thought stagnates in my head as the ink in my pen—and this will never do!—I must rouse myself to occupation; and if I cannot find it without, I must create it from within. There are yet four months of winter and leisure to be disposed of. How?—I know not; but they must be employed, not wholly lost.

February 17

"There is no society in Toronto," is what I hear repeated all around me—even by those who compose the only society we have. "But," you will say, "what could be expected in a remote town, which forty years ago was an uninhabited swamp, and twenty years ago only began to exist?" I really do not know what I expected, but I / will tell you what I did not expect. I did not expect to find here in this new capital of a new country, with the boundless forest within half a mile of us on every side,—concentrated as it were the worst evils of our old and most artificial social system at home, with none of its *agrémens,* and none of its advantages. Toronto is like a fourth or fifth rate provincial town, with the pretensions of a capital city. We have here a petty colonial oligarchy, a self-constituted aristocracy, based upon nothing real . . .

There reigns here a hateful factious spirit in political matters, but for the present no public or patriotic feeling, no recognition of general or generous principles of policy: as yet I have met with none of these. Canada is a colony, not a country; it is not yet identified with the dearest affections and associations, remembrance, and hopes of its inhabitants: it is to them an adopted, not a real mother. Their love, their pride, are not for poor Canada, but for high and happy England; but a few more generations must change this.

Source: Anne Brownell Jameson, excerpts from *Winter Studies and Summer Rambles in Canada,* in *An Anthology of Canadian Literature in English,* edited by Russell Brown, Donna Bennett, and Nathalie Cooke (Toronto: Oxford University Press, 1990), 51–52.

Excerpt 2

Each for a moment faces them all and stands
In his little desperate ring; like a tired bull moose
Whom scores of sleepless wolves, a ravening pack,
Have chased all night, all day
Through the snow-laden woods, like famine let loose;

. . . .

But afar in the ring of the forest,
Where the air is so tender with May
And the waters are wild in the moonlight
They lie in their silence of clay.
The numberless stars out of heaven
Look down with a pitiful glance;
And the lilies asleep in the forest
Are closed like the lilies of France.

Source: Excerpted from Archibald Lampman, "At the Long Sault: May, 1660," in Russell Brown, Donna Bennett, and Nathalie Cooke, eds., *An Anthology of Canadian Literature in English* (Toronto: Oxford University Press, 1990), 159–60.

PART 2

Here is the passage you are asked to punctuate correctly. You need use only quotation marks, ellipses, brackets, and the slash to do so. Pay particular attention to quotations that have been changed from their original form, whether by deletion or substitution.

As Douglas Jones once observed, Canada's problem, through much of its history, has been the absence of a central and sustaining mythology. If a country is to have a culture, it must have a mythology, a central set of images, narratives, and perspectives through which it defines itself. This problem is greatly magnified for a country formed by immigrants who refused to accept the mythology of the indigenous inhabitants.

We see the outlines of the problem when we read an early Canadian writer like Anna Brownell Jameson, whose *Winter Studies and Summer Rambles in Canada* was written expressly for an English audience. She states unequivocally

> Canada is a colony, not a *country;* not yet identified with the dearest affections and associations, remembrances, and hopes of its inhabitants: it is to Canadians an adopted, not a real mother. Their love, their pride, are not for poor Canada, but for England; but a few more generations must change all this. (52)

Her confidence that this would change quickly was misplaced. It was to take longer than a few generations to accomplish the creation of a national mythology. Part of the means by which it was accomplished was for Canadians to build a sense of their land as unique. If we think of wilderness village town city as a continuum, the general scene for the new country, the town city part of it evolved more slowly. Here again Jameson is instructive. She says, There is no society in Toronto, I hear even from those who compose the only society we have (51). Later, she describes Toronto as a fourth or fifth rate provincial town, with the pretensions of a capital city (52). The very terms she uses in this description reveal her inability to see Toronto or Canada on its own terms, and the inability of the inhabitants to attempt anything more than an awkward transplant of English perspectives and constructs into the new land.

Not surprisingly, then, when Jameson describes the brute physical facts of the new country, it is as though she were talking about an adversary rather than a friend. She complains, I could almost wish myself a dormouse, or a she-bear, to sleep away the rest of this cold, cold winter and The cold is at this time so intense, that the ink freezes while I write a glass of water by my bedside is a solid mass of ice in the morning (50). Here the country and its weather is merely something to be endured.

Fifty years later, the mythmaking capacity is much more in evidence when we read a poet like Archibald Lampman. In his poem At the Long Sault: May, 1660, he consciously tries to create a mythic version of the defence, by sixty Frenchmen, Hurons, and Algonquins, of a fort on the Ottawa River, against a vastly superior force of Iroquois numbering five hundred. Here the wilderness is spoken of as a friend. The small group of defenders are even compared to a tired bull moose Whom scores of sleepless wolves, a ravening pack, Have chased all night (158). They are, naturally, overcome in the end, but Lampman tries to persuade us that they are heroes of a new land. This simple attempt to mythologize is one means of building a mythology in which the new country has its own validity and presence. The poem has many weaknesses, including its rhetorical heightening, but its intention is a necessary one. Heroes are a part of any mythology, and heightening is a necessary part of their presentation. Thus, we leave the dead defenders in the following lines:

> But afar in the ring of the forest,
> Where the air is so tender with May

They lie in their silence of clay.
The numberless stars out of heaven
Look down with a pitiful glance;
And the lilies asleep in the forest
Are closed like the lilies of France. (160)

Of course, this may seem overdone by today's standards. But we should not miss the attempt to fuse the old country with the new, and to create heroes out of actions in Canada rather than import them from France or England. In an awkward but honest way, lilies and forest are brought together. The slow effort to construct our own mythology has begun. Here, the wilderness village part of the continuum is addressed; later writers could create the town city mythology.

Mechanics

62-a Titles of Works

In word-processed documents, titles of complete works are italicized. In hand-written work, whether on exams or in-class tests, underlining is used to indicate italics (<u>The English Patient</u>). Quotation marks are used for short poems and titles that are parts of complete works, such as essays and short stories (see 55-c).

BOOKS	*Great Expectations, The Last Crossing*
CHOREOGRAPHIC WORKS	Balanchine's *Agon*, Alvin Ailey's *Revelations*
COMIC STRIPS	*Sherman's Lagoon, Doonesbury*
FILMS	*There Will Be Blood, Juno*
JOURNALS	*New England Journal of Medicine, Canadian Historical Review*
LONG MUSICAL COMPOSITIONS	Handel's *Messiah*, Puccini's *La Bohème*
LONG POEMS	*The Prelude, Seed Catalogue*
MAGAZINES	*Maclean's, Canadian Business*
NEWSPAPERS	*The Globe and Mail, Le Devoir*
PAMPHLETS	Paine's *Common Sense, Facts about the Flu*
PLAYS	*Hamlet, Coming Up for Air*
RADIO PROGRAMS	*Ideas, As It Happens*
TELEVISION PROGRAMS	*Friends, Canada: A People's History*
WORKS OF VISUAL ART	Michelangelo's *David*, Colville's *Horse and Train*

NOTE: Do not italicize the titles of (1) sacred books, such as the Bible, the Talmud, or the Koran; (2) legal and political documents, such as Magna Carta, the Charter of Rights and Freedoms, the Criminal Code, or the Canadian Environmental Protection Act; and (3) software, such as Microsoft Word or WordPerfect.

62-b Other Uses

In the following cases, underlining can be used in lieu of italics in handwritten work.

1. Italicize the names of aircraft, spacecraft, ships, and trains.

    In May 1927, Charles Lindbergh made the first solo transatlantic flight in a monoplane named *Spirit of St. Louis.*

    It was the flight of the space shuttle *Discovery* in 1992 that made Roberta Bondar the second Canadian astronaut in space.

    Sir Ernest Shackleton's polar exploration vessel, the unfortunately named *Endurance,* was crushed in ice in 1914 and sank months later.

    In the 1960s, a train called the *Rapido* took passengers from Toronto to Montreal in a little over four hours.

    NOTE: Do not use italics for vehicle types (Boeing 747, Avro Arrow).

2. Italicize foreign words and phrases.

    The long collaboration between Margaret Atwood and Charles Pachter, which began in the mid-1960s, brought into Canada the tradition of the *livre d'artiste.*

    NOTE: Do not italicize foreign words that are frequently used by English speakers and thus are considered part of the English language (e.g., "ad infinitum," "bona fide," "habeas corpus," "noblesse oblige," "per capita," "tour de force," and "vice versa").

3. Use italics for the biological classifications of plants, animals, insects, and microorganisms. Note that the genus name but not the species name is capitalized.

    Rosa acicularis

    Felis domesticus

4. Italicize words, letters, and numbers referred to as words.

    The word *NIMBY* sums up that neighbourhood lobby group.

    He thought *committed* was spelled with one *m* and one *t.*

    A circled *46* appeared at the top of his math test.

    NOTE: Quotation marks may be used instead of italics for this purpose. (See 55-d.)

5. Italicize the names of legal cases.

   R. v. Morgentaler

   Bhinder v. Canadian National Railway

   Saint John (City) v. McKenna

6. Italics may be used to create emphasis.

   Antidepressants can mask feelings and can also *cause* depression.

63 CAPITALIZATION

63-a Sentence Capitals

1. The first word of a sentence is capitalized unless the sentence is contained within another sentence and enclosed in parentheses or dashes.

   The thunderhead darkened the prairie sky.

   The author follows his introduction with a historical overview of the right wing in Canada (a decline in racist activity after the Second World War ended in a "virtual explosion" in the 1970s and 1980s) and detailed sections on the Canadian Nazi Party and the Edmund Burke Society.

   NOTE: A sentence in parentheses that is not part of another sentence begins with a capital letter: *The board of directors met on Monday. (No details concerning the meeting were released to the press.) On Thursday they voted to fire the CEO.*

2. A quoted complete sentence that is blended into the writer's sentence begins with a lowercase letter.

   George Orwell believed that "modern English, especially written English, is full of bad habits."

   If the quoted complete sentence has a more remote syntactic relation to the rest of the sentence, the initial capital is retained.

   As George Orwell said, "Modern English, especially written English, is full of bad habits."

3. If a quoted sentence is interrupted by a speaker tag (*he said, she wrote*, etc.), do not capitalize the first word after the speaker tag.

"After one of these storms," she said, "the sky looks like pink cotton candy."

4. When two complete sentences are linked by a colon, the second sentence does not begin with a capital letter unless it is a quotation.

The government took drastic measures: it imposed martial law.

Jack McClelland's response to the failure of *The Stone Angel* to capture a Governor General's Award was characteristically blunt: "It's a goddamn disgrace."

NOTE: A sentence that follows a dash always starts with a small letter: *There's no doubt about it—the honeymoon's over.*

63-b Proper Nouns

1. Proper nouns name particular persons, places, and things. Common nouns name generic classes of persons, places, and things.

PROPER NOUNS	COMMON NOUNS
Judith Thompson	playwright
Mount Logan	mountain
Jupiter	planet
Giller Prize	book award

2. Capitalize all proper nouns and the adjectives derived from them. Do not capitalize common nouns unless they begin a sentence. The following categories of words are always capitalized:

• personal names
• days of the week and months of the year
• official and popular names of geographic areas
• official names of organizations
• names of deities, religions, and religious writings
• names of racial, linguistic, religious, and other groups of people
• names of civic holidays and holy days
• names of historical periods
• names of specific aircraft, spacecraft, ships, and trains
• names of structures
• names of planets, stars, and other bodies in space

Here are some specific examples:

CIVIC HOLIDAYS/ HOLY DAYS	Canada Day, Yom Kippur
GEOGRAPHICAL AREAS	Maritimes, the Canadian North, Ottawa Valley
HISTORICAL EVENTS	Riel Rebellion, October Crisis
ORGANIZATIONS	New Democratic Party, Canadian Centre for Policy Alternatives
PERSONAL NAMES	Pierre Trudeau, Jeremy Wotherspoon
RELIGIOUS REFERENCES	Judaism, Catholic Church, Buddhist
STRUCTURES	Westminster Abbey, CN Tower
TRADE NAMES	Aspirin, Coke, Kleenex, Styrofoam, Xerox

3. Capitalize titles of persons that directly precede a proper name. Do not capitalize titles used alone or following a proper name.

> Prime Minister Martin first met with President Bush in the spring of 2004.

> Paul Martin, the prime minister, first met with the U.S. president in the spring of 2004.

63-c Titles of Works

In MLA style, capitalize the first and last words in titles of works and all other words except for articles, prepositions, coordinating conjunctions, and the *to* part of an infinitive. MLA also recommends that a title for a work be italicized.

MLA *The Ingenuity Gap: How We Can Solve the Problems of the Future*

APA style requires that the first word of a title or subtitle and all proper nouns be capitalized. It also recommends that a title be italicized. Chicago style allows you to follow either the MLA or APA format in capitalizing a title but recommends that the title be italicized.

APA *The ingenuity gap: How we can solve the problems of the future*

64-a Titles of Persons

1. Academic, religious, political, and military titles are usually abbreviated when they directly precede a full name and spelled out when they precede a surname alone.

Prof. Ali Ghazal	Professor Ghazal
Rev. Douglas Chambers	the Reverend Chambers
Sen. Gail Ling	Senator Ling
Rear-Adm. Michael Sykes	Rear-Admiral Sykes
Gov. Gen. Michaëlle Jean	Governor General Jean

2. A title that stands alone is not abbreviated.

    professor

    My English ~~prof.~~ says that Walt Whitman is considered the greatest American poet.

3. Do not use a title before a name if another title follows the name. The title *Dr. Yetta Abramsky, Ph.D.* is redundant. Either *Dr. Yetta Abramsky* or *Yetta Abramsky, Ph.D.* would be acceptable depending on the context.

64-b Geographical Names

1. The names of countries are usually spelled out in running text. A common exception is *U.S.*, which may appear in text as an adjective but not as a noun.

UNACCEPTABLE	Canada's largest trading partner is the U.S.
ACCEPTABLE	Many Canadians are troubled by our dependence on the U.S. economy.

2. In bibliographical citations, the names of provinces, territories, and states are abbreviated. Listed below are the traditional abbreviations for provinces/territories and the two-letter abbreviations used by Canada Post.

	TRADITIONAL	CANADA POST
Alberta	Alta.	AB
British Columbia	B.C.	BC
Manitoba	Man.	MB
New Brunswick	N.B.	NB
Newfoundland and Labrador	Nfld. and Lab.	NL
Northwest Territories	N.W.T.	NT
Nunavut	—	NU
Nova Scotia	N.S.	NS

	TRADITIONAL	CANADA POST
Ontario	Ont.	ON
Prince Edward Island	P.E.I.	PE
Quebec	Que. or P.Q.	QC
Saskatchewan	Sask.	SK
Yukon Territory	Y.T.	YT

64-c Acronyms and Initialisms

1. *Acronyms* are abbreviations that can be pronounced as words (*PEN, NAFTA, RAM*). *Initialisms* are abbreviations that are pronounced letter by letter (*MP, VHS, IBM*). Here are some examples of acronyms and initialisms:

CBC	Canadian Broadcasting Corporation
CNR	Canadian National Railways
CRTC	Canadian Radio-television and Telecommunications Commission
CSA	Canadian Standards Association
CUPE	Canadian Union of Public Employees
NATO	North Atlantic Treaty Organization
NDP	New Democratic Party
NFB	National Film Board of Canada
RCMP	Royal Canadian Mounted Police
UNESCO	United Nations Educational, Scientific, and Cultural Organization

2. If you think your audience is unlikely to know what an acronym or initialism stands for, write the full name at the first use, followed by the acronym or initialism in parentheses; in subsequent mentions, use the acronym or initialism by itself. If you are using an acronym or initialism only once or twice in an essay, write the full name at each mention.

3. Geographical initialisms may be written with or without periods (*U.K.* or *UK, U.S.* or *USA*).

64-d Era Designations and Time of Day

1. The abbreviation A.D. precedes a date, and B.C. follows a date. Acceptable alternatives are B.C.E. and C.E.

1000 B.C.   before Christ

A.D. 1700   *anno Domini* (in the year of our Lord)

1000 B.C.E.   before the common era

1700 C.E.   common era

NOTE: Era designations are often set in small caps with or without periods (A.D./AD).

2.   The abbreviations A.M. and P.M. are acceptable only when used with figures.

6:45 A.M.   *ante meridiem* (before noon)

10:30 P.M.   *post meridiem* (after noon)

NOTE: A.M. and P.M. are often set in lowercase letters (a.m./p.m.) or in small caps (P.M.).

64-e Scholarly Abbreviations

General abbreviations such as *etc.*, *e.g.*, and *i.e.* are appropriate in informal writing. Some authorities consider the use of such abbreviations acceptable in formal writing, but only within parentheses or in tables.

Scholarly abbreviations are appropriate in notes and other forms of documentation. Here are some common scholarly abbreviations:

anon.	anonymous
b.	born
©	copyright ("© 2005")
cf.	compare (from the Latin *confer*)
d.	died
diss.	dissertation
ed.	editor (*pl.* eds.); edition; edited by
e.g.	for example (from the Latin *exempli gratia*)
esp.	especially
et al.	and others (from the Latin *et alii*)
i.e.	that is (from the Latin *id est*)
ms., mss.	manuscript, manuscripts
N.B.	note well (from the Latin *nota bene*)
n.d.	no date of publication
no., nos.	number, numbers
n.p.	no place of publication; no publisher; no page
p., pp.	page, pages
pref.	preface
pub.	publisher; publication; published by
ser.	series
supp.	supplement
rev.	review; revised; revision
vol., vols.	volume, volumes

XI MECHANICS

65-a Spelling Out

1. Numbers that can be expressed in one or two words should be spelled out in formal writing. (In technical and business writing, figures are often preferred, although usage varies.) Use figures for numbers that require more than two words to spell out.

   three
   The movie tells the story of ~~3~~ missionaries caught up in the turmoil of China's Boxer Rebellion.

   My mutual fund's investment portfolio includes holdings in *forty-seven* ~~47~~ Canadian blue-chip companies.

   894
   Wayne Gretzky scored ~~eight hundred and ninety-four~~ goals in the course of his NHL career.

   EXCEPTIONS: (1) Related numbers should be expressed in the same style: *Dalton McGuinty captured 71 of 107 seats in the 2007 Ontario election.* (2) To express sums of money in the millions or billions of dollars, you may use a combination of numbers and words accompanied by the dollar sign (*$15 billion*).

2. Do not begin a sentence with a figure, even when other numbers in the sentence are expressed in figures.
   Five
   ~~5~~ employees are responsible for processing between 80 and 120 application forms.

   A sentence that begins with a long number can be revised to avoid awkwardness.

UNACCEPTABLE	175 people attended Bob and Lynn's wedding.
AWKWARD	One hundred and seventy-five people attended Bob and Lynn's wedding.
REVISED	There were 175 people at Bob and Lynn's wedding.

65-b Punctuation of Numbers

In traditional English style, commas are used to separate groups of three digits. In SI (*Système international d'unités*) style, a space is used to mark the separation. The traditional style is appropriate for academic and general-interest materials. SI usage is usually restricted to technical or scientific writing.

85,000 [traditional]

85 000 [SI]

NOTE: In four-digit numbers, the use of a separating comma is optional: *Mount Everest is 8863* (or *8,863*) *metres above sea level.*

65-c Uses of Numbers

Numbers are appropriate in the following instances:

ADDRESSES	215 Pacific Avenue, Suite 1407
DATES	August 24, 2008 (*or* 24 August 2008)
DECIMALS, FRACTIONS	0.09, 3/4
DIVISIONS OF BOOKS	Chapter 8, Volume 2, page 63
DIVISIONS OF PLAYS	Act II, Scene iv (*or* Act 2, Scene 4), lines 5–13 (*or,* in MLA style, 2.4.5-13)
EXACT SUMS OF MONEY	$4829, $2.51
SCORES	a 6–5 victory
RATIOS	a ratio of 3 to 1, 2-to-1 odds
TIME OF DAY	9:00 A.M., 2:58 P.M. (*but* four o'clock)

65-d Symbols and Units of Measurement

Symbols (such as %, ¢, =, @, and #) and units of measurement (such as *cm, g, km, kg, L,* and *m*) are appropriate in tables but not in the body of an essay, according to MLA.

percent
Finding an investment with a guaranteed annual return of ten % is no easy task these days.

metres
Rising to a height of 290 m, First Canadian Place is Canada's tallest office building.

In APA style, it is appropriate to use the symbol in the body of the essay, but Chicago style recommends that "percent" be written out in humanities essays unless the essay contains many references to "percent," in which case the symbol is acceptable.

EXCEPTIONS: (1) The dollar sign is always used with figures: *At the time of her death, the Toronto-born poet Gwendolyn MacEwen had a bank account balance of $2.02.* (2) Symbols may be used to express temperature (18°C, 102°F).

XI MECHANICS

66-a Compound Words

A compound word is a word made up of two or more words. Compound words occur as separate words, as single words, or with hyphens.

SEPARATE WORDS	free trade, lowest common denominator, hard disk
SINGLE WORD	makeup, grandfather, textbook, workplace
WITH HYPHENS	medium-sized, first-class, hard-hitting, ex-wife

Following are some guidelines concerning the use of hyphens in compound words:

1. Use hyphens to connect the parts of compounds that function as adjectives (*well-known writer, six-year-old boy, large-scale project*).

2. Use a hyphen after the prefixes *all-, self-, ex-,* and *quasi-* (*all-inclusive dinner, self-appointed leader, ex-convict, quasi-scientific theory*). Do not, however, use a hyphen in the words *selfish, selfhood, selfless,* and *selfsame*.

3. Use a hyphen with prefixes that precede a capital or a figure (*non-Native, post-1945*).

4. Use hyphens to prevent readers from misunderstanding the relationship between adjectives and the words they modify. *Light blue coat*, for example, could mean either a blue coat that is light in weight or a coat that is light blue in colour. Adding a hyphen would clarify the latter meaning (*light-blue coat*).

5. Do not use a hyphen to connect adverbs ending in *-ly* to the words they modify (*highly developed society*, not *highly-developed society*).

6. Use a hyphen in spelled-out fractions and in number compounds from twenty-one to ninety-nine (*fifty-two, one-seventh*).

7. A hyphen may be used to separate paired terms (*author-critic, parent-child, French-English*). A slash is also used for this purpose. (See Chapter 57.)

8. Use a hyphen to separate identical vowels or consonants in some compounds (*anti-inflation, de-emphasize, bell-like*).

9. Use a hyphen to distinguish between such words as *recover* and *re-cover, coop* and *co-op, overage* and *over-age, reform* and *re-form*.

66-b Word Division

Hyphens are used to link parts of a word divided between lines of text. Canadian practice regarding word breaks is to follow the pronunciation by dividing between syllables. (The entries in most dictionaries indicate the syllable breaks in words.) Here are some guidelines:

1. Do not divide one-syllable words (*strength*, not *stren/gth*).

2. Do not divide words of fewer than five letters (*also*, not *al-/so*).

3. Divide compounds (whether otherwise hyphenated or solid) only between the parts of the compound (*long-/distance*, not *long-dis-/tance*; *counter-/attack*, not *counterat-/tack*).

4. Leave at least two letters at the end of a line and at least three letters at the beginning of a line.

5. Do not divide initials preceding a name (*S. J.-/Tanaka*, not *S.-/J. Tanaka*).

6. Do not divide acronyms and initialisms (*NAFTA*, not *NAF-/TA*; *CRTC*, not *CR-/TC*).

COMPUTER TIP

Most frequently, students set up their computers so that only the left margin is justified. This eliminates the problem of hyphenating words that don't fit at the end of a line, since any word that does not fit on a line is automatically pulled to the next line. This does, of course, result in your paper having a ragged right margin.

If you wish to avoid a ragged right margin, you can set up your page so that it is justified on both the left and right side. When your page is set up to be fully justified, your word-processing program will allow you to hyphenate words and eliminate gaps that would otherwise appear. In most programs, this feature is automatic. Your program will also contain a manual hyphenation feature that allows you to control where a word breaks it if falls at the end of a line. As well, it will contain a feature that allows you to use optional hyphens to break special words or prevent a hyphenated word from breaking.

XI
MECHANICS

EXERCISES

EXERCISE XI-1   NUMBERS

Study each of the following sentences. Write a C at the end of each sentence that demonstrates a correct handling of numbers. Make the necessary corrections to those sentences that do not.

1. A recent article on income distribution in the Western industrialized countries showed that Canada was number three on the list of places where the distribution of wealth was most unequal.

2. In Canada, 1% of the population controls twenty-eight point seven percent of the total wealth of the country.

3. An even more startling figure is the fact that five % of the population holds 47% of the total wealth.

4. The top 20% of Canadian earners take home just under seventy percent of the available wealth.

5. This leaves only two point one % of the wealth for the bottom twenty percent of Canadian wage earners.

6. Average real wages have fallen since their peak, in 1976, of $15.31 an hour; by 1990, that average had fallen to $14.98.

7. An interesting part of the overall picture is the stagnation of family income. There are now more income earners per family, since women increased their participation in the workforce from eleven point two percent in nineteen-fifty to 50.5% in 1976 and sixty-one point one % in 1990, yet family income has not changed since the 1970s.

8. It is clear, therefore, that four-fifths of the population have to fight over less than 1/2 of the country's money, and it is not surprising that the median income of thirty-five thousand, seven hundred and ninety-five dollars for 1990 was less than the median income of 1981, thirty-six thousand, two hundred and forty-nine dollars.

9. It is actually worse in the United States, where the top one percent of income earners enjoyed a larger increase in their wealth, between 2002 and 2005, than the entire income of the bottom 20% of employed earners.

10. Therefore, 5.8% unemployment and $803, 502, 000,000 in purchased goods and services are shared unequally among Canada's more than fourteen million workers.

EXERCISE XI-2 PROBLEM SENTENCES

NOTE: This exercise lends itself to group discussion or board work. Seeing how others attack a problem will give you insight into your own problem-solving strategies. After completing the exercise, compare your answers with those of other students. Use any major discrepancies you find as an opportunity for discussion.

Each of the sentences in the following two parts either contains one or more errors or is error-free. The errors reflect not only problems in mechanics but also problems addressed in previous sections of the book. Place a C after the sentences that are error-free and then work toward correcting the problem sentences. Let meaning be your guide as you unravel the problems in punctuation, grammar, word choice, clarity, and coherence. As you discuss your answers with other students, keep in mind that there may be more than one way to correct a problem sentence.

PART 1

1. To a person leaving school and attempting to live on their own this is simply not sufficient.

2. Education, a strengthening of the spirit and physical well-being must be made available to all in order to enable the individual to deal with life in a constructive, nonviolent manner.

3. Colin Wilson's statement talks about fear being the cause of violence.

4. Layton tells us that poetry is freedom because you can do anything with it.

5. The use of landscape is shown in 3 poems from 3 different Canadian authors: "Tantramar Revisited", by Charles G. D. Roberts; "Lakeshore" by F. R. Scott; and "The Lonely Land" by A. J. M. Smith.

6. Kip realizes this, he sees James's strengths and weaknesses and how much mischief coyote can make.

7. They should not expect to have it handed to them they should have a fair understanding of the knowledge on completion of their education.

8. At the end of that session, I was still hopelessly lost and quit.

9. People tend to take a passive acceptance of all that is organized around us.

10. Many of these people obtained a high-school diploma while remaining completely illiterate. These people must have accepted a teacher's wisdom without questioning the validity of his judgment.

1. These people do not look at education as a pursuit of knowledge to attain a specific goal but rather as an environment where they feel safe and secure.

2. It would seem quite obvious that a cat would have to be crazy to fight a dog; But fear quite often makes people and animals crazy.

3. People, whether right or wrong the taking in a trusting of leaders and role models is a part of society.

4. If we do, our ability to express oneself may be tarnished.

5. From kindergarten through college the student is conformed by every teacher. The ideas of pupils are therefore hindered and individual thought seems impossible when so many ideas have already been suppressed on them.

6. For others though, it is copying others goals because they have not made up their own career and follow their peers objectives without any care for what knowledge they could heap from the education supplied to them.

7. I have problems with writing skills like gramer, spelling and make the sentence together.

8. This is mostly to do with the fact that we have made higher education too excessible. Think about it, the only entrance examination into any Canadian college or university is the professor holds up a mirror to your face.

9. Passive acceptance is a problem that is taught to our society's young unnoticeably while they our young and effects them subconsciously throughout their life.

10. With out teachers and their knowledge to pass on to the students that want to learn, would be very disastrous.

Job-Related Writing

Writing and communication have been central to the conducting of business for centuries. Business writing, also called transactional writing, has the same purpose as other kinds of writing (to clearly and persuasively communicate information, instruction, and positions), but it employs distinctive forms to achieve that purpose. Memos, letters, and reports are the primary forms.

67-a Memos and E-mails

One of the simplest documents you will be asked to write is the inter-office memo, an in-house document directed to a person or group of people in the same organization. Although you will conduct a fair amount of internal business by phone, there will be times when you have to be more formal. The memo is the appropriate medium. It may be the only way to reach people who are hard to contact or who work for the same organization but at a different location. The memo enables you to retain a hard copy of your communication to act as a reminder or as proof that you have made a request or voiced an opinion.

Between the phone call and the paper memo, in terms of formality, is the e-mail (see Figure 67-1). There will be many occasions when an e-mail is sufficient for the business you wish to conduct. E-mail also furnishes you with a record you can recall. Increasingly, e-mail is taking the place of memos, especially in large firms.

COMPUTER TIP

The simplicity and convenience of using an e-mail program encourages spontaneous and informal communication. Indeed, research has shown that we say things in an e-mail we would never say to a person's face. Be wary of this pitfall. In everything you write—including e-mail—use language that is appropriate for your audience.

Memos are sent for a number of reasons. Like letters, they may be used to ask questions, distribute information, make requests, and transmit good or bad news. They may even be used to persuade someone to do something. However, memos should be brief and to the point. No one likes getting internal mail that is verbose.

The memo is sufficiently important in business writing that many of the better word-processing programs have templates for memos built right into them. You may find that the template has been modified to suit the needs of an individual organization. However, if an organization uses a preprinted memo form, it will look something like the one in Figure 67-2 on page 382.

As you can see from the size of these examples, memos are often printed on half-sheets of paper. This encourages people to be brief and focused in their interoffice communications. The memo's subject line introduces the reader to the subject immediately and allows the writer to get right to the point in the body of the memo. Figure 67-2 shows how brief a memo can be.

Figure 67-1 Brief E-mail

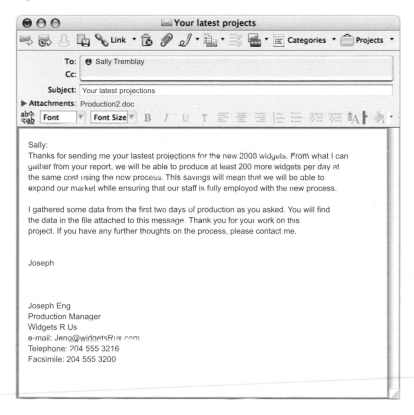

Like a business letter, a memo is brief and to the point. Unlike a business letter, a memo lacks a salutation and a formal close. You should sign your memo, though, either with your initials or, if your organization tends to be informal, with your first name. Your signature goes either at the end of the memo, as in Figure 67-2, or at the top of the memo at the end of the *From* line.

COMPUTER TIP

If you are using e-mail for communications, consider setting up a formal closing block that includes your name, title or position, your organization's name, your phone and fax numbers, and your e-mail address. This block of information, called a *signature block,* functions as the signature at the end of a traditional memo. Format your e-mail so that the signature block is automatically added to all of your outgoing mail.

Figure 67-2 Brief E-mail

MEMO
Aardvark Educational Materials

To: Lee Rendall, Director of Operations
From: James Hong, Purchasing Manager
Date: March 12, 2009
Subject: *Business Communications Handbook for Employees*

The Handbook's publication date has been pushed back to August 1. Would you like us to place a standing order or, given the delay, would you prefer to investigate alternative titles?

James

Direct your correspondence to a specific audience. Be action-oriented. Memos and business letters tend to use *I*, *we*, and *you* more than formal essays or written reports. It is useful to direct your message to a specific reader or set of readers and be reader-oriented. Similarly, in business letters or memos, state what action, if any, you or others will take. Action-oriented writing makes your correspondence strong and direct.

67-b Formal Letters

Letters, like memos, should be clear and concise. Both letters and memos may be used for a number of purposes. Common letter types include the following:

- good-news letters
- bad-news letters
- letters of inquiry
- persuasive letters

A letter has distinct parts that give its recipient all the necessary information. The fact that letter styles are predictable in construction makes it easy for a reader who is familiar with standard letter styles to find information in a letter. The parts of a letter are separated by at least one blank line and the letter's text or body is usually single-spaced.

The main parts of a formal letter are as follows:

- Letterhead/return address
- Date line
- Recipient's address
- Salutation
- Subject line
- Body or text
- Complimentary close
- Signature block
- Reference initials
- Enclosure notation
- Copy notation

If you use the letterhead of the organization you work for, the return address for your letter is usually preprinted on the organization's stationery. If you are writing a letter that is not on letterhead, you should place your return address at the top of the page.

The placement of the return address, like the placement of other parts of the letter, varies according to the format you use. At present, four letter formats are commonly used. The traditional letter format is gradually being replaced by the simpler and more functional full-block, modified-block, and simplified formats. Each of these formats is associated with one of the two punctuation styles outlined below.

1. *Mixed punctuation*
   - In addresses, punctuation is used between elements in a line (*Toronto, ON*) but not at the end of a line.
   - Salutations end with a colon. (A comma is acceptable in personal letters.)
   - Complimentary closes end with a comma.

2. *Open punctuation*
   - In addresses, punctuation is used between elements in a line (*Toronto, ON*) but not at the end of a line.
   - Neither the salutation nor the complimentary close have end punctuation.

TRADITIONAL FORMAT (MIXED PUNCTUATION)

The traditional format, shown in Figure 67-3, has the following characteristics:

- The *letterhead*, consisting of the organization's name and return address, is centred at the top of the page. If letterhead stationery is not available, a

XII
JOB-RELATED WRITING

FORMAL LETTERS |

return address consisting of the writer's mailing address is placed just to the right of the centre of the page (see Figure 67-4 on page 386).

- Two to six lines below the letterhead is the *date line*, which is placed just to the right of the centre of the page. If a return address is used, it is placed immediately above the date line.
- The *recipient's address*, the *salutation*, and the *subject line* are flush with the left margin. Each is separated from the element nearest to it by two blank lines. The subject line is emphasized by using underlining.
- The first line of each paragraph in the *body* or *text* of the letter is indented five spaces. The text is single-spaced with one blank line between paragraphs.
- The *complimentary close* appears two lines below the last line of text. Like the date line, it is placed to the right of the centre of the page.
- Four or five lines below the complimentary close is the *signature block*, which contains the writer's signature, typed name, and title. Like the date line and the complimentary close, the signature block is placed to the right of the centre of the page.
- *Reference initials* (the writer's initials and the typist's initials) are two lines below the last line of the signature block and flush with the left margin.
- Immediately below the reference initials is the *enclosure notation*.
- Two lines below the enclosure notation is the *copy notation*, which lists all individuals (in addition to the addressee) receiving the letter.

NOTE: Although the letterhead shown in Figure 67-3 shows only the company's name and mailing address, most businesses now also include their telephone number, fax number, and website address on their stationery. Whether their letterhead is pre-printed or electronically generated, some organizations also leave a place for individual employees to insert their e-mail address, as more and more business correspondence is being done electronically.

FULL-BLOCK FORMAT (OPEN PUNCTUATION)

The full-block format (see Figure 67-5 on page 387) differs from the traditional format in two respects: (1) all elements in the letter—except for the letterhead, which is centred at the top of the page—are flush with the left margin; and (2) the paragraphs in the body of the letter are not indented. At present, this is the most common style in use.

MODIFIED-BLOCK FORMAT (MIXED PUNCTUATION)

The modified-block format is the same as the full-block format except that the date line, complimentary close, and signature block are placed to the right of the centre of the page (see Figure 67-6 on page 388).

Figure 67-3 Traditional-Formal Letter (Mixed Punctuation)

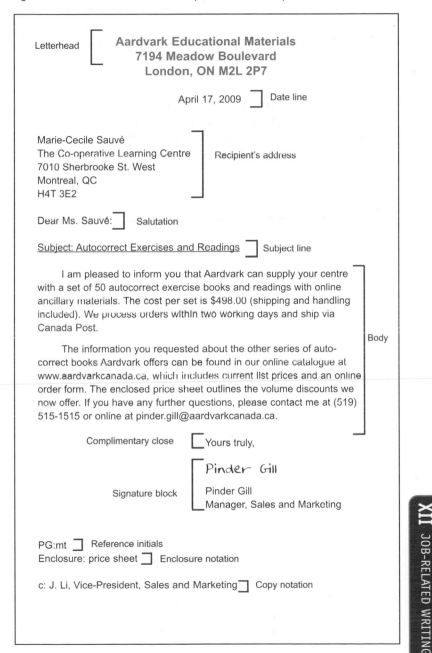

Letterhead

**Aardvark Educational Materials
7194 Meadow Boulevard
London, ON M2L 2P7**

April 17, 2009 — Date line

Marie-Cecile Sauvé
The Co-operative Learning Centre — Recipient's address
7010 Sherbrooke St. West
Montreal, QC
H4T 3E2

Dear Ms. Sauvé: — Salutation

Subject: Autocorrect Exercises and Readings — Subject line

   I am pleased to inform you that Aardvark can supply your centre with a set of 50 autocorrect exercise books and readings with online ancillary materials. The cost per set is $498.00 (shipping and handling included). We process orders within two working days and ship via Canada Post.

   Body

   The information you requested about the other series of auto-correct books Aardvark offers can be found in our online catalogue at www.aardvarkcanada.ca, which includes current list prices and an online order form. The enclosed price sheet outlines the volume discounts we now offer. If you have any further questions, please contact me at (519) 515-1515 or online at pinder.gill@aardvarkcanada.ca.

Complimentary close — Yours truly,

Pinder Gill

Signature block — Pinder Gill
Manager, Sales and Marketing

PG:mt — Reference initials
Enclosure: price sheet — Enclosure notation

c: J. Li, Vice-President, Sales and Marketing — Copy notation

Figure 67-4 Placement of Return Address in Traditional-Format Letter

7194 Meadow Blvd.
London, Ontario
M2L 3P7
April 17, 2009

Marie-Cecile Sauvé
The Co-operative Learning Centre
7010 Sherbrooke St. West
Montreal, QC
H4T 3E2

SIMPLIFIED FORMAT (OPEN PUNCTUATION)

The simplified format is the same as the full-block format except that the salutation and the complimentary close are omitted and the subject line appears in capital letters (see Figure 67-7 on page 389). The simplified format is appropriate when you are directing the letter to an organization in general rather than to a specific person in the organization.

SEQUENCING ELEMENTS IN A LETTER

All letters contain a main idea, details, and a close. The order in which you present these different elements depends on the purpose of your letter. If you are conveying *neutral news* or *good news*, you should start with the main idea, follow it up with any supporting details, and end with a positive closing remark (see Figure 67-8 on page 390). If you are conveying *bad news*, start with a neutral comment, explain your position, present the bad news, and end with a positive comment (see Figure 67-9 on page 391). The opening explanatory comment and the concluding positive comment help to offset the negative effects of the bad news.

Figure 67-5 Full-Block Format Letter (Open Punctuation)

Aardvark Educational Materials
7194 Meadow Boulevard
London, ON M2L 2P7

2009 04 17

Marie-Cecile Sauvé
The Co-operative Learning Centre
7010 Sherbrooke St. West
Montreal, QC
H4T 3E2

Dear Ms. Sauvé

Subject: Autocorrect Exercises and Readings

I am pleased to inform you that Aardvark can supply your centre with a set of 50 autocorrect exercise books and readings with online ancillary materials. The cost per set is $498.00 (shipping and handling included). We process orders within two working days and ship via Canada Post.

The information you requested about the other series of autocorrect books Aardvark offers can be found in our online catalogue at www.aardvarkcanada.ca, which includes current list prices and an online order form. The enclosed price sheet outlines the volume discounts we now offer. If you have any further questions, please contact me at (519) 515-1515 or online at pinder.gill@aardvarkcanada.ca.

Yours truly

Pinder Gill

Pinder Gill
Manager, Sales and Marketing

PG:mt
Enclosure: price sheet

c: J. Li, Vice-President, Sales and Marketing

Figure 67-6 Modified-Block Format Letter (Mixed Punctuation)

Aardvark Educational Materials
7194 Meadow Boulevard
London, ON M2L 2P7

April 17, 2009

Marie-Cecile Sauvé
The Co-operative Learning Centre
7010 Sherbrooke St. West
Montreal, QC
H4T 3E2

Dear Ms. Sauvé:

Subject: Autocorrect Exercises and Readings

I am pleased to inform you that Aardvark can supply your centre with a set of 50 autocorrect exercise books and readings. The cost per set is $498.00 (shipping and handling included). We process orders within two working days and ship via Canada Post.

The information you requested about the other series of autocorrect books Aardvark offers can be found in our online catalogue at www .aardvarkcanada.ca, which includes current list prices and an online order form. The enclosed price sheet outlines the volume discounts we now offer. If you have any further questions, please contact me at (519) 515-1515 or online at pinder.gill@aardvarkcanada.ca.

Yours truly,

Pinder Gill

Pinder Gill
Manager, Sales and Marketing

PG:mt
Enclosure: price sheet

c: J. Li, Vice-President, Sales and Marketing

Figure 67-7 Simplified-Format Letter (Open Punctuation)

Aardvark Educational Materials
7194 Meadow Boulevard
London, ON M2L 2P7

April 17, 2009

The Co-operative Learning Centre
7010 Sherbrooke St. West
Montreal, QC
H4T 3E2

SUBJECT: AUTOCORRECT EXERCISES AND READINGS

Aardvark Educational Materials offers a full range of autocorrect exercise books and readings that may meet the educational needs of your centre. If you check our website at www.aardvarkcanada.ca, you should be able to find texts that are suitable for your purpose.

If you have any questions about Aardvark's product line, you may contact me on my direct line at (519) 515-1516 or e-mail me at pinder.gill@aardvarkcanada.ca. I look forward to hearing from you.

Pinder Gill

Pinder Gill
Manager, Sales and Marketing

PG: mt

c: J. Li, Vice-President, Sales and Marketing

XII JOB-RELATED WRITING

Figure 67-8 Good-News Letter

Kaleidoscope Research Associates
823 Ste-Croix Blvd. St. Laurent, Quebec H4L 3X9
Tel: (514) 555-8700 Fax: (514) 555-8800
www.kaleidoscopecanada.ca

March 12, 2009

Paul Stonjcer
1534 Poplar Street
Prince Albert, SK
S6V 4H2

Dear Mr. Stonjcer:

Subject: Availability of Quebec/Canada Studies Modules

I am very pleased to report that Kaleidoscope Research Associates
offers course modules that we believe will meet your stated curriculum
needs. I am enclosing overviews of the first five modules in the series for
your perusal. The other modules in the series may be previewed at our
website (www.kaleidoscopecanada.ca).

If you require further information, you may reach me on my direct line at
(514) 555-8701 or contact me by e-mail at rsmith@kaleidoscopecanada.ca.
I look forward to hearing from you.

Yours truly,

Renée Smith

Renée Smith
Sales Manager

RS:hb
Enclosure: Module overviews

Figure 67-9 Bad-News Letter

Kaleidoscope Research Associates
823 Ste-Croix Blvd. St. Laurent, Quebec H4L 3X9
Tel: (514) 555-8700 Fax: (514) 555-8800
www.kaleidoscopecanada.ca

March 12, 2009

Paul Stonjcer
1534 Poplar Street
Prince Albert, SK
S6V 4H2

Dear Mr. Stonjcer:

Subject: Availability of American Studies Modules

Kaleidoscope Research Associates offers a wide range of modules that are designed for postsecondary courses on various aspects of Canada–U.S. relations.

At present, we do not carry a module that deals specifically with the effects of NAFTA on U.S. ownership in Canada. However, that subject will be addressed in a module Kaleidoscope is currently developing that will examine the history of NAFTA and its effects on Canada's economy. For more information about this module, please refer to the description in the enclosed flyer, or visit our online catalogue at www.kaleidoscopecanada.ca.

As noted in the flyer, the module's release date is November 17, 2009. You can reserve a copy by filling out our online request form or by contacting me directly at (514) 555-7816 or rsmith@kaleidoscopecanada.ca. I look forward to hearing from you.

Yours truly,

Renée Smith

Renée Smith
Sales Manager

RS:hb
Enclosure: flyer

67-c Reports

There are two types of business reports: *formal reports* and *informal reports*. Formal reports are long and comprehensive, and are often circulated outside an organization by mail, courier, and/or Internet. Informal reports are less detailed and are usually written for internal circulation only.

FORMAL REPORTS

A formal report contains most or all of the following elements:

1. *Letter of transmittal.* Some formal reports require a letter of transmittal, which introduces the report to readers. This element is especially important if the report is written in response to an advertised request for a proposal (RFP).

2. *Title page.* The title page includes the title of the report, the name of the organization the report was written for (including the file number if the report was written in response to an RFP), the date on which the report is submitted, and the names of the author and his or her organization.

3. *Abstract or executive summary.* This critical part of a report highlights the report's most important points, including the author's conclusions or recommendations. An abstract or executive summary should run no longer than one-tenth the length of the report.

4. *Table of contents.* The table of contents lists headings and other major parts of the report, as well as the page number on which each listed element begins.

5. *Problem statement.* The problem statement identifies the problem or issue addressed in the report.

6. *Background.* The background section of the report explains circumstances surrounding the problem. Depending on the nature of the report, you may also use this section to define elements of the analysis, set limits, and review material relevant to the analysis.

7. *Body of the report.* The body of the report is where you present analysis, evaluation, observations, and data relating to the problem. This part of the report may contain figures, tables, or graphs.

8. *Conclusion and recommendations.* The conclusion summarizes the main elements of the report and makes recommendations. Both the conclusion and the recommendations should be clear and concise. If your recommendations are extensive, you may wish to format them as items in a list.

9. *Appendix or appendixes.* Appendixes present material that is not an essential part of the body of the report but is nevertheless helpful to readers seeking further information. Tables that support the main text are often presented in this part of a report.

10. *List of figures, tables, and graphs.* Appropriate only when the report contains a substantial number of these elements.

11. *Bibliography.* The bibliography is a list of the works cited in the report.

12. *Index.* Appropriate only when the report is very long and contains enough names, subjects, and key terms to justify an index.

COMPUTER TIP

Using a word-processing program, you can create customized tables. A table—which may contain numbers, text, graphics, or combinations of these—allows you to present information in a clear and concise fashion.

PROPOSAL REPORTS

The proposal report, a special type of formal report, seeks to persuade a client of the benefits of following a specified course of action. It may be unsolicited or it may be written in response to a request for a proposal (RPF). Proposal reports contain the following elements:

1. *Introduction.* The introduction identifies the problem and explains why the author's organization is best suited to deal with the problem. The introduction's main purpose is to interest readers in the contents of the report and to provide some indication of the validity and cost-effectiveness of the author's proposed solution.

2. *Background.* In this section, the author presents an analysis of the problem. The objective here is to demonstrate a thorough understanding of the problem and its associated issues.

3. *Plan.* This part of the proposal report sets forth the author's plan for addressing the problem and details the benefits to the client of implementing the plan. A plan usually includes a preliminary budget and schedule. All aspects of the plan should be feasible.

4. *Request for approval.* In the final stage of the proposal report, the author asks the client to approve the plan and reminds the client of the plan's main benefits.

INFORMAL REPORTS

Usually three pages or less in length, an informal report has a narrower focus than a formal report. Informal reports may take the form of a memo or letter, or they may be written on an organization's preprinted report form. Here are some common types of informal reports:

analytical report   feasibility report
compliance report   information report

XII JOB-RELATED WRITING

investigative report	recommendation report
justification report	research report
periodic report	situation report (non-recurring)
progress report	summary report

Although the elements that make up an informal report vary, reports of this type usually include an introduction, background information, a proposal (including budget requirements), and a request for approval. The preparaton of most informal reports involves, at least one of the following activities:

- checking sources for information
- reviewing records
- making observations
- designing interviews, questionnaires, and surveys
- conducting interviews, questions, and surveys
- doing inventories
- using a library's resources
- conducting electronic searches
- examining government documents

COMPUTER TIP

For material on the job search, visit this book's website:
www.canadianwritersguide-4e.nelson.com

EXERCISES

EXERCISE XII-1 MEMOS AND LETTERS

You work in the research and development wing of the production department of Smith & Lubelski Ltd., a company that manufactures and sells coat hangers. You have just discovered a new process for making coat hangers that will cut the company's production costs by half while increasing production capability. The new process is less labour-intensive than the current one, so half of the sixty people who work in production will have to be laid off if the process is adopted. If current production rates are maintained, the $250,000 cost of conversion to the new process will be recovered within one year as a result of the savings in labour costs.

1. Using the standard memo format, write a memo to your production manager, Al Martinez (the former president of the local Metal Fabricators Union), outlining your position on the new process.

---

2. Not long after Al Martinez receives your memo, you are promoted to the position of vice-president of production. Your first task as vice-president is to write a letter to the union explaining that implementing the new process will necessitate layoffs and worker reassignments. However, Smith & Lubelski's sales and marketing department anticipates that workers who are laid off will eventually be re-hired by the company. The reasoning behind this projection is as follows: the cost savings resulting from the new process will allow Smith & Lubelski to sell coat hangers at a lower price; the lower price is expected to increase sales by an estimated fifty percent; the increased demand will, in turn, necessitate the re-hiring of all laid-off employees. Using modified-block format and mixed punctuation, write a letter to the president of the Metal Fabricators Union, Michelle Strong, outlining your position.

3. Michelle Strong responds to your letter with a letter of her own in which she points out that, under the current union contract, laid-off employees are entitled to (1) layoff pay for the duration of the layoff period, and (2) free training in the mechanics of the new process. Write a bad-news letter to the company president, Theo Lubelski, in which you explain the potential costs involved in the transition to the new process.

4. Theo Lubelski comes up with a compromise. He is willing to keep all of the workers on during the transition period at regular hours. He knows that, for at least half of the two-month transition, he will need workers to make hangers the old way. He also knows that, if he retrains his staff during the transition, he will be fully prepared to take on the extra volume that the new process will allow him to generate and sell. His sales staff has assured him that it can generate the business, so he is willing to pay his employees to retrain during the downtime when they are not needed to produce hangers using the old process. He figures that, by staggering the training period over the two months, he will be able to train one-quarter of his staff every eleven days (including one day for a review of the process) and thus allow for a gradual increase in the use of the new procedure, a gradual increase in production to meet new sales demands, and a gradual decrease in the use of the old method over the two-month period. Using simplified style and open punctuation, write a good-news letter to Michelle Strong outlining the details of your boss's proposal.

EXERCISE XII-2 INFORMAL REPORT

You have been asked by your manager to find out why there was a fifty percent increase in the use of your department's photocopier over the past year. Your investigation turns up the following information:

- Employees from other departments sometimes use your department's photocopier.

- Some employees in your department have been using the photocopier to copy documents, such as magazine articles, for personal rather than company use.

Write a one-page memo in which you report your findings and make recommendations.

EXERCISE XII-3 FORMAL REPORT

You work in Halifax for a group that studies the effects of industry on the environment. The provincial government in Nova Scotia has had an increase in the number of applications from people who want to operate salmon farms along the southeast coast of Nova Scotia. The government is concerned by reports that intensive fish farming affects tidal basins and could cause pollution harmful to other marine species. Thus, the government has announced a request for a proposal to study the economic and environmental effects of increased salmon fish farming in Nova Scotia. The request for a proposal is entitled "The Future of Salmon Aquaculture in Nova Scotia"; the competition number is F1054–7. You are asked to submit a brief proposal report for your company. You discover the following information in doing preliminary research:

- Aquaculture is over two thousand years old and has roots in Japan's oyster industry and Egypt's fish industry.
- The first known book on aquaculture was written in China in the fifth century B.C.
- In 1992, worldwide, aquaculture harvested 19.3 million tonnes of fish, 19 percent of the fish production for that year.
- In 1982, aquaculture accounted for 10 percent of fish production.
- Between 1992 and 2002, fish production from aquaculture increased 42 percent
- The United Nations Food and Agricultural Organization predicts a doubling of aquaculture production between 2000 and 2025.
- 48.9 percent of aquaculture production is related to trout, salmon, and carp.
- 80 percent of current aquaculture production occurs in Southeast Asia.
- Atlantic salmon are raised in floating nylon cages that are on average 20 metres by 20 metres in size.
- The pens are most successful in protected bays along coastal areas.
- Tanks made out of plastic that allow farmers to control the fish's environment have become more common over the last decade, but these pens recycle water into the bays where they are set up.
- In 1994, aquaculture in Canada produced 54,500 tonnes of finfish, about 10 percent of the total value of commercial fisheries in Canada.

- A powerful lobby has been active on both coasts of Canada to maintain wild fish stocks and limit the growth of aquaculture. This lobby has been led by commercial fishers, canning companies, and consumers who are concerned with what they perceive of as the possibility of genetically engineered fish raised on fish farms.

- Local communities on the east and west coasts of the country have been active in both the promotion of aquaculture and lobbying against aquaculture. Some communities claim that aquaculture is a threat to the environment; others claim that farming salmon risks mixing farmed fish with wild stock and destroying the traditional fishing industry. Other communities are happy to see a new employment base in their community.

- Studies of aquaculture along the coast of Chile over the past decade have shown that fish farms have had to relocate their base of operation every two to five years as bays become polluted (William Lim, *Studies on the Fish Farm Habitat of Chile,* Department of Fisheries, Canada, 1998).

- Small towns in Chile experienced a strong initial growth in prosperity when fish farms were located close by. When the fish farms relocated, towns not only lost one of their main employers but also a portion of their population, which relocated with the fish farm (interview with William Lim, July, 2000).

- Norwegian fish farms have not experienced the same effect. The currents in Norwegian fiords seem to be able to sustain the long-term presence of fish farms.

- Studies have not been made on the tidal systems and water conditions off Nova Scotia relative to Chile and Norway, although data are available on both the Chilean and Norwegian experiences.

- In 2002, aquaculture in Nova Scotia produced 1,950,609 kg of salmon worth $12,503,969, 43.9 percent of the aquaculture production for the province. In 1994, aquaculture produced 540,759 kg of salmon worth $3,836,385, 53 percent of the aquaculture production of the province. www.gov.ns.ca/nsaf/aquaculture/stats

- In 2002, the market value of all non-aquaculture fisheries in Nova Scotia was $739,429,000. http://www.dfo-mpo.gc.ca/communic/statistics/main_e.htm

- In New Brunswick in 2002, the value of all fish landed by fishers was $198,096,000, whereas the value of salmon aquaculture production was $202,574,000. In 1995, fish landed accounted for $188,072,000, whereas salmon aquaculture accounted for $111,574,000. http://www.dfo-mpo.gc.ca/communic/statistics/main_e.htm

Your report must have a letter of transmittal, a title page, an introduction, background information relevant to the proposal, a proposal plan (including a schedule and a budget), and a request for approval. You estimate that a study of the subject will take three months and that the report will take one month to write. You estimate that the budget for this study will include the following cost factors:

- Although your company bills at a rate of $6,000 per month per researcher, two full-time researchers will cost the company $5,000 per month.
- Office materials and fixed costs are $2,000.
- Transportation expenses travelling to and from Halifax are $3,000.
- Miscellaneous expenses are $2,000.
- Printing, telephone, and postage costs are $1,000.

SELECTED ANSWERS FOR EXERCISES

EXERCISE IV-1   PARENTHETICAL CITATIONS

(2) **MLA**   Smith contends that "there are only four major rules for the use of the comma" (45).

   APA   Smith (2003) contends that "there are only four major rules for the use of the comma" (p. 45).

   Chicago   Note: The questions in this exercise ask for the parenthetical citation. In the humanities, you would be asked to use a footnote or endnote reference system.
Smith (2003) contends that "there are only four major rules for the use of the comma" (p. 45).

(5) **MLA**   According to one authority, "The semicolon is easy to use once you have mastered the comma" (Adams and Smith 93).

   APA   According to one authority, "The semicolon is easy to use once you have mastered the comma" (Adams & Smith, 1995, p. 93).

   Chicago   According to one authority, "The semicolon is easy to use once you have mastered the comma" (Adams and Smith, 1995, p. 93).

EXERCISE IV-2   BIBLIOGRAPHY ENTRIES

5.

MLA

Huseman, Richard, et al. *Business Communication: Strategies and Skills.* 2nd ed. Toronto: Holt, Rinehart and Winston, 1988. Print.

APA

Huseman, R., Stockmayer, D., Hatfield, J., Lahiff, J., & Penrose, J. (1988). *Business communication: Strategies and skills* (2nd ed.). Toronto: Holt, Rinehart and Winston.

CSE

Huseman R, Stockmayer D, Hatfield J, Lahiff J, Penrose J. 1988. Business communication: strategies and skills. 2nd ed. Toronto: Holt, Rinehart and Winston.

Chicago

Huseman, Richard, Dixie Stockmayer, John Hatfield, James Lahiff, and John Penrose. *Business Communication: Strategies and Skills.* 2nd ed. Toronto: Holt, Rinehart and Winston, 1988.

EXERCISE V-1 PARTS OF SPEECH I

1 = noun, 2 = pronoun, 3 = verb

1. Samuel Hearne's diary(1) of his journeys(1) leaves(3) us(2) an account(1) of the rigours(1) faced(3) by the early explorers(1).

2. His account(1) of the efforts(1) he(2) made(3) to locate the Coppermine River(1) is(3) full of details(1) about the Barren Lands(1) he(2) traversed(3).

EXERCISE VI-4 CLAUSES

The dependent and independent clauses in the following passage are identified by underlining and the appropriate number before each: 1 = independent clause, 2 = dependent clause.

     2   1   2

As Canada matures as a country, its sense of what it means to be Canadian

                                              1   2

changes. In the mid-twentieth century, the accepted view was that Canadians

were, for the main part, of European heritage, looking to western Europe and, in

particular, Great Britain and France for a sense of identity and culture. The

 1

history taught in schools pointed to European exploration and focused on how

 2

the fur trade was important to that exploration.

EXERCISE VI-2 IDENTIFYING SENTENCE TYPES

1 = simple, 2 = compound, 3 = complex, 4 = compound-complex.

[4] Canada has a significant export business with China, but it pales in comparison with the mass of goods that Canada imports from China. [1] Recently, this trade relationship has suffered in several key areas. [3] The first challenge came from the tainted wheat gluten found in pet food that was exported to Canada from China. [2] Menu Foods sold this food to Procter and Gamble, and they in turn marketed it in North American pet stores under names like Iams and Eukanuba.

EXERCISE VIII-1 FRAGMENTS

(The second and third sentences should be combined to read)
This leads them inevitably to conclude that either the net income attached to each job has declined or it has declined for a significant proportion of these jobs.

(What was originally the fourth sentence should read)
The second reason furnishes a more likely scenario than the one that has every job declining in net value.

(What was originally the sixth sentence should read)

In fact, Starbucks learns from McDonald's and Safeway teaches Wal-Mart the lesson of using hours and titles and myths to disguise the fact that the employer is not paying a living wage.

EXERCISE IX-1   SLANG EXPRESSIONS

Part A

My buddies [friends] and I agree that it is mega fun [fun] to get together on a Saturday night to shoot the breeze [to gossip] and watch the boob tube [television].

Part B

Nine times out of ten [Frequently], it is easier to find a good DVD [video *or leave as DVD*] to watch than to find a good movie at a local theatre. Why is it that all the good movies are at cinemas on the opposite side of town? It seems the only movies that come to the local cinema are either for boppers or Echo Boomers[teenagers or young adults]. How interesting can a film be when it goes on and on about who is going to or wants to shag [make love to] whom?

EXERCISE IX-2   PRETENTIOUS LANGUAGE

(1) You're fired.

EXERCISE IX-4   IDIOMATIC LANGUAGE

(1) on

(2) from

(3) of

(4) with

EXERCISE IX-5   PRONOUN CASE

The pronouns in bold are the correct choice.

Although the odds against **our** winning a lottery are almost ludicrously high, we collectively invest millions in this new form of tax invented by revenue-hungry provincial governments, hospitals, and charities. No matter **whom** we talk to, they will tell **us** that they just buy the tickets because the charity is a deserving one or because it's a cheap form of pleasure.

EXERCISE IX-6   *WHO, WHOM, THAT,* AND *WHICH*

The errors are underlined and the corrections appear after them in brackets.

Although you would think that people would no longer embrace *Cinderella*—the story of a pretty young woman that [who] is rescued from a life of poverty and servitude by a handsome, young, wealthy prince—the story remains popular. It may not be as popular as it once was when the storybooks <u>which</u> [that] every child in Canada had included a rendition of the story. It was Walt Disney's animated film version of the story, of course, <u>which</u> [that] embedded the story in the minds of the last three generations of North Americans.

EXERCISE IX-7   AGREEMENT WITH COLLECTIVE NOUNS

(1)   its, it

EXERCISE IX-8   INCLUSIVE LANGUAGE

- <u>his gavel</u> Try *a gavel* to avoid the gender exclusion here.

- <u>his bench top</u> Perhaps *the bench top*—or simply delete *on his bench top*, as it is not an essential detail.

EXERCISE IX-10   COMPARATIVE AND SUPERLATIVE FORMS

(1)   greedier

(2)   better

EXERCISE IX-11   ACTIVE AND PASSIVE VOICE

Section A

Clauses in passive voice are underlined and their verbs appear in bold type. The rewritten passages, in active voice, appear in the brackets.

Yet at the stroke of midnight on 31 March 1949, <u>Newfoundland **was led** into the Canadian Confederation by Joseph R. Smallwood, its first premier</u> [Joseph R. Smallwood, Newfoundland's first premier, led the province into the Canadian Confederation]. <u>It **is said**</u> [Some people say] <u>that Newfoundland was abandoned by Britain</u> [that Britain abandoned Newfoundland].

Section B

In the following exercise, the active-voice passages that were to be changed are underlined, the subjects and verbs affected by the change to passive voice are in bold print, and the rewritten passages in passive voice appear in brackets.

In periods <u>when **the government lays off** people who work in the public sector</u> [when people who work in the public sector are being laid off/ being laid off by the government], **it handles** <u>the layoffs very carefully</u> [the layoffs are handled very carefully].

EXERCISE X-1 COMMA, SEMICOLONS, AND COLONS

A. Commas to Set Off

Large multinational corporations have had a larger effect on the way we live than we think. The most evident signs of their presence in our communities are the large malls and big box stores. It doesn't matter where you go in North America these days; the big box stores and the large malls are everywhere.

At first[,] we think of the large stores[,] the so-called big box stores[,] as having better prices than the small[,] family-run stores that used to dominate communities. We still use the term "mom and pop corner store" to describe these small community businesses. In most cases[,] these small stores serve a local community and know their clients. When you entered a small business[,] you could be assured of personal service by someone who knew what was in the store and would be able to help you if you were searching for a solution to a problem. Indeed[,] personal service was one of the cornerstones of small businesses. If they were not able to keep their customers happy[,] they knew they would lose that business.

B. Commas to Separate and Commas to Set Off

Newfoundland[,] the last province in Canada to join Confederation[,] joined on March 31[,] 1949. Today[,] Newfoundlanders still comment on how distinct Newfoundland is and how mainlanders are diffcrent from them.

C. The Semicolon and the Colon

In 2000[,] 150 years after the beginning of immigration from China to Canada[,] the complexity of the history of the Chinese in Canada is still unfolding. The titles of the books on the Chinese in Canada are in themselves an indication of some of the trials and tribulations the Chinese faced[:] *In the Sea of Sterile Mountains*, *A White Man's Province*, and *White Canada Forever: Popular Attitudes and Public Policy Toward Orientals in British Columbia* are evocative of the attitudes of the Euro-Canadian population toward immigration from China. The Opium Wars between the Chinese and Western powers from 1839 to 1869 not only was a sad period in China's history, but it also revealed, as James Morton points out in his book[ ] *In the Sea of Sterile Mountains*, the attitude of major Western powers toward China. Morton notes that there is no small irony in the fact that the Chinese had to[ ] "be beaten senseless because they would not allow the importation of opium" (xiii).

EXERCISE X-2 PUNCTUATION

In his 2003 Massey Lectures[,] *The Truth About Stories*[,] Thomas King remarks repeatedly[,] "The truth about stories is that that's all we are." King's assertion sounds like an oversimplification at first. How could we simply be stories[?] Aren't we more than that[,] more than the sum of the parts[,] more than the individual highlights[,] more than the people we meet[,] the places we visit[,] the books we read[,] the films we see[,] the music we listen to[?]

EXERCISE X-3   QUOTATION MARKS, BRACKETS, ELLIPSES, AND SLASHES

Part 2

Canada is a colony, not a country; ... not yet identified with the dearest affections and associations, remembrances, and hopes of its inhabitants: it is to [Canadians] an adopted, not a real mother. Their love, their pride, are not for poor Canada, but for ... England; but a few more generations must change all this.(52)

EXERCISE XI-1   NUMBERS

Sentences that showed a correct handling of numbers are reflected here with a C. Those that needed correction are reproduced here but with their errors corrected and set in bold type.

(1)   C

(2)   In Canada, 1% of the population controls **28.7%** of the total wealth of the country.

EXERCISE XI-2   PROBLEM SENTENCES

(agr = agreement, cap = capital, cs = comma splice, p = punctuation, ref = problem reference, sp = spelling, ww = wrong word)

Part 1

(1)   To a person leaving school and attempting to live on their [agr] own [,p] this [ref] is simply not sufficient.

(2)   Education, a strengthening of the spirit and physical well-being [a poor definition] [,p] must be made available to all in order to enable the individual to deal with life in a constructive, nonviolent manner.

Part 2

(1)   These people do not look at education as a pursuit of knowledge to attain a specific goal [poor expression] but rather as an environment [ww] where they feel safe and secure.

(2)   It would seem quite obvious that a cat would have to be crazy to fight a dog [,p but] [cap] fear quite often makes people and animals crazy.

INDEX

CREDITS

This page constitutes an extension of the copyright page. We have made every effort to trace the ownership of all copyrighted material and to secure permission from copyright holders. In the event of any question arising as to the use of any material, we will be pleased to make the necessary corrections in future printings. Thanks are due to the following authors, publishers, and agents for permission to use the material indicated.

CHAPTER 3

Pages 15–16: From Reinhold Kramer, "Nationalism, the West and *The Englishman's Boy*," in *Essays on Canadian Writing* Spring 1999 (5–6). Reprinted with the kind permission of *Essays on Canadian Writing*.

PART 1 EXERCISES

Page 27: Steve Kerstetter, Table: Distribution of Personal Wealth among Family in B.C., 1999, from "BC Home to Greatest Wealth Gap in Canada," *Behind the Numbers*, 28 November 2001. Reprinted by permission of the Canadian Centre for Policy Alternatives, BC Office.

Page 28: **Table (2):** Steve Kerstetter, Table: Regional Differences in Personal Wealth, 1999, from "BC Home to Greatest Wealth Gap in Canada," *Behind the Numbers*, 28 November 2001. Reprinted by permission of the Canadian Centre for Policy Alternatives, BC Office. **Table (3):** "Income Shifts 1989 to 1998." Adapted from Statistics Canada, *Income in Canada*, 75-202-XIE, 1998, page 90. (http://www.statcan.ca/cgi-bin/downpub/listpub.cgi?catno=75-202-XIE1998000).

CHAPTER 10

Page 75: Andrew Lipsman, "comScore Releases December 2007 U.S. Search Engine Rankings." Press release. Reprinted by permission of ComScore, Inc.

CHAPTER 17

Pages 82–83: From *The Rise and Fall of the Great Powers*, by Paul Kennedy, copyright © 1987 by Paul Kennedy. Used by permission of Random House. Reprinted by permission of HarperCollins Publishers Ltd, © Paul Kennedy 1987.

CHAPTER 22

Pages 132–138: Reprinted by permission of Daryl Kroell.